Transgender Identities

Routledge Research in Gender and Society

Transgender Identities

Towards a Social Analysis of Gender
Diversity

Edited by Sally Hines and Tam Sanger

Routledge
Taylor & Francis Group
New York   London

First published 2010
by Routledge
711 Third Avenue, New York, NY 10017

Simultaneously published in the UK
by Routledge
2 Park Square, Milton Park, Abingdon, Oxon OX14 4RN

Routledge is an imprint of the Taylor & Francis Group, an informa business

First issued in paperback 2012

© 2010 Taylor & Francis

Typeset in Sabon by IBT Global.

Library of Congress Cataloging-in-Publication Data

Transgender identities : towards a social analysis of gender diversity / edited by Sally Hines and Tam Sanger.
   p. cm. — (Routledge research in gender and society ; 24)
   Includes bibliographical references and index.
   ISBN 978-0-415-99930-4
   1. Transgender people—Identity.   2. Gender identity.   I. Hines, Sally.   II. Sanger, Tam.
   HQ77.9.T7158 2010
   306.76'8—dc22
   2009037544

ISBN13: 978-0-415-99930-4 (hbk)
ISBN13: 978-0-203-85614-7 (ebk)
ISBN13: 978-0-415-81058-6 (pbk)

Contents

Figures

Tables

Acknowledgments

Sally: Thank you to Tam Sanger for her initial enthusiasm for the book and for her on-going commitment as co-editor. Many thanks to each of the contributing authors for their attentiveness throughout the various stages of the book-and for producing such vibrant and engaging work. This book has only been possible because of you. Thanks to Ben Holtzman at Routledge for his support for this project in its first stages and to others at Routledge, especially Jennifer Morrow, who saw the book through to completion. Thank you to Yvette Taylor for ongoing conversation and friendship. I would like to thank Zowie Davy, who worked with me on the ESRC project on the Gender Recognition Act during the year that this book was in production, for being such a great colleague. Many thanks, as always, to other friends and family for their time and support; in particular to Margaret Hines, Barry Hines, Mark Jackson and Gil Jackson-Hines.

Tam: Thank you to Sally Hines for being a great co-editor, and the contributing authors for their hard work and ability to stick to deadlines despite other commitments. I would also like to thank my friends and family who gave their support during the various stages of the coming together of this volume.

Introduction

Sally Hines

Transgender Identities: Towards a Social Analysis of Gender Diversity emerges from, and speaks to, recent sociological considerations of 'transgender.' The term 'transgender' denotes a range of gender experiences, subjectivities and presentations that fall across, between or beyond stable categories of 'man' and 'woman.' 'Transgender' includes gender identities that have, more traditionally, been described as 'transsexual,'[1] and a diversity of genders that call into question an assumed relationship between gender identity and presentation and the 'sexed' body.

This introduction serves three purposes. First it seeks to provide a historical and political context to recent sociological analyses of transgender. In the section titled 'Transgender Debates: Reflections and Futures' I frame some of the central ways in which transgender debates have developed and changed over time. I consider the different ways in which social analysis has problematised a medical understanding of gender diversity as pathological: beginning with ethnomethodology in the 1960s and ending with a discussion of the emergence of 'transgender studies' as a distinct field of scholarship in the late 1990s. Such theoretical considerations intersect with shifts in political and social movements around gender and sexuality. Thus I move on to address the relationship between transgender and feminist and lesbian and gay movements; looking at how trans movements have productively affected these political sites. I end this section of the introduction by considering the impact of theoretical and political developments on law and policy; addressing particularly recent legal interventions around gender recognition in the UK. Each of these areas is extensive and each deserving of full-length discussion. These themes are taken up in the subsequent chapters, which are outlined in the last part of this introduction.

In the second part of the introduction I turn my attention to 'a sociology of transgender.' I sketch out what such an approach may entail; considering what sociology has to bring to transgender studies, and moreover, what transgender studies has to offer sociology. The final part of the introduction provides an overview of the four parts of the book, and outlines the main themes and arguments of the forthcoming chapters.

TRANSGENDER DEBATES: REFLECTIONS AND FUTURES

Theoretical Developments

Sexual historians have illustrated how medicine took an increasingly dominant role in understandings of sexuality during the nineteenth century
(Weeks 1977; Foucault 1978). Alongside homosexuality—and a range of
other non-normative sexual acts—practices that we now discuss as transgendered were separated from heterosexuality and classified as deviant.
The 'naming' of gender diverse practices during the first half of the nineteenth century produced distinct ways of thinking about gender diverse
individuals. Prior to this, cross-dressing and cross-living practices had
been understood as fetishistic behaviours and described through the terms
'sexual inversion' or 'contrary sexual feeling,' which were applied to non-
heterosexual acts (Ekins and King 1996: 80). Studies by Hirschfeld (1910)
and Ellis (1938) were seminal in distinctly classifying gender diverse practices. Their work was significant in separating practices of gender diversity from those of sexuality. Moreover, practices of gender diversity were
distinguished from each other. In particular, 'transsexuality' was isolated
from 'transvestism.' The work of sexual reformer Harry Benjamin was
instrumental in distinctly categorising transsexuality and in positioning
surgical reconstruction as the appropriate 'treatment' for the 'transsexual
condition' (Benjamin 1953). As surgical techniques of gender reconstruction developed during the 1960s, access to surgery widened. Speaking to
such medical developments, this period witnessed the growth of research
into transsexuality from the fields of sexology (Benjamin 1966), psychology and psychiatry (Money and Green 1969). Here, dysfunctional socialisation was identified as the 'cause' of transsexuality. Significantly, gender
was conceptualised independently of biological 'sex.'

Throughout the 1970s the term 'gender dysphoria' replaced that of 'transsexuality' in medical and psychological writing. Locked into the notion of
'gender dysphoria' is the idea of the 'wrong body,' which suggests a state of
discord between 'sex' (the body) and gender identity (the mind). In match-
ing the gendered body and the gendered mind, surgery was (and still is)
positioned as a route to gendered harmony. Here a further shift in understandings of gender diversity is witnessed. Rather than a privileging of the
'sexed' body, the mind is seen to hold the key to a coherent gendered 'self.'
The site of pathology was thus transferred from the body to the mind.

The theoretical underpinnings of the notion of 'gender dysphoria,' which
point to a 'true' gendered identity, were first critiqued through the ethnomethodological work of Garfinkel (1967). Garfinkel's (1967) seminal
study of 'Agnes,' a woman born with both 'male' and 'female' genitalia,
was written in collaboration with American psychiatrist Stoller. Through a
focus on Agnes' gendered speech and behaviour, the study examined how
intersex people articulate their chosen gender within the constraints of

medical gendered discourse. Garfinkel critiqued the pathological assumptions that underscored medical and psychiatric thinking by showing how Agnes exercised agency in her chosen gender; resisting and managing social and medical stigmatisation. Moreover, Garfinkel linked Agnes' techniques of gender management to the wider silent 'rules' of gender:

> The experiences of these intersexed persons permits an appreciation of these background relevancies that are otherwise easily overlooked or difficult to grasp because of their routinized character and because they are so embedded in a background of relevancies that are simply 'there' and taken for granted.
>
> (Garfinkel 1967: 16)

Garfinkel's work makes an important intervention in shedding light on how gender 'rules' not only impact on intersex people, but work to structure all gendered subjects. Kessler and McKenna (1978) built on Garfinkel's work to further develop social analyses of gender diversity. By the late 1970s feminist scholarship had identified gender as a constraining mechanism and multi-faceted feminist studies were examining how gendered norms impacted upon women's experiences. As a result of feminist theory, the social sciences were increasingly conceptualising 'gender' as a social construction. Yet it was still generally assumed that 'sex' was a fixed biological determinant. Notably, Kessler and McKenna (1978) posited that 'sex' was as equally constructed as were the social characteristics of masculinity and femininity. Viewing certain body parts as essentially male or female, they argued, was a social and cultural process. This significant theoretical development drew attention to ways in which 'sex' and 'gender' were collapsed in academic discourse.

Ethnomethodology provided an important critique of the pathological positioning of gender diverse people within dominant medical frameworks. It recognised the social construction of gendered bodies, and was attentive to the subjective understanding and negotiation of gender norms. While the potentials of moving between the categories of gender are brought into being, though, it is only possible to move from one gender category to another within this analysis. As Kessler and McKenna later acknowledged, the binary framework of early ethnomethodological studies are thus limited for contemporary social understandings of gender diversity[2]:

> What we did not consider 25 years ago was the possibility that someone might not want to make a credible gender presentation-might not want to be seen as clearly either male or female. [. . .] In other words, we did not address what has come to be called 'transgender.' Transgender was neither a concept nor a term 25 years ago. Transsexual was radical enough.
>
> (Kessler and McKenna 2000)

Throughout the 1980s plural feminist approaches attended to the complexities of gender and to its relationship with sexuality. Whilst radical feminists have argued that sexuality is key to theorising gender—thus understandings of gender are developed from experiences of sexuality (MacKinnon 1982), other feminist writers have foregrounded gender in theorising the relationship between sexuality and gender—here experiences of sexuality are determined by experiences of gender (Jackson 1999). A different approach to the relationship between gender and sexuality has been developed by theorising gender and sexuality as distinct but overlapping categories (Hollibaugh 1989; Rubin 1989; Vance 1989; Sedgwick 1990). This framework distinguishes between gender and sexuality in order to independently theorise gender and sexual difference. Although this body of work did not explicitly address transgender, it was significant for developing accounts of gender plurality in which erotic desire does not automatically fit preconceived binary identities of either gender (man/woman) or sexuality (homo/hetero).

The development of poststructuralist feminist theory and queer theory through the 1990s brought issues of gender and sexual plurality to the fore. In taking the discursive formations of gender and sexuality as their starting point, these approaches have engaged directly with transgender. Butler's (1990) work is central here. Echoing Kessler and McKenna (1978), Butler argues against a biological understanding of 'sex.' Rather, 'sex' is socially and culturally produced. Poststructuralist feminist interventions were key to developing analytical frameworks that moved beyond an understanding of gender as a binary opposition (man/woman). Alongside post-colonial theory, this body of work brings a richer understanding of gender as socially relational; enabling a more complete analysis of 'difference' across and between gender categories. Moreover, poststructuralist work advanced feminist analyses of gender as a social experience by focusing attention on how 'gender' is discursively produced. Thus gender is understood as a central categorising device. From here on in, the gender binary is conceptualised as a social and political organising principle.

In similar ways, the development of queer theory moved forward social constructionist accounts of sexuality. Seidman (1996) traces the influence of social constructionism on lesbian and gay studies; pointing out the agenda of lesbian and gay studies to '[. . .] explain the origin, social meaning, and changing forms of the modern homosexual' (Seidman 1996: 9). As feminists mapped the social factors that impacted upon the experience of women, lesbian and gay scholars examined the social production of a modern homosexual identity. Queer theory, as Seidman notes, shifted the focus from an explanation of modern homosexuality to a discursive interrogation of the hetero/homosexual binary; bringing a shift from 'a politics of minority interest to a politics of knowledge and difference' (Seidman 1996: 9). It is the latter departure—a politics of difference—that brought theories of sexuality into conversation with transgender.

Queer theory argues against the representation of identity categories as authentic. Rather, identities are unstable and multiple. Queer theory's politics of difference seeks to dissolve the naturalisation of dominant identities and to challenge the pathologisation of minority identities. From a queer framework, transgender cultures are seen to rupture dominant identity categories; as I have argued elsewhere (Hines 2005, 2007), queer theory has often highlighted transgender as epitomising categorical instability. Queer theory thus embraced transgender practices as a deconstructive tool.

Throughout the 1990s trans scholars engaged with the theoretical debates of feminism, lesbian and gay theory and queer theory; providing explicit critiques of medical discourse and practice. 'Transgender Studies' is interdisciplinary (including academic fields as diverse as the humanities, arts, sociology, psychology, law, social policy, literature, anthropology, history and politics) and intertextual (often mixing academic scholarship with autobiography and political commentary). While some trans writers (for example, Stone 1991; Bornstein 1994) reflected a queer subjectivity in positioning themselves outside of gender, many trans scholars have been critical of queer theory's lack of material analysis. Reflecting this critique, Whittle states:

> It is all very well having no theoretical place within the current gendered world, but that is not the daily lived experience. Real life affords trans people constant stigma and oppression based on the apparently unreal concept of gender. This is one of the most significant issues that trans people have brought to feminism and queer theory.
>
> (Whittle 2006: xii)

In arguing for a reinstatement of materiality in analyses of transgender, Whittle's intervention is deeply political. As I suggest later in this introduction, his emphasis on 'lived experience' is requisite for a sociology of transgender. Whittle's points here are also significant in indicating how trans scholarship developed through and alongside trans politics. Indeed, the broad theoretical developments around gender and sexuality that I have outlined in this section are each tied up with shifting understandings and methods of organising within political and social movements. It is these shifts to which I now turn.

POLITICAL DEVELOPMENTS

It is unfeasible to isolate the development of theories around gender and sexuality from the politics of these social movements. Thus developments in feminist theory interweave with the histories of feminism as a political movement, while the disciplines of lesbian and gay theory and queer theory reflect shifts in social movements around sexuality. Further, as I will address, the development of transgender studies over the last decade is inseparable from the growth of a visible trans movement.

The relationship between feminism and transgender has been far from smooth. In the 1980s, Janice Raymond's (1980) critique of trans women as servile constructions of a patriarchal medical system instigated a politics of hostility towards trans people. More recently, other feminist writers (Jeffreys 1997; Greer 1999; Bindel 2003, 2004) have supported Raymond's proposition that trans practices are inherently un-feminist. At the core of feminist discussions around trans femininity is the concept 'woman.' As Feinberg states:

> The development of the trans movement has raised a vital question that's being discussed in women's communities all over the country. How is woman defined? The answer we give may determine the course of women's liberation for decades to come.
>
> (Feinberg 1996: 109)

In addressing the marginalised histories, experiences, and social and political demands of women, the women's movement applied 'woman' as a fixed category, which was distinct from 'man.' For the most part, feminism has assumed an inherent identity, understood through the category 'woman.' 'Woman' not only initiated feminist interests and goals, it also constituted the subject for whom political representation was pursued. Questions around the position of trans women within feminism cut to the heart of discussions around the constitution of 'woman.' In problematising a unified concept of gender, trans practices challenge feminist politics of identity. Strands of radical feminism responded to these complexities by defending the category of 'woman' through recourse to both biological 'sex' and gendered socialisation (Raymond 1980; Jeffreys 1997; Greer 1999; Bindel 2003). From either basis, trans women were not 'real' women. Trans women, therefore, could not be feminists and had no place in the 'women's' movement.

Autobiographical and activist work by trans writers (Stone 1991; Feinberg 1992; Bornstein 1994; Riddell 1996; Califia 1997; Wilchins 1997) has articulated the ways in which trans people were excluded from feminist movements during the 1980s and 1990s. Riddell explicitly links the publication of Raymond's (1980) book to the emergence of a wider anti-transgender feminism; setting out the personal and political consequences of such a politics:

> My living space is threatened by this book. [. . .] its attacks on transsexual women, its dogmatic approach and its denial that female experience is our basic starting point are a danger signal of trends emerging in the whole women's movement.
>
> (Riddell, cited in Ekins and King 1996: 189)

Recent empirical research into the relationship between transgender and feminism (Hines 2007) has articulated the impact of exclusionary politics on the lives of both trans women and trans men. While trans women were positioned as 'outsiders' because they were not 'born women,' trans men were often viewed as feminist traitors; the argument being that, in transitioning, they were denouncing their feminist politics for male privilege (Halberstam 1998; Monro and Warren 2004; Hines 2005, 2007).

Writing against a politics of identity based upon gendered authenticity, trans scholarship and activism has mapped out the common ground between feminism and transgender (Rubin 1996; Hale 1998; Cromwell 1999; Wilchins 2002; Koyama 2003; Monro and Warren 2004; Hines 2005). Hale (1998), for example, discusses how the themes of bodily autonomy and freedom of choice run through both feminist and transgender politics. Wilchins (2002) draws parallels between the projects of feminism and transgender; proposing that transgender has much to offer feminism:

> 'gender-queerness' would seem to be a natural avenue for feminism to contest Woman's equation with nurturance, femininity, reproduction: in short to trouble the project of Man.
>
> (Wilchins 2002: 57)

In discussing the role of trans men in feminism, Cromwell also suggests that transgender has much to bring to feminism:

> Female-to-male transpeople constitute a prime subject for feminist thought and methods, if for no reason than being born biologically female or assigned at birth as female. Feminists should be concerned that male-dominated discourses have made female-to-male transpeople virtually invisible.
>
> (Cromwell 1999: 9)

For Rubin, such mutuality requires dislodging gender biology or socialisation as cornerstones of identity—what he terms an 'ideal feminist identity paradigm,' (1996: 308). Alternatively, Rubin proposes an 'action paradigm' in which feminist identity arises out of political commitment rather than female biology: '"Womanhood" is no longer a necessary, nor sufficient qualification for feminist identity. A feminist is one who acts in concert with feminist ideals' (Rubin 1998: 308). A feminist identity thus arises from political commitment, not gendered biology or history.

Corresponding with feminist communities, there is a history of exclusion of trans people within lesbian and gay cultures. In the 1960s, trans people played a visible role in pivotal moments of lesbian and gay liberation such as the 'Stonewall riots,' and worked alongside lesbian and gay activists to form seminal organisations such as 'Gay Activists Alliance' and the 'Gay Liberation Front' (Wilchins 2002, 2004; Hines 2009). Yet, as Devor and Matte argue, their involvement has been marginalised in lesbian and gay histories:

> People who are today known as transgendered and transsexual have always been present in homosexual rights movements. Their presence and contributions, however, have not always been fully acknowledged or appreciated.
>
> (Devor and Matte 2006: 387)

During the 1970s, lesbian and gay organisations increasingly adopted a politics of social reform. Trans people were seen to be a political liability to this assimilationist agenda; as explicitly illustrated by the recollections of US activist Matt Foreman:

> There was a time when nobody wanted to even mention transgender issues or have transgender people accompany you on lobbying visits to members of your state assembly because that was pushing the envelope too far [. . .] There was a myth in our community, and frankly I was part of that myth, that including transgender people would set our cause back.
>
> (Foreman quoted by Leff n.d.)

While identity-based feminist politics developed around the uniform concept of 'woman,' lesbian and gay identity politics were based around the shared experiences of 'lesbians' and 'gay men.' However, these sexual identity categories were understood through gender: so that a lesbian identity mapped onto a female body and a gay male identity that of a male body. Moreover, sexual identity categories did not simply denote the gender of the identifying subject, but also that of her/his object of desire: thus a 'lesbian' desired 'women' and a 'gay man' desired 'men.' As much trans scholarship has addressed, trans identities problematise straightforward readings of the relationship between gender and sexuality; showing the limitations of sexual identity categories as well as those of gender (Devor 1989; Feinberg 1996; Nataf 1996; Halberstam 1998; Cromwell 1999; Monro 2005; Boyd 2006; Devor and Matte 2006; Schrock and Reid 2006; Stryker 2006; Hines 2007; Sanger 2008). Thus as transgender complicated the notion of a universal gender identity, it challenged a unitary notion of sexuality. As Devor and Matte (2006) detail:

> Homosexual collective identity, especially in the days before queer politics, was largely framed as inborn, like ethnicity, and based primarily on sexual desires for persons of the same sex and gender. However, such definitions make sense only when founded on clearly delineated distinctions between sexes and genders. It becomes considerably harder to delineate who is gay and who is lesbian when it's not clear who is

male or a man, and who is female or a woman. Like bisexual people, transgendered and transsexual people destabilize the otherwise easy divisions of men and women into categories of straight and gay because they are both and/or neither. Thus there is a long standing tension over the political terrain of queer politics between gays and lesbians, on the one hand, and transgendered and transsexual people, on the other.

(Devor and Matte 2006: 387)

As trans scholars and activists countered the exclusion of trans people from feminist communities, they sought to carve out a cooperative politics of sexuality. Rubin (1992) appealed for a greater tolerance towards trans people within lesbian and gay communities and traced historical points of commonality between these communities. Feinberg (1996) also argued for a coalition politics in support of transgender civil rights. For Stryker, the 'transgender phenomena' productively invites: '[. . .] queer studies, and gay and lesbian communities, to take another look at the many ways bodies, identities and desires can be interwoven' (Stryker 2006: 8).

While empirical research (Hines 2007; Sanger 2008) points to exclusions of trans people in feminist and lesbian and gay communities, it also evidences how, more recently, these communities are moving towards a more inclusive politics. The shift away from restrictive gender identity politics within feminism, then, is mirrored by less restrained understandings of sexual identity politics (Hines 2009). As I have argued elsewhere (Hines 2005; 2007), queer politics may be encouraging both contemporary feminism and political movements around sexuality to pay greater attention to gender variance. Moreover, as this discussion has indicated, a move towards diversity within feminist and sexual political movements came out of the interventions of trans activists.

Stryker (2006) traces the advent of transgender studies to two publications from the early 1990s. First, Sandy Stone's (1991) *Posttranssexual Manifesto* called for transsexuals to leave behind claims of authenticity and to come out as trans men and women. Second, in a political pamphlet entitled *Transgender Liberation: A Movement Whose Time Has Come*, Leslie Feinberg (1992) envisaged a united movement of all individuals who fell outside gendered social conventions and embodied norms. In turn, these publications reflected the organisation of a visible trans movement beyond the academy; demonstrating again how theory and politics interconnect.

The emergence in the US of what Stryker terms 'politicized communities of identity' (Stryker 2006: 5) is evident throughout the 1990s in the formation of activist groups such as 'Transgender Nation' and 'FtM International,' community cultural productions such as the zines 'Gender Trash' and 'The Transsexual News Telegraph,' and trans community activism around AIDS (Stryker 1996). In the UK, the trans political lobbying group 'Press for Change' was formed after trans man Mark Rees lost his case for the rights to privacy and marriage in the European Court of Human Rights. The decade also witnessed the growth of trans support groups. In developing community networks of care, these groups articulated a movement-based critique of a medical system of care (Hines 2007). The growth of home computers was also significant in bringing together a '[. . .] geographically dispersed, diverse trans community [. . .]' (Whittle 1996: xii).

The conceptual, cultural and social shifts discussed here form the backdrop to significant legislative developments in recent years. In the US, debate over the inclusion of gender identity in the 'Employment Non-Discrimination Act' (ENDA) continues, while in the UK, the 'Gender Recognition Act' (2004), enables transgender people to change their birth certificates and to marry in their gender of choice. Much then has changed since this introduction's point of departure in the nineteenth century. The key intersecting shifts that I have identified here are the 'queering' of both theory and politics of gender and sexuality; the emergence of a visible trans movement; and a changing social and political climate in the UK, Europe and the US, which has led to legal recognition of the rights of trans people.

This book arises from, and reflects, the growing interest in practices of gender diversity within the social sciences. This book seeks to consider the social dynamics of gender diversity through a range of inter-connected ethnographic, theoretical and policy questions. From this juncture, the book has two central aims. First it strives to give voice to the breadth and variety of sociological studies emerging around transgender; reflecting original work that addresses current social, cultural and legal shifts around gender and sexuality. Second, it seeks to articulate and develop a distinctly sociological perspective on gender diversity. With these points in mind, I move on to consider what a sociology of transgender might look like.

A SOCIOLOGY OF TRANSGENDER

Throughout the 1990s much of the scholarly work on transgender was developed out of the field of humanities, particularly in the US (for example, Devor 1989; Butler 1990; Epstein and Straub 1991; Stone 1991; Garber 1992; Prosser 1998; Wilchins 1997; Halberstam 1998; Stryker 1998; Cromwell 1999). This body of work was instrumental in questioning medical constructions of transsexuality and, thus, in challenging the pathologisation of trans people. Moreover, these wide-ranging analyses focused attention on a diversity of non-normative gendered practices; illuminating the weakness of a binary gender model. Since then, scholarly work on transgender from the humanities and social sciences has developed at a rapid pace. The socio-biological focus on transsexuality evident in medical and psychological approaches has been challenged. Rather than concentrating on aetiologies of gender diversity—as do medical and psychological studies of transsexuality—considerations of transgender from disciplines such as sociology, social policy, gender studies, sexuality studies, law, politics, human geography, cultural studies and anthropology, attend to cultural, legal and spatial configurations of transgender, and to the social experiences and concerns of trans people themselves.

Over the past decade, analyses of transgender have moved from the margins and transgender studies has established itself as one of the most creative sites of debate within gender and sexuality studies. As the previous discussion addressed, the interventions of trans scholars affected strong critiques of the organising principles and theoretical signifiers of feminism and lesbian and gay theory/politics, and articulated the productive challenges of transgender for feminist and queer theory and politics. The preceding discussion also mapped the ways in which transgender has emerged as a subject of increasing social, cultural and legal interest. Alongside a 'cultural turn to transgender'—signified by a rising focus on transgender within the media and popular culture—shifting attitudes towards transgender people are evident in law (Hines 2007). These social, cultural and legislative developments reflect the ways in which transgender is acquiring increasing visibility in contemporary society, and mark transgender as an important and timely area of social and cultural inquiry.

Sociological scholars have begun to turn their attention to practices of gender diversity. The publication of several sole-authored monographs (Ekins 1997; Ekins and King 1996, 2006; Monro 2005; Hines 2007) and a recent Reader (Stryker and Whittle 2006) reflect a flurry of academic interest in transgender from social scientists. Further, there are numerous doctoral and post-doctoral projects on transgender in progress in universities across the UK, Europe and the US.

'Identity' has long been a building block in the sociological project to link the individual and society. From here on in, gender identity—alongside identity markers such as class and race, and more recently, sexuality—has featured as a primary site of sociological investigation. As Gilroy states, from a sociological perspective, 'we live in a world where identity matters. It matters both as a concept, theoretically, and as a contested fact of contemporary political life.' (Gilroy 1997: 301) Sociology, then, has utilised the concept of identity in order to examine dimensions of social inequality, and to explore the relationship between structure and agency in the formation of collective identities. Further, the influence of post-structuralism affected an, albeit controversial, 'cultural turn' in sociology. As Friedland and Mohr elaborate:

> Problems of meaning, discourse, aesthetics, value, textuality, and narrativity, topics traditionally within the humanists' purview, are now coming to the fore as sociologists increasingly emphasize the role of meanings, symbols, cultural frames, and cognitive schema in their theorizations of social process and institutions. This is happening across the intellectual landscape.
>
> (Friedland and Mohr 2004: 1)

Considering these developments, it is noteworthy that sociological analyses of gender diversity are a very recent development. Sociological work on gender—and sexual—identity formation and experience has, in the main, taken the gender binary as read.[3] Despite poststructuralism's stress on the discursive production of power, then, and the turn to 'difference' within post colonialist scholarship and queer theory, until recently, the gender binary has been naturalised within social theory.

Transgender raises questions about the formation of *all* gender identities; particularly concerning the extent to which we can shape and re-shape individual and collective identities. These matters are central to sociological concerns around identity broadly, and, more specifically, key to debates around contemporary gender and sexual identities and the materiality of the body within gender and sexuality studies. Transgender has much, then, to bring to social analysis. Conversely, sociology provides a pertinent site through which to consider key conceptual and substantive issues around transgender.

A 'sociological imagination' (Mills 1959) links individual experience to social institutions, and sheds light on how experience is culturally and historically situated. Such epistemological and ontological considerations provide productive theoretical tools through which to examine transgender. Linking 'experience' to social and cultural formations enables a material and corporeal analysis of transgender that avoids indiscriminate projections of fluidity or autonomy. An emphasis upon gender as socially relational, as well as peformatively constructed, is particularly important in accounting for gender identities that are subjectively positioned as neither fluctuating nor unstable, but, rather, as corporeally experienced. Moreover, an analysis of 'lived experience' not only brings richer possibilities for theory-building, it also enables a political project that works to shed light on systems of oppression within dominant frameworks of social organisation.

A sociology of transgender requires that practices of gender diversity are analysed in relation to wider social positionings and divisions, and should work to counter universal theorising; what Roen (2001) describes as the ethnocentrism of much trans theory. A sociological analysis should not work to simply 'add in' variables of class, gender, race, ethnicity, location, age, sexuality, and so on, but needs to critically attend to how structures of difference are mutually constructed and lived out in the 'everyday.' Much work on transgender has lacked such an intersectional analysis with the effect that 'trans people' are often represented as *only that*—as only trans. Hence trans people are disconnected from their intimate, material, geographical and spatial surroundings, and from other significant social signifiers. This problematic is not only (mis)representational, it also acts to homogenise and de-politicise. Thus privileging/de-privileging forces, such as the economic resources to pay privately for surgery, geographical access to 'trans friendly' social spaces, levels of support from intimate networks, which structure transgendered experiences are unaccounted for.

These considerations link to a further strength of a sociology of trans-gender: the development of theory through empirical research. This enables a move beyond the representational; as Plummer argues 'There are impor-tant studies to be done in the empirical world, and an obsession with texts is dangerous indeed. It is time to move beyond the text—and rapidly' (1998: 611). Similar concerns are evident in calls for non-representational theory within critical human geography. From this position, Thrift discusses non-representational theory as '[. . .] a radical attempt to wrench [research] out of contemplative models of thought . . . and towards theories of prac-tice which amplify the potential flow of events' (Thrift 2000: 556). Yet this development does not, I believe, have to signpost a move beyond or away from discourse. In arguing against a dichotomous political theorising that seeks to emphasise 'redistribution' over 'representation,'[4] Butler (1995) stresses the unstable and interconnected relationship between the material and the cultural (or discursive). From this position, empirically grounded theory can be developed from a framework that is attuned to the intersec-tions of discursive and material formations. Such a methodology may serve as a corrective to textual analyses of transgender that, again, often evade 'lived experience,' as well as enabling an intersectional consideration of transgender as previously discussed .

In taking a sociological perspective of transgender as the framework of the collection, this book has much in common with the move towards mate-riality within deconstructive approaches to gender and sexuality (Seidman 1996; Weed and Schor 1997; Monro 2005; Richardson, McLaughlin and Casey 2006; Hines 2007; Taylor 2007; 2009). While influenced by poststruc-turalist deconstructions of binary categorisations, such a framework maps the formations of power within and through gender and sexual categories. From this juncture, this book explores the ways in which (trans) gender shifts feed into wider theoretical debates around the meanings of gender, sexuality and embodiment, and considers the challenges transgender projects bring to current discourses around gender and sexuality. These debates are central to contemporary sociological theory. In empirically addressing the forma-tion of collective identities, the book also examines the relationship between transgender communities and the history and contemporary organisation of lesbian and gay activism, queer and feminist politics and spaces.

Existing theoretical and empirical work foregrounds this project. In mapping a diversity of transgender practices in contemporary society, the body of work developed by Ekins and King has employed a sociological imaginary that is finely attuned to diversities amongst, and lines of connec-tion between, transgender identities. Hird (2000, 2006) is also concerned with developing a social analysis to account for gender variance. In trac-ing the different ways that transsexuality has been conceptualised, Hird examines how intersexed and transsexed bodies bring binary frameworks of sex and gender into question. Such issues, Hird (2002) argues, are deeply sociological. Monro's (2005) notion of gender pluralism is also significant in developing a social model of gender as a spectrum. Also influencing this book are calls for a queer sociology (Seidman 1996; Roseneil 2000; Hines 2007) and Namaste's (2000) proposal of a poststructuralist sociology. These frameworks seek to develop approaches to gender and sexual difference by grounding deconstructionist analyses within a sociological framework.

This book aims to go beyond simply 'showcasing' new identities. Rather, the identities explored throughout the book have implications for understanding and living gendered lives more widely in the twenty-first century. Furthermore, these emerging identities have key significance for the future developments of theory on gender and sexuality. Sociological studies of transgender lives offer the tools to transform existing theories of gender and sexuality.

AN OVERVIEW OF THEMES AND CHAPTERS

The book is organised around four themes: Emerging Identities; Trans Governance; Transforming Identities; Transforming Theory, which reflect the overarching concerns of the book.

First, the book seeks to consider the emergence of distinctive transgender identities in the twenty-first century, and to examine how social and cultural developments shape these identities on both an individual and collective level. These themes are reflected in the first part of the book: *Emerging Identities*. In *The Emergence of New Transgendering Identities in the Age of the Internet* (Chapter 1), Ekins and King consider the role of the Internet in the emergence of new transgendering identities. They identify three 'sites' within which transgendering identities were previously fashioned: firstly, the medical knowledge and practice that developed from the late 1800s to the 1950s; secondly, the sub-cultural knowledge and organisations that developed in the 1960s through to the 1980s; and thirdly, the transgender rights movements which emerged in the 1990s. From the mid-1990s onwards, these sites became interconnected in new ways through the emergence and development of the Internet. Ekins and King detail the proliferation of new transgendering identities enabled by the new technologies of the Internet. In illustration they consider the rise of the virtual identity and address the emergence of new identities, such as the autogynephilic transsexual identity and the Internet sissy, following interrelations between medical and 'member' knowledge.

Westbrook's chapter turns to print media to examine shifting meanings of 'transgender.' In *Becoming Knowably Gendered: The Production of Transgender Possibilities and Constraints in the Mass and Alternative Press from 1990–2005 in the United States* (Chapter 2), Westbrook analyses the 'content' of 'transgender' as it has moved into popular discourse. Westbrook first examines what she calls 'teaching transgender' articles—which appeared in trans community publications and the mainstream news media in the United States between 1990 and 2005—in order to explore the possible ways of being gendered the term 'transgender' produces. Although 'transgender' expands possible ways of living, Westbrook argues that, like all categories, it also constrains. For example, as 'transgender' was (re)produced within the mainstream press, it came to mean people who were not 'real women' or 'real men'. Moreover, as 'transgender' replaced and encompassed 'transsexual' in the mainstream press, people who had 'sex-change' surgeries were understood as transgender rather than, as they had previously been recognised, men and women. Westbrook argues that although 'transgender' made more ways of doing gender legitimate, in the process of making previously illegible genders readable, it reproduced the idea that all people have a 'knowable' gender.

In *Telling Trans Stories: (Un)doing the Science of Sex* (Chapter 3) Rooke examines the ways in which young trans people 'make sense' of scientific and cultural discourse. Rooke presents a case study of the 'Sci:dentity Project,' an inter-disciplinary participatory arts and research project, which engaged 18 young transsexual and transgendered people from across the UK in a series of creative workshops to explore the science of sex and gender. Findings from the project are employed to bring a sociological focus of subjectivity to queer theory. Thus Rooke argues for the importance of locating a critique of gender norms within the complexity of trans people's lives as they navigate the gendered and sexual normativity of schools, care systems and youth groups, and liberatory queer identities and medical governmentality. Competing narratives of trans subjectivities are juxtaposed throughout the chapter so that grassroots political understandings of trans identities, informed by queer politics and theory, rub up against medical diagnosis of transsexuality as a psychiatric disorder. Here, the politics of storytelling are interrogated within a creative cultural setting that enables trans youth to narrate their gender in new creative ways.

The second concern of the book is to examine how law and social policy have responded to contemporary gender shifts. Such questions are explored in the second part of the book: *Trans Governance*. In *Recognising Diversity? The Gender Recognition Act and Transgender Citizenship* (Chapter 4) Hines draws on empirical research to explore the impact of the UK 'Gender Recognition Act' (2004) upon the construction of individual and collective transgender identities. The chapter asks why recognition 'matters' to some trans people and why it does not to others. In examining this recent legislation, Hines considers individual and community understandings and practices of a new framework of citizenship. The chapter suggests that while the 'claims' of citizenship of some trans people are now being met, deep divisions over a politics of recognition mean that transgender citizenship remains a contested terrain. Moreover, Hines concludes, the schism between 'claims' and 'transgressions' of citizenship have widened further as 'deserving' and 'undeserving' gendered and sexual citizens are constructed anew through law.

Davy's chapter *Transsexual Agents: Negotiating Authenticity and Embodiment within the UK's Medicolegal System* (Chapter 5) looks at the complex relationships trans people have with medicolegal institutions. The narratives that form Davy's research are considered in relation to the phenomenology of authenticity to explore the negotiations between general practitioners and trans people at the initial stages of transition. As these encounters materialise around the notion of authenticity, Davy examines the experiences of trans people's treatment in both the NHS and private healthcare settings. Her analysis moves on temporally to consider policy implementations and how 'treatment' is affected. Davy also discusses the UK Gender Recognition Act (2004) and its effects on transsexual subjectivities and identities. By incorporating transsexuals' narratives into the structure-agency debate, Davy moves beyond a dichotomous argument of authenticity (as tangible) and inauthenticity (as arbitrary).

The law and social policy are examined in relation to the workplace in Rundall and Vecchietti's chapter *(In)Visibility in the Workplace: The Experiences of Trans-Employees in the UK* (Chapter 6). Rundall and Vecchietti explore employees' self-reported experiences of inclusion, protection and discrimination in UK workplaces, and suggest that these issues link to questions of visibility or invisibility. Although the options for employees to feel included and protected whilst being visibly trans/gender-diverse continue to increase, they argue that many individuals still face discrimination and prejudice. Their findings highlight the restrictions to inclusion and protection in the workplace, which have wider implications for policy debates around inclusivity in the UK.

The third aim of the book is to articulate diverse ways of living gender and sexual lives in contemporary society. These concerns are reflected in the third part of the book: *Transforming Identities*. In *Racialising Gender Performance and Performing Racialised Genders: The Impact of Race in a Drag King Community* (Chapter 7) Shapiro presents an in-depth case study of feminist drag troupe 'The Disposable Boy Toys' (DBT) from Santa Barbara, US. Shapiro examines the extent to which the relationship between drag and gender identity is mediated by race. Shapiro asserts that the gendered meaning of drag performances cannot be understood without viewing drag as a gendered process in which the performance itself—as well as the organisational and ideological context in which it takes place—transforms the gender identity of the drag performer. Her research shows that the process of participating in drag communities may function as a form of consciousness-raising and a site of identity transformation. In addition, the case study explores how racialised performances, a white collective identity, and the lack of racial diversity mediate the gender identity shifts of participants in DBT. Thus Shapiro argues that gender identity development is affected in fundamental ways by racial demographics within oppositional communities.

Gregory's chapter, Transgendering in an Urban Dutch Streetwalking Zone (Chapter 8) examines the experiences of transgendered sex workers in the Netherlands. Gregory explores how these sex workers negotiate divergent expressions of their gendered and sexual selves in both the professional and private sphere. As such, in some instances, gender performance does not always inform potential sexual customers or personal partners of what role each party will play during the act of sex. Gregory suggests that what emerges from this is a disjuncture between gender performance, the customised sexual desires of clients, and their lived emotional experiences with personal partners. Yet, there is no language or utterance through which to categorise these sexual acts or performances because they exist outside of a gendered Westernised binary. The chapter works to suggest ways in which compulsory heterosexuality influences sex worker relations with clients and lovers, and how, in turn, the services provided by transgendered sex workers transform client expectations of female-born sex workers.

In *Beyond Borders: Lived Experiences of Atypically Gendered Transsexual People* (Chapter 9) Davidmann first examines the lived experiences of self-identified non-binary transsexual people in relation to the medical and popular view of transsexuality. Second, she addresses concerns around visibility and invisibility in the social domain by looking at differences between 'private' and 'public' gender presentations. These concerns are analysed through case studies of two atypically gendered transsexual people; one born female-bodied and the other born male-bodied. Davidmann suggests that contrary to the popular belief that a desire for genital surgery is an essential criterion of a transsexual identity, increasing numbers of transsexual people do not wish to have 'sex change' operations. She thus proposes an alternative perspective to the medical and popular view that the 'cure' for transsexuality is the exchange of a male body for a female one, or vice versa. In doing so, she offers a counter narrative to the notion of 'being born in the wrong body,' which has come to symbolise the transsexual condition and configures around the genitalia as the signifier of female-ness or male-ness (Stone, 1991). Davidmann's case studies demonstrate the complex ways in which transsexual people experience their bodies, and bring to the surface the 'policing' of gender in public spaces and medical practice.

The final aim of the book is to theoretically reflect on the increasing visibility of trans people in contemporary society and, particularly, to examine the increasing impact of transgender theory upon the social sciences. These issues are examined in the fourth part of the book: *Transforming Theory*. This section traces the challenges and the contributions transgender theory has brought to gender theory, queer theory and sociological approaches to identity and citizenship. In keeping with the aims of the book, this section points to the importance of incorporating transgender into sociological theory and empirical sociological research.

In *Who Put the 'Hetero' in Sexuality?* (Chapter 10), Fee examines how people who define as transgender experience sexuality and gender. Her research illustrates how sex, gender and desire are grounded and organised within the heterosexual matrix. From this departure, comes the telling of transgender narratives, which, Fee suggests, structures how experiences are described and influences what is experienced. Fee highlights the silences around the complexities of gender and sexuality and maps the constraints, and effects, of the current classification systems within the heterosexual paradigm.

Hammers' chapter, *Corporeal Silences and Bodies that Speak: The Promises and Limitations of Queer in Lesbian/Queer Sexual Spaces* (Chapter 11) is based on her ethnographic study of two Canadian lesbian/queer bathhouses. Hammers explores the centrality of 'queer,' and the concomitant promises and limitations of a queer project in relation to gender diversity, bodily speech and sexual agency. Her chapter complicates the debate surrounding queer theory by showing how queer operates 'on the ground.' She outlines how the bathhouse organisers espouse and utilise queer theory in combination with feminist principles to enable the discursive and physical conditions for intelligibility and sexual agency among bathhouse patrons. While the philosophical underpinning of queer is one of indeterminacy, flux, instability and, thus 'liberation,' within these bathhouse spaces transgendered individuals and queers of colour have had difficulty experiencing these supposed 'queer' ideals. Thus Hammers takes up Stein and Plummer's (1996) assertion that sociology can give to queer theory 'a more grounded, more accessible approach' (185) to ask: how does the queering of space impact and shape the bathhouse environment? Who remains marginalised and why? Where bodies are front and centre of the spatial landscape, can queer be an effective strategy for gender diversity and sexual/bodily agency?

In *Towards a Sociology of Gender Diversity: The Indian and UK Cases* (Chapter 12), Monro presents a snap shot of theoretical developments leading up to the formation of a sociology of transgender and intersex, and provides an empirically-driven overview of an intersectional approach to a sociological theorising of gender diversity. Monro's contribution speaks to Roen's (2001) important critique of the ethnocentrism of much trans theorising. Thus she addresses the importance of cultural specificity in theorising gender diversity. Her chapter is set within the context of cross-cultural work concerning gender diversity. By taking two localities—the UK and India—as comparative sites, and ensuring that complexity in both sites is made evident, Monro works against cultural 'idealising', which privileges a non-Western 'primordial location' where gender diversity flourished before the 'Fall into Western Modernity.' (Towle and Morgan 2006: 666)

In the final chapter *Beyond Gender and Sexuality Binaries in Sociological Theory: The Case for Transgender Inclusion* (Chapter 13), Sanger explores the potentialities of transgender studies for challenging the binary notions of gender and sexuality that continue to undergird mainstream sociological research. In considering recent social and legal developments relating to trans people, Sanger argues that sociologists have not taken on board the importance of these shifts in contemporary theorisations of identity. In bringing the collection to a close, she examines how empirical studies of trans people's lives may engage sociology in new and illuminating discursive frameworks. In addition, the usefulness of sociological theory and method to transgender studies is reflected upon. Here Sanger emphasises the value of bringing transgender studies and sociology together in order to more fully engage with the important questions raised by studies of trans lives and identities.

Of course, the organising themes of the book also work as a traditional structuring device in the preparation of a 'coherent' and 'accessible' manuscript. Such a device, however, may work to problematically *dis*connect—isolating considerations that emerge across and between the chapters. As the chapter summaries indicate, there are many areas of overlap in the book's contributions to which these categorising themes do not do full justice.

NOTES

1. The term 'transsexual' articulates the experiences of people who alter their bodies through the use of hormones and/or surgery and identify as an alternative gender to that which they were assigned at birth.
2. Kessler's more recent work develops her earlier analysis in addressing how medical and surgical procedures work to construct a binary model in the case of intersex children (see Kessler 2000).
3. Exceptions to this are UK sociologists Ekins and King who, individually and collaboratively, have been producing sociological work on transgender since the 1970s.
4. See the exchanges between Butler (1997) and Fraser (1998) in Social Text.

REFERENCES

Benjamin, H. (1953) 'Transvestism and transsexualism', *International Journal of Sexology*, 7: 12–14.
Benjamin, H. (1966) *The Transsexual Phenomenon*, New York: Julian Press.
Bindel, J. (2003) 'I changed for all the wrong reasons, and then it was too late', *The Telegraph*, 15 December. http://www.parakaleo.co.uk/article9.html (accessed 27 May 2009).
Bindel, J. (2004) 'Gender benders, beware', *The Guardian*, 31 January. http://www.guardian.co.uk/world/2004/jan/31/gender.weekend7 (accessed 27 May 2009).
Bornstein, K. (1994) *Gender Outlaw: On Men, Women and the Rest of Us*, New York: Routledge.
Boyd, N. A. (2006) 'Bodies in motion: lesbian and transsexual histories', in S. Stryker and S. Whittle (eds) *The Transgender Studies Reader*, New York and Abingdon: Routledge.
Butler, J. (1990) *Gender Trouble: Feminism and the Subversion of Identity*, New York and London: Routledge.
———. (1995) 'For a careful reading', in S. Benhabib, J. Butler, D. Cornell, N. Fraser and L. Nicholson *Feminist Contentions: A Philosophical Exchange (Thinking Gender)*, London and New York: Routledge.
Butler, J. (1997) 'Merely Cultural', *Social Text*, 52–53: 265–277.

Califia, P. (1997) *Sex Changes: The Politics of Transgenderism*, San Francisco: Cleis Press.

Cromwell, J. (1999) *Transmen and FTMs: Identities, Bodies, Genders and Sexualities*, Champaign: University of Illinois Press.

Devor, H. (1989) *Gender Blending: Confronting the Limits of Duality*, Bloomington: Indiana University Press.

Devor, A. H. and Matte, N. (2006) 'One Inc. and Reed Erickson: the uneasy collaboration of gay and trans activism, 1964–2003', in S. Stryker and S. Whittle (eds) *The Transgender Studies Reader*, New York and Abingdon: Routledge.

Ekins, R. (1997) *Male Femaling: A Grounded Theory Approach to Cross-Dressing and Sex-Changing*, New York and London: Routledge.

Ekins, R. and King, D. (1996) *Blending Genders: Social Aspects of Cross-Dressing and Sex-Changing*, London: Routledge.

———. (2006) *The Transgender Phenomenon*, London: Sage.

Ellis, H. (1938) *The Dance of Life*, Grosset and Dunlap.

Epstein, J. and Straub, K. (1991) *Body Guards: The Cultural Politics of Gender Ambiguity*, New York and London: Routledge.

Feinberg, L. (1992) *Transgender Liberation: A Movement Whose Time Has Come*, New York: World View Forum.

———. (1996) *Transgender Warriors: Making History from Joan of Arc to Dennis Rodman*, Boston: Beacon Press.

Foucault, M. (1978) *The History of Sexuality, Volume 1: An Introduction*, New York: Random House.

Fraser, N. (1998) 'Heterosexism, misrecognition, and capitalism: a response to Judith Butler', *Social Text*, 53/54: 279–289.

Friedland, R. and Mohr, J. (2004) *Matters of Culture: Cultural Sociology in Practice (Cambridge Cultural Social Studies)*, Cambridge: Cambridge University Press.

Garber, M. (1992) *Vested Interests: Cross-Dressing and Cultural Anxiety*, New York: Routledge.

Garfinkel, H. (1967) *Studies in Ethnomethodolgy*, Englewood Cliffs, N.J: Prentice Hall.

Gilroy, P. (1997) 'Diaspora and the detours of identity', in K. Woodward (ed.) *Identity and Difference: Culture, Media and Identities*, London and Thousand Oaks, California: Sage (in association with the Open University).

Greer, G. (1999) *The Whole Woman*, London: Random House.

Halberstam, J. (1998) *Female Masculinity*, Durham, NC: Duke University Press.

Hale, J. (1998) 'Tracing a ghostly memory in my throat: reflections of ftm feminist voice and agency', in T. Digby (ed.) *Men Doing Feminism*, New York and London: Routledge.

Hines, S. (2005) '"I am a feminist but . . . ": transgender men, women and feminism', in J. Reger (ed.) *Different Wavelengths: Studies of the Contemporary Women's Movement*, New York and London: Routledge.

———. (2007) *TransForming Gender: Transgender Practices of Identity and Intimacy*, Bristol: Policy Press.

———. (2009) 'A pathway to diversity? human rights, citizenship and politics of transgender', *Contemporary Politics*, 15(1): 87–102.

Hird, M. J. (2000) 'Gender's nature: intersexuals, transsexuals and the "sex" / "gender" binary', *Feminist Theory*, 1(3): 347–364.

———. (2006) 'Animal trans', *Australian Feminist Studies*, 21(49): 35–48.

Hirschfeld, M. (1910) *Die Transvestiten*, Berlin: Pulvermacher.

Hollibaugh, A. (1989) 'Desire for the future: radical hope in passion and pleasure', in C. Vance (ed.) *Pleasure and Danger: Exploring Female Sexuality*, London: Pandora.

Jackson, S (1999) *Heterosexuality in Question*, London: Sage.

Jeffreys, S. (1997) 'Transgender activism: a feminist perspective', *The Journal of Lesbian Studies*, 1(3/4): 55–74.

Kessler, S. J. and McKenna, W. (1978) *Gender: An Ethnomethodological Approach*, New York: Wiley.

Kessler, S. and McKenna, W. (2000) 'Who put the "trans" in transgender? gender theory and everyday life', *The International Journal of Transgenderism*, 4(3). http://www.symptosion.com/ijt/gilbert/kessler.htm (accessed 27 May 2009).

Koyama, E. (2003) 'Transfeminist manifesto', in R. Dicker and A. Piepmeier (eds) *Catching a Wave: Reclaiming Feminism for the 21st Century*, Northeastern Press.

Leff, L. (n.d.) 'As gay pride hits stride, transgendered find more acceptance', Associated Press. http://www.usatoday.com (accessed 10 July 2008).

MacKinnon, C. (1982) 'Feminism, Marxism, and the state: an agenda for theory', *Signs: Journal of Women in Culture and Society*, 7: 515–544.

Mills, C. W. (1959) *The Sociological Imagination*, Oxford: Oxford University Press.

Money, J. and Green, R. (eds) (1969) *Transsexualism and Sex-Reassignment*, Baltimore: The Johns Hopkins University Press.

Monro, S. (2005) *Gender Politics: Citizenship, Activism and Sexual Diversity*, London: Pluto Press.

Monro, S. and Warren, L. (2004) 'Transgendering citizenship', *Sexualities*, 7(3): 345–362.

Namaste, V. K. (2000) *Invisible Lives: The Erasure of Transsexual and Transgendered People*, Chicago: The University of Chicago Press.

Nataf, Z. (1996) *Lesbians Talk Transgender*, London: Scarlet Press.

Plummer, K. (1998) 'The past, present and future of the sociology of same-sex relations', in P. M. Nardi and B. E. Schneider (eds) *Social Perspectives in Lesbian and Gay Studies*, London: Routledge.

Prosser, J. (1998) *Second Skins: The Body Narratives of Transsexuality*, New York: Columbia University Press.

Raymond, J. (1980) *The Transsexual Empire*, London: The Women's Press.

Richardson, D., McLaughlin, J. and Casey, M. (2006) *Intersections Between Feminist and Queer Theory*, Basingstoke: Palgrave Macmillan.

Riddell, C. (1996) 'Divided sisterhood', in R. Ekins and D. King (eds) *Blending Genders: Social Aspects of Cross–Dressing and Sex–Changing*, London: Routledge.

Roen, K. (2001) '"Either/or" and "both/neither": discursive tensions in transgender politics', *Signs: Journal of Women in Culture and Society*, 27(2): 501–522.

Roseneil, S. (2000) 'Queer frameworks and queer tendencies: towards an understanding of postmodern transformations of sexuality', *Sociological Research Online*, 5(3). http://www.socresonline.org.uk/5/3/roseneil.html (accessed 27 May 2009).

Rubin, G. (1989) 'Thinking sex: notes for a radical theory of the politics of sexuality', in C. Vance (ed.) *Pleasure and Danger: Exploring Female Sexuality*, London: Pandora.

———. (1992) 'Of Catamites and kings: reflections on butch, gender and boundaries', in J. Nestle (ed.) *The Persistent Desire: A Femme-Butch-Reader*, Boston: Alyson.

Rubin, H. (1996) 'Do You Believe in Gender?' *Sojourner*, 21: 6.

Sanger, T. (2008) 'Trans governmentality: the production and regulation of gendered subjectivities', *Journal of Gender Studies*, 17(1): 41–53.

Schrock, P. and Reid, L. (2006) 'Transsexuals' sexual stories', *Archives of Sexual Behaviour*, 35(1): 75–86.

Sedgwick, E. K. (1990) *Epistemology of the Closet*, Berkeley: University of California Press.

Seidman, S. (ed.) (1996) *Queer Theory/Sociology*, Oxford: Blackwell.

Stein, A and Plummer, K (1996) '"I can't even think straight": 'queer' theory and the missing sexual revolution in sociology', in S. Seidman (ed.) *Queer Theory/Sociology*, Oxford: Blackwell.

Stone, S. (1991) 'The *empire* strikes back: a posttranssexual manifesto', in J. Epstein and K. Straub (eds) *Body Guards: The Cultural Politics of Sexual Ambiguity*, Routledge.

Stryker, S. (1998) 'The transgender issue: an introduction', *GLQ*, 4(2): 145–158.

———. (2006) '(De)subjucated knowledge: an introduction to transgender studies', in S. Stryker and S. Whittle (eds) *The Transgender Studies Reader*, New York and Abingdon: Routledge.

Stryker, S. and Whittle, S. (2006) (eds) *The Transgender Studies Reader*, London and New York: Routledge.

Taylor, Y. (2007) *Working-Class Lesbian Life Experiences: Classed Outsiders*, Basingstoke: Palgrave.

———. (2009) *Lesbian and Gay Parenting: Securing Social and Educational Capital*, Basingstoke: Palgrave Macmillan.

Towle, E. B. and Morgan, L. M (2006) 'Romancing the transgender native: rethinking the use of the "third gender" concept', in S. Stryker and S. Whittle (eds) *The Transgender Studies Reader*, London, New York: Routledge.

Thrift, N. (2000) 'Non-representational Theory', in R. J. Johnston, D. Gregory, G. Pratt and M. Watts (eds) *The Dictionary of Human Geography*, Blackwell: Oxford.

Vance, C. (ed.) (1989) *Pleasure and Danger: Exploring Female Sexuality*, London and New York: Routledge.

Weed, E. and Schor, N. (1997) *Feminism Meets Queer Theory*, Bloomington, IN: Indiana University Press.

Weeks, J. (1977) *Coming Out: Homosexual Politics in Britain from the Nineteenth Century to the Present*, London: Quartet.

Whittle, S. (1996) 'Gender fucking or fucking gender? Current cultural contributions to theories of gender blending', in R. Ekins and D. King (eds) *Blending Genders: Social Aspects of Cross-Dressing and Sex-Changing*, London: Routledge.

———. (2006) 'Foreword', in S. Stryker and S. Whittle (eds) *The Transgender Studies Reader*, New York and Abingdon: Routledge.

Wilchins, R. A. (1997) *Read My Lips: Sexual Subversion and the End of Gender*, Firebrand Books.

———. (2002) 'Gender rights are human rights', in J. Nestle, C. Howell and R. A. Wilchins (eds) *GenderQueer: Voices from Beyond the Sexual Binary*, Los Angeles: Alyson Books.

———. (2004) *Queer Theory, Gender Theory: An Instant Primer*, Los Angeles: Alyson Books.

Part I
Emerging Identities

1 The Emergence of New Transgendering Identities in the Age of the Internet

Richard Ekins and Dave King[1]

INTRODUCTION

This chapter is a case study of the emergence of two new transgendering identities in the age of the Internet, situated within the conceptual frameworks we have developed elsewhere for the sociological analysis of the full range of transgender diversity in contemporary Euro-American societies (Ekins 1997; Ekins and King 2001a, 2006). These conceptual frameworks were based, principally, on extensive life history work with several hundred Euro-American transgender informants and ethnographic work with several thousands of transpeople worldwide, since the mid-1970s, as guided by the methodology of grounded theory. Grounded theorists follow the research strategy of 'theoretical sampling'. Informants and research sites are sampled on the basis of developing theory. Emerging data is analysed using the 'constant comparative method' (Glaser and Strauss 1967; Glaser 1978).

Ekins (1993, 1997) considered 'male femaling' identities in terms of their emergence within three sets of interrelations: those of sex (the body), sexuality, and gender; those of self, identity and social world; and those of 'scientific' (expert), 'member' and 'common sense' (lay) formulations of transgendering phenomena. He set forth an ideal-typical career path within which a range of male femaling identities emerged from 'beginning', through 'fantasying', 'doing', 'constituting', and 'consolidating'.

Ekins (1997) did not consider 'female maling'; neither did he give due weight to the (then) recent emergence of 'transcending' gender identities. In particular, in relation to this chapter, Ekins (1997) only touched upon 'demaling' and 'ungendering' trans identities. We addressed these various omissions in Ekins and King (2001a) and more fully in Ekins and King (2006). In that book, we argued that all transgender identities emerge within one of four modes of transgendering: those of 'migrating', 'oscillating', 'negating', and 'transcending'. We identified five principal sub-processes variously operative within each mode: those of 'erasing', 'substituting', 'concealing', 'implying' and 'redefining'. Where the privileged sub-process is 'substituting', we are likely to be evidencing the 'migrating' mode, as with the 'transsexual' who migrates across the gender border. In the oscillating mode, 'implying' is privileged, as with the male 'transvestite', who temporarily wishes to imply that he is a woman. 'Transcending' the binary divide privileges the sub-process of 're-defining', as part of a radical critique of gender polarities. Least identified and understood in the medical, research, academic, and sub-cultural literatures is the mode of transgendering we term 'negating'. When the sub-process of 'erasing' is privileged, we are likely to be witnessing the 'negating' mode of transgendering, and, where relevant, the emergence of a negating identity, as with the female to 'ungendered' person (O'Keefe and Fox 2003: 40–41) and the 'male sissy maid' (Ekins and King 2006: 152–158). Some 'negators' seek to become as 'gender less' as possible. Others, like many male sissy maids, may be feminised or feminise themselves, in the service of their sex, sexuality and gender demaling (Ekins and King 2006: 143–180).

As Plummer points out, 'Solitary "experiences" are converted into "beings" through the construction of *stories of identity*' (1995: 118, emphasis in original). The emergence of new stories of identity depends on the appearance of those we term 'identity innovators'. In the transgender field the dominant tendency has been for innovators within medico-psychiatric communities of 'experts' to construct new categorisations and typologies. However, some trans identities have emerged as a result of collaborations between 'experts' and 'members', and sometimes the line between them is blurred (Ekins and King 2006). The extent to which particular stories of identity are accepted by both 'experts' and 'members' is variable, and the struggles to promote or discredit them can sometimes be strenuous and bitter. Recent years, as we shall see, have been marked by 'members' increasingly becoming 'experts'.

At various times and places, certain stories 'cannot be told' (Plummer 1995). These stories are taboo and attempts are made to silence their tellers. Such stories, in the context of this chapter, we term 'unwelcome stories'. All stories may, of course, be variously welcome or unwelcome depending on the audience, but in this chapter we focus on two stories that are particularly unwelcome in the context of the dominant transgender narratives that have achieved a degree of respectability since the end of the twentieth century. Principally, these stories—those of the 'autogynephilic transsexual' and the 'male sissy'—are unwelcome because they privilege sexuality (the erotic) which has been underplayed, often to the point of extinction, as the 'acceptable faces' of transvestism and transsexualism have come to be characterised, increasingly, in terms of 'gender', both by most 'experts' and most 'members' (Ekins and King 2006).

In particular, as we shall see, the 'acceptable faces' of transgender have emerged in large measure through a symbiotic relationship between 'experts' and 'members', which has adopted a 'gender identity story' of transgender phenomenon. The 'autogynephilia story' has been read by many 'experts' and 'members' as potentially undermining the gains made by the 'gender identity' story, whether in terms of the latter story's potential to incorporate a biological basis for transsexualism, the theory of the sexed brain (Swaab and Garcia-Falguera 2009), or its potential to lead to a non-medicalised, non-pathological conceptualisation of transgender phenomenon, as favoured by many contemporary trans activists (James 2008) and their supporters.

At the time Plummer (1995) was writing, he could only hint at the role that the personal networked computer might come to play in the telling of sexual stories. Today, the Internet has become a major, indeed, to many, *the* major medium through which stories of all kinds, not just sexual stories, are told. Most importantly, for unwelcome stories, it offers the teller of such stories anonymity. Tellers, as it were, can put their heads above the parapet in comparative safety. Secondly, it enables the stories to reach others who might identify with them to an extent that would have been impossible before the development of the Internet. By the same token, the Internet enables unwelcome stories to be heard by those who would rather not hear them and who would seek to silence them. A corollary of this, of course, is that the researcher has easy access both to the stories, and in some cases, as in this chapter, to the teller of the stories.

Hirschfeld (1991 [1910]) distinguished the 'transvestite' from the 'homosexual'. Benjamin (1966) popularised the division of Hirschfeld's 'transvestite' into two: the 'transvestite' and the 'transsexual', thus facilitating the development of the three major transgendering identities available from the 1960s through to the late 1980s: the transsexual, the transvestite and the gay drag queen. Following the work of trans community activist, Virginia Prince, the principal 'transvestite' identity available from the 1960s onwards, in an emerging trans sub-culture, privileged a gender motivation, as opposed to a sexual (erotic) motivation for cross-dressing (Ekins and King 2005). The male cross-dresser was said to be expressing the 'woman within', thus reformulating Hirschfeld's categorisation, and the medico-psychiatric work that built upon it. It was a 'member' (sub-cultural) as opposed to a 'scientific' (medical) story. Virginia Prince was a trans person. The Benjamin (scientific) story of changing the body to fit the mind, and the Prince (member) story of developing the 'woman within', as well as the gay drag emphasis upon performance and theatricality, entailed a downplaying of the relevance of unwelcome sexuality in all the major transgendering stories.

The end of the 1980s and beginnings of the 1990s ushered in a paradigm shift in the conceptualisation and theorisation of transgender phenomena. In the first place there was the move to a 'beyond the binary' view of gender, which we consider in terms of 'transcending' (Ekins and King 2006). This shift had both modernist and postmodernist variants. Feinberg (1992), for instance, reconceptualised transgender in terms of a Marxist modernist 'grand narrative'. Bornstein (1994) and Wilchins (1997), on the other hand, situated their work within postmodernist readings of gender performance and fluidity. In the second place, the greater awareness of transgender diversity, combined with a critique of the major medico-psychiatric categorisations, lessened the need for many trans people to 'find themselves' with reference to an available medico-psychiatric categorisation, as had been the norm prior to the end of the 1980s. For many, acceptance of a broad 'trans' or postmodernist 'gender queer' label sufficed (Nestle, Howell and Wilchins 1997). For others, however, the move to the acceptance of greater diversity led to the emergence of new refinements of categorisation and identity, as they sought to identify precisely who and what they were. It was within this latter backdrop that the two identities of the autogynephilic transsexual and the male sissy emerged.

Significantly, this latter paradigm shift coincided with developments in Internet technology that made the Internet an increasingly accessible resource for trans people.[2] Those at the vanguard of the postmodernist movement in transgender identity deconstruction (Bornstein 1994) often linked their arguments to the Internet as an aspect of post modernity. Here was a virtual world which to the participants might be 'more real than my real life', as one participant put it, 'who turns out to be a man playing a woman who is pretending to be a man' (Turkle 1995: 10). Certainly, there seemed to be an elective affinity between the postmodern-identifying trans people who were 'playing with' and 'performing' their gender(s) and the Internet within which it was possible to present in any gender (or none) that one wished (Whittle 1996; see also, Stryker 2000).

As social constructionist sociologists, however, we do not think there is anything inherently 'modern' or 'postmodern' about any technology, let alone the Internet. Neither do we believe that the use made of any technology is necessarily either modernist or postmodernist. Rather the task of the empirically-inclined social constructionist is to investigate that use with detailed empirical studies (e.g., Kendall 1998; Hegland and Nelson 2002; Hill 2005, Lin 2006; Shapiro 2004). We find particularly striking the fact that the Internet enabled an emerging voice for unwelcome identities; including the two unwelcome transgender identities that we focus upon in this chapter. Neither of these two identities would have developed in the way they did without the Internet. Janice, the self-identified autogynephilic transsexual we considered in Ekins and King (2001b), put it this way: 'Virtual contact creates critical mass. It was the Internet effect: that no matter how small a minority you belong to, you could at last find your community.'

The particular significance of focusing upon our chosen two identities is that one, the autogynephilic transsexual, provides an excellent illustration of a near 'taboo' medico-psychiatric categorisation initially formulated pre-Internet, in the 'old' academic sphere, and only subsequently promoted as an identity through the Internet. While the other identity, the male sissy, is dependent on the Internet for widespread dissemination of its formulation and development as a new identity distinct from the transvestite, the transsexual, the homosexual, or the transgendering sado-masochist. In the case of each identity, we focus on the way the Internet is used both for identity promulgation and development by two significant contemporary 'gender identity innovators'; Anne Lawrence (2008a), through her website *Transsexual Women's Resources* and Sissy Jaunie (2005–2008), through her blog *Emasculinization and Feminization*. In particular, the autogynephilic material on *Transsexual Women's Resources* illustrates identity promotion through the Internet, insofar as Anne Lawrence had identified as an autogynephilic transsexual prior to her use of the Internet and then used the Internet to promote that identity. Whereas Sissy Jaunie's blog, *Emasculinization and Feminization*, illustrates identity construction through the Internet, insofar as it was through his use of the Internet that Jaunie first constructed his identity as a male sissy.

ANNE LAWRENCE, THE AUTOGYNEPHILIC TRANSSEXUAL AND TRANSSEXUAL WOMEN'S RESOURCES: THE INTERNET AND IDENTITY PROMOTION

In May 1996, transactivist (later clinician and researcher) Anne Lawrence launched her site *Transsexual Women's Resources* (TWR). This site was to have a major impact in many areas of importance to transgender theory and practice. It is primarily a medical resource site for (male to female) trans women. As Lawrence puts it: 'Its purpose is to empower transsexual women by providing factual information, informed opinion, and personal narratives. I hope these resources will help transsexual women make decisions that will best serve their individual needs' (Lawrence 2008a). The listing of 'Medical and other resources for transsexual women' includes sections on such matters as hormone therapy, sex reassignment surgery, orchidectomy (castration), breast augmentation, facial feminisation surgery, voice feminisation surgery, and more controversially autogynephilia and sexuality.

The TWR site was a major influence on a number of our informants, who came to identify as autogynephilic transsexuals, largely through their reading of the relevant material on the site. Lawrence's site is important for illustrative purposes, not only because it straddles the pre-Internet and Internet ages and links the two periods. It is also an excellent example of an Internet site that builds upon pre-Internet modernist formulations of trans phenomena. It accepts a positivist theory and methodology in science and social science, and a psychopathological model of sex and gender variations, for instance. Yet it deliberately uses the Internet to develop its theorisations and to rapidly expand its sphere of influence in a way that would have been impossible in the pre-Internet age.

It is the extensive sections on autogynephilia and sexuality on the site that concern us in this chapter. It was through these sections that Lawrence championed the earlier writings of psychologist Ray Blanchard on autogynephilia ('love of oneself as a woman') (1989a, 1989b, 1991, 1993a, 1993b), which had been largely ignored outside of Blanchard's immediate circle. Blanchard was primarily concerned to construct a typology of transsexualism built upon erotic object choice, thus privileging sexuality in his formulations of transsexual motivation.[3] Lawrence adopted a transsexual identity that was built upon Blanchard's work and, as an identity innovator, she made the new trans identity of the 'autogynephilic transsexual' easily available on the Internet for others to identify with.

Lawrence says that on reading Blanchard's journal articles she experienced the 'kind of epiphany' that trans people often feel when first coming across words and formulations that fit and work for them' (Lawrence 1999a). Not only do they feel empowered to make sense of their predicament, but the formulations are proof to them that they are not alone. Lawrence began to categorise herself as an 'autogynephilic transsexual', and conceptualised autogynephilic feelings as one of her principal motivations for seeking sex reassignment surgery. Moreover, following her surgery in 1996, she maintained both her autogynephilic feelings and her autogynephilic identity.

Lawrence's first attempts to transmit her enthusiasm for Blanchard's ideas, however, fell on stony ground. She recalls talking about the concept of autogynephilia at a TV/TS (Transvestite/Transsexual) convention called 'California Dreamin' in 1995. 'Almost no one had heard of the concept and those who had dismissed it out of hand' (Lawrence 2008, personal communication). These TV/TS 'members' were not interested. She made similar observations in Lawrence (1999a): 'As I discussed Blanchard's theory with colleagues, I discovered two surprising things. First his theory was not widely known. Second, many of those who did know about it, thought it was not so much wrong, as heretical.'

The years 1994 to 1996 saw Lawrence straddling the pre-Internet and Internet ages in a particularly striking way. Having come to her autogynephilic self-understanding from hard copy academic journal articles in 1994, she began, from 1996 onward, to use the Internet to further develop her self-understanding, to publicise Blanchard's work, and to solicit informants for her developing research projects on transsexualism.

Furthermore, her site not only catapulted Lawrence into public awareness within the transgender community, but also facilitated her entrance into the field of academic sexology. Following the time line of principal events is highly instructive in this latter regard. It illustrates how a 'member' (a trans person) also became an established 'expert' (a sexologist) in the space of a few highly productive years, a process greatly facilitated by the use of the Internet.

Lawrence's entrance into the professional arena may be marked by her presentation of a poster session at the Harry Benjamin International Gender Dysphoria Association (HBIGDA) Conference held in Vancouver, Canada, in September 1997. Ironically, this was the first HBIGDA conference at which trans activists demonstrated their wrath at being excluded on account of their alleged lack of academic and professional expertise, and their inability, often, to pay the high fees and related expenses of medical and professional conferences.[4] Lawrence's (1997) poster session was on the satisfaction of trans people who had not completed the standard 'real life' test period normally required for trans surgery. Significantly, all the data gathered (other than from her self-reporting) was through her website; from trans people who had responded to her appeals for informants on the Internet.

In 1998, Lawrence published her article 'Men trapped in men's bodies: an introduction to the concept of autogynephilia' in the USA 'member' magazine *Transgender Tapestry*, which brought before a 'member' audience Blanchard's formulations on autogynephilia. MTF 'members' had long spoken of themselves in terms of being girls/women trapped in men's bodies, to some the so-called 'feminine essence' narrative (Dreger 2008). The construction and adoption of the medico-psychiatric terminology of transsexuals' 'gender identity' being at odds with their morphology had provided 'expert' authentication of this 'member' conceptualisation. Lawrence's deliberately provocative title would have none of this. Her autogynephilic transsexuals were *men* who were trapped in men's bodies. Insofar as they became 'women' they were actualising their sexually driven wishes and fantasies of being women. In short, they were men who wanted to be women, and not women trapped in men's bodies.

Lawrence was a medical doctor (MD) and had practiced as an anesthesiologist before her gender transition. However, she had no university-affiliated position and was, in effect, writing as a freelance (some said) politically motivated, scholar. Through her website, however, she was able to immediately self-publish her early work to a wide audience; thus circumventing the time-consuming procedures associated with publishing in academic journals (Lawrence 1999b, 1999c, 1999d).

At the 1999 Harry Benjamin International Gender Dysphoria Association (HBIGDA) conference, Lawrence put forward her developing position on autogynephilia to a professional and specialist audience (Lawrence 1999a, 1999e). This led us to write the first sociological article on autogynephilia, which was published in 2001 (Ekins and King 2001b). In that article, we argued that we were observing a new transsexual identity being constructed; a 'migrating' identity built upon a privileging of sexuality (erotic object choice), as opposed to those that privileged either sex (the body) or gender.

The controversy surrounding the concept of autogynephilia developed further in 2003 with the publication of Bailey's popular science book *The Man Who Would Be Queen* (Bailey 2003), part of which provided material illustrative of Blanchard's classification, based on Bailey's own ethnographic work with a number of transsexuals. Much of its content could hardly have been more unwelcome, indeed offensive, to those who sought to expunge sexuality (eroticism) from transsexuality, and adopt the, by this time, conventional transsexual 'gender identity' story.

When the book was published in 2003 its most vocal and vitriolic critics speedily launched an attack, principally on the Internet.[5] They linked Ray Blanchard, Anne Lawrence and Michael Bailey as the proponents of work that they felt sought to undermine the 'gender identity' story of transsexualism that they subscribed to. Lynn Conway (2003–2007) and Andrea James (2008), in particular, proceeded to muster all the support they could to discredit Bailey's book, and to use every means available to them to attack the book, its author, and those who supported it. One of the effects of the ensuing debate was to give the book huge publicity, particularly within the trans community. As a result, by August 2006, the book had sold approximately 4,200 copies and had received some 900,000 visits online to its electronic version, again, indicative of the impact of the Internet (Dreger 2008: 412).

Having used her website as a springboard to publicise her writings on autogynephilia, Lawrence began to publish in (what she regards as) significant refereed academic journals on various aspects of transsexualism from 2003 onwards (Lawrence 2003, 2004, 2007, 2008b). By this time, she had also obtained a Ph.D. in sexology. In 2004, Blanchard published an article in a 'member' publication, the Internet based *AG (Autogynephilia) Resource.* A year later, he also published a paper in an academic journal, reviewing his own previous work (Blanchard 2005). Whereas the interrelations between 'expert' and 'member' knowledge (Blanchard and Lawrence) had led to the 'new' transsexual identity, now the 'member' (Lawrence) had become 'expert' and the 'expert' (Blanchard) was writing for 'member' Internet sites, in addition to presenting in academic forums. Interestingly, as Lawrence's career as an academic writer took off, she began to write less and less for TWR. She sacrificed speed of publication in order to gain greater respectability (in some circles), influence, and, so she hopes, longevity (Lawrence 2008, personal communication). However, insofar as the members of the so-called 'axis of evil' (Bailey, Blanchard, and Lawrence) all consider some forms of transsexuality to be a paraphilia (a psychosexual disorder), it is questionable how 'respectable' (welcome) this story will ever be in a climate which seeks increasingly to depathologise matters of sex, sexuality and gender (Dreger 2008: 416).

Lawrence's most vociferous critics continued to accuse her of projecting her 'sex-fueled mental illness' (James 2008) onto transsexualism and onto other transsexuals. From the standpoint of this chapter, however, her significance is that she had in the space of a few short years established a third major migrating trans identity: an identity based upon sexuality, as opposed to sex (the body), or gender (Ekins and King 2006: 43–96).

EMASCULINIZATION AND FEMINIZATION: SISSY JAUNIE'S BLOG 14 AUGUST 2005, CONTINUING: THE INTERNET AND IDENTITY CONSTRUCTION

When Anne Lawrence launched her web site, which has never included a blog, the terms 'web log' and 'blog' were not in use and the numbers of such sites were very small. However, by 2005 there were countless million blogs,[6] and a burgeoning academic literature on them (Brady 2005). In that year a new blog called *Emasculinization and Feminization* was launched by a male sissy who used the name 'Jaunie'.

Unlike many blogs that are short-lived, Jaunie's blog is three-years-old, at the time of this writing. It is one of the most highly regarded of the hundreds of male sissy blogs currently up and running, many of which focus on aspects of 'unwelcome sexuality'.

Within the terms of our conceptual framework, the male sissy identity that Jaunie's blog sets forth and develops is an example of a gender negating identity. Jaunie, as a male sissy, is systematically 'erasing' his masculinity. Whereas the transsexual seeks to migrate across the gender divide (permanent substitution) and the transvestite oscillates betwixt and between the divide (temporary crossing), Jaunie seeks to do neither of these things. Rather, he comes to identify permanently as a male sissy, as a sissyboy/sissy girl, and seeks to increase his sissification with its two prongs, those of emasculinisation and feminisation. Jaunie considers himself a male sissy, not a woman, however much feminised. The emphasis is on him 'erasing' his masculinity, preferably permanently. His feminisation is an important part of this process, but never to the point of passing as a woman. Indeed, it is as a feminised *male* sissy that Jaunie seeks public humiliation, thus consolidating his sissification, still further. For this reason, we will refer to Jaunie as 'he' throughout this chapter.

In the pre-Internet age, what we term 'negating' identities were largely unidentified and unavailable. Steps had been taken within the trans community to argue for the role of 'demaling' and 'ungendering' as part of a vision which sought to give greater voice to the great range of diversities within the trans community, but these steps were small and little known about. Debra Rose was the leading writer in this area and published a series of booklets and magazines through the fantasy fiction publisher Sandy Thomas (e.g., Rose 1994–1996). These publications articulated a rather complete ideology for the 'sissy maid' who moved increasingly towards an emasculated/feminised asexual state of service to his mistress (Ekins and King 2006). However, the impact of such writings, except on a small minority of devotees, was minimal. Rather, such phenomena were almost always considered in terms of other more widely available categorisations; most typically those of transvestism or sadomasochism. Thus it was that Jaunie had to wait until the age of the Internet to find his distinctive voice, both, as we shall see, in terms of his surfing the Internet which led to his 'constituting' his identity (Ekins 1997: 107–129) as a male sissy, and then using his blog to 'consolidate' (Ekins 1997: 130–162) that identity. Moreover, Jaunie, unlike Lawrence, is constituting and consolidating an identity that barely appears on medical (expert) radars at all.

A review site for 'Sissy blogs: sissy, cuckold, forced fem and chastity blog reviews' (2008) refers to Jaunie's blog as 'a great read for aspiring sissies'. It notes that the site documents a sissy named Jaunie's full feminization training and it covers all aspect of becoming the perfect sissy. Although not frequently updated (posts number in the one or two a month region) Jaunie's posts are always interesting. Jaunie illustrates many posts with relevant photographs, none of which are explicit. The blog is well written, with a light, charming tone and it is a shame that it's author doesn't post more frequently, the only downside that I can see.

(http://sissyblogs.blogspot.com/>)

Jaunie's User Profile lists his interests as 'Feminine training, becoming "girlie", learning to be a good sissy, strap on play, BDSM, humiliation, being exposed'. His single profile page, at the time of writing, features a single photo of part of his body, including a hairless midriff with a belly-button piercing. He has placed his right hand to the side of his midriff and the photo shows just his fingers and thumb. His finger nails have had a French manicure and he is wearing a gold ring on his index finger. It was not until Jaunie's blog was well advanced that he acquired the belly-button piercing and placed this picture on his profile page. It marked an important transitional point in his sissification. The blog is entitled *Emasculinization and Feminization* and these are the two interrelated underlying themes that he explores in his blog that opens thus:

> This seemed like a great time to start a blog of my training that I and my mistress are pursuing. I realised a while back that I was a sissyboy/ sissygirl and recently started embracing it honestly. Within my mistress' directions, my masculine traits are being removed to make me less of a 'real man'. I am being feminized in my appearance, behavior, and thinking. Big changes are taking place over time and I will share them here.
>
> (Sissy Jaunie 2005–2008, 14 August 2005)

Prior to Jaunie's use of the Internet,[7] he was unable to categorise himself within any publicly available transgender category that he felt adequately 'fitted and worked' to describe his sex, sexuality and gender. He felt himself to be heterosexual and his sexual life with his girlfriends was important to him. He had no homosexual fantasies and had no interest in either cross-dressing, or changing sex. Put another way, none of the pre-Internet publicly available categories of homosexual, transvestite, and transsexual seemed to fit him. Insofar as he did try to constitute a meaning for his sexual interests, he tended to see himself as a person with multiple fetishes. In terms of the career path of male femaling developed in Ekins (1997), Jaunie never 'constituted' himself as any sort of male femaler, let alone a sissy, in his pre-Internet years.

In retrospect, we might say Jaunie's 'beginning phase' (Ekins 1997) took place before the age of five with the occasional cross-gender incident. He would hear his mother talking about lipstick, and occasionally put lipstick on in private. He also recalls noticing polished nails on girls and women and putting lipstick on his nails to see what it would look like.

In his early teens, Jaunie's interests begin to focus upon the removal of body hair, which was to remain a central preoccupation throughout his life. The removal by a male of his body hair presents an interesting issue in terms of both body and gender male femaling. Body hair is culturally coded as masculine, and removal of body hair is coded as feminine. Jaunie is erotically aroused both by girls/women removing their body hair, and by the fantasy and practice of removing or having his own body hair removed.

It is important to note that Jaunie, at this time, did not have any cross-dressing fantasies 'just a little envy and excitement noticing the "girlie" things like painted nails on women'. A significant incident occurred with a girlfriend to whom he revealed that his favourite fantasy was shaving his legs. 'She laughed at me when I told her and I found I enjoyed being laughed at by her about it'. From thenceforth, the aspect of humiliation became intertwined with his 'fetish', as he referred to it then.

Later Jaunie began going to beauty salons for leg waxes. His first such experience could not have been more exciting for him: 'I could not believe the experience, *better than sex*!' He also started waxing or shaving his chest during this time. He then began to develop his 'eyebrow waxing fetish', as he called it, which, in his early 20s, became a major preoccupation. Later on with the support of a sympathetic girlfriend, Jaunie began to wax his arms, legs, chest and eyebrows. In his mid-20s, he meets his wife, who he now refers to as his mistress and who apparently was aware of and happy for him to remove his body hair.

Several years after his relationship with his wife/mistress began, Jaunie happened to hear something about chastity devices. He bought one via the Internet and began to incorporate it into his sexual relationship with his wife. As Jaunie puts it: 'We already had great sex (always throughout our relationship) but with me kept locked, it got even better'. The couple went through periods when he would be locked, 'such as weekends or a couple of days before a planned night together.' This has continued.

There is still no 'constituting' of a more particular meaning to his various activities. Rather, he begins to try out with his wife/mistress what he is reading about on the web. He is still in his 'doing' phase. He talks to his wife about her giving him 'strap-on training' to cement the relationship, an idea that his reading on the Internet had suggested to him. This entails the mistress strapping on a dildo and anally penetrating her submissive sissy.

Many dominant mistresses make a specialty of emasculating and feminising submissives. Now aware of such material on the Internet, quite soon Jaunie comes across the two sissy Internet sites that will become most important in his self-understanding as a sissy, namely 'Girl-a-matic' (1997–2008) and 'Sissy Station' (2000–2008). The 'Girl-a-matic' site set the main trends for many of the sissy sites and sissy blogs that followed it since its inception in 1997.

During its first three years, Girl-a-matic received some three million hits (Marlissa [Girl-a-matic website master] 2000, personal communication). There was clearly a huge interest in male sissification presented in the format pioneered by Girl-a-matic, which featured images of beautiful female models fantasised as male sissies. But Girl-a-matic was not an interactive site in any way at all. Sissy Station, on the other hand, was launched in 2000 and introduced the interactive element in a small way. Besides 'galleries' of sissies with captions and sissy stories, it featured various sissy 'assignments'. Assignments range from buying nail varnish of a specified colour and painting your toe nails, to buying a dildo and getting used to 'sucking cock', to going to a tanning studio and acquiring bikini tan lines. However, common to all of them is the theme of humiliation. The sissy assignments make it evident to anyone who observes the assignment being carried out that this is a male carrying out the assignment. He can expect to be scorned and humiliated for his unmanly conduct.

Jaunie found these Sissy Station assignments both stimulating and educational. They introduced him to many aspects of sissification that he had previously not thought about or had not found of interest. Now he felt ready to cross-dress as the assignments frequently insisted. He began to self-identify as a sissy, with the cross-dressing featuring as an important aspect of his sissification.

Jaunie's various activities, those that he had previously considered in terms of 'fetishes', now begin to cohere within the identity of the male sissy he was exploring on the web. He begins to see all his sexual 'fetishes' in terms of an identity as a male sissy interested in both 'emasculinisation' and 'feminisation'. In terms of our framework, he is 'constituting' the meaning of his identity as a male sissy. His 'constituting' phase is short. Quite soon, Jaunie feels ready to 'consolidate' his life as a sissy and take increasingly public steps that will involve his displaying as a sissy, and decides to start a blog to document the process.

Jaunie's blog may be divided into a number of phases. In the first phase, the emphasis is upon detailing his experience of leg waxes and eyebrow shaping that have been an almost life-long preoccupation of his. He then begins to detail his sissy experiences that are new to him while blogging, such as nipple stimulation to maximise nipple sensitivity, breast pumping, and the acquisition of tanning bikini lines. Other sissies who had blogs of their own would leave comments on such matters on Jaunie's blog: where to buy the most effective breast pumps, and so on, and Jaunie would relate her own experience in following suggestions made by commentators.

In the second phase, the frequency of the blogs reduces, but the blogs tend to be longer. There are more frequent long summaries that detail the main foci of his particular sissy lifestyle. More recently, as we write, a third phase is beginning which is preoccupied with fantasying that his wife/mistress should look to a 'real man' man for sexual satisfaction, now that he has become so emasculated. Significantly, Miss D, a dominatrix and humiliatrix, who is a regular commentator on a number of sissy blogs, including Jaunie's, adds her advice with a characteristic comment (Miss D 2008):

> If there is something on your mind, even something like Mistress taking a Real Man as Her lover, you are obligated to speak of it to Her. If and when She decides to start dating Real Men you will still be Her gurl won't you femmed and waiting at home for Her to return late at night utterly satisfied by a Real Man or maybe Real Men. Let's see what would that make you jaunie? Yes a sissy gurl cucky [cuckold].
>
> Miss D[8]

This is the point at which we will leave Sissy Jaunie's blog.

FANTASIES, REALITIES AND FUTURES

Sherry Turkle introduced her 1995 tour de force *Life on the Screen: Identity in the Age of the Internet* with the following paragraph. 'A rapidly expanding system of networks, collectively known as the Internet, links millions of people in new spaces that are changing the way we think, the nature of our sexuality, the form of our communities, our very identities' (Turkle 1995: 9).

We are not futurologists and it is still too early to say with certainty whether the Internet has heralded a phase in trans development that marks the sort of sea change that occurred at the end of the nineteenth century with the 'medicalization of the sexually peculiar' (Foucault 1979). We suspect it might have done. What is certain, however, is that the virtual contact enabled by the Internet has created critical mass and the formation of new virtual social worlds within which new trans identities, both 'virtual' and 'real', have emerged.

The autogynephilic transsexual identity looks set to stay as one of the major trans migrating identity-options for the foreseeable future, albeit an unwelcome one. Moreover, it will remain as an excellent case study in the interrelations between pre-Internet and Internet age trans identity formation. The widespread availability of a coherent male sissy identity has in large measure been an Internet creation. We have only touched upon the surface of this phenomenon.

What then of Jaunie's future? When we asked Jaunie to try to distinguish a 'fantasy' future and a 'reality' future, the differences were marked.

> The fantasy:
> Were circumstances not what they are, if I could jump back in time . I [would] become the sissy maid to a kind, loving, but firm mistress (my own wife with a little different personality perhaps). To a mistress that is truly dominant, independent, and has an agenda for transforming my

mind, interests, and body much like the TV-Trainer website steps and others. She'd cuckold me but rarely. I would be her sissy lesbian hubby but obviously not the one who wears the pants in the family. She'd force me into a bi-curious or bisexual role. She might have me dressed as a woman 24/7 although I think I would prefer to be an obvious 'sissy boi/fag.' Her training would certainly involve strict chastity, hormones (to a point), and me receiving orgasms in only a sissy way. There would be a lot of psychological training and reshaping of me. My job would be to serve her by taking care of her home and needs.

The reality:

So here I am, what will the REAL future hold? Well, it will be subdued compared to the past few years. I have a young family. As they get older, it's important I show more of a 'manly' image to them . I'll be a sissy more privately over time. This may be fun as mistress and I have a way of planning events that provide a great deal of pleasure even if they are fewer and farther between! Without the responsibilities of parenthood, I'd guess we'd keep going in the direction of making me a public sissy. She's enjoying dressing me in a pink shirt and having me wear this or that to show off my feminine attributes. Not liking it at first, now she enjoys parading me around. She's not interested in cuckolding or changing our normal sexual activities, so who knows?

(Jaunie 2008, personal communication)

Who knows? Indeed!

NOTES

1. We wish to thank Anne Lawrence for her helpful comments on earlier versions of this chapter.
2. The impact of the Internet and the World Wide Web on the transgender world is under researched and requires book length treatment. The first transgender webpages appeared in 1994–1995 (Roberts 2008; Sand 1995) and were basically online versions of what was then currently available in a printed format. In the documentation for the HBIGDA conference in 1995 there are few email addresses and no websites in evidence. But things were changing quickly and by 1996 the importance of the Internet for the transgender community was the subject of comment (Ekins and King 1996; Whittle 1996). As we wrote then: 'Transgender web pages offer shopping opportunities and (like the traditional media) access to pornography, information and entertainment. More importantly, perhaps, they offer a means of quickly disseminating ideas and information democratically to a massive, global audience' (Ekins and King 1996). In the last few years of the twentieth century the transgender world, like the rest of the world, developed a major virtual presence. By the 1999 HBIGDA conference in London, all the transgender organisations participating in the conference had websites listed at the end of the programme. With few technical resources and skills, most people could produce their own home pages and have an online presence expressing and exploring their transgendered identities (Hegland and Nelson 2002).

3. We discuss Blanchard and the concept of autogynephilia in more detail in Ekins and King (2001b, 2006). Blanchard argues that there are only two fundamentally different types of transsexualism in males: homosexual and non-homosexual and that the common characteristic shared by members of the non-homosexual category is their tendency to be sexually aroused by the thought or image of themselves as women. In Ekins and King (2006: 90), we summarised the views of many of his critics thus: 'In the main, Blanchard's less disciplined critics tend to conflate a number of rather different criticisms. These are the pathologizing and heteronormative trends in clinical psychology; the explanatory trends in Blanchard's work; [and] the political (and in some instances, personal) unacceptability of his "findings"'. In particular, many opponents of Blanchard's autogynephilic story 'find it objectionable on personal, political and "scientific" grounds to reduce MTF "transsexuals" to two categories: homosexual and autogynephilic'.

4. Lawrence, herself, demonstrated sympathy for the demonstrators by wearing a black 'Transsexual Menace' T-shirt under her silk suit.

5. The Bailey controversy and the debates over autogynephilia should be seen in a historical context as the latest in a number of struggles between competing stories concerning transsexualism. Since the development of medical methods to 'change sex' in the middle of the twentieth century the main focus of the competing stories has been the legitimacy or otherwise of such methods. What Dreger (2008) calls the 'feminine essence narrative' views as legitimate or tenable (King 1993, 2001) the claims of some people to somehow belong to the gender category which is not conventionally indicated by their bodies. This then in turn acknowledges the entitlement to medical interventions to alter the body to fit the mind. This story was initially a minority one within the medical profession but by the late 1970s, early 1980s it had acquired a degree of respectability and had become the dominant story in many parts of the world (Ekins and King 2006). Alongside the dominant story there have been a number of 'dissenting stories' (Ekins and King 2006). Initially the dominant psychiatric story depicted the transsexual as deluded, denied the reality of the claimed gender and condemned the use of medical procedures to alter the body. Gradually this story lost influence but it has not disappeared and there have been similar stories told from feminist and religious perspectives (Ekins and King 2006). Not surprisingly the autogynephilia story is seen by its opponents to undermine the 'feminine essence' narrative and thus endanger the provision of what are termed 'gender confirming' medical interventions. However, the promoters of the autogynephilia story have not universally condemned such interventions. And, whilst the feminist, religious and psychiatric stories that would outlaw medical reassignments are told by those who are 'outsiders' to the transgender community, the autogynephilia story has been embraced and promoted by some 'insiders' (Merton 1972).

6. Developments in software technology enabled the proliferation of blogging in the early years of the twenty-first century. According to Drezner and Farrell, the number of blogs in 1999 was estimated to be a mere 50, but by 2004 estimates suggested that there were between 2.4 and 4.1 million (Drezner and Farrell 2004). Blogs are sometimes grouped alongside developments such as social networking sites and photo and video repositories such as YouTube and Flickr under the umbrella term 'Web 2.0' (Beer and Burrows 2007; Burrows 2007). There are a number of distinctions that are made between 'Web 1.0' (1993–2003) and 'Web 2.0' (2004 onwards) but for our purposes here one that is particularly important is the greater interactivity characterising 'Web 2.0' with the blurring of the distinction between producers and consumers.

7. The details of Sissy Jaunie's pre-Internet life, as well as Jaunie's offline life after starting his blog, are taken from a series of email interviews we conducted with Jaunie between 23 September 2007 and 18 August 2008. We thank Jaunie for granting us these interviews and for giving us permission to use material from them for the purposes of this chapter. We have made a number of changes of detail to protect Jaunie's privacy. As we went to press, Jaunie had made no blog entries since January 2009.

8. Note that Miss D follows the common femdom/sissy practice of using a capital letter as the first letter of Mistresses and Real Men, and lower case when referring to the sissy another aspect of erasing and negating.

REFERENCES

Bailey, J. M. (2003) *The Man Who Would Be Queen: The Science of Gender-Bending and Transsexualism*, Washington, DC: John Henry Press.

Beer, D. and Burrows, R. (2007) 'Sociology and, of and in Web 2.0: some initial considerations' *Sociological Research Online*, 12(5). http://www.socresonline.org.uk/12/5/17.html (accessed 17 December 2008).

Benjamin, H. (1966) *The Transsexual Phenomenon*, New York: Julian Press.

Blanchard, R. (1989a) 'The classification and labeling of non-homosexual gender dysphoria', *Archives of Sexual Behavior*, 18: 315–334.

———. (1989b) 'The concept of autogynephilia and the typology of male gender dysphoria', *Journal of Nervous and Mental Disease*, 177(10): 616–623.

———. (1991) 'Clinical studies and systematic observations of autogynephilia', *Journal of Sex and Marital Therapy*, 17: 235–251.

———. (1993a) 'The she-male phenomenon and the concept of partial autogynephilia', *Journal of Sex and Marital Therapy*, 19: 69–76.

———. (1993b) 'Varieties of autogynephilia and their relationship to male gender dysphoria', *Archives of Sexual Behavior*, 22(3): 241–251.

———. (2004) 'Origins of the concept of autogynephilia'. http://www.autogynephilia.org/origins.htm (accessed 17 December 2008).

———. (2005) 'Early history of the concept of autogynephilia', *Archives of Sexual Behavior*, 34(4): 439–446.

Bornstein, K. (1994) *Gender Outlaw: On Men, Women and the Rest of Us*, London: Routledge.

Brady, M. (2005) 'Blogging: personal participation in public knowledge-building on the web', *Chimera Working Paper*, 2. http://www.essex.ac.uk/chimera/ (accessed 17 December 2008).

Burrows, R. (2007) 'Web 2.0', in G. Ritzer (ed.) *Blackwell Encyclopedia of Sociology*, Blackwell Publishing. http://www.sociologyencyclopedia.com/subscriber/tocnode?id=g9781405124331_chunk_g978140512433129_ss1-32 (accessed 17 December 2008).

Conway, L. (2003–2007) 'An investigation into the publication of J. Michael Bailey's book on transsexualism by the National Academies'. http://ai.eecs.umich.edu/people/conway/TS/LynnsReviewOfBaileysBook.html (accessed 17th December 2008).

Dreger, A. (2008) 'The controversy surrounding *The Man Who Would Be Queen*: a case history of the politics of science, identity, and sex in the Internet age', *Archives of Sexual Behavior*, 37(3): 366–421.

Drezner, D. W. and Farrell, H. (2004) 'The power and politics of blogs', paper presented at the American Political Science Association annual meeting, Chicago, September 2004. http://www.utsc.utoronto.ca/~farrell/blogpaperfinal.pdf (accessed 17 December 2008).

Ekins, R. (1993) 'On male femaling: a grounded theory approach to cross-dressing and sex-changing', *The Sociological Review*, 41: 1–29.
——. (1997) *Male Femaling: A Grounded Theory of Cross-Dressing and Sex-Changing*, London: Routledge.
Ekins, R. and King, D. (1996) 'Is the future transgendered?', in A. Purnell (ed.) *Conference Report on the 4ᵗʰ International Gender Dysphoria Conference*, London: BM Gendys.
——. (2001a) 'Tales of the unexpected: exploring transgender diversity through personal narrative', in F. Haynes and T. McKenna (eds) *Unseen Genders: Beyond the Binaries*, New York: Peter Lang.
——. (2001b) 'Transgender migrating and love of oneself as a woman: a contribution to a sociology of autogynephilia', *International Journal of Transgenderism*, 5(3). Symposion Publishing. http://symposion.com/ijt/vo05_301 (accessed 17 December 2008).
——, (eds) (2005) *Virginia Prince: Pioneer of Transgendering*, New York: Haworth Press.
Ekins, R. and King, D. (2006) *The Transgender Phenomenon*, London: Sage.
Feinberg, L. (1992) *Transgender Liberation: A Movement Whose Time Has Come*, New York: World View Forum.
Foucault, M. (1979) *The History of Sexuality, vol. 1*, London: Allen Lane.
Girl-a-matic Corporation (1997–2008) Home Page. http://www.geocities.com/WestHollywood/Heights/8036/ (accessed 2007–2008).
Glaser, B. (1978) *Theoretical Sensitivity: Advances in the Methodology of Grounded Theory*, Mill Valley, CA: Sociology Press.
Glaser, B. and Strauss, A. L. (1967) *The Discovery of Grounded Theory: Strategies for Qualitative Research*, Chicago: Aldine.
Hegland, J. E. and Nelson, N. J. (2002) 'Cross-dressers in cyber-space: exploring the Internet as a tool for expressing gendered identity', *International Journal of Sexuality and Gender Studies*, 7(2/3): 139–161.
Hill, D. B. (2005) 'Coming to terms: using technology to know identity', *Sexuality and Culture*, 9(3): 24–52.
Hirschfeld, M. (1991 [1910]) *Transvestites: the Erotic Drive to Cross-Dress*, New York: Prometheus Books.
James, A. (2008) 'Categorically wrong: a Bailey-Blanchard-Lawrence clearing house'. http://www.tsroadmap.com/info/bailey-blanchard-lawrence.html (accessed 17 December 2008).
Kendall, L. (1998) 'Meaning and identity in cyberspace: the performance of gender, class, and race online', *Symbolic Interaction*, 21(2): 129–153.
King, D. (1993) *The Transvestite and the Transsexual. Public Categories and Private Identities*, Aldershot: Avebury.
——. (2001) 'Condition, orientation, role or false consciousness? Models of homosexuality and transsexualism', in K. Plummer (ed.) *Sexualities: Critical Concepts in Sociology, Volume 2*, London: Routledge.
Lawrence, A. (1998) 'Men trapped in men's bodies: an introduction to the concept of autogynephilia', *Transgender Tapestry*, 85 (Winter): 65–68.
——. (1999a) 'Lessons from autogynephiles: eroticism, motivation, and the standards of care', paper presented at the 16ᵗʰ Harry Benjamin International Gender Dysphoria Association Symposium, London, August 1999.
——. (1999b) '28 Narratives about autogynephilia', *Transsexual Women's Resources*. http://www.annelawrence.com/agnarratives.html (accessed 17 December 2008).
——. (1999c) '31 new narratives about autogynephilia plus five revealing fantasy narratives', *Transsexual Women's Resources*. http://www.annelawrence.com/twr/31narratives.html (accessed 17 December 2008).

Lawrence, A. (1999d) 'Autogynephilia: frequently-asked questions', *Transsexual Women's Resources*. http://www.annelawrence.com/twr/agfaqs.html (accessed 17 December 2008).

———. (1999e) 'Men trapped in men's bodies: autogynephilic eroticism as a motive for seeking sex reassignment', paper presented at the 16th Harry Benjamin International Gender Dysphoria Association Symposium, London, August 1999.

———. (2003) 'Factors associated with satisfaction or regret following male-to-female sex reassignment surgery', *Archives of Sexual Behavior*, 32: 299–315.

———. (2004) 'Autogynephilia: a paraphilic model of gender identity disorder', *Journal of Gay and Lesbian Psychotherapy*, 8(1/2): 68–87.

———. (2007) 'Becoming what we love: autogynephilic transsexualism as an expression of romantic love', *Perspectives in Biology and Medicine*, 50(4): 506–520.

———. (2008a) *Transsexual Women's Resources*. http://annelawrence.com/twr/ (accessed 17 December 2008).

———. (2008b) 'Shame and narcissistic rage in autogynephilic transsexualism', *Archives of Sexual Behavior*, 37: 457–461.

Lin, D. C. (2006) 'Sissies online: Taiwanese male queers performing sissiness in cyberspaces', *Inter-Asia Cultural Studies*, 7(2): 270–288.

Miss D. (2008) 'Comment' on 'All I can hope for now'. Sissy Jaunie's Blog Entry for Sunday 27 April 2008.

Merton, R. K. (1972) 'Insiders and outsiders: a chapter in the sociology of knowledge', *American Journal of Sociology*, 78: 9–47.

Nestle, J., Howell, C. and Wilchins, R. A. (eds) (2002) *GenderQueer*, Los Angeles: Alyson Books.

O'Keefe, T and Fox, K. (eds) (2003) *Finding the Real Me: True Tales of Sex and Gender Diversity*, San Francisco: Jossey Bass.

Plummer, K. (1995) *Telling Sexual Stories: Power, Change and Social Worlds*, London: Routledge.

Roberts, J. (2008) *JoAnn Roberts Home Page*. http://www.cdspub.com/jar.html (accessed 17 December 2008).

Rose, D. (1994–1996) *The Sissy Maid Quarterly*, vols 1–5, Capistrano Beach, CA: Sandy Thomas.

Sand, J. (1995) 'Who in the world is Jenny Sand?' http://home.online.no/~jane1/vanity.html (accessed 17 December 2008).

Shapiro, E. (2004) 'Trans'cending barriers: transgender organizing and the Internet', *Journal of Gay & Lesbian Social Services: Issues of Practice, Policy, and Research*, 16(3/4): 165–179.

Sissy Blogs: Sissy, Cuckold, Forced Fem and Chastity Blog Reviews (2008) http://sissyblogs.blogspot.com/ (accessed 17 December 2008).

Sissy Jaunie (2005–2008) 'Emasculinization and feminization' http:jauniestraining.blogspot.com (accessed 17 December 2008).

Sissy Station (2000–2008) http://www.sexyadulthost.com/users/sissystation/ (accessed 17 December 2008).

Stryker, S. (2000) 'Transsexuality: the postmodern body and/as technology', in D. Bell and B. M. Kennedy (eds) *The Cybercultures Reader*, London: Routledge.

Swaab, D. F. and Garcia-Fulgueras, A. (2009) 'Sexual differentiation of the human brain in relation to gender identity and sexual orientation', *Functional Neurology*, 24(1): 17–28.

Turkle, S. (1995) *Life on the Screen: Identity in the Age of the Internet*, New York: Simon and Schuster.

Whittle, S. (1996) 'The trans-cyberian mail way', *Radical Deviance*, 2(2): 61–68.

Wilchins, R. A. (1997) *Read My Lips: Sexual Subversion and the End of Gender*, Ithaca, NY: Firebrand Books.

2 Becoming Knowably Gendered

The Production of Transgender
Possibilities and Constraints in the
Mass and Alternative Press from
1990–2005 in the United States

Laurel Westbrook[1]

The advent and rise of the term 'transgender' as both an identity category separate from 'transsexual' and 'transvestite,' and as an umbrella category representing a wide variety of non-normative gender practices, has been well documented by scholars (Whittle 1998, 2006; Meyerowitz 2002; Denny 2006; Stryker 2006, 2008; Valentine 2007; Currah 2008). Historians and other academics have carefully detailed how, in the early 1990s in the United States, trans people began using the term as a way to fight the medical monopoly on classification of trans practices and identities, as well as to unify a diverse population of people whose non-normative gender practices were unaccepted by many members of both straight and gay communities (Denny 2006; Valentine 2007; Spade and Currah 2008). What has not yet been examined is the content of the term 'transgender' as its meaning has moved into popular discourse, as well as some of the unintended consequences of the methods used to institutionalise the term both within and outside of trans communities. In this chapter I examine what I call 'teaching transgender articles'—articles which explicitly try to teach the term 'transgender' to readers—that appeared in trans community publications and the mainstream news media in the United States between 1990 and 2005. I analyse these articles in order to explore what possible ways of being gendered the deployment of the term 'transgender' has produced, as well as foreclosed. I argue that these teaching transgender articles constructed transgender as a knowable category of personhood and I examine how this production impacted upon understandings of gender in the United States.

Because no term is immediately apparent to an audience unfamiliar with it, all terms must be implicitly or explicitly defined to become knowable. After the invention of the term 'transgender,' three types of articles within print media appeared in the early 1990s that had the primary intention of defining it. First, in trans community publications, self-identified trans people wrote articles to explain 'transgender' to other trans people. Second, trans people taught non-trans people about 'transgender' in articles published both within and outside of trans community publications. Finally, non-trans people composed articles for the mainstream press in which they explained 'transgender' to a primarily non-trans audience. These articles offer a rich site through which to trace the meaning of transgender as it was produced within the trans community and then taken up by mainstream journalists.

I suggest that all three types of articles construct very similar versions of 'transgender.' Although it was originally coined as a term for people who wanted to change gender but not engage in surgical body modification practices, 'transgender' quickly came to be an umbrella category encompassing a wide variety of ways of doing gender, from the more well known 'transsexual' and 'transvestite,' to the less well known 'he-she' and 'gender queer.' Moreover, transgender was defined so broadly as to include a number of previously unnamed gender practices, thus making these ways of doing gender knowable and those who do them recognisable as human.[2] In contrast to many scholars who argue that transgender people are socially abject (e.g. Besnier 2004 and Lloyd 2005)—seen as not human because their gender practices render them socially illegible—I suggest that these teaching transgender articles made audiences literate in previously unreadable gender practices. Thus, these practices became knowable, their practitioners became recognisable as human, and social understandings of 'gender' changed significantly.

Although the usage, and ultimate acceptance, of 'transgender' expanded the possible ways of living, like all categories, it also constrained these in a number of ways, four of which I highlight here. First, contrary to those who argue that 'transgender' will dismantle 'gender' (e.g. MacKenzie 1994; Bornstein 1995), I argue that these articles reinforced the idea of gender while at the same time challenging the current rules of the gender system. Second, in their attempts to legitimate the new term 'transgender,' authors often attempted to naturalise the category and provided rigid definitions for it, which may have discouraged debate over the content of the term. Third, as 'transgender' was (re)produced within the mainstream press, it came to mean people who were not 'real women' or 'real men' and functioned as a category outside of 'man' or 'woman.' Finally, although 'transgender' made more ways of doing gender legitimate, the process of making previously illegible genders readable reproduced the idea that all people have a knowable gender, thus reinforcing the norm of knowability.

In the conclusion, I elaborate on my argument that transgender people are not universally 'abject'. I also engage with the ongoing debate among scholars about whether trans identities and practices 'stabilise' or 'destabilise' the 'gender system' to argue that this, fundamentally, is the wrong question to ask. I argue, using my exploration of teaching transgender articles for evidence, that new ways of doing gender will not undo the existence of gender but can, instead, change how gender is done. The questions to ask, then, are how trans terms and practices change understandings of gender, and how are they expand and/or constrain possible ways of living gendered lives. These are the questions that I take up here.

CONTRIBUTION TO KNOWLEDGE

Poststructuralist Theory and the Discursive Production of Gender

Poststructuralist theorists, particularly Michel Foucault and Judith Butler, argue that language, including categories of thought and the systems of meaning that contain them, create social realities, including identities, desires, and the materiality of bodies. Language both produces potential ways of being as well as restricts ways of being. These theorists argue that the study of discourse must be central to our study of society because everything we think or do is filtered through language. If we want to understand social actions, we must first look at the language around those actions, including embedded ideas about how the world works. Butler (1993) argues that these discourses come to seem natural through their repetition, and thus often remain unquestioned, taking on the label of truth. But, she argues, these languages are not static; they are processes and sites of struggle between subjects. Although those subjects themselves are shaped through discourses, they are not determined by them, and can create social change through the processes of language. This chapter aims to add to poststructuralist scholarship on the discursive production of gender by examining the construction of a new gender category by a non-dominant gender group, and by exploring how this category was adopted by the mainstream news media.

Transgender Studies

Much empirical research on people who are labelled as doing non-natal gender has taken place within the field of transgender studies.[3] Because transgender studies is a relatively new field, most of the research has focused on establishing that transgender people exist, categorising the many practices within the transgender umbrella, and arguing that the current gender system is too restrictive (e.g. Devor 1997; Halberstam 1998; Prosser 1998). Many transgender studies scholars, both those working inside and outside of academia, have argued that transgender people have always existed, that the desire to engage in cross-gender practices is biological and natural, and that modern societies have attempted to subjugate non-normative ways of doing gender (e.g. Feinberg 1992, 1996). Thus, most of the work within transgender studies focuses on what Foucault (1978) called 'repressive power,' paying little attention to the workings of 'productive power.'[4] Most examine how diverse ways of being gendered are constrained and repressed in society and see trans people as challenging norms in a way that will eventually lead to freedom from the tyranny of the gender system. Very few scholars within transgender studies look at how identity categories and ways of being, including transgender identities and practices, are *produced* through discourses.

In recent years, several scholars have published work that is an exception to this rule, finally bringing an analysis of productive power to transgender studies (e.g. Parlee 1996; Meyerowitz 2002; Valentine 2007). Many of these exceptional pieces have included examinations of the production of the categories 'transsexual' and 'transgender.' At the forefront of this new turn in transgender studies is Joanne Meyerowitz, whose 2002 book is a genealogy of the category of 'transsexual.' Through an analysis of the history of sex-change surgeries starting in the 1950s, she examines how this term became a medical category and then a social identity in the United States. She argues that transsexuality emerged as an option and identity through intense, although informal, negotiations between doctors and those seeking hormones and surgery.

A number of other scholars have examined the production of the category 'transgender' (e.g. Whittle 1998; Valentine 2007; Stryker 2008). The most accepted history of the term is that Virginia Prince coined it as an alternative to the then dominant 'transsexual' and 'transvestite.' It is said that she wanted 'transgenderist' to describe someone who wanted to change gender but not have sex change surgery (Papoulias 2006). 'Transgender' was quickly adopted as an umbrella category that included transsexual, transvestite, transgenderist and other non-normative gender practices after the publication of Leslie Feinberg's *Transgender Liberation* (1992), in which ze uses it in that way (Stryker 1998; Valentine 2007). Most scholars focus on the positive outcomes of the creation of 'transgender' (e.g. Stryker 1998; Whittle 1998), but several scholars have noted that the implementation of the term was controversial within the trans community (e.g. Broad 2002; Denny 2006; Valentine 2007). Similarly, a few researchers have noted the unintended exclusions produced by the term transgender as well as the forced inclusions (e.g. Currah 2006). For example, Valentine (2007) details how, in the struggle for the right to identify as transgender, many other identities are belied. He describes how numerous people who do not identify as transgender are nevertheless named as such by leaders in the community and service providers.

In this chapter, I build on this body of scholarship, asking: What was the process by which 'transgender' became the accepted term for those labelled as doing non-natal gender? What possible ways of living did this process produce and what did it constrain? How has the advent of 'transgender' as a knowable category of personhood impacted understandings of gender in the United States? To fully explore these questions, I not only examine the production of 'transgender' within the trans community, but expand on current understandings by also investigating the production of 'transgender' within the mainstream news media.

Media Studies

The mainstream news media are a prime source of public information and, thus, an important site for studying the discursive production of reality. Media scholars have convincingly argued that the media do not simply reflect or represent reality; instead, the media construct reality (e.g. Gamson et al. 1992; Jansen 2002; Macdonald 2003). The media do this by providing audiences with narratives, frames, and belief systems that shape interpretations of the world as well as actions within it. Given that the media are such powerful distributors of discourse (Berns 2001), it is surprising that poststructuralist scholars of gender have not yet turned to the media as a site in which to study the discursive production of the idea of sexual difference, the categories of sex, and the criteria with which the categories are applied. The media is a particularly important site because of its power to influence all media consumers' understandings of gender, including those held by trans people themselves, since the media has been shown to have a significant effect on the ways in which some people form identities as trans (Gagne, Tewksbury, and McGaughey 1997; Meyerowitz 2002; Ringo 2002). A study of the production of transgender by trans people and the adoption of the term in the mainstream media is vital to understanding how gender identities, both 'normal' and 'deviant', are socially constructed. This project begins to fill the current gap in scholarship by examining the production of the category *transgender* by the trans community press and its usage in media coverage.

METHODS

This chapter draws from a larger study based on a systematic collection of non-fiction texts produced about people labelled as doing non-natal gender in the United States between 1990 and 2005 in two forums: the mainstream news media, and transgender community publications and activist groups. In my analysis of these texts, I discovered the phenomenon of what I call 'teaching transgender articles.' Within both mainstream and trans community news publications, journalists wrote articles explicitly defining the term transgender and attempting to teach their audience about the term and the people it is said to represent. Often, these articles followed a classic textbook style of definition, including bold-facing the term transgender and then providing a clear, authoritative definition. For example, in an article published in *TV-TS Tapestry* in 1994:

> *Transgendered*—an umbrella term encompassing one or more individuals dealing with transsexual, transvestite, transgenderist or androgyne issues.
>
> (Israel 1994: 11)

Other typical styles of presentation of these types of articles include the explicit question 'What is Transgender?' followed by, as with the textbook style, a clear, authoritative definition.

I collected teaching transgender articles from the two most influential U.S. trans community publications that published continuously between 1990 and 2005: *Transgender Tapestry* and *FTM. Transgender Tapestry*, which changed its name from *TV-TS Tapestry* in 1995, endeavors to appeal to the entire transgender community, although it primarily features transwomen both as writers and as subjects of articles. *FTM* is a publication of FTM International and exclusively targets its publication at transmen. For the purposes of this chapter, I will refer to the authors and intended audiences of these publications as 'trans.' Although this term is often used as an identity category, here I use it not to describe a person's self identity or their essence, but to describe their practices as those that could be seen as possibly *trans*forming gender, *trans*gressing gender norms, or *trans*itioning from one gender to another. I gathered these articles by paging through archived copies of all the issues of each magazine published between 1990 and 2005; I found 243 articles that explicitly defined 'transgender,' each of which I photocopied and then scanned into an image file. In 2003, for its 101st issue, *Transgender Tapestry* published a 'Transgender 101' issue intended for a non-transgender audience. I gathered and analysed 26 articles from that issue to explore how 'transgender' was produced for non-transgender audiences by the trans community press.

For the mainstream news media articles, I searched the two largest databases of U.S. news publications: Access World News and Lexis Nexis. These databases include newspaper and news magazine articles produced for a 'general' audience.[5] I collected the stories by searching for the term 'transgender' and skimming each story to determine whether it overtly defined transgender. From those, I selected a random sample of 250 stories. I analysed all articles with the support of Atlas.ti, a qualitative data analysis program. Atlas.ti assists researchers by organising data and codes. Although it does have an automatic coding function, I did not use it, as I have found that personally coding each text is better suited to my research goals.

I examined each article with a focus on how the authors defined 'transgender,' who they explicitly included within the term and who they implicitly excluded, mentions of struggles over definitions, the form and style of the texts, their beliefs about gender, sex, and sexuality, and their definitions of other identity terms of interest, including cross-dresser, transsexual, and transvestite. For texts produced by trans people for a non-trans audience, I also explored which terms the authors felt needed to be defined for a non-trans audience and which were assumed to be known. For texts produced by non-trans authors, I noted similarities and differences between definitions inside and outside the trans community. Finally, for all texts, I investigated whether and how the definitions changed over time. An examination of all of these aspects of the texts helped me explore the central questions of this chapter: How was 'transgender' produced as a knowable category of personhood and how did this impact upon understandings of gender in the United States?

PRODUCING 'TRANSGENDER' IN THE TRANS COMMUNITY PRESS

In their production of the category 'transgender,' authors for the trans community press both challenged dominant understandings of gender and naturalised the new gender category. In so doing, they worked to expand the number of acceptable ways of being gendered and make previously unnamed gender practices legible. In the process, these teaching transgender articles also reinforced the idea of gender as something that is both real and desirable. Although challenging one regime of knowability—medical understandings of 'transsexual' and 'transvestite'—these articles produced another, reinforcing the norm that gender is knowable.

Challenging Dominant Understandings of Gender

Teaching transgender articles in the trans community press often challenge dominant understandings of gender, arguing that the current gender system is too rigid and that gender is a continuum. One typical article argues that, as part of the struggle for transgender rights, ze wants to:

> defend the rights of each person today to shape their bodies, identities and self-expression. I want to show that although gender has been expressed differently in diverse historical periods, regions, cultures, classes and nationalities, there has always been gender diversity in the human population. And people have always determined, defined and changed their sex.
>
> (Feinberg 1994)

In challenging dominant understandings of gender, teaching transgender articles promote an idea of gender as 'a continuum,' as 'diverse,' and as 'fluid.' These understandings explicitly argue against a belief that the world is comprised of two mutually exclusive genders.

Besides challenging current gender norms, these teaching transgender articles dispute dominant understandings of gender by arguing that all people should be allowed to choose their gender and that gender should not be determined by sex. For example, in her highly influential piece 'The Transgender Alternative,' Holly Boswell reasons:

> The term gender has recently become accepted as defining one's personal, social, and legal status independent of biological sex, e.g.

ascribing traits of aggressiveness, nurturance, competitiveness, expressiveness, etc. Many people confuse sex with gender. Sex is biological, gender is psycho/social. If biology does not truly dictate gender or personality, then dichotomies of masculinity and femininity may only serve to coerce or restrict the potential variety of ways of being human.

(Boswell 1991: 31)

Finally, authors often framed transgender itself as challenging gender norms and argued that changing the rules of gender would benefit everyone. For instance, in a story in *TV-TS Tapestry*, the author writes:

We can see that our earliest ancestors, working cooperatively in communal societies, treated each member of society as valuable. I believe our liberation is tied to the freedom of humanity and that the revolutionary role of the transgender movement will leave its imprint on the kind of just society we all are working to bring to birth. The right to be ourselves, love whomever we choose, and control our own bodies will be fundamental rights.

(Rothblatt 1993: 40)

As I will discuss later, these challenges to dominant understandings of gender often rely on making claims in terms of history and nature.

Expanding the Number of Acceptable Ways of Being Gendered

Before the invention and acceptance of transgender in the trans community, the groups of people said to be served by both *FTM* and *TV-TS Tapestry* were transsexuals and transvestites. With the rise of 'transgender,' the view of who is included in the community widened dramatically, both in terms of specific identity labels and in terms of gender practices. By far, the most common definition of transgender given within the teaching transgender articles written by trans community members is that transgender is an 'umbrella category' including a wide variety of people. Often, definitions consist of a list of known identities, as well as a statement that defines transgender broadly in such a way as to allow for countless previously unnamed practices to be legible to a large number of people in a way that they were not previously. For example, these articles often define transgender as 'all persons who cross traditional gender boundaries' (e.g. Green 1994: 9) or 'anyone and everyone . . . who *transgresses gender* lines even slightly in their behavior or attitudes' (Staff 1995: 1). By defining the term not only by using existing identity categories, but instead also by offering an expansive definition marking *practices* instead of identity, a large number of people became potentially knowable as people.

Many definitions listed examples of already named identity categories and practices. The specific identity categories most commonly explicitly included under the umbrella are transsexuals and crossdressers. In the early years of the usage of the term as an umbrella category (1993–1995), 'transvestite' is also commonly included (transvestite was rarely used after 1995, except in publications for non-trans audiences). Very often included are also drag queens, androgynous people and androgynes, transgenderists, masculine women and feminine men, and intersex people. But, the definitions are frequently even more expansive. The following is a complete list of all the categories ever included in the transgender umbrella as defined in the trans community publications I studied: 'androgynous' or 'androgyne,' 'bi-gendered,' 'bisexuals,' 'butches,' 'crossdressers,' 'drag kings,' 'drag queens,' 'everyone,' 'female impersonators,' 'femmes,' 'gays,' 'gender-benders,' 'he-shes,' 'homosexuals,' 'intersex,' 'lesbians,' 'male impersonators,' 'masculine women,' 'feminine men,' 'MtFs,' 'FtMs,' 'multi-gendered,' 'non-operative transsexuals,' 'passing women,' 'post-operative transsexuals,' 'pre-operative transsexuals,' 'pre-transsexuals,' 'radical faeries,' 'shapeshifters,' 'she-males,' 'single parents,' 'transgenderists,' 'transsexuals,' 'transvestites,' and 'two-spirits.' This extensive list shows how diverse the group of people claimed by the promoters of the term 'transgender' is.

Besides its definition as an umbrella category, the definition of transgender as a specific *identity* category underneath that umbrella also expanded the number of acceptable ways of being gendered. In these stories, transgender as an identity category is defined as people who change gender but do not have body modification surgeries. When this meaning is intended, authors often use 'transgenderist' rather than 'transgender.' For example, in an article produced for a non-trans audience, the author defines transgenderist as:

> TRANSGENDERIST: Person living as gender opposite to anatomical sex, i.e. a person with a penis, who is living as a woman. Sexual orientation varies.
>
> (Nangeroni 2003: 23)

This definition is the one said to have been intended by Virginia Prince when she first coined the term as an identity category for people who were neither transsexuals nor transvestites. This promotes an alternative to the two previously dominant identity categories of 'transsexual' and 'transvestite,' both of which were created within medical discourse.

Reinforcing Gender

Although the authors of teaching transgender articles in the trans community press often challenge dominant understandings of gender, arguing that the current gender system is too rigid, they do not work to 'dismantle' gender, as some scholars and trans activists have argued will be the consequence of transgender activism (e.g. MacKenzie 1994; Bornstein

1995). While the authors of 'teaching transgender articles' challenge the current rules of gender, very rarely do they suggest that the entire system of gender should be eliminated. Instead, authors call for a gender system in which there is more room for different ways of doing gender, and in which there are not such severe consequences for doing gender differently from the norm. Moreover, even if they were interested in dismantling gender, the way they portray gender and define transgender in these articles will not do so.

Teaching transgender articles reinforce the idea of gender by offering explicit definitions of the term which, although challenging the way gender is constructed now, do not question the idea that gender exists. In a typical article for the 'Transgender 101 Issue,' the author defines gender (and gender identity) in this way:

> **Gender Identity:** Gender is a social construct that divides people into "natural" categories of men and women that are assumed to derive from their physiological male and female bodies. Gender attributes vary from culture to culture, and are arbitrarily imposed, denying individuality. Most people's gender identity is congruent with their assigned sex but many people experience their gender identity to be discordant with their natal sex. A person's self concept of their gender (regardless of their biological sex) is called their gender identity.
>
> (Rainbow Access Initiative 2003: 28)

Similarly, by basing their self-identity on the existence of gender, transgender authors reinforce the idea of gender. Transgender, as either an umbrella category or an individual identity that means crossing the current boundaries of gender, relies on the existence of gender in order to make cultural sense. In sum, groups that understand themselves in terms of gender, and who give authoritative definitions of gender, are highly unlikely to dismantle the gender system. I explore this further in the conclusion.

Naturalising Transgender

Through their tone and formatting, as well as explicit claims that transgender practices come from nature, these teaching transgender articles naturalise the concept of 'transgender.' Thus, in their attempt to construct transgender as a legitimate and knowable category of personhood, they risk placing 'transgender' outside the realm of the challengeable, possibly reducing the likelihood of re-examining the term to check and see if it produces the kinds of livable lives it strives for.[6]

As is seen from some of the examples of definitions from teaching transgender articles I have given so far, many of these adopt the form and tone of textbooks. At first glance, these articles look like scientific textbooks because of their use of bold font in the word being defined, followed by a brief definition. Similarly, they are written with the tone of textbooks—that of authority—rarely qualifying the definitions given. Although highly effective for establishing and legitimising 'transgender' as a new category, this use of tone and form also discourages struggles over the definitions of the terms. This form implies that the discussions of both what transgender is and who should be included are already done and that the definition is now 'known.'

Like the tone and form, the content of these articles often worked to naturalise the concept of 'transgender.' For example, as you can see from quotations given earlier in this chapter, these articles often argue that transgender practices have existed throughout history. Similarly, authors frequently argue that transgender is natural and biological. For example, Holly Boswell writes: 'It is our culture that has brainwashed us, and our families and friends, who might otherwise be able to love us and embrace our diversity as desirable and natural-something to be celebrated' (Boswell 1991: 31). Echoing this, another author argues:

> The last 30 years of the Benjamin/Prince model of transgender has been an important start, but it is time to move to new models that acknowledge and celebrate our deep, consistent transgendered nature. I have a button, This Is What A Transgendered Person Wears, and it doesn't matter if I wear it on a suit or a dress. I am transgendered, and that is important, not simply what I wear or how I act.
>
> (Williams 1995: 67)

Finally, authors of these stories often claim that people are transgender, whether or not they see themselves as fitting the category. For instance, in an article on the 'Transgender Revolution,' Miqqi Alicia Gilbert tells readers that, 'like it or not,' they have been 'drafted' into the revolution, which started with the invention of the term transgender. She concludes by writing:

> So, when you woke up that morning and discovered that you were transgendered, I hope you realized that it was a good thing. I hope you embraced and worked to understand its significance. It's time to be proud of yourselves, and it's time to embrace your comrades, all of them. It's time for the revolution to begin.
>
> (Gilbert 1999: 24)

By arguing that people can be transgender without self-identifying as such, these authors produce an idea of 'transgender' as a natural category. Thus, in sum, these articles tend to—through form, tone, and content—discourage continued debate over the meaning and usage of 'transgender.' But, for the term to function so as to challenge dominant rules of gender, it must be constantly reinterogated for exclusions and other ways it (unintentionally) reinforces structures its users are opposed to.[7]

(Re)Producing Gender as Knowable

'Transgender' was coined in opposition to the, then dominant, medical model of understanding trans practices. In these teaching transgender articles, authors often explicitly challenge the medical model, criticising its demands that trans people fit strict definitions in order to be legible (and eligible for surgery) and its tendency to try and 'know' trans people. But, by providing unqualified definitions of transgender combined with the use of textbook formatting, these teaching transgender articles produce their own regime of knowability. In claiming the right to become the knowers rather than the known, these trans authors produce their own set of truth claims and define and delineate what people 'really' are.[8] This, of course, is neither entirely positive nor negative, for we (academics) often call for oppressed groups to speak for themselves. But, as I detailed previously, the way in which the claim to being a speaking subject is done in these articles often forecloses future debates about the terms they defined.

'TRANSGENDER' IN THE MAINSTREAM PRESS: A NEW CATEGORY OF PERSONHOOD

The term 'transgender' has occasionally been used within the mainstream news media since 1993, but did not become widespread until the early 2000's and has now been institutionalised with an entry in the *Associated Press Stylebook* in 2005.[9] In many ways, mainstream journalists adopted the understanding of transgender developed within the trans community. For example, they saw transgender people as people, they defined transgender as not following dominant gender norms, and they characterised transgender people as at risk of discrimination and violence because they are transgender. But, in their adoption of the term, there were also modifications made, the most important being that, unlike the trans community, mainstream journalists defined transgender people as not 'real' men and not 'real' women. This is in contrast to previous mainstream understandings of trans possibilities, such as the belief held before the early 2000s that if a person had genital surgery, they could transition from being a real man to a real woman (or from a real woman to a real man). The rise in use of transgender in the mainstream media and its explicit definition in teaching transgender articles represent two changes in the dominant understandings of gender: first, an increased acceptance of another way to do gender besides being a gender-conforming man or woman, and, second, an understanding that people are able to *choose* their gender.

Teaching transgender articles in the mainstream news media often open with or centre around a vignette about an out transgender person and his or her struggles in mainstream society. These articles demonstrate a high level of sympathy for the discrimination and violence experienced by transgender people, occasionally explicitly condemning the perpetrators and often including quotes from people critical of attacks on transgender people. For example, in a story on transgender and the fight for anti-discrimination laws, only quotes in favor of the proposed legislation are given, including:

> "Transgender people are being treated like dirt and it's disgraceful," said Steven Goldstein, the group's chairman. "The passage of this legislation would rank right up there with legalizing marriage of gay couples as one of the top two priorities of New Jersey's gay and lesbian community."
>
> (Verrinder 2005)

These articles further promoted the idea that transgender people are human by describing their everyday activities as similar to most individuals in the United States. For example, transgender people are depicted going to work, hanging out with friends, and spending time with family. In these ways, transgender people are portrayed much as the trans community sees itself: as humans who wrongly face discrimination from mainstream society.

Mainstream journalists repeatedly define 'transgender' as referring to 'people whose internal sense of gender doesn't match with their biological gender' (e.g. Marech 2003:A19). Unlike the trans community, mainstream journalists describe transgender people as not 'real' men or women. For example, although writers in the trans community press generally use 'transgender' as a modifier on the gender categories of man and woman, journalists for the mainstream news media almost never coupled the term with man or woman and, instead, used it as a category separate from 'man' and 'woman.'[10]

Before the rise of 'transgender,' mainstream news journalists used body-based criteria to determine someone's gender. As defined in the *Associated Press Stylebook*, people who had surgery on their genitals had changed sex/gender, whereas without surgery they had not. For example, the stylebook instructed journalists to do the following in the case of transsexuals:

> Follow these guidelines in using proper names or personal pronouns when referring to an individual who has had a sex-change operation:
>
> - If the reference is to an action before the operation, use the proper name and sex of the individual at that time.
> - If the reference is to an action after the operation, use the new proper name and sex.
>
> For example:
>
> Dr. Richard Raskind was a first-rate amateur tennis player. He won several tournaments. Ten years later, when Dr. Renee Richards applied

to play in tournaments, many women players objected on the ground that she was the former Richard Raskind, who had undergone a sex-change operation. Miss Richards said she was entitled to compete as a woman.

(Goldstein 1994: 223–4)

Following this criteria, transsexuals could move from one binary gender category to the other with proper surgery. This allowed them to be seen as the gender with which they self-identified. By contrast, with the adoption of 'transgender' in the mainstream press, transsexuals were no longer seen as men or women and were, instead, labelled transgender.

By embracing the category of transgender, journalists did not just define what it meant to be transgender, they also defined what it meant to be a (non-transgender) man or a woman. If to be transgender is to be neither a man nor a woman because your body and identity do not 'match,' then to be a man or a woman, you must have an identity and a presentation of self that always 'matches' with the shape of your body. In previous time periods, when the categories of 'man' and 'woman' were defined solely by the shape of genitals, as illustrated by the *Associated Press Stylebook* rules before 2000, people could engage in a wide variety of behaviours and still be considered a man or a woman (albeit a 'deviant' man or a 'bad' woman) (see Westbrook 2007). Whereas before, all people with vaginas were labelled as women, whether or not they identified as or felt like women, and all people with penises were labelled as men, whether or not they believed themselves to be men. Starting in the early 2000's, only people whose bodies and perceived self-identities could be said to 'match' were labelled men or women. People whose bodies did not match who they felt themselves to be were labelled 'transgender.' The adoption of the term transgender narrowed the realm of behaviours men and women could engage in before their membership in those categories was questioned.

CONCLUSION

There are two trends of theorising within transgender studies that I would like to address and challenge. First, is the common argument that transgender people are 'abject.'[11] This term is often used to explain violence or discrimination experienced by trans people. But, its deployment in these, and other, contexts actually damages scholars' abilities to understand, and work to prevent, oppression of transgender people. Judith Butler, the scholar most often cited by those labelling transgender people as abject, defines abject as the 'constitutive outside' of the category of human; it is the category of 'not human' that makes the category of 'human' possible (Butler 1993). She argues that gender norms both 'produce the domain of intelligible bodies'—those who are legibly gendered and, therefore, seen as human—and 'a domain of unthinkable, abject, unlivable bodies'—the illegibly gendered (Butler 1993: xi).[12]

As I argue in this chapter, through the invention and promotion in the mainstream and alternative press of the term 'transgender,' transgender becomes a legible gender practice within those realms; moreover, authors for both types of media I examine see transgender people as human. As such, it is clearly false to label transgender as a *universally* abject category; if this was ever an accurate classification, it is no longer. The argument that it is inaccurate to call a speaking subject abject (or, the associated term subaltern) is, of course, not new (e.g. Spivak 1988). But, as 'abject' is still commonly applied to transgender subjects, it bears repeating here.

The counter argument to mine might be that given the high level of fatal violence against transgender people, they are clearly not seen as human by mainstream U.S. society. But, although it may be correct to say that a trans person was abject in the mind of their assailant when they were killed, this does not help our understanding of the position of trans people in current society, for it would be similarly accurate to say that anyone who is murdered is seen as abject by their killer. Moreover, simply because trans people are killed, and some are killed specifically because they are trans, does not mean the group has abject status in society. For example, non-trans men are killed everyday; in fact, men comprise more than 75 percent of U.S. homicide victims (Bureau of Justice Statistics 2007), some are killed precisely because they are men, and they are killed at a much higher rate than women, but we would never claim that non-trans men are an abject group. Moreover, although 'transgender' may function as the constitutive outside for the categories 'men' and 'women,' that does not necessarily mean it is the constitutive outside for the category 'human.' Indeed, as detailed before, mainstream journalists writing about transgender people clearly portray them as human.

Arguing that 'transgender' is a universally abject category is ultimately damaging in at least two ways. First, the label is inaccurate and so applies a set of theoretical reasonings that will not help improve understandings of the position of trans people in society. Second, doing so makes it difficult, if not impossible, to see how transgender people are treated as human. By labelling trans people as abject—an inaccurate and extreme description— scholars blind themselves to moments of successful constructions of trans subjecthood. If one of our goals as academics is to improve people's lives and increase livability, we must be mindful of successes of the groups we study, for those accomplishments—whether they are decreasing violence against the group, achieving policy or legislative goals, or increasing the social acceptance of the group—are the key to continuing to improve lives. As evidenced within this chapter, such a moment of success, as partial as it was, occurred in the early 2000s with the acceptance by mainstream journalists of an idea of gender as something not necessarily solely determined by genitals. Thus, a more productive line of inquiry than claiming abject status for trans people is to look at inequalities in access to subjecthood, as well as to investigate successes in such access.

Another trend in transgender studies is to investigate whether transgender people 'destabilise' or 'stabilise' gender.[13] Almost always, scholars come to the conclusion that transgender identities and practices, despite having the potential to destabilise, actually stabilise gender. Based on the evidence they use to argue that transness does not 'destabilise' but, actually, 'stabilises' gender, it is clear that by 'destabilise,' scholars often mean, not 'shake up,' but 'dismantle.'[14] As demonstrated here, many transgender people construct a sense of self in terms of gender. The authors producing teaching transgender articles for the trans community press see themselves as gendered beings engaging in gendered practices. Similarly, mainstream journalists and, most likely, their audience, understand transgender people in terms of gender. As such, transgender existence, in its current form, reinforces the idea of gender. It is highly unlikely that transgender people, or understandings of their practices in this form, will ever dismantle gender, although they are quite likely to change it.

This is not to argue that conceptions of 'transgender' do not challenge current hegemonic forms of gender. Indeed, transgender practices often destabilise the idea of binary gender, the belief that sex determines gender, and the understanding that gender is not fluid and cannot change over time (Broad 2002; Roen 2002; Monro 2005; Hines 2007; Sanger 2008). My contention here is that, while transgender identities and practices as they are presented within the trans community and mainstream press, do challenge current ways of doing gender, they do not challenge the idea of *gender* itself. By this I mean the belief that all people have at least one gender, that gender is knowable and should be made known to others (whether through behaviours or through explicit self-labelling), and that behaviours of the self and to the self by others should be shaped by membership in a gender category (whatever that category may be, whether woman or gender queer or fluid).

It can be argued that transgender, as represented in these articles, actually reinforces the idea of gender, while at the same time destabilising the content of the gender system. Although transgender works to expand the number of ways of doing gender, it does not challenge the idea that we all must do (at least one) gender. A proliferation of gender categories will not dismantle the gender system. Like non-transgender men and women, the transgender people portrayed in the articles examined here claim to have at least one gender, including man, woman, androgynous, and multi-gendered. In both the descriptions of 'transgender' in *Transgender Tapestry* and *FTM,* as well as in the adoption of 'transgender' by the mainstream media, the idea of transgender is never used to question gender itself, or the idea that all people have a gender. Instead, it is used to question the rules of gender that require all people to be men or women and which determine that gender based on the shape of genitals at birth.

Thus, the focus on whether transgenderists will 'dismantle' gender is the wrong question to ask about the effects of non-normative *gender* practices on the gender system.[15] Many trans activists struggle for a change in the rules of gender, rather than for the end of gender, and most trans people make claims to gendered identities. As a result, the existence of trans possibilities does not challenge popular beliefs that gender does and should exist, but, rather, shapes ideas about categories and conventions of gender. Thus, a better line of inquiry is into *how* trans practices change dominant understandings of gender. In this chapter, I demonstrated that between 1990 and 2005 trans people shaped mainstream media's production of gender, causing a consideration of *identity* rather than genitals in determining someone's gender and introducing 'transgender' as a viable category of personhood.

NOTES

1. I am extremely grateful to Sally Hines and Tam Sanger for their detailed and thoughtful feedback. In addition, I wish to thank Wendy Brown, Dawne Moon, Barrie Thorne, David Valentine, Mel Stanfill, Brett Stockdill, Diana Anders, Mona Bower, George Ciccariello Maher, Jack Jackson, Asaf Kedar, Sara Kendall, and Yves Winter for comments on previous versions of this work.
2. Judith Butler (1993, 2004) argues that those bodies that do not have a recognisable gender are not seen as human. Practices or other ways of being that render one's gender unknowable or indefinable within the current system of two binary genders move one into the realm of the 'abject,' which is the constitutive outside of the category 'human.'
3. 'Labelled as doing non-natal gender' is a phrase I have coined to mean labelled by oneself or others as 'doing gender' (West and Zimmerman 1987) so as to be seen as a sex other than one is presumed to have been assigned at birth. I feel that using a phrase that points to the practice of labelling both the self and others with gender categories is important when examining the construction of gender categories.
4. Repressive power is power that says 'no,' limits ways of acting, and focuses on controlling the body. In contrast, productive power is power that says 'yes,' produces ways of thinking and acting, and focuses on affecting the mind. Foucault (1978) argued that most people see only the workings of repressive power and ignore the much more effective workings of productive power.
5. For example, the data for this project comes from both larger general-audience newspapers such as the Washington Post, The New York Times, the San Francisco Chronicle, the Chicago Tribune, and the Los Angeles Times as well as smaller general-audience newspapers like the Watertown Daily Times, the Omaha World Herald, and the Tri-Valley Herald.
6. For the argument that the purpose of new categories should be to expand the possibility of livable lives and that categories must be constantly reexamined to ensure maximum livability, see Butler (1993, 2004).
7. The need to (re)interrogate terms such as 'transgender' comes from the tendency of such terms to move from describing acts or practices to being seen as representing people's essences or identities. When terms move in

this essentialising direction, they lose their potential to destabilise existing (restrictive) social structures. For example, as the term 'queer' has moved from meaning a challenge to binaries and category boundaries (i.e. 'queer theory') to an identity (i.e. an umbrella term for lesbian, gay, bisexual, transgender, and so on), it has lost its dexterity at denaturalising the modern system of 'sexuality,' and, ironically, tends to reify the idea of an essential sexuality.

8. For poststructuralist theories of 'truth' and knowledge as a claim to truth see Foucault (1972, 2001).
9. See Goldstein (2005). Note that in the 2005 edition, the 'transgender' entry simply directs readers to 'see sex changes.'
10. Trans journalists often write 'transgender man' or 'transman' to describe someone who was labelled female at birth and identifies as a man.
11. For examples of authors who label transgender people as abject, see Besnier (2004) and Lloyd (2005).
12. To elaborate, she argues that 'The abject designates here precisely those "unlivable" and "uninhabitable" zones of social life which are nevertheless densely populated by those who do not enjoy the status of the subject, but whose living under the sign of the "unlivable" is required to circumscribe the domain of the subject' (Butler 1993: 3).
13. For examples of this approach, see Gagne et al. (1997), Gagne and Tewksbury (1998), Kessler and McKenna (2001), Sloop (2004), Taylor and Rupp (2004), and Willox (2003).
14. There are also a group of theorists who examine whether and how transgender identities and practices 'destabilise' gender in the sense of challenging gender as binary and the belief that sex determines gender (for example, Broad 2002; Roen 2002; Hines 2007; Monro 2007; Sanger 2008).
15. The exception to this argument would be people who consciously claim no gender identity at all. Those people who reject any and all gender identities (including highly radical gender identities such as 'gender queer') engage in a 'disidentification' with the gender system which may work to dismantle the idea of gender (while at the same time potentially temporarily abjectifying the subjects engaged in such practices). For theories of 'disidentification,' see Butler (1993) and Munoz (1999). For an analysis of the similar concept of 'anti-normalization,' see Meeks (2001).

REFERENCES

Berns, N. (2001) 'Degendering the problem and gendering the blame: political discourse on women and violence', *Gender & Society*, 15(2): 262–281.

Besnier, N. (2004) 'The social production of abjection: desire and silencing among transgender Tongans', *Social Anthropology*, 12(3): 301–323.

Bornstein, K. (1995) *Gender Outlaw: On Men, Women, and the Rest of Us*, New York: Vintage.

Boswell, H. (1991) 'The transgender alternative', *TV-TS Tapestry* 58: 31–33.

Broad, K. L. (2002) 'GLB+T? Gender/sexuality movements and transgender collective identity (de)constructions', *International Journal of Sexuality and Gender Studies*, 7(4): 241–264.

Bureau of Justice Statistics (2007) 'Homicide trends in the U.S.: trends by gender'. <http://www.ojp.usdoj.gov/bjs/homicide/gender.htm> (accessed 7 March 2009).

Butler, J. (1993) *Bodies that Matter: On the Discursive Limits of 'Sex'*, New York: Routledge.

———. (2004) *Undoing Gender*, New York: Routledge.

Currah, P. (2006) 'Gender pluralisms under the transgender umbrella', in P. Currah, R. M. Juang, and S. Price Minter (eds) *Transgender Rights*, Minneapolis: University of Minnesota Press.

———. (2008) 'Stepping back, looking outward: situating transgender activism and transgender studies—Kris Hayashi, Matt Richardson, and Susan Stryker frame the movement', *Sexuality Research and Social Policy* 5(1): 93–105.

Denny, D. (2006) 'Transgender communities of the United States in the late twentieth century', in P. Currah, R. M. Juang, and S. Price Minter (eds) *Transgender Rights*, Minneapolis: University of Minnesota Press.

Devor, H. (1997) *FTM: Female-To-Male Transsexuals in Society*, Bloomington: Indiana University Press.

Feinberg, L. (1992) *Transgender Liberation: A Movement Whose Time Has Come*, New York: World View Forum.

———. (1994) 'Leslie Feinberg's transgender pride project', *FTM* July: 11.

———. (1996) *Transgender Warriors: Making History from Joan of Arc to Dennis Rodman*, Boston: Beacon Press.

Foucault, M. (1972) *The Archaeology of Knowledge*, trans. S. Smith, London: Tavistock.

Foucault, M. (1978) *The History of Sexuality. Volume 1: An Introduction*, trans. R. Hurley, New York: Pantheon Books.

———. (2001) *Fearless Speech* (ed. J. Pearson), Los Angeles: Semiotext(e).

Gagne, P. and Tewksbury, R. (1998) 'Conformity pressures and gender resistance among transgendered individuals', *Social Problems,* 45(1): 81–101.

Gagne, P., Tewksbury, R. and McGaughey, D. (1997) 'Coming out and crossing over: identity formation and proclamation in a transgender community', *Gender & Society,* 11(4): 478–508.

Gamson, W. A., Croteau, D., Hoynes, W. and Sasson, T. (1992) 'Media images and the social construction of reality', *Annual Review of Sociology,* 18: 373–393.

Gilbert, M. A. (1999) 'On the edge of revolution', *Transgender Tapestry,* Summer, Issue 87: 23–24.

Goldstein, N. (1994) *The Associated Press Stylebook and Briefing on Media Law*, Cambridge: Perseus Publishing.

———. (2005) *The Associated Press Stylebook and Briefing on Media Law*, New York: Basic Books.

Green, J. (1994) 'What is transgender?' *FTM*, July.

Halberstam, J. (1998) *Female Masculinity*, Durham, NC: Duke University Press.

Hines, S. (2007) '(Trans)forming gender: social change and transgender citizenship', *Sociological Research Online,* 12(1). http://www.socresonline.org.uk/12/1/hines.html (accessed 26 May 2009).

Israel, G. E. (1994) 'Coming out for the transgendered individual: transsexuals, transvestites, transgenderists, androgynes', *TV-TS Tapestry,* Summer: 11–12.

Jansen, S. C. (2002) *Critical Communication Theory: Power, Media, Gender, and Technology*, New York: Rowman & Littlefield.

Kessler, S. and McKenna, W. (2001) 'Who put the "trans" in transgender? gender theory and everyday life'. *The International Journal of Transgenderism: Special Issue on What is Transgender?* 4(3). http://www.symposion.com/ijt/gilbert/kessler.htm (accessed 12 October 2005).

Lloyd, A. (2005) 'Defining the human: are transgender people strangers to the law?', *Berkeley Journal of Gender, Law & Justice,* 20: 150–195.

Macdonald, M. (2003) *Exploring Media Discourse*, London: Arnold.

MacKenzie, G. O. (1994) *Transgender Nation*, Bowling Green, OH: Bowling Green State University Popular Press.

Marech, R. (2003) 'S.F. school's day of remembrance', *San Francisco Chronicle*, November 21: A19.

Meeks, C. (2001) 'Civil society and the sexual politics of difference', *Sociological Theory*, 19(3): 325–343.

Meyerowitz, J. (2002) *How Sex Changed: A History of Transsexuality in the United States*, Cambridge: Harvard University Press.

Monro, S. (2005) 'Beyond male and female: poststructuralism and the spectrum of gender', *International Journal of Transgenderism*, 8(1): 3–22.

———. (2007) 'Transmuting gender binaries: the theoretical challenge', *Sociological Research Online* 12(1). http://www.socresonline.org.uk/12/1/monro.html (accessed 10 December 2008).

Muñoz, J. E. (1999) *Disidentifications: Queers of Color and the Performance of Politics*, Minneapolis: University of Minnesota Press.

Nangeroni, N. (2003) 'Transgenderism', *Transgender Tapestry*, Spring, Issue 101: 23–24.

Papoulias, C. (2006) 'Transgender', *Theory, Culture and Society*, 23(2/3): 231–233.

Parlee, M. B. (1996) 'Situated knowledges of personal embodiment: transgender activists' and psychological theorists' perspectives on "sex" and "gender"', *Theory and Psychology*, 6(4): 625–645.

Prosser, J. (1998) *Second Skins: The Body Narratives of Transsexuality*, New York: Columbia University Press.

Rainbow Access Initiative (2003) 'A glossary of terms', *Transgender Tapestry*, Spring, Issue 101: 28.

Ringo, P. (2002) 'Media roles in female-to-male transsexual and transgender identity formation', *The International Journal of Transgenderism*, 6(2). http://www.symposion.com/ijt/ijtvo06no03_01.htm (accessed 12 October 2005).

Roen, K. (2002) '"Either/or" and "both/neither": Discursive tensions in transgender politics', *Signs*, 27(2): 501–522.

Rothblatt, M. A. (1993) 'Considering transgender liberation', *TV-TS Tapestry*, Issue 64: 40–41.

Sanger, T. (2008) 'Trans governmentality: the production and regulation of gendered subjectivities', *Journal of Gender Studies*, 17(1): 41–53.

Sloop, J. (2004) *Disciplining Gender: Rhetorics of Sex Identity in Contemporary U.S. Culture*, Amherst: University of Massachusetts Press.

Spade, D. and Currah P. (2008) 'The state we're in: locations of coercion and resistance in trans policy, part 2', *Sexuality Research and Social Policy*, 5(1): 1–4.

Spivak, G. C. (1988) 'Can the subaltern speak?' in C. Nelson and L. Grossberg (eds) *Marxism and the Interpretation of Culture*, Urbana: University of Illinois Press.

Staff (1995) 'Welcome to Transgender Tapestry: celebrating the diversity of gender expression', *Transgender Tapestry*, Winter, Issue 74: 1.

Stryker, S. (1998) 'The transgender issue: an introduction', *GLQ: A Journal of Lesbian and Gay Studies*, 4(2): 145-58.

———. (2006) '(De)subjugated knowledges: an introduction to transgender studies', in S. Stryker and S. Whittle (eds) *The Transgender Studies Reader*, New York: Routledge.

———. (2008) *Transgender History*, Berkeley, CA: Seal Press.

Taylor, V. and Rupp, L. J. (2004) 'Chicks with dicks, men in dresses: what it means to be a drag queen', *Journal of Homosexuality*, 46(3/4): 113–133.

Valentine, D. (2007) *Imagining Transgender: An Ethnography of a Category*, Durham, NC: Duke University Press.

Verrinder, M. (2005) 'N.J. group buys airtime for ad backing transgender rights', *The Associated Press State & Local Wire*, December 1.

West, C. and Zimmerman, D. (1987) 'Doing gender', *Gender & Society,* 1(2): 125–51.

Westbrook, L. (2007) 'One person's he is another person's she: the mind, the body, and the "truth" of gender', paper presented at the American Sociological Association Conference, New York City, New York, August.

Whittle, S. (1998) 'The trans-cyberian mail way', *Social Legal Studies,* 7(3): 389–408.

Whittle, S. (2006) 'Foreword', in S. Stryker and S. Whittle (eds) *The Transgender Studies Reader,* New York: Routledge.

Williams, C. (1995) 'Thoughts: a speech given at Atlanta Action '95 convention', *Transgender Tapestry,* Summer, Issue 72: 64–70.

Willox, A. (2003) 'Branding Teena: (mis)representations in the media', *Sexualities,* 6(3/4): 407–425.

3 Telling Trans Stories
(Un)doing the Science of Sex

Alison Rooke

INTRODUCTION: FROM TRANS SUBJECTS TO TRANS LIVES

A significant body of trans[1] theory (see, for example Bornstein 1994, 1998; Feinberg 1996, 1998; Wilchins 1997) investigates the specificity of trans experience and what this can tell us about the relationships between embodied difference, cultural norms and social power (Stryker 2006). This work, together with the work of Stone (1991), Prosser (1998), Namaste (2000), Whittle (2006), Whittle Turner, Al Alami (2007), Halberstam (2005) and Hines (2006, 2007a) emerged from the 1990s at the conjunction of feminist, poststructuralist and queer theory. This body of theory works against the more abstract theorisations of gender, where the transgendered have, in many ways, functioned as the emblematic ideal postmodern subjects; multiple in their narratives, produced through a range of sometimes contradictory stories, scripts, and accounts. As Stryker argues '"transgender" became an over determined construct, like "cyborg" through which contemporary culture imagined a future filled with new possibilities for being human, or posthuman' (Stryker 2006: 8). This turn to the specificity of experience within trans theory can be located in a broader critique of postmodern and specifically queer theory, in particular of its textuality and theoretically driven writing as a retreat from empirical engagement with the messiness of the social world (see Seidman 1995, 1996; Hines 2006b, 2007; Back 2007; Rooke 2009).

This chapter contributes to an emerging body of trans theory which has offered a critique of the dematerialisation of the trans subject within queer theory and has 'established what was effectively a new paradigm for the conceptualization and study of transgender phenomenon' (Ekins and King 2006: 21). It is concerned with the ways in which transgendered identities are realised and expressed. It takes as its focus a participatory arts project entitled Sci:dentity, which was aimed at young trans people. The chapter explores the ways that the project opened up a space where gendered identities were formed relationally with others. It explores the artwork that emerged from the project, which is concerned with gendered relations in the social world. It foregrounds young trans people's experiences of gender relations in their everyday life, and examines the various ways that trans lives are storied. The chapter asks: what is at stake in listening to these stories for our theorisation of trans lives and the consequences of gendered relations?

SCI:DENTITY: EXPLORING THE SCIENCE OF SEX THROUGH ART

The Sci:dentity project was funded by the Wellcome Trust and took place between March 2006 and March 2007 in London, UK.[2] The project aimed to investigate the science of sex and to explore how sex and gender are understood by both transsexual and transgendered people (and in society in general[3]). The participants were encouraged to creatively respond to the science of sex and gender through art. The project brought together academics, arts practitioners, medical professionals and a group of 18 young transgendered and transsexual people between the ages of 15 and 22 from across the UK who were living their sex and gender with a degree of complexity.[4] Together, the project team shared their knowledge and put theories of gender to work.[5] Here young trans people could form their questions, explore, deepen and express their understandings of gender and sex, interrogate scientific discourses of sex, gender and transsexuality and respond to the 'authority' and apparent certainties of science creatively through a variety of media and performing arts.[6] The project examined explanations of sex and gender differences found in contemporary medical science such as endocrinology, neurology and biology. As the project progressed, bio-ethics were also discussed in relation to hormonal and surgical sex reassignment.

The project had two main phases: firstly a creative engagement phase, which consisted of a series of four weekend workshops. This first phase of the project was documented on video and culminated in an exhibition and performance to an invited audience of approximately 150 people, including the participants' families and friends, youth workers, trainee teachers, teachers, LGBT[7] youth and community workers, people from trans networks, academics and funders. This chapter focuses on this creative engagement phase. The project's second phase consisted of a series of 16 outreach workshops about sex and gender, which were delivered to a variety of audiences including school and college teachers and students, trainee drama teachers, young people including LGBT youth, youth workers, arts practitioners, educationalists, activists and those working in the area of equalities and diversity policy and delivery. The documentary film about the arts workshops was shown in some of the outreach workshops with an aim of communicating the outcomes of the project and the life experiences of the participants to a wide range of people. Many of these were coming across the notion and the lived experience of transgender for the first time. In keeping with the project's participatory ethos, several of the young people who took part in the creative workshops went on to co-facilitate some of the outreach workshops.

FROM PARTICIPATIVE ART TO RELATIONAL AESTHETICS

Before discussing the story telling which came out of the project, I want to briefly set out some ways in which the project can be understood in terms of its practice. Both participatory arts and participatory action research are fields where academics, together with a range of collaborators, such as artists and activists, have found an area of common ground. Through participatory practice academics, artists, activists and associated agencies have worked together to formulate research questions, identify priorities and produce work which connects art and lived experience as social processes. In this way, whether through art or research, participants are engaged in collaborations that emphasise collective creativity, and the ways in which this can contribute to wider social and political agendas (see Freire 1972; Hall 1982; Park 1993; Cooke and Kothari 2001; Butler and Reiss 2007 for more discussion). Recently contemporary art theorists have turned their attention to community-based and participative arts inspired by social issues and have began to interrogate some of the questions raised by such encounters (see Kester 1995; Bishop 2004; Downey 2007).

Bourriaud's (2002) seminal text *Relational Aesthetics* argues that some of the most innovative contemporary art can be understood not as an artistic object or product, but rather as a form of social exchange and encounter, producing what he describes as a 'relational aesthetic' (2002). The significance of such relational art is the process of participation rather than the production of art objects per se. The relationality of such work is found in both its inter-subjective character and the collective elaboration of meaning that these encounters produce. It is also worth noting that this relational art frequently takes place in social settings rather than the 'white cube' of the art gallery. One of the important functions of relational aesthetics is to offer a break from everyday life and the modes of communication and participation it structures. More specifically, relational art represents a branch of artistic practice that is largely concerned with producing and reflecting upon the interrelations between people and the extent to which such relations—or communicative acts—need to be considered as an aesthetic form. The aestheticisation of relationality was central to the Sci:dentity project in several ways. Firstly, relationality characterised the space that the creative workshops provided. This was a space where the participants could relate with other young trans people and explore their own identities through these relations with others. The process of engaging in creativity provided the conditions for interpersonal encounters and sociability. Secondly, Sci:dentity provided an interstitial space where participants could reflect on the gender normativity they encountered in their everyday lives. Finally, the gendered inter relations in the participants' everyday lives were a central theme of the artwork produced. I now explore each of these dimensions by examining the stories that were told as the project unfolded and how these relate to other trans narratives.

TELLING TRANS STORIES

The Sci:dentity project sat at a nexus between several contemporary sites where trans identities are discursively formulated. These include; medico-psychiatric practices regarding transgenderism and transsexualism; on-line identity spaces such as trans community message boards, support groups, and photo-sharing sites; off-line trans social spaces, and the narratives of transsexuality found in popular culture, in particular the 'spectacular' material of talk shows, makeover and reality television (Gamson, 1998; Dovey 2000; Biressi and Nunn 2005; Heller 2006; Oullette and Hay 2008). These are all sites where trans stories are told and where investments in versions of trans identities are played out, struggled over and realised. The practice and pedagogy of the Sci:dentity Project, raises the question 'Who "tells" trans stories, and to whom?' It also asks 'What does this story telling do?' The project engaged with this story telling on several levels. Firstly, it created a space for the narration of gendered identities. Here the participants were able to narrate their felt sense of their own gender to each other and, later, to a wider audience. It also interrogated how the truth of sometimes overlapping and contradictory discourses about sex and gender are constituted and performed in a variety of sites. In particular, the scientific basis of sex was interrogated.

There was a clear sense of the compulsion to tell one's story to others among the group of young people working on the project. This story telling was part of the process of coming to an understanding of one's own trans identity (Mason-Schrock 1996; Gagne and Tewksbury 1998). In the act of giving an account of their own personal experience to another, the participants produced meaning and understanding for the other individuals involved. This led into the production of artistic work. However, this was not unproblematic for the facilitators, as Catherine McNamara the project co-coordinator has stated elsewhere:

> As a staff team, we understood that the act of story telling within sessions is not straightforward: not *everyone* wants to tell theirs, or feels the compulsion to make their personal experience public. We were interested in finding ways for individuals to mediate the extent to which the synthesis of scientific discourses and personal experiences became 'public', either within the sessions among their peers or as part of an exhibition of work derived from these explorations. Our responsibility as arts practitioners was to provide choices in terms of methods of exploration, modes of expression and media of communication such that participants were able to use autobiography and draw on personal stories, but in a way that wouldn't expose their vulnerability, or even lead them to perform something they may later regret in terms of revealing the personal in a public arena.
>
> (McNamara and Rooke 2006: 86)

Clearly, this presented the facilitators with the challenge of encouraging expression and creativity, whilst balancing this with a consideration of the participants' vulnerability. So for example, some participants were selecting aspects of their personal narrative to create work that aimed to make a statement to a wider audience, while others worked in a more insular, processual way. Some of these accounts were included in the final exhibition, others were not. This points to the ethical issues that were present throughout the project process. These included a consideration of the project's impact on the participants and the need for confidentiality and anonymity, balanced with an impetus to produce project outcomes.

NARRATING A TRANS SELF

The creativity which emerged allowed the participants to tell their personal stories to each other, and in many cases to a wider audience. In this way, the young people did considerable identity work within the workshop as they developed their own identity narratives and explored accounts of transsexuality and transgenderism. By responding creatively to science, the trans young people told their own stories and interacted with each other's. The participants' own histories and experiences were transformed through challenging the authority of the science of sex and gender, and by exploring their perceptions of transgenderism in society as they worked to develop a group show. These autobiographies became the raw materials in the creation of art. At the heart of this process was a biographical narrating of being transsexual and transgendered as participants communicated their experience of the far-reaching consequences, difficulties and pleasures of living as a young trans person. Simultaneously, they developed critiques of the scientific and medical practices that reproduce the coherence of sex and gender in the figure of the 'man' or 'woman'. Through this process, the project created an opportunity for the young people to interrogate the incitements to intelligibility they were likely to encounter in medical discourses, and the associated practices in the diagnosis and treatment of the condition of transsexuality as they began the process of transitioning.

Being together in a group with other transgendered young people provided a space where many of the participants became comfortable with their transgendered identities, as the following quote illustrates:

> I expected to feel a bit weird initially 'cos I'm not transitioning via surgery/hormones like it seems like the vast majority of everyone else is. So I didn't think I'd feel as accepted and liked as I did. Speaking to a few leaders and participants about my own lack-of-gender path was freeing because I was understood and not ridiculed or misunderstood. I could

also relate to other people saying their bodies went the wrong way at puberty or social expectations didn't fit with their view of themselves.

(Shannon, genderqueer, age 19)

The sense of ease or comfort sat in contrast to the medical diagnosis of transsexuality as a type of disorder or dysphoria.[8] In group discussions participants considered the ways that the story of being transgendered is subject to medical scrutiny and associated ethical dilemmas, as Shannon goes on to discuss here:

> I've pondered how gender and transition relate with other body modifications (piercings, tattoos, cosmetic surgery) because to get your tits enlarged you just need money, but to get them cut off you need a gender shrink. That's bloody weird! Where do you draw the line between someone who wants non-genital cosmetic surgery and someone who wants genital cosmetic surgery? Why is one more of a problem for society than the other? Why does society require that we have an either/or gender?
>
> (Shannon, genderqueer, age 19)

While we might question the extent to which gender reassignment can be considered 'cosmetic', here Shannon questions why some gender expressions are acceptable while others are placed discursively in the realm of psychiatry. This was also apparent in a session where the participants had an opportunity to formulate questions for a private doctor who was a gender specialist. The following question also revealed the extent to which participants were aware of the ethics surrounding their potential access to 'treatment':

> How do you feel about the rightness and wrongness of a person's transition? How do you feel about having the responsibility of making decisions about a person's transition process?
>
> (Question formulated by participants for a GP and gender specialist)

FROM DIAGNOSIS TO IDENTITY

By combining art and science the project opened up a space that sat at the nexus between psychiatric discourses, which consider transsexuality to be a symptom of an individuals 'gender dysphoria', and the identitarian discourses of a growing global queer and trans social justice movement, which brings together identities organised around the modalities of gender, sex, sexuality, ethnicity, desire and location in unpredictable, dynamic and playful ways. It is worth noting that these narratives of a gendered self and a transsexual identity are not always distinct from each other. As Hines points out, there is a correspondence between the medical inception of the concept of being 'trapped in the wrong body' and many transgender identity narratives: 'The epistemological power of medical discourse has thus worked to structure specific aetiologies of transgenderism' (Hines 2007: 59). These correspondences overlap in complex ways which are neither straightforward nor unproblematic. On-line communities and community support spaces and the informal practices of sharing one's story with others who identify themselves as a community constitute a 'novel form of authority' in the fields of medicine and health. As Rose and Novas point out in a discussion of debates among those at risk of developing Huntington's disease and their relatives, recounting one's experience (rather than formal training, status or possession of specialist skills) is the basis of this kind of authority which is 'folded into the self' (Rose and Novas 2000: 503). The project can be understood as a site where this folding took place as medical science, experience and community knowledge combined as the participants developed coherent narrations of their trans selfhood.

Crucially, this story telling is relational. One's experience is converted into authority through a social interaction with others. This was apparent in a short film made by one participant called Liam, a young FTM man age 22, which interrogated and responded to medical versions of the transsexual person. Liam's film exemplifies how the creativity opened up a space to respond to medical discourses about the science of sex and articulate a developing self-understanding. After the first weekend of the creative workshops, Liam expressed some ambiguity about the science of sex presented that weekend when he wrote the following in the evaluation blog, 'the most challenging aspect of the weekend for me was the science talk and the thoughts and feelings it always evokes in me when biology is mentioned'. However, by the end of the creative workshops he had used these ambivalent feelings to critique the authority of science. Liam made a short film based on an encounter with his GP when he requested a referral to a gender identity clinic. The encounter was less than satisfactory, revealing his GP's lack of awareness of trans identities and current NHS procedures. Liam took this encounter and used it as the raw material of a short film. Liam took the content of a letter written by his GP which discussed his lack of 'normal' biological development. He re-wrote this text, re-narrating the encounter until it reflected his sense of his gender. This text was used in a video which explored the notion of 'transition'. It begins with Liam clean-shaven, and as it plays backwards, we see Liam seemingly shaving, then with a beard prior to the shave, and finally putting a beard on (with the use of glue and hair clippings). The visual dimension of the video works to achieve a transition from male to female (or at least imbue in the viewer some uncertainty). Simultaneously, a voice-over which accompanies these visuals begins with Liam's (pre-transition) female-sounding voice reading out the doctor's letter referring to 'her', 'she' and female biology (such as menarche and a lack of hirsuitism). As the film progresses the voice-over becomes deeper and the words of the letter change, until at the end, a deep male-sounding voice states:

> This 22-year-old asked me to refer him as he has not been feeling fully male, has felt more male gender in his physical and mental activities. His menarche started late 14, and his sexual organs showed unreasonable development. He denies any hirstuitism, would you kindly see him for further investigations.

This statement is an account of a transsexuality narrated from the perspective of the trans person. Liam's film is just one example of the ways in which relationality was explored creatively in the project. Liam worked to unfix the determinism of biology and re-narrate his gendered self-hood in the very terms which had been used to dismiss it. This demonstrates a performative understanding of the medical discourses, which challenge his self-understanding as male. This short film reflexively worked on the power of words to produce realities. It contests the unexamined habits of the GP's ways of seeing gender, and their ontological power in determining that which is real or not.

RELATIONAL SPACE, RELATIONAL IDENTITIES

The relational space of the workshops offered a performative space where gendered expressions and trans identities could be reflected upon, worked on and re-worked. Here the materiality of bodies as hard biological facts was folded into the ways in which bodies are somatically felt and produced relationally through affective communication. Contemporary theorists concerned with embodiment have argued that bodies are not the biological facts of distinct separate physical entities, but rather they are constituted through relationality. This relationality may be with 'open-ended objects' (Fraser, Kember and Lury 2005: 3), with images (Coleman 2008) and with other bodies (Sheets Johnston 1992; Browne 2006; Blackman 2009). In regard to sexed bodies then, as Browne (2006) suggests in a discussion of masculine appearing women who are mistaken for men, it is not the case that the sexed body is an essential element of the self. Instead the sexed body is produced performatively in relation to others. As Browne argues '[Thus] the creation of the sexed body is not a sole individual endeavor, rather it is produced through a nexus of interrelations' (Browne 2006: 137). Bodies are processual. They come into being through their affective relations with others.

As the project progressed, the participants interrogated the ways in which the certainties of sexed bodies are constituted through scientific and medical discourses regarding the materiality of sex. For example, science lessons examined hormones and their effect on behaviour, chromosomes and their

function, debates on the evidence for male and female brains, sex reassignment and the 'conditions' of intersexuality and transsexuality. Simultaneously, through intersubjective encounters in the workshops, participants'
own sexed bodies were constituted through their relations with others who
were transgendered and transsexual. In this way, the participants worked
on their own identities, as the following extracts illustrate:

> I learnt a lot about the *lack* of scientific/medical understanding about
> sex, or rather that understanding became less of a concept and more of
> a reality. It has driven me to learn more about sex and intersex. I think
> it has made me feel less like the female assignment and characteristics
> I have *make* me female. I think once you shed the ideal images of what
> a man and woman should be away it's easier to accept your own body,
> when you realise there is no clear line. It's like ok, I'm a short, unusual
> guy, and there's lots of them about and not all of them are even trans!
> The challenge becomes less of an internal battle (mind vs. matter), more
> of a process of getting the recognition of who you are!
>
> (Paul, FtM, age 20)

Many participants echoed these sentiments when discussing the workshops.
They spoke of how relationships within the project impacted on their self-
understandings and crucially, their ability to articulate these in the social
world. This was frequently compared to their on-line interactions. Existing research (Whittle 2006) shows how transgender identities are often
formed in isolation from other trans people through virtual encounters in
cyberspace. This was evident in the participants' stories. Sixteen of the 18
participants had never met another trans person in 'real life' before coming
along to the workshops. Most of the participants had developed their self-
understanding as trans through gathering information and forming text
based relationships in virtual trans spaces such as Internet forums, message
boards and chat spaces. In these spaces, trans people receive and pass on
embodied (trans)gendered cultural knowledge and form collective identities, through sharing photographs and information on hormone regimes,
surgery and NHS procedures, discussing the standard of care and crafts-
manship of various surgeons in the UK and beyond. This is reflected in
John's discussion of the project here:

> David said to me at the end of the project, "I am going home now and
> I am not going to get called 'he' for months and months". Obviously
> someone can call you he on the Internet but it is not the same as that
> real experience that you are wanting to have.
>
> (John, FtM, age 22)

The participants found these 'real life' off-line interactions validating,
enabling their felt 'sense of gender' (Browne and Lim 2009) to be realised

(however temporarily). So, for example, when asked 'What are the most important things you have got out of this project?' one participant stated:

> The chance to be entirely yourself for the duration of the weekends, to not have to hide anything or be worried about being misunderstood. That for me has been the most important thing I think and has contributed to a massive surge in confidence, in being myself and being out, [ ] actually the most important thing I've got is friends.
>
> (Eddie, FtM, age 20)

Participants also discussed the ways the project offered the possibility of self-expression, of 'being who you are', which differs from merely being 'who you want to be'. Aiden identifies as male, dresses in a feminine way at weekends for club nights and parties but dresses as a man in his everyday life:

> [W]hen you're allowed to express yourself more and more as who you are, it becomes more apparent who you're not and who you weren't when you were trying to act a different way. So having this full weekend where you can just without question be yourself and be who you are was a first for me. Like I've gone to bars where for the night I can be who I wanna be—I've got friends who know me as who I am, but they still don't know the gender thing yet, don't know the sex thing yet, they just know who I am. The pronoun stuff . . . grating. But being here, for like a solid two days and being completely in this space is like one of the first times for the longest period of time that I've been able to do that, and feel better and better about it, and it being more comfortable with me.
>
> (Aiden, genderqueer, age 22)

Aiden's experience speaks to the possibilities of realisation of one's felt gender identity in the spatiality and temporality of the workshops. However, the project's safe ontological space simultaneously highlighted how the navigation of a binary gendered social world routinely foreclosed a relational confirmation of participant's felt gender. This had emotional consequences, as Shannon discusses here:

> It's a nasty shock leaving that safe environment and going in to a challenging one again that looks at you and sees something else. It was severely unpleasant going home sometimes. And I know, speaking to Julie (a participant) she said, "I want to stay in there because that's the life that I want and life can't be like that". It was deeply disturbing for me as well. I remember going home the first time and thinking, "I am glad there are three more weekends of that 'cos that was fantastic." I will really miss it.
>
> (Shannon, genderqueer, age 19)

While this participant speaks of the possibilities that the relational space of the project allowed, it also speaks to the ways in which these are foreclosed in the binary gendered everyday, which does not afford cultural space for those who are transgendered. Most of the participants were returning to worlds where their felt sense of gender would be contested repeatedly. This was expressed by Fred age 15 who identified as FtM. Fred composed several songs and performed these at the final weekend performance. His songs poignantly communicated his struggles with the ways in which he was received as male by his family.

> Don't tell me that I'm not old enough to know
>
> the one thing that I have always known
>
> and no one's dead so why're you grieving?
>
> you say I'm in denial when you're the one who won't believe me
>
> you're so blinded by love that you don't even see me.

The participants' creative work also emphasised the pleasures of being recognised in their felt gender or 'passing'. The Sci:dentity 'zine' which was produced for the art exhibition included several accounts of being read in public in their felt gender. Here Aiden discussed a trip he took to a queer club with a friend:

> Anyway while at the club a bi-sexual girl came up to me telling me how hot n cute I looked (I was wearing six inch white stilettos, a short white mini skirt, white top with devil written on as well as angel wings, which got me a lot off attention). She came onto me strong, so we started snogging. She was really into it so she put her hand up my top. She stopped and pulled away. She looked at me and said "I thought u was a girl", she was really shocked and surprised by it all but was really cool with it.
>
> (Aiden, genderqueer, age 22)

Steven also wrote about the pleasures of passing in LGBT spaces:

> Last month I was at my local pub and they had a drag queen in. He came over and talked to me and my mates. He said that he was just a gay man, cross dressed for a living. He identified all my mates correctly as gay, lesbian, or bi. So, impressed, I asked him what I was and he said a young sexy bi man. I was so hyped by that!!! My mates left, so me and him kept chatting. He was trying to score with me so bad, even though I was trying to explain about my 'situation'! I was amused!!! I

set off to get in my taxi and he said "wait!" turned around to his manager, and said "get my number I need this young man in my life!" I had to tell him I wasn't physically what he was looking for but we still chat and text loads. I was just so amazed I passed that well!

(Steven, FtM, age 18)

Eddie discusses another example of passing although in a different context. He describes boarding a train in a hurry with no ticket and being caught by the ticket inspectors:

"You got a ticket mate?" Inwardly I groan. I passed, he thinks I'm a boy, usually a cause for celebration, but sooner or later he's going to realise. "No" I mutter. He asked me why not. He still hasn't had that little look of surprise . . . So when he asked me my name I tell him the one that isn't on my ID cards, the one that just my friends use. I can't bear to let him think I'm a girl. He starts to fill out a ticket, asking me questions and my heart's hammering like anything at the possibility that he'll realise and I'll have to explain to him. But he doesn't realise and neither does his colleague, he fills out the report with Mr and He and describes me as a young man, age 19, 5ft 4. I get off the train in a bit of a daze, I pause and grin, and I practically dance home.

(Eddie, FtM, age 20)

These accounts point to the complex ways that young trans people are continuously navigating the web of gender normativity while negotiating their own developing gendered and sexual identities on an everyday basis. They speak of the pleasures of passing in their felt gender (see Garfinkel 1967; Stone 1991; Feinberg 1992; Bornstein 1994; Hines 2007 for further discussion of passing).

CREATIVE METHODOLOGIES

I now want to briefly discuss some of the art created in the workshops, and specifically the exhibition and performance which took place at the end of the project. Here I focus on the ways this art expressed and explored the relational aspects of gender. The methodologies employed included drawing, animation, painting, song writing, performance and film making. These media gave the young people an opportunity to narrate their self understanding and crucially, their sense of their own gender in creative ways which combined community narratives of trans selfhood such as female-to-male (FtM), male-to-female (MtF) and genderqueer, with medical discourses of transsexuality to narrate a coherent trans-self (McNamara and Rooke 2008). The participants' art work questioned the overlapping popular narratives of transsexuality found in medicine and television documentaries, such as 'Sex Change Hospital', which presents transsexuality as the process of having a 'sex change' by transitioning from one sex to another. This is a process often understood as having a distinct beginning, middle and end.

The dominant narrative here, as discussed earlier, is that of the trans person trapped in the 'wrong body', who, in the process of undergoing psychiatry will be diagnosed as gender dysphoric, undergo hormonal treatment, have surgery and arrive at the destination of their new 'sex'. While these versions of the trans self may make sense of many transsexual people's self understandings, they do not leave room for the possibility of being transgendered, of identifying as neither male or female, or both male and female. In their creative explorations, the participants reflected their self-understandings and the ways they are positioned within medical discourses and associated procedures. The young people's response to the 'authority' of scientific knowledge was clearly communicated in the Sci:dentity art exhibition and performance, which explored the participants' transgendered identities and critiqued a medical model of transsexuality and the more sensational representations of trans people in the media. Early workshop sessions, which focused on representations of sex and gender in the media and art, employed the ambiguity of artistic representations. This was in contrast to the apparent certainties of science. This ambiguity was utilised to produce nuanced autobiographical artwork. The themes of the exhibition reflected the young people's concerns, passions and experiences. These included, 'passing', relationships with family, friends, coming out, feeling different from the 'norm' and negotiating places such as clubs, bars, toilets and public transport. The artwork focused on the variety of the participants' experience of their gendered identities as a variety of different journeys and potential life trajectories.

IN THE GREY ZONE

In curating the exhibition the participants developed the idea of a 'grey room' that was designed to explore the grey area between the gender binaries of male and female - thereby opening up a trangendered space. The exhibits here drew attention to the participants' everyday spatialities. (see Rooke 2009 for further discussion) and the ways in which gender is continuously reiterated and negotiated. The exhibition's grey room contained a series of sculptures and projections, which undid gender and explored the ways that gender is 'done' in the social world. Installations included a collage titled 'Buying into Gender', showing gendered consumer goods such as children's toys and clothes, typically coded in pink and blue colors. A video installation showed a participant playing with clothes and gender stereotypes in a shop changing-room, while a sculpture featured gender stereotypical clothes which had been ripped and burnt. One installation in the grey room consisted of a large toilet with walls on three sides that were covered with the young people's writing. This writing spoke of their experience of binary gendered spaces and the ways that their navigation of these was particularly treacherous. As well as transcriptions of overheard questions such as "Mummy, is that a boy or a girl?" and "Is he a girl?", some of the participants' writing speaks of the impact of gender normativity on trans people's navigation of such 'public conveniences' and the inconvenience they afford trans people who do not easily pass as one gender or another:

> I have yet to go to the 'gents' but now that I am 'going over to the other side' I find it hard when I am in the 'ladies.' It's true that I don't really fit into one category and one box so therefore I get looks and whispers. I have had remarks but even when there is no one in the toilets I can still hear them.
>
> (Anonymous contribution to Sci:dentity zine)

> Women looking at me disgusted. Others confused. But all of them, ALL of them looking, thinking. If not saying something to me with words, it all comes out in their eyes. Their body language . . . Wouldn't you think twice about which toilet to go into? Sometimes I hold it in for hours until I get home. Or until I can find toilets that aren't separated to male/female.
>
> (Steven, FtM, age 18)

These quotes speak of the ways in which sexed and gendered spaces are maintained and policed through what we might call the visual regimes of gender normativity. (For further discussion of the negotiation of the toilet as a site which is sexed in regulatory ways see Sibley 1995; Halberstam 1998; Munt 1998, 2001; Browne 2004).

CONCLUSION

This chapter has offered one example of sociological research that balances an understanding of the inter-relation between gendered lives as they are lived at the level of everyday relations, guided, as Butler argues, 'by the questions of what maximizes the possibilities for a liveable live, what minimizes the possibility of an unbearable life, or indeed social or literal death' (Butler 2004: 7). It has foregrounded the situated, embodied materiality of being trans in order to work against theoretical abstraction. Participative projects, such as Sci:dentity, speak to the small differences that engaged empirical research can make, not just to individuals, but also to a wider queer political project of social justice, opening up what Butler describes as 'a place in a regime of truth' (Butler 2005: 22). The Sci:dentity project developed capable, informed and skilled trans youth, who were willing and able to participate in existing spaces of representation. So for example, London's Metropolitan Police LGBT Advisory Group (an independent group of LGBT people who advise and monitor the metropolitan police) went on to work with the participants in the development of a Trans subgroup. Four Sci:dentity youth went on to be involved in the development of the Department of Health's Sexual Orientation and Gender Identity Advisory Group's (SOGIAG) Trans work stream, a group which was established as part of the Department of Health's Equality and Human Rights team, in order to make healthcare in the UK more accessible to LGBT people. At the close of the project the parents of some of the young people participating also contacted us to tell us about happier children, and their own new found confidence when it came to speaking to schools and colleges about their children's gender identity and asking for changes in the care and treatment of their child (for example being able to request that the appropriate pronouns were used in these spaces).

While these are small successes, the Sci:dentity project can be located in an emerging body of empirical research into the materiality of trans lives (see for example the sociological work of Namaste, 1996a, 1996b, 2000; Hines, 2006a, 2006b, 2007; and the politically informed writing of Feinberg 1996, 1998; Califia, 1997; Green 2004; Currah, Juang and Minter 2006; Whittle 2006; Whittle et al. 2007) and a sociological engagement with queer theory (Foucault, 1979; Fuss, 1991; Rubin, 1993; Sedgwick, 1993; Halberstam, 1998), which asks questions about the shape of theory: is it in good enough shape to make sense of the lives of trans people as they navigate the gendered relations of the social world? What can we learn about the struggles and pleasures of young trans people as they navigate the sexual normativity of schools, care systems and youth groups, as well as liberatory queer identities and medical govermentality? One of the strengths of these approaches to the social world is their ability to locate a queer critique of gender norms (see Butler 1991, 1993, 1996, 1997, 1999[1990], 2004; Garber, 1993) *within* the complexity of the lives of those who are living the consequences of not fitting neatly within its regimes of intelligibility (Butler 1999[1990], 2004, 2005). One of the strengths of the sociological imagination (Mills 1959, Back 2007) is that it can ground postmodern philosophical speculation in the materiality and intimacy of everyday life, following C. Wright Mills' plea for the development of the kind of sociological imagination which pays attention to the relationship between private troubles or the traps of everyday life, and those matters which become public issues. Sex, gender and sexuality occupy a special relationship between the private troubles and public issues of which Mills speaks. They are simultaneously the stuff of our private intimate worlds, the raw materials of popular entertainment and the focus of moral debates in the 'new politics of intimacy and everyday life' (Donovan, Heaphy and Weeks 2001). This raises the question of the ways that transgender and transsexuality become a public issue. While some queer theorists celebrate the possibilities of active 'transgression', we must remind ourselves that this is an ontological and social space which is often not available for some individuals and groups.

NOTES

1. Throughout this article certain terms are used which need explanation for the sake of clarity. *Trans* is used in this report to include transsexual and transgender. *Transsexual* is a medical term used to refer to a person who identifies as a gender which is different from that which they were assigned at birth. Transsexuals usually undergo a medical process of sex reassignment through the use of surgery and the administration of hormones. *Transgender* is a more colloquial term used to describe a person who feels that the gender assigned to them at birth is not a correct or complete description of what they feel. Transgender can be used to describe a wide range of gender expressions, which are a variation from the norms of society (for example including masculine or 'butch' women, feminine men, cross-dressers). *Genderqueer* is also a colloquial or community term that describes someone who identifies as a gender other than 'man' or 'woman,' or someone who identifies as neither, both, or some combination thereof. In relation to the male/female genderqueer people generally identify as more 'both/and' or 'neither/nor,' rather than 'either/or.' Some genderqueer people may identify as a third gender in addition to the traditional two. The commonality is that all genderqueer people are ambivalent about the notion that there are only two genders in the world.
2. The project was formulated by three academics, myself included, whose backgrounds are in queer theory, visual arts, participatory research and performance. The project was conceptualised and led by Catherine McNamara. Jay Stewart was the documentary maker for the project. Together the project team had training and professional experience in applied theatre, participative arts, mental health work and youth and community work with LGBT and non LGBT youth. I was responsible for the participatory evaluation of the project.
3. Many transgendered and transsexual people invest time in conducting research into the scientific and biological basis of sex and gender in the process of identity formation, (Whittle 2006: xii) in order to make sense of their feelings of discomfort with gender normativity and assumptions about the coherence between biology and gender which exist in wider society.
4. Four of the participants were already living in relation to medical understandings of sex and gender, as they were either being referred to, or were already clients of, gender identity clinics. Several others had formed their trans identities in virtual spaces in isolation from off-line social contact with other trans people
5. The two reports on the participatory evaluation reports of the project can be accessed at http://www.goldsmiths.ac.uk/cucr/research/res29 (Rooke 2006, 2007)
6. For a more extensive discussion of the significance of the transgendered space that was created by the project see Rooke 2009.
7. LGBT is a common acronym for Lesbian, Gay, Bisexual and Transgender.
8 Gender Identity Disorder (GID) is the formal diagnosis used by medical professionals to describe persons who experience significant gender dysphoria.

The current guidance for medical practitioners is produced by the General Medical Council and contained in the Harry Benjamin Guidelines on the Treatment of Transsexuals (2001). In regard to the treatment of young people, these suggest caution. Medical practitioners are faced with ethical decisions as to whether to administer reversible treatments such as hormone blockers to the trans adolescent prior to irreversible treatments such as hormone administration and surgery. Guidelines published in 2005 by the British Society for Paediatric Endocrinology and Diabetes, which have since been updated—laid down that treatment should not start until puberty is complete. This practice in the UK stands in contrast to the situation in countries such as the US, Australia, Canada, the Netherlands, Germany, Belgium and Norway. This is now under review following on from considerable campaigning by academics, legal experts and grassroots organisations. A report in 2008 by an expert in the field of medical ethics (Giordano 2007) criticised medical practice in the UK, arguing that UK doctors are 'depriving children relief from "extreme suffering" caused by their condition, leading to self harm and suicide and forcing their families into seeking help outside the UK'. The publication of this report, and two subsequent conferences in 2008, led to considerable press attention, debate and activism around the treatment of 'gender variant adolescents'.

REFERENCES

Back, L. (2007) *The Art of Listening*, London: Berg.

Biressi, A. and Nunn, H. (2005) *Reality TV: Realism and Revelation*, London: Wallflower Press.

Bishop, C. (2004) 'Antagonism and relational aesthetics', *October* 110: 51–79.

Blackman, L. (2009) *The Body: The Key Concepts*, Oxford and New York: Berg.

Bornstein, K. (1994) *Gender Outlaw: On Men, Women and the Rest of Us*, New York and London: Routledge.

———. (1998) *My Gender Workbook*, New York: Routledge.

Bourriaud, N. (2002) *Relational Aesthetics*, Dijon: Les presses du rebel.

Browne, K. (2004) 'Genderism and the bathroom problem: (re)materialising sexed sites, (re)creating sexed bodies', *Gender, Place and Culture—A Journal of Feminist Geography*, 11(3): 331–346.

———. (2006) 'A right geezer bird (man-woman): the sites and sights of "female" embodiment', *Acme*, 5(2): 121–143.

Browne, K and Lim, J. (2009) 'Senses of gender', *Sociological Research Online*, 14(1). http://www.socresonline.org.uk/14/1/6.html (accessed 12 January 2009).

Butler, D. and Reiss V. (2007) *Art of Negotiation*, Manchester: Cornerhouse Publications.

Butler, J. (1991) 'Imitation and gender insubordination', in D. Fuss (ed.) *Inside/Out: Lesbian Theories, Gay Theories*, London: Routledge.

———. (1993) *Bodies that Matter: On the Discursive Limits of 'Sex'*, London: Routledge.

———. (1996) *Excitable Speech: A Politics of the Performative*, New York: Routledge.

———. (1997) 'Merely Cultural', *Social Text*, 52–53: 265–277.

———. (1999 [1990]) *Gender Trouble: Feminism and the Subversion of Identity*, New York: Routledge.

———. (2004) *Undoing Gender*, London: Routledge.

Butler, J. (2005) *Giving an Account of Oneself*, Bronx, New York: Fordham University Press.
Califia, P. (1997) *Sex Changes: The Politics of Transgenderism*, San Francisco: Cleis Press.
Coleman, B. (2008) 'The becoming of bodies', *Feminist Media Studies*, 8(2): 163–179.
Cooke, B. and Kothari, U. (eds) (2001) *Participation: The New Tyranny?* London: Zed Books.
Currah, P., Juang, R.M., and Minter, S.P. (2006) *Transgender Rights*, Minneapolis: University of Minnesota Press.
Donovan, C., Heaphy, B. and Weeks, J. (2001) *Same Sex Intimacies: Families of Choice and other Life Experiments*, London: Routledge.
Dovey, J. (2000) *Freakshow*, London and Sterling, VA: Pluto Press.
Downey, A. (2007) 'Towards a politics of (relational) aesthetics', *Third Text*, 21(3): 267–275.
Ekins, R. and King, D. (2006) *The Transgender Phenomenon*, London, Thousand Oaks and New Delhi: Sage Publications.
Feinberg, L. (1992) *Transgender Liberation: A Movement Whose Time Has Come*. New York: World View Forum.
———. (1996) *Transgender Warriors: Making History from Joan of Arc to Dennis Rodman*, Boston: Beacon Press.
———. (1998) *Transliberation: Beyond Pink or Blue*, Boston: Beacon Press.
Foucault, M. (1979) *Discipline and Punish*, New York: Vintage Books.
Fraser, M., Kember, S. and Lury, C. (2005) 'Inventive life: approaches to the new vitalism', *Theory, Culture and Society*, 22: 11–14.
Freire, P. (1972) *Pedagogy of the Oppressed*, Harmondsworth: Penguin.
Fuss, D. (1991) *Inside/Out: Lesbian Theories, Gay Theories*, London: Routledge.
Gagne, P. and Tewksbury, R. (1998) 'Conformity pressures and gender resistance among transgendered individuals', *Social Problems*, 45(1): 81–101.
Gamson, J. (1998) *Freaks Talk Back: Tabloid Talk Shows and Sexual Nonconformity*, Chicago: University of Chicago Press.
Garber, M. B. (1993) *Vested Interests: Cross-dressing and Cultural Anxiety*, London: Penguin Books.
Garfinkel, H. (1967) *Studies in Ethnomethodology*, Englewoodcliffs, NJ: Prentice Hall.
Giordano, S. (2007) 'Gender atypical organisation in children and adolescents: ethico-legal issues and a proposal for new guidelines', *International Journal of Children's Rights*, 15(3/4): 365–390.
Green, J. (2004) *Becoming a Visible Man*, Nashville: Vanderbilt University Press.
Halberstam, J. (2005) *In A Queer Place and Time: Transgendered Bodies Subcultural Lives*, London: NYU Press Hill.
———. (1998) *Female Masculinity*, Durham, NC: Duke University Press.
Hall, B. (1982) 'Breaking the monopoly of knowledge: research methods, participation and development', in B. Hall, A. Gillette and R. Tandon (eds) *Creating Knowledge: A Monopoly? Participatory Research in Development*, New Delhi: PRIA.
Harry Benjamin International Gender Dysphoria Association (2001) *Harry Benjamin Standards of Care for Gender Identity Disorders*, Sixth Edition. http://www.pfc.org.uk/medical/scc2001.htm (accessed 3 November 2009).
Heller, D. (2006) *The Great American Makeover: Television, History, Nation*, Basingstoke: Palgrave Macmillan.
Hines, S. (2006a) 'Intimate transitions: transgender practices of partnering and parenting', *Sociology* 40(2): 353–371.
———. (2006b) 'What's the difference? Bringing particularity to queer studies of transgender', *Journal of Gender Studies*, 15(1): 49–66.

———. (2007) *TransForming Gender: Transgender Practices of Identity, Intimacy and Care*, Bristol, UK: Policy Press.

Kestler G. H. (1995) 'Aesthetic evangelists: conversion and empowerment in contemporary community art', *Afterimage* 22: 5–11.

Mason-Schrock, D. (1996) 'Transsexuals' narrative construction of the "true self"', *Social Psychology Quarterly*, 59(3): 176–192.

McNamara, C. and Rooke, A. (2008) *Creative Encounters*, London: Wellcome Trust Publications.

Mills, C. W. (1959) *The Sociological Imagination*, Oxford: Oxford University Press.

Munt, S. (1998) *Butch and Femme*, London: Cassell.

———. (2001) 'The butch body', in R. Holliday and J. Hassard (eds) *Contested Bodies*, London: Routledge.

Namaste, K. (1996a) 'The politics of inside/out: queer theory, poststructuralism and a sociological approach to sexuality', in S. Seidman (ed.) *Queer Theory/ Sociology*, Oxford: Blackwell.

———. (1996b) 'Tragic misreadings: queer theory's erasure of transgender subjectivity', in B. Beemyn and M. Eliason (eds) *Queer Studies: A Lesbian, Gay, Bisexual and Transgender Anthology*, New York and London: NYU Press.

———. (2000) *Invisible Lives: The Erasure of Transsexual and Transgendered People*, Chicago: University of Chicago Press.

Oullette, L. and Hay, J (2008) *Better Living through Reality TV: Television and Post-Welfare Citizenship*, Carlton, Victoria: Blackwell.

Park, P. (1993) 'What is participatory research? A theoretical and methodological perspective', in M. Brydon-Miller, B. Hall and T. Jackson (eds) *Voices of Change: Participatory Research in the United States and Canada*, Westport, CT: Bergin & Garvey.

Prosser, J. (1998) *Second Skin: The Body Narratives of Transsexuality*, New York: Columbia University Press.

Rooke, A. (2006) *The Sci:dentity Project Evaluation Report: Phases 1 and 2*, Goldsmiths University, Centre for Urban and Community Research. http:// www.goldsmiths.ac.uk/cucr/publications.php (accessed 16 February 2009).

———. (2007) *The Sci:dentity Project Evaluation Report: Phases 3 and 4*, Goldsmiths University, Centre for Urban and Community Research. http://www. goldsmiths.ac.uk/cucr/publications.php (accessed 16 February 2009).

———. (2010) 'Trans youth, science and art: creating (trans)gendered space', *Gender, Place and Culture*, Forthcoming.

Rose, N and Novas, C. (2000) 'Genetic risk and the birth of the somatic individual', *Economy and Society*, 29(4): 485–513.

Rubin, G. S. (1993) 'Thinking sex: notes for a radical theory of the politics of sexuality', in H. Abelove, M. A Barale, and D. Halperin (eds) *The Lesbian and Gay Studies Reader*, New York: Routledge.

Sedgwick, E. K. (1993) *Tendencies*, London: Routledge.

———. (1995) 'Deconstructing queer theory or the under theorising of the social and the ethical', in L. Nicholson and S. Seidman (eds) *Social Postmodernism*, Cambridge: Cambridge University Press.

Seidman, S. (1996) *Queer Theory/Sociology*, Oxford: Blackwell.

Sheets Johnston, M. (1992) *Giving the Body its Due*, Albany, New York: SUNY Press.

Sibley, D. (1995) *Geographies of Exclusion*, London: Routledge.

Stone, S. (1991) 'The empire strikes back: a post-transsexual manifesto', in K. Straub and J. Epstein (eds) *Body Guards: The Cultural Politics of Gender Ambiguity*, New York: Routledge.

Stryker, S. (2006) '(De)subjugated knowledges: an introduction to transgender studies', in S. Stryker and S. Whittle (eds) *The Transgender Studies Reader*, London: Routledge.

Whittle, S. (2006) 'Foreword', in S. Stryker and S. Whittle (eds) *The Transgender Studies Reader*, London: Routledge.

Whittle, S., Turner, L. and Al-Alami, M. (2007) 'Engendered penalties: transgendered people's experience of inequality and discrimination', *Communities and Local Government Publications*. http://www.pfc.org.uk/files/EngenderedPenalties.pdf (accessed 12 March 2009).

Wilchins, R. A. (1997) *Read My Lips: Sexual Subversion and the End of Gender*, Ithaca, NY: Firebrand Books.

Part II
Trans Governance

4 Recognising Diversity?

The Gender Recognition Act and Transgender Citizenship

Sally Hines

INTRODUCTION

This chapter explores the impact and the significance of the UK 'Gender Recognition Act' (GRA 2004) on trans individuals and trans communities.[1] The GRA came into being in 2004; enabling trans people to legally change their birth certificates and to marry or civilly partner in their acquired gender. In order to contextualise the GRA within shifting conceptualisations of gender more broadly, the chapter first examines understandings of gender—and of transgender—within feminist, queer and transgender theory. I move on to examine how these theoretical shifts were mirrored in trans activism, and, particularly, evident in the legal challenges brought by trans people, which formed the backdrop to the GRA. Yet, as I explore in my discussion of medical understandings of transsexuality, such conceptual and political frameworks contrast sharply with medical thinking, which is also woven into the GRA. I thus suggest that the GRA embodies on-going tensions between very different ways of understanding (trans) gender.

From this juncture, the chapter explores these tensions at an experiential level by considering how trans people variously experience the legal process of the GRA (see 'Case Studies'). Here I draw on my qualitative research, which is exploring the meanings and significance of the GRA, and the impact of 'recognition' on individual and community identity practices.[2] The last section of the chapter situates these substantive reflections within debates around rights and recognition, and theoretical considerations of sexual citizenship. I suggest that while the 'claims' of citizenship of some trans people are now being met, the schism between 'deserving' and 'undeserving' gendered and sexual citizens may have widened. Moreover, these divisions link back, I argue, to the GRA's incompatible positioning of social and medical understandings of gender.

UNRAVELLING 'SEX' AND 'GENDER': THEORETICAL CHALLENGES

The law, of course, does not exist in isolation from social and cultural discourse. Rather, legal discourse and practice is inextricably tied up with social and cultural understandings. To contextualise the GRA within epistemological frameworks and sites of political organisation, this section examines understandings of gender within feminist theory, queer theory and transgender studies. These disciplinary areas have been selected for analysis as each has enacted challenges both to dominant conceptualisations of gender, and to medical discourse and practice on transsexualism. I move on to address the link between these theoretical fields and trans activism; looking finally at legal challenges brought by trans people in the UK to a pre-GRA legal framework.

Theoretically and politically, trans practices have been the subject of much contestation within feminism. As Hird (2002) has illustrated, second-wave feminism was one of the first academic fields to respond to the growing public awareness of modern western transgender practices. Radical feminism's hostility to transgender is best exemplified by Raymond's (1980) book *The Transsexual Empire: The Making of the She-Male*. Raymond positioned transsexuality as a fabrication of a patriarchal medical system, which, through practices of surgical reconstruction, constructs servile women. Raymond's biological perspective of gender as mapped on to sex as defined at birth denied trans female identity positionings: 'It is biologically impossible to change *chromosomal* sex. If chromosomal sex is taken to be the fundamental basis for maleness and femaleness, the man who undergoes sex conversion is *not* female.' (1980: 10 italics in original). Raymond's position established an anti-transgender line within some strains of feminism that has been hard to break (Hines 2007a, 2007b). In *The Transsexual Empire* Raymond delivered a personal attack on academic and feminist activist Sandy Stone; identifying Stone by name, using the pro-noun 'he' and challenging her membership of the women's recording collective 'Olivia Records.' Members of 'Olivia' initially defended Stone's position in the collective, though public threats from some within feminist and lesbian communities to boycott 'Oliver' records led Stone to resign from the collective. In her reply to Raymond, and to anti-transgender feminist cultures more broadly, Stone (1991) spoke of the need for trans visibility and collective organisation. For Stryker and Whittle, Stone's intervention established a distinct trans subject position:

> Stone exacts her revenge more than a decade later, not by waging an anti-feminist counterattack on Raymond, but by undermining the foundationalist assumptions that support Raymond's narrower concept of womanhood, and by claiming a speaking position for transsexuals that cannot be automatically dismissed as damaged, deluded, second-rate, or somehow inherently compromised.
>
> (Stryker and Whittle 2006: 221)

Moreover, Stryker and Whittle (2006) read 'The Empire Strikes Back: A Post-Transsexual Manifesto' (Stone 1991) as the foundational text of transgender theory, situating it as:

The protean text from which contemporary transgender studies emerged. In the wake of (the) article, a gradual but steady body of new academic and creative work by transgender people has gradually taken shape, which has enriched virtually every academic and artistic discipline with new critical perspectives on gender.

(Stryker and Whittle 2006: 221)

During the 1990s queer scholars also developed strong critiques of the naturalisation of gender within feminist thinking. This body of work, and that of Butler (1990) in particular, sought to untie understandings of gender from those of 'sex.' Thus Butler argued that a binary model of 'sex' and 'gender'—wherein 'sex' constitutes the biological body and 'gender' denotes the social meanings attached to bodies—has restricted feminist understandings of gender as distinct from sex:

> The presumption of a binary gender system implicitly retains the belief in a mimetic relation of gender to sex whereby gender mirrors sex or is otherwise restricted by it. When the constructed status of gender is theorized as radically independent of sex, gender itself becomes a free-floating artifice, with the consequence that *man* and *masculine* might just as easily signify a female body as a male one, and *woman* and *feminine* a male body as easily as a female one.
>
> (Butler 1990: 6, italics in original)

Further, Butler, challenges feminist understandings of 'sex' as stable. Rather, 'sex', like gender, is discursively constructed. From a queer framework, transgender cultures bring to light the discord between 'sex' and 'gender'; signposting 'gender trouble.' For Butler, drag cultures, in particular, reveal the instability of the sex/gender binary:

> The performance of drag plays upon the distinction between the anatomy of the performer and the gender that is being performed. But we are actually in the presence of contingent dimensions of significant corporeality: anatomical sex, gender identity, and gender performance. If the anatomy of the former is already distinct from the gender of the performer, and both of those are distinct from the gender of the performance, then the performance suggests a dissonance not only between sex and performance, but sex and gender, and gender and performance.
>
> (Butler 1990: 137)

From a queer reading, then, certain transgender cultures rupture dominant ways of understanding gender more broadly. Trans writers such as Bornstein (1994) and Stone (1991) reflect a queer subjectivity in positioning themselves not as transsexuals, but as 'gender outlaws' (Bornstein 1994) who 'speak from outside the boundaries of gender, beyond the constructed oppositional nodes which have been predefined as the only positions from which discourse is possible.' (Stone 1991: 351) For other trans theorists though, queer perspectives are problematically partial; lacking the corporeal and material analysis to fully account for trans, and especially transsexual, emotion and experience (Felski 1996; Rubin 1996; Namaste 1996; MacDonald 1998; Prosser 1998, Hines 2007b). These debates indicate further how understandings of transgender within feminism, queer studies and transgender theory were deliberated during the 1990s and beyond, and, moreover, signal how these diverse theoretical fields—and related sites of political activism—spoke to each other.

Considerations of gender within feminism, queer theory and transgender theory were often epistemologically divergent. Strands of radical feminist hostility to transgender were based on the ontology of 'woman', which was tied to both biological 'sex' and to socialisation; transgender women lacked both the biological basis and the experience of 'womanhood.' Thus trans femininity was categorically false. Queer theory developed against a politics of identity; situating both gender and 'sex' as discursively constructed and inherently unstable. Transgender theory offered varied epistemological and political positions; while some trans theorists articulated a queer gender politics, which transgressed gender binaries and challenged notions of gendered entitlement, others spoke of the inherent sensibilities and corporealities of transsexualism (Prosser 1998). Common to these different schools of thought, though, were the challenges brought to medical discourse and practice. Whereas feminists such as Raymond (1980) and Jeffreys (1997) held the medical establishment responsible for generating stereotypical femininities in trans women, both queer theory and transgender theory challenged the medical pathologisation of transgender and the intrinsically related deviant positioning of trans people. Furthermore, throughout the 1990s, a number of transgender writers outside the academy articulated their personal gender trajectories, and, in turn, engaged with the theoretical debates of feminism and queer theory, again presenting an explicit critique of medical discourse. Significantly, such textual articulations were closely aligned with trans rights based politics.

UNRAVELLING 'SEX' AND 'GENDER': LEGAL CHALLENGES

Before the GRA (2004), Britain was one of four European countries that failed to legally recognise the acquired gender of transsexual people (Whittle 2000). Until 2004, then, the law saw gender as biologically fixed at birth. Practically this meant that while trans people modified their bodies and physical appearances, changed their names, and constructed new social identities, they were unable to change key legal documents. The impact of the rift between self identity and legal status was far-reaching and bled into all areas of life. This climate disabled legal rights in relation to work and welfare (for example, pensions and tax rights); those related to relationships and parenting (for example, next-of-kin status, marriage and partnership recognition and parental responsibility); and impacted upon the social and cultural fabric of everyday life (for example, trans people were required to use opposite-sex toilets and changing rooms, were treated in opposite sex hospital wards and were sent to opposite sex prisons). Moreover, legal non-recognition brought the psychological—and very tangible—effects of 'disclosure' (so that a trans person may be publicly outed if, for example, they were called by their original name in a public place, such as a GP surgery or benefit office).

These issues had long been at the forefront of rights-based trans politics. Within a UK context, such concerns were at the forefront of the campaigning agenda of political lobbying organisation 'Press for Change,' who, since the early 1990s, had petitioned the government for legal recognition and campaigned against the wide-ranging forms of discrimination faced by trans people. 'Press for Change' advised on a number of petitions to the European Court of Human Rights (ECHR) brought by trans people who argued that the law was discriminatory and in violation of their human rights. The issues of parenting recognition and the right to family life, privacy and freedom from discrimination were cited in three separate cases heard at the ECHR in 1997 (the case of X, Y and Z),[3] 1998 (the case of Sheffield & Horsham)[4] and 2002 (Goodwin & I v. United Kingdom Government).[5] Though petitions to the ECHR were unsuccessful in the first two cases, in respect of Goodwin & I v. United Kingdom Government, in 2002 the ECHR held that the UK government's failure to alter the birth certificates of transsexual people and to allow them to marry in their acquired gender was a breach of the European Convention on Human Rights. This proved to be a landmark case, which was instrumental to the development of the GRA. On the back of the ECHR's ruling, 'Press for Change' stepped up their campaign for legal recognition:

> [...] [t]here is good reason to think that English courts if asked to address any question of legal status recognition or marriage, will interpret English law to follow the ECHR's [European Court of Human Rights] decision. Consequently we are encouraging everyone to go ahead now, and take advantage of the wonderful ECHR court victory by claiming their rights. The government needs to change the law in order to clarify it.
>
> (Whittle 2002)

The conceptual significance of ECHR's ruling—and the subsequent legal significance of the GRA—lies in the challenges brought to a biological model of gender, which presumes a fixed relationship between 'sex' and gender identity. In this way, the ruling maps on to contemporary conceptualisations of gender within much social theory, as discussed above. Yet, as I move on to address, an understanding of gender as distinct from 'sex,' and as precariously experienced, continues to conflict with medical perspectives on transsexuality. As the chapter will later explore, these conceptual tensions play out within the GRA itself, and, in turn, generate uneven access to rights.

THE MEDICALISATION OF TRANSSEXUALITY

From the 1970s, the concept of 'gender dysphoria' became central to medical understandings of transsexualism. Locked into the notion of 'gender dysphoria' is the idea of the 'wrong body.' Transsexualism is read as a state of discord between 'sex' (the body) and gender identity (the mind). Reconstructive bodily surgery was seen as the route to gender harmony; enabling the 'true' self to emerge. The theoretical shifts that accompanied the increasing acceptance of reconstructive surgery thus effectively strengthened the role of the medical practitioner. Exemplifying this, psychologists Money and Green (1969) argued that medical opinion should dictate public policy and legislation on transsexualism. By the end of the 1970s surgical procedures had become the orthodox method of 'treatment' (Cromwell 1999) and 'gender dysphoria' a curable 'condition'. Significantly, notions of 'gender dysphoria' continue to inform medical understandings and practices.

The ways in which medical discourse on transsexualism structures trans identities, subjectivities and experiences has been subject to much critique (Stone 1991; Nataf 1996; Califia 1997; Halberstam 1998; Cromwell 1999, Monro 2005; Hines 2007b). Though later medical insights represent a more complex understanding of gender than were offered within founding medical perspectives, the problematic correlation of transsexuality and biological pathology remains; as illustrated by the 1996 report for the *Parliamentary Forum on Transsexualism*:

> weight of current scientific evidence suggests a biologically based, multifactoral aetiology for transsexualism. Most recently, for example, a study identified a region in the hypothalamus of the brain which is markedly smaller in women than in men. The brains of transsexual women examined in this study show a similar brain development to that of other women.
>
> (Press for Change 1996)

Significantly, the concept of 'gender dysphoria' remains a key classificatory term within medical discourse and practice, and, moreover, is seen as symptomatic of 'gender identity disorder', which is a listed category in the *Diagnostic and Statistical Manual of Mental Disorders* (DSM) (American Psychiatric Association 1968). The DSM—a handbook for mental health professionals on diagnosing mental illnesses—utilises the following criteria for diagnosis:

There must be evidence of a strong and persistent cross-gender identification, which is the desire to be, or the insistence that one is of
the other sex (Criteria A). This cross-gender identification must not
merely be a desire for any perceived cultural advantages of being the
other sex. There must also be evidence of persistent discomfort about
one's assigned sex or a sense of inappropriateness in the gender role of
that sex (Criteria B). The diagnosis is not made if the individual has
a concurrent physical intersex condition (e.g., androgen insensitivity
syndrome or congenital adrenal hyperplasia) (Criteria C). To make
the diagnosis, there must be evidence of clinically significant distress
or impairment in social, occupational, or other important areas of
functioning (Criteria D).

(Exhibit 2 Gender Identities Disorder Section in DSM IV TM: 576)

While gender identity may be read as distinct from sex as defined at birth
within current medical discourse and practice, then, this framework presents a confounded mix of biology and psychology, which variably positions
transsexualism as a congenital trait, a neuro-developmental condition, and
a consequence of dysfunctional socialisation. Aetiologies of transsexualism
thus continue to position practices of gender diversity as manifest of *atypical* 'sexed' biological or psychological development. A clear line is etched
between gender normativity—the 'right' body—and gender diversity—the
'wrong' body. Such understandings clearly do not inscribe either 'sex' or
'gender' as social formations. Yet, as the next section explores, medical discourse and practice has influenced, and, indeed, is written into the GRA,
thus sharply contrasting with elements of the GRA which articulate a social
model of gender diversity.

ODD COUPLINGS: SOCIAL AND MEDICAL
UNDERSTANDINGS OF GENDER IN THE GRA

To achieve legal gender recognition, an application is submitted to the 'Gender Recognition Panel,' which is made up of legal and medical members; the
latter including psychologists. Successful applicants are considered legally
in their 'acquired gender' and given a gender recognition certificate reflecting this. The term 'acquired gender' is used to refer to the gender in which
a person identifies and presents, as distinct from the gender that they were
registered and recognised as at birth. Such a distinction is considerable.
This reflects the separation of gender and biological 'sex' as articulated
by the stands of social and cultural theory discussed above, and the goals
of trans political organisations as previously examined. The granting of a
gender recognition certificate enables a new birth certificate and affords the
right to marry someone of the opposite gender or to form a civil partnership with someone of the same gender.

Further to untying gender from 'sex,' the Act is significant here in allowing for a more complex understanding of the relationship between 'sex,' gender and sexuality. Thus dominant configurations of a 'heterosexual matrix,' (Butler 1990), which assumes correlation between the male or female 'sexed' body, gender identity and sexual desire, are fractured somewhat in the recognition that these variables may be ambiguously experienced and diversely practiced. The legal standpoint on existing marriages, however, is less progressive. If a successful applicant for gender recognition is married, she/he receives an interim certificate, with the full certificate being granted when the marriage is annulled through the divorce courts. The applicant has six months in which to divorce. For married people, then, the legislation is problematic; bringing a stark choice between the recognition of gender and recognition of relationship (Hines 2007b, 2009; Sanger 2008).

The divorce criteria in the GRA was challenged by 'Press for Change,' however, it was argued by Ministers that the Civil Partnership Act (CPA 2004) enabled the 'continued right to family life,' (European Convention on Human Rights, Article 8) as married couples could register for a civil partnership following divorce. Thus the GRA and the CPA are co-positioned. Yet same-sex civil partnerships are unintelligible for people who wish to remain married to their long term partner (and often co-parent) and do not identify as lesbian or gay (Hines 2007a, 2009). What the GRA does not take account of here, are the multifarious intersections—and points of disconnection—between gender, sexuality and intimacy. Marriage may be significant for a range of reasons—symbolising intimate vows, emotional commitment, financial obligation, and parenting responsibilities—which are distinct from sexual identity. A civil partnership does not afford the same rights as marriage, nor does it necessarily reflect the reason why two people wish to have their relationship recognised. Moreover, linking the GRA and the CPA carries a set of assumptions about gender and sexuality, and intimate relationships, which are constructed through a hetero/homo binary; one can be heterosexual (marry) *or* homosexual (civilly partner). So while the GRA aims to protect the 'right to a family' (European Convention on Human Rights, Article 8), it reinforces inequality for those who are married or whose sexualities or intimate relationships transgress the homo/hetero binary (Hines 2007b, 2009; Sanger 2008). The problematics of binary understandings are also apparent in the Act's understandings of gender.

While the Act complements social constructionist concerns to free gender from biological understandings of 'sex,' a binary model of gender (male/female) is written into law. The Act demands that an applicant: 'has lived in the acquired gender throughout the period of two years ending with the date on which the application is made' and 'intends to continue to live in the acquired gender until death.' (Gender Recognition Act 2004). Those who do not firmly and permanently identify as male or as female—androgynous, intersex, bi-gendered, polygendered people, for example—remain 'unrecognised' in law. Thus, as I have previously argued (Hines 2007b, 2009), the GRA is unable to recognise the diversity of masculinities and femininities as they are variously experienced. Further problematics arise when the evidence required for successful applications is examined.

Although the GRA does not require surgical reconstruction, it does demand evidence that the applicant has lived in their acquired gender for two years prior to appplication—the 'real life test.' Moreover, the determination of applications is based on the Gender Recognition Panel being satisfied that the applicant: 'has or has had gender dysphoria,' (Gender Recognition Act 2004) evidence for which is based upon:

(a) a report made by a registered medical practitioner practising in the field of gender dysphoria and a report made by another registered medical practitioner (who may, but need not, practise in that field), or

(b) a report made by a chartered psychologist practising in that field and a report made by a registered medical practitioner (who may, but need not, practise in that field).

(Gender Recognition Act 2004).

In both instances, the continued influence of medical understandings and the persistent role of the medical practitioner are starkly evident. Thus the notion of 'gender dysphoria' still figures large and the medical practitioner maintains the role of expert. Accordingly, transsexuality remains pathologised. As the next section will address, the ramifications of binary understandings of gender and sexuality within the GRA, and the continued influence of a medical model of transsexuality within the legal process for gaining recognition, are sharply felt by those considering gender recognition.

TO SEEK OR NOT TO SEEK GENDER RECOGNITION? CASE STUDIES

The data on which this section draws has been collected by ESRC funded research, which seeks to explore the meanings and significance of the Gender Recognition Act for people who seek gender recognition and for those who choose not to, and to consider the impact of the GRA on individual and collective identity practices. The project employed a range of qualitative research methods, including textual/policy analysis, one-to-interviews, focus group interviews, and analysis of virtual material. The data that is drawn on here emerges from individual interviews in the form of four case studies. A 'case study' approach enables individual experience to be extrapolated to consider broader themes (McCall 2005; Valentine 2007; Taylor 2009). While the data in this chapter is based upon four cases that have been chosen for particular reflection, the analysis is based upon wider knowledge and narratives from the project as a whole.[6] The four case studies have been selected as they represent varied views about, and experiences of, the Gender Recognition Act as evident in the project more broadly.

Tasha is 42-years-old and lives in a city. She is white and British. Tasha works as a benefits rights adviser. She is in a relationship with a trans woman, although says she finds it difficult to define her sexuality. Tasha has applied to the Gender Recognition Panel and has been successful in gaining a gender recognition certificate. Amanda is 42-years-old and lives in a large city. She is white and British. Amanda works as an IT project manager. She is separated from her wife and has a young daughter. She describes her sexuality as 'straight with bi-tendencies.' Amanda wishes to register for a gender recognition certificate, but is restricted by the criteria for recognition. Heather is 30-years-old and lives in a large city. She is white and British. Heather is single and identifies as heterosexual. She has had two applications for gender recognition turned down, though has recently been granted a certificate. Christie is white and lives in a large city. She did not want to discuss her occupation, relationship status or sexuality. Christie chooses not to register for gender recognition.

Tasha locates her transition as beginning in 2002.[7] In 2004 she had gender reassignment surgery and in 2006 received her gender recognition certificate. Tasha describes the process of applying for gender recognition as being fairly straightforward; saying that it was: 'simple enough. As long as you had all the bumph, there was a lot of bumph. A lot of the bumph was easy enough to deal with.' (Tasha, Age 42). Tasha fulfilled the criteria for gender recognition and was able to provide the Gender Recognition Panel with the required evidence: she had been on an approved medical programme of gender transition[8] and had lived in her acquired gender role for the required time. Yet the ways in which Tasha discusses her gender identity are far from straightforward; as the following interview extract illustrates:

Interviewer: Could you tell me a little about your gender identity? How do you identify?

T: Depends on the mood. I don't like being classified. For the GRC I'm a lot happier being classified as female than I am being classified as male, but I certainly don't want to be classified as male, but I feel that I have some male characteristics, so in between that's where I see myself. But if someone can't get his head round that then I'm female.

(Tasha, age 42)

Far from articulating an inherent gender identity, which conflicts with her biological 'sex', Tasha discusses the variability of gender expression. Further, she rejects binary gender classification, instead presenting gender as a spectrum. While she suggests that she identifies more as female than male, she does not rule out elements of masculinity. As has been explored though, such complexities of gender identification and expression are unrecognised in the GRA. Thus she must 'choose' how she wants to be officially classified. Significantly, Tasha presents an account that separates her official classification from her other gendered 'moods'; demonstrating awareness of legal restraints.

In reflecting on the significance of the GRA—on why gender recognition mattered—Tasha focuses upon the practical benefits of state recognition:

> Some things do feel nice. The driving licence form; 'use this form to announce a change of address, name or sex'; great! I remember that because that pleased me. Yes, it lightens the load doesn't it? I think yes, it lightens the load. It is on the whole better that the State thinks of me as a female.
>
> (Tasha, age 42)

For Tasha, a gender recognition certificate makes life smother on a practical level. In using the phrase 'on the whole,' though, she offers a somewhat reluctant attitude to the significance of recognition. This is further apparent when she considers legal understandings of gender as an either/or (male/female) binary:

> Let's see; the state says I am a man—definite no-no. I don't like that at all. The state says I am a woman . . . I'm much keener on that but it's not perfect [. . .] What I would want is that the state admits that my retirement age is 65 whatever gender I am and that the state has no interest *at all* what sex I am.
>
> (Tasha, age 42)

Again, then, what matters to Tasha are the practical legal benefits afforded by the GRA. The importance of state recognition of gender is complexly related and Tasha is ambivalent, rather than affirmative, about the importance of legal recognition as female.

Amanda talks of rejecting male gender roles when she was six-years-old, though she positions her 'transition' as starting 14 months before her involvement in the research. Amanda is on a recognised 'gender transition programme' and is just over a year into her two year 'real life test'—living 'full time,' as the GRA demands, as a woman. Amanda wishes to register for a gender recognition certificate, however, she must wait until the period of two years is over. Yet while Amanda is 'proving' herself as a woman, she is unable to change her birth certificate and is denied the rights of privacy and state benefits afforded by gender recognition. Amanda has a three-year-old daughter with her ex-partner. Though separated, Amanda and her partner remain married. Amanda expresses disquiet that the law demands divorce before gender recognition is granted:

The fact that you're living with somebody and you've got to divorce them, you've got to go through all this kind of process that your marriage is being annulled [. . .] [t]he vows that I made in the church were very important to me you know. [. . .] I would imagine that would be very very hard for both people. And then you know, you can go through a civil partnership ceremony after it but for me personally there is a thing about being married as opposed to having a civil partnership. [. . .] And I would have to have a civil partnership because of my background. That would make me feel very second class in terms of that relationship.

(Amanda, age 42)

Amanda demonstrates the problematics of a legal co-positioning of the GRA and the CPA. For Amanda, the marriage vows taken in church carry greater weight than civil recognition. In instating civil partnerships as 'second class,' then, Amanda suggests that the Civil Partnership Act does not bring equivalent significance or equality of rights when compared to marriage. Such disparities are subject to critical debate within lesbian and gay political movements, particularly around the construction of a two-tier system of relationship recognition whereby heterosexual 'marriage' is privileged above lesbian and gay 'partnerships.'

Heather officially transitioned in 2000. She unsuccessfully applied for a gender recognition certificate in 2006 and again in 2007. Heather refused to disclose personal and medical information as required by the Gender Recognition Panel, and became involved in a legal dispute with the Panel that lasted for two and a half years. Following her legal challenge, her third application was successful in 2008. Central to the GRA is the 'respect of privacy.' As explored previously, privacy was a central campaigning issue for trans rights organisations, who spoke out about the impact forced disclosure of gender status and history had on the lives of trans people. On applying for a gender recognition certificate, however, Heather objected to the amount of personal and medical information she was required to disclose to the Gender Recognition Panel:

I felt that the Gender Recognition Act was asking for a level of personal disclosure that was a breach of your medical confidentiality; in terms of the medical evidence that they were requiring. And I took umbrage at that really on a couple of different levels; firstly the personal level; being a patient I thought it was the level of medical confidentiality that they were asking—because these are highly personal issues, you know, when you go into a counselling session with a gender therapist and you're talking about things to do with your family life, your love life, your sex life, how you felt as a child [. . .] And I thought, "no," that's just wrong, that's inherently wrong. And I thought I'm not willing to do that. It all kind of swung on their interpretation of one line in the

Gender Recognition Act which says that an applicant must provide details of the diagnosis of gender dysphoria. [...] And that's very intrusive. And that was a step I wasn't willing to take really.

(Heather, age 39)

In particular, Heather objected to the Panel's demand to read her case history. She argued that such a requirement was in breach of her respect to privacy and contradicted her human rights:

You're having to swap one universally accepted human right, to gain another set. Your right to medical confidentiality is protected in European Law, yet we're being asked to swap that right for the right to marry and, you know, pension rights and whatever else that comes along with the Gender Recognition Certificate. But I don't think that we should be put in the position where we have to swap one set of human rights in order to gain another [...] You know actually in the past two years I've had to make more self-disclosures in terms of the GR act than I have in my entire transition.

(Heather, age 39)

Like Tasha, Heather's desire to gain gender recognition was led by the practical benefits the certificate brings. Significantly, for both these participants, gender recognition was not linked to self- affirmation. In this way, Heather said:

In terms of gender identity I don't think it has any effect because you don't need a bit of paper to tell you who you are [...] I've always been quite secure in who I am and you know, where I'm going in life.

(Heather, age 39)

These narratives indicate the nuances of gendered and intimate lives. Challenges are brought to the GRA's reinforcement of a binary gender model and to the role of the medical expert. Further, Tasha, Amanda and Heather make apparent the inequalities around marriage, offering strong points of critique concerning the extent to which the GRA affords citizenship rights for trans people. Each of these participants, however, recognises that the GRA affords benefits that they were previously denied, and each, however, cautiously, wish to access these rights. For other people though, the binary gender framework is incomprehensible and explicitly rejected.

Christie's gender definition is 'non-gendered' and Christie uses the title 'Pr', an abbreviation of 'Person.' Christie's rejection of a gender binary means that Christie is denied the rights afforded by the GRA. Initially, Christie welcomed the GRA: 'I had hoped this might prove to be the first stage towards improving the lives of all transpeople.' As the Act proceeded through Parliament, however, Christie became aware that the rights afforded by the GRA did not extend to non-gendered people:

> I was not encouraged by the fact the proposed legislation appeared to exclude so many people, including me. [...] There did not appear to be any follow-up plan or intention insofar as I could see to help those groups who would receive no benefit from the GRA. Once the GRA became law, these fears were truly confirmed and it was as though the shutters had come down. I felt there was no further interest on the part of those who had fought to get the GRA on the statute book in securing same legal rights for others within the 'transgendered' umbrella. Transpeople who were let down by GRA already suffered a much greater level of social marginalisation when compared with those who benefited.
>
> (Christie)

Christie's argument here is imperative in addressing how a binary gender model excludes those who cannot, or will not, identify as male or as female. As Christie further explains:

> I could only successfully apply for gender recognition if I were to identify within the gendered societal construct and also having been through the relevant statutory procedures and met the criteria as stated within the GRA. The GRA has made no positive impact on my life and I have felt until fairly recently that I was in a worse position than before, as the GRA at least appeared to offer some hope of a better future for everybody but this was clearly never the intention.
>
> (Christie)

Here Christie suggests that the new framework of citizenship, as enacted by the GRA, may actually disable access to rights for some trans people. In the following quotation, Christie discusses how the GRA explicitly reproduces a gender binary, which discriminates against people whose gender presentation and identity falls outside the dualities of male/female:

> The law does not recognise human existence outside the gendered societal structure [...] Many transpeople, including some transsexuals, do not meet the criteria to have their birth certificate amended under the statutory terms of the GRA. For a successful application, the applicant should have undergone, or partly undergone, gender reassignment through a recognised gender clinic with the intention of living full time within their chosen gendered role. The GRA opens up citizenship rights for transsexuals who can tick all the right boxes [...] preferably heterosexual within their chosen gendered role and able to blend into gendered society without much risk of being 'read'. The GRA does not

benefit any 'transgendered' individual who does not identify as either 100 per cent male or 100 per cent female. The Act does not benefit anyone who is transsexual but, for whatever reason, does not live full time within their chosen gendered role. The GRA does not benefit transsexuals who, for whatever reason, choose not to interact with the gender clinics. The Act does not benefit anyone whose case is not accepted by the medical profession as having fulfilled the criteria to undergo reassignment treatment.

(Christie)

As Christie details, the evidence required by the gender recognition panel means that the law affords rights to a specific trans population—people who are under the care of a gender identity clinic, who conform to normative gendered appearance, and who permanently identify as male or female. Conversely, those trans people whose gender identities and presentations are less straightforward, and those who are not part of a medical system of care, fall outside the law. Thus, while the GRA opens up access to citizenship for some trans people, many others fall outside of the evidence-based system of rights. As I move on to explore, such issues are central to theoretical debates around sexual citizenship, and to politics of recognition and difference.

GENDER RECOGNITION AND GENDER DIVERSITY: IMPLICATIONS FOR (TRANS) GENDERED CITIZENSHIP

The narratives considered here bring to light the ways in which the law not only reflects a gender binary, but reproduces it anew. To gain access to rights, trans people must firmly situate their identities within a binary framework of male/female. Yet, as the narratives of research participants indicate, gendered subjectivities are rarely this clear-cut. Moreover, trans people must redefine their relationships through a hetero/homo binary. As has been explored, this stifles the nuances of intimate practices. Regulatory frameworks thus fashion practices of self-regulation, which, in the case of the GRA, constrains gender and intimate diversity. While some people are able to benefit from this new system of rights, others, who, through factors of structure (not meeting the evidence based criteria for recognition), or agency (refusing to accept a medical diagnosis, refusing to divorce, refusing to fit into a gender binary), are further marginalised. As Christie suggested, the effects of this may fragment a minority community, working to construct 'deserving' and 'undeserving' citizens.

Such issues are also pertinent to recent UK legislative moves to grant rights to lesbians and gay men. Critical readings of rights discourse show how understandings and practices of sexuality are constructed. In considering sexual citizenship, scholars such as Stychin (1998), Richardson (1998, 2000), Bell and Binnie (2000) and Phelan (2001) argue that discourses of citizenship are constructed along a heterosexual model—so that the notion of citizenship itself is heterosexualised. Richardson argues that the granting of lesbian and gay rights leads to the privatisation and circumscription of these sexual identities: 'Lesbians and gay men are granted the right to be tolerated as long as they stay within the boundaries of that tolerance [. . .].' (1998: 90) Since notions of citizenship are heterosexualised, such boundaries of tolerance depend upon rights based claims (such as the right to marry), which fit with a heterosexual model of the 'good citizen.' Thus Stychin points to the problematics of a politics of recognition: '[. . .] lesbians and gays seeking rights may embrace an ideal of "respectability," a construction that then perpetuates a division between 'good gays' and (disreputable) "bad queers."' (1998: 200). It is the latter who are excluded from notions of citizenship (Hines 2007b; Taylor 2009). Problematics of claiming sexual citizenship map on to the paradoxes of claiming gender recognition. While the GRA developed to broaden the rights of citizenship for trans people, the influence of medical discourse and practice, and binary conceptualisations of gender and sexuality, effect a division between the trans citizen who is able and/or willing to fulfil the requirements of law, and the trans person who is unable or unwilling to meet the demands of recognition.

CONCLUSION

I began this chapter by contextualising the GRA in relation to shifting understandings of gender within the fields of feminism, queer theory and transgender theory; exploring in particular the challenges brought by each of these disciplinary areas to medical understandings of transsexuality. I linked these theoretical moves to the goals of trans activism, and discussed the legal challenges brought by trans political movements, which preceded—and led to—the formation of the GRA in 2004. I argued that the GRA represented a significant legal moment in which gender and 'sex' were decoupled. Yet, as I moved on to explore, the influence of medical discourse and practice, particularly in relation to the evidence based criteria for gender recognition, enacts an inconsistent framework of rights.

Later sections of the chapter explored these tensions at an experiential level through the use of four research case studies. These case studies and the research findings more broadly, signpost diverse experiences of seeking gender recognition and offer varied understandings of the significance of the GRA. I suggested that while citizenship claims of some trans people are now being met, other trans people are constructed outside of law. As I discussed, such issues map on to the concerns of critical sexual citizenship scholarship, which highlights the political and personal compromises inherent in rights based claims. Binary understandings of gender and sexuality within the GRA, and the continued influence of a medical model of transsexuality within the legal process for gaining recognition, thus enact divisions between those who are able to access the new framework of rights—namely trans people on a recognised medical programme of gender transition who are single or willing to divorce—and those who remain situated outside of law; thus residing as non-citizens. As Stychin (2004) has argued, the law may act as a disciplining force; working against 'difference' to normalise and civilise. In this way, trans people may find themselves fitting into gendered categories that are (still) not their own.

Yet, as the case studies considered here indicate, trans people are actively engaging with legal processes of gender recognition; speaking out against the annulment of existing marriages; challenging requirements of medical evidence, and enacting claims based on the rights of 'difference.' Though acts of resistance are apparent in each of the four cases studies considered in this chapter, Christie offers an explicit politics of resistance in campaigning for an extension of the rights afforded by the GRA to all trans people. Christie states:

> What I am advocating is provision within gendered society for people who do not identify as male or female. I would propose that the privileged gendered majority and its legislators considered the fact that gender is a societal construct and that there should be more radical thinking towards an alternative to a gendered societal structure that denies the existence of, and socially excludes, individuals whose core identity is neither male nor female.
>
> (Christie)

Christie's argument here does not represent an academic call for a gender*less* society. Rather, more strategically, Christie argues for a system that recognises that not all citizens are able to, or wish to, define as male or female. From this position, the GRA may be viewed positively as a stepping-stone to a future legislative framework that protects the rights of all gender diverse people. Yet, as Christie's demand that gender be recognised as a social construction infers, such a move depends upon uncoupling law and medical discourse and practice; the latter which, as I have argued through this chapter, continues to pathologise practices of gender. From this juncture, *all* gendered identities and expressions could, in law at least, be deemed equal.

NOTES

1. 'Trans' is an abbreviation of 'transgender,' which is used to include a diversity of diverse gender identifications, including, but not restricted to, transsexual, transvestite, intersex, gender queer, female and male drag, cross-dressing and some butch/femme practices
2. The project is entitled 'Gender Diversity, Recognition and Citizenship.' ESRC funding began in May 2008 and is on-going until 2010. I would like to thank and acknowledge the ESRC for providing the funding for this research. I am

hugely grateful to the people who participated in the research. I would like to acknowledge the important contribution of Zowie Davy who worked as Research Assistant on the project and who carried out the interviews. Thanks Zowie for bringing so much to the project—and for good times shared along the way. Thanks also to Yvette Taylor who offered feedback on an early version of this chapter.

3. In the case of X, Y and Z, in 1997, a transgendered man (X) took his case to European Court of Human Rights to be recognised as the father of the child (Z) of his female partner (Y), who had conceived through donor insemination.

4. In this case, two trans women argued that inability to change their birth certificates violated Article 8 (right to respect for private and family life) of the European Convention on Human Rights and Article 12 (right to marry and to found a family).

5. Christine Goodwin argued as above.

6. Twenty five one-to-one interviews have been completed with a diversity of trans people across the UK. While the sampling strategy was not designed to be representative of a whole population, variables of gender, class, age, sexuality, relationship and parenting status were build into the sampling strategy to encourage diversity. The sampling strategy included people who had successfully registered for a gender recognition certificate, those who planned to register, and those who did not seek recognition. The interviews took place over a six month period between 2008–2009.

7. Here 'transition' is used to represent acceptance on a medical programme of gender transition.

8. Under such a programme the 'patient' is placed under the care of a gender 'specialist'—usually a psychologist specialising in 'gender identity disorders'—who monitor their 'real life test'; assessing progress for two years.

REFERENCES

American Psychiatric Association (1968) *DSM-II: Diagnostic and Statistical Manual of Mental Disorders* (2nd ed.), Washington, DC: American Psychiatric Association.

Bell, D. and Binnie, J. (2000) *The Sexual Citizen: Queer Politics and Beyond*, Cambridge: Polity Press.

Bornstein, K. (1994) *Gender Outlaw: on Men, Women and the Rest of Us*, New York: Routledge.

Butler, J. (1990) *Gender Trouble: Feminism and the Subversion of Identity*, New York and London: Routledge.

Califia, P. (1997) *Sex Changes: The Politics of Transgenderism*, San Francisco: Cleis Press.

Cromwell, J. (1999) *Transmen and FTMs: Identities, Bodies, Genders and Sexualities*, Champaign: University of Illinois Press.

Felski, R. (1996) 'Fin de siecle, fin de sexe: transsexuality, postmodernism and the death of history', *New Literary History*, 27(2): 137–153.

Gender Identities Disorder Section in DSM IV TM: 576. http://72.3.233.244/images/asset_upload_file155_30369.pdf (accessed 11 Feburary 2008).

Gender Recognition Act (2004). http://www.opsi.gov.uk/acts/acts2004/ukpga_20040007_en_1 (accessed 11 February 2008).

Halberstam, J. (1998) *Female Masculinity*, Durhan, NC: Duke University Press.

Hines, S. (2007a) '(Trans)forming gender: social change and transgender citizenship', *Sociological Research Online*, 12(1). http://www.socresonline.org.uk/12/1/hines.html (accessed 26 May 2009).

———. (2007b) *TransForming Gender: Transgender Practices of Identity and Intimacy*, Bristol: Policy Press.

———. (2009) 'A pathway to diversity? Human rights, citizenship and politics of transgender', *Contemporary Politics* 15(1): 87–102.

Hird, M. J. (2002) 'For a sociology of transsexualism', *Sociology*, 36(3): 557–595.

MacDonald, E. (1998) 'Critical identities: rethinking feminism through transgender politics', *Atlantis*, 23(1): 3–12.

McCall, L. (2005) 'The complexity of intersectionality', *Signs*, 30(3): 1771–800.

Money, J. and Green, R. (eds) (1969) *Transsexualism and Sex-Reassignment*, Baltimore: The Johns Hopkins University Press.

Monro, S. (2005) *Gender Politics: Citizenship, Activism and Sexual Diversity*, London: Pluto Press.

Namaste, V. K. (1996) 'The politics of inside/out: queer theory, poststructuralism, and a sociological approach to sexuality', in S. Seidman (ed.) *Queer Theory/ Sociology*, Malden, MA and Oxford: Blackwell.

Nataf, Z. (1996) *Lesbians Talk Transgender*, London: Scarlett Press.

Phelan, S. (2001) *Sexual Strangers: Gays, Lesbians and Dilemmas of Citizenship*, Philadelphia: Temple University Press.

Press for Change (1996) 'Transsexualism: the current medical viewpoint'. www. pfc.org.uk (accessed 12 December 2008).

Prosser, J. (1998) *Second Skins: The Body Narratives of Transsexuality*, New York: Columbia University Press.

Raymond, J. (1980) *The Transsexual Empire*, London: The Women's Press.

Rubin, H. (1996) 'Do you believe in gender?' *Sojourner: The Women's Forum*, 21(6): 7–12.

Richardson, D. (1998) 'Sexuality and citizenship', *Sociology*, 32(1): 83–100.

———. (2000) 'Constructing sexual citizenship: theorizing sexual rights', *Critical Social Policy*, 20(1): 105–135.

Sanger, T. (2008) 'Transpeople's intimate partnerships and the limits of identity politics', in Z. Davy, J. Downes, L. Eckert, N. Gerodetti, D. Llinares and A. C. Santos (eds) *Bound and Unbound: Interdisciplinary Approaches to Genders and Sexualities*, Cambridge: Cambridge Scholars Publishing.

Stone, S. (1991) 'The *Empire* Strikes Back: A Posttranssexual Manifesto', in J. Epstein and K. Straub (eds) *Body Guards: The Cultural Politics of Sexual Ambiguity*, New York and London: Routledge.

Stryker, S. and Whittle, S. (2006) *The Transgender Studies Reader*, New York and Abingdon: Routledge.

Stychin, C. (1998) *A Nation By Rights: National Cultures, Sexual Identity Politics and the Discourse of Rights*, Philadelphia: Temple University Press.

Stychin, C. (2004) 'Same-sex sexualities and the globalisation of human rights discourse', *McGill Law Journal*, 49: 953–968.

Taylor, Y. (2009) 'Complexities and complications: intersections of class and sexuality', *Lesbian Studies*, 13(2): 189–203.

Valentine, G. (2007) 'Theorizing and researching intersectionality: a challenge for feminist geography', *The Professional Geographer*, 59(1): 10–21.

Whittle, S. (2000) 'Legal limbo' *Law.co.uk: In Practice/ Human Rights*. http:// uk.law.com/cgi-bin/gx.cgi/AppLogic+FTContentServer?pagename=FutureTe nse/Apps/Xcelerate/Render&c=lc_article&cid=ZZZKBB5KL8C (accessed 10 March 2008).

———. (2002) 'Goodwin & I v. United Kingdom government: what does it mean? Analysis of the implications of the ECtHR judgments in the cases of Goodwin v. UK and I v UK', *Press for Change*. http://www.pfc.org.uk/node/352 (accessed 10 March 2008).

5 Transsexual Agents
Negotiating Authenticity and Embodiment within the UK's Medicolegal System

Zowie Davy

INTRODUCTION

In this chapter, I look at the complex encounters transpeople have with onto-logical claims made by experts within medical and legal institutions, and how transpeople dynamically shape their negotiations with them. I will be using the term 'medicolegal' following Butler (1993) to conceptualise the relationship between medical and legal regulatory norms, which function to constitute 'authentic' transmen and 'authentic' transwomen in society. Trans-people often foster relationships with medicine in order to negotiate aesthetic interventions through technology, and/or to receive legal recognition in their acquired gender. During these relational negotiations, both transpeople and medicolegal representatives construct, deconstruct and reconstruct vari-ous narratives of (trans) authenticity, deserving of medical interventions and legal recognition. Sociological theorisations about these relationships, such as those from radical feminist perspectives, which are antagonistic to socio-legal recognition of transpeople (Millot 1990; Jeffreys 2005, 2008), often call into question the 'authenticity' of transpeople's experiences without questioning their own 'authentic' experiences. This questioning becomes a self-confirming logic based on moralising dichotomies that foreclose who, and how, (trans) men and women should be i.e. 'good (real) wo/men'/'bad (trans)wo/men'; 'natural wo/men'/'constructed (trans)wo/men,'; having 'authentic agency' (wo/men who exercise the same choices as radical feminists)/being 'dupes' ((trans) wo/men who make (pseudo) choices directed by patriarchal forces). These dichotomies simplify what we (could) know about transsexual negotiations surrounding embodiment. Furthermore, as Rita Felski warns us:

> [t]here is something troubling, both ethically and politically, about a view that would deny *any* genuine insight or agency to those with whom one disagrees.
>
> (Felski 2006: 274, emphasis added)

In my research, nine participants had various body modification technolo-gies as National Health Service (NHS) patients. Gregory who could not have any surgeries was prescribed hormones on the NHS, and two other transmen had decided not to receive body modification procedures at the time of their interviews. Ten private patients had all undergone various body modifications. Addressing participants' narratives phenomenologically—that is a study of experiences, actions and practices and their meanings (Heinamaa 1997)—this chapter explores how participants understand and negotiate their 'authentic' subject positions when seeking body modification and legal recognition. The first aim of this chapter is to refrain from falling into the trap of reducing authenticity to essentialism, which rests on a biological notion of a core 'sex' being the natural basis for 'gender.' Secondly, I do not want to reduce 'authenticity' to poststructuralist understandings of gender identity formation, in which subjects are often seen as passive and culturally determined by coercive forces, which constitute their mental and behavioural characteristics. I argue that we should regard transsexual subjectivities as intentionally 'situational' (Rubin 2003) and understand the agentic negotiations that are intrinsic to trans subjectivity, to get at a deeper understanding of how the medicolegal fields are negotiated in the UK.

In providing a complex assortment of transsexual narratives as situational, I aim to incorporate transsexuals' subjectivities into an agentic framework. The narratives of participants show how their desire for body modification and legal recognition needs to be negotiated through medical discourses, and requires working 'with' doctors and psychiatrists when approaching the services in relation to bodily modification and legal recognition that constitute them. Transsexuals acknowledge that the medicolegal discourses that are interpreted by the doctors and psychiatrists require perceptive manipulation. Thus, transsexuals' own discourses have both agentic and subjugating elements to them, which the participants utilise and/or rework at a discursive level as well as a phenomenological level.

GENDER RECOGNITION THROUGH THE MEDICAL GAZE(S)

Diagnosis of Gender Dysphoria by medical authorities is required not only to actualise body modification required by a transperson, but also to actualise legal recognition of their acquired gender. The processes of referrals to Gender Clinics began through participants presenting their narratives to their General Practitioner (GP), a psychiatrist or a counsellor. In my research, a GP was usually the first port of call for those experiencing 'gender issues' and participants were often confronted with problems of ignorance in these meetings, resonating with the findings of Hines (2007a). In relation to clinical care for transpeople, Hines (2007a) argues that education for doctors is paramount in order to provide better care. Some GPs had very little experience with trans issues and some had none at all. Nonetheless, participants attempted to pre-empt or surpass the lack of knowledge

GPs had surrounding 'gender identity disorders' and sought medical knowledge themselves. For example, Daniel suggested,

> if you are a T person, she [psychiatrist] tells you to get these books published in the States by Dr. Sheila Kirk. They are very good books about testosterone and oestrogen for transpeople and they tell you far more than you would ever find out from the doctors I have come across here [. . .] That helped me a lot and it all came from me, it didn't come from medical professionals because they didn't really know.
>
> (Daniel, transman)

Rather than being straightforwardly inflexible gatekeepers to transsex treatments, Daniel and Gregory's experiences reflect GPs' lack of training and authoritative knowledge around 'gender issues.'

According to most of the participants, both the GPs and psychiatrists at the Gender Identity Clinic (GIC) need to cooperate in the treatment of transsexuality. The cooperation will enable a smoother transition to the primary trans-sexing stage of hormone therapy, and the Real Life Experience (RLE)[1] and eventual legal recognition if so sought. The lack of integrated services from the GIC and GP resulted in inconsistent support that transpeople believed was necessary for their care needs according to this research. Participants suggested that it was sometimes the GPs that were at fault and sometimes the fault was with psychiatrists at the GICs. GPs often did not know about the 'Standards of Care' for transsexuals (HBIGDA 2001), modified five times since the original version 1 in 1979 to standardise professional key principles and treatments in the area of transgender and transsexualism.[2] There was very little correspondence about treatment protocol between the clinics and the GPs, if any at all. In a few cases, GPs did not recognise transsexualism as an authentic condition. This was illustrated by the GPs' reluctance to treat their patients, for example, Raymond said:

> I had a doctor who struck me off because he couldn't treat something like me because he was a good Catholic.
>
> (Raymond, transman)

In Raymond's narrative, the GP's religious convictions seemed to outweigh professional codes and medical diagnoses, such as the DSM (American Psychiatric Association 1994) classification of Gender Identity Disorder. The refusal of treatment also suggests that this GP did not accept the psychiatric diagnosis as an authentic medical condition, but rather conceptualised it as 'sinful' because of his faith.

Many of the participants who related negative experiences of GPs suggested that they were not taken seriously and their requests for treatment were seen as absurd. Regular visits to their GP, or different GPs, were required either to demonstrate their determination to transition or to find a sympathetic GP who would prescribe hormones and provide regular health checks. For example, Courtenay suggested that at first she was put off talking about how she was feeling about her 'gender issues,' because of not knowing the GP well enough and not knowing his professional position on transsexualism. She said:

> Why I had not gone earlier was because this new doctor didn't really know me, I hadn't seen him more than two or three times. I think he did say to me, "how has this come out of the blue," and I said, "I don't think it has come out of the blue" and had to explain this. I kind of left it a while after that.
>
> (Courtenay, transwoman)

Following this encounter with her GP, Courtenay consulted an experienced and well-known psychiatrist in the field of transsexualism who subsequently diagnosed her with GID. However, Courtenay continued to have problems with her GP. She stated:

> I went to my GP and he [my psychiatrist] had given me a letter. So I gave him [GP] the letter and I said "would you prescribe hormones for me" and he said to me "well how would your relatives feel if you drop down dead" and this sort of thing and I said "well I would hope that they would be upset" and then he basically said "no." I thought he would be nice about saying no but he was adamant about it. I think he thought I was mad taking this health risk which he felt I did not need to take.
>
> (Courtenay, transwoman)

Courtenay needed to respond strategically in a way that reduced the chances of her being denied hormone therapy. For Courtenay, the hypothetical question from her GP was unrelated to her diagnosis and contradicted what the gender identity specialist had written in the letter. No matter what Courtenay had said at this meeting, she would have been denied hormone treatment. There was no correct response that Courtenay could have offered, which suggests that her GP, like Raymond's, was not influenced by the experts' diagnosis or convinced of the authenticity of GID. Furthermore, the question both undermined Courtenay's phenomenological experiences and the psychiatrist's diagnosis, thus rendering them inauthentic.

Courtenay subsequently approached a different GP in the same medical practice, where she was approved for prescription hormones. Here we witness different approaches from GPs arising from their perceptual differences of GID and the hormone therapy required for transition. These procedural differences, far from being grounded in medical diagnosis, may be subject to non-medical influences such as religious beliefs. Each GP asserted their beliefs in relation to the patient presenting to them; however, the second GP accepted GID as authentic and treatable, unlike the first.

Other GPs did, however, accommodate the GICs guidelines and patients concerns, both during the referral process and the administering of hormones and, this led to a smoother transition and RLE for transpeople. For example, Anna-Marie said:

> I had no problem whatsoever with any of the staff, they were all very helpful and never gave me a cause for concern. We always hear so much about the badness of NHS staff and how someone was unjustly treated; you never hear anything about the successes, perhaps because it is not news if everything is going well. The problem with only the bad news making it to press is that it perpetuates a negative stereotype.
>
> (Anna-Marie, transwoman)

Anna-Marie's account was very positive. Similarly, another participant Samantha was pleased with her GP's understanding of her and, in both instances, this led to a situation of mutual respect. It is possible that Samantha (33-years-old) and Anna-Marie (25-years-old) were treated better than others because of their age and ability to 'pass' successfully as attractive women, allowing them recognition as authentic candidates for body modification technology and legal recognition. During the interview, both Anna-Marie and Samantha inferred that their gender presentation influenced the psychiatrists' view of them and their suitability for clinical intervention. Kessler and McKenna (1978) suggested that clinicians' diagnostic process was not based, so much, within science, but was a highly subjective endeavour, which may depend on the aesthetic presentation of transpeople. They stated that one clinician:

> said that he was more convinced of the femaleness of a male to female transsexual if she was particularly beautiful and was capable of evoking in him those feelings that beautiful women generally do.
>
> (Kessler and McKenna 1978: 118)

Factors of age and beauty then, influence the diagnostic process, and create a tiered system, in which transpeople who manage to appropriate the necessary aesthetic and presentational markers of gender marks their authenticity.

AUTHENTICITY AND AUTHENTICATION

Recognition in order to trans-sex both physically and legally requires authentication by a qualified psychiatrist, usually from a gender identity clinic. The participants spoke about this authentication process in different ways: Anna-Marie believed that her psychiatrist asked her clandestine questions in relation to her childhood experiences to see her reactions and to search out the truth about her transsexuality. She said:

> I believe all they are looking for is someone who is balanced in what they are doing, what risks are involved and what is ahead of them. To know that along with knowing what role you will play in life afterwards. If you go in with the notion of changing sex for pleasure, let's say, or sexual gratification, they will be able to tell that immediately.
>
> (Anna-Marie, transwoman)

More important for Anna-Marie was the clinician's expertise in differentiating sexually motivated sex changing from the 'balanced' type who understands the situation they are getting themselves into and who are 'dedicated' to the social role that they will perform once they have transitioned. Anna-Marie's authentication is provided by the psychiatrist on the basis that she would be successful through her RLE and show her commitment to live in an authentic 'woman's' role.

Anna-Marie sees the questions that the psychiatrist asked her as establishing authentic markers between transsexualism and other diagnoses of 'gender deviancy,' such as autogynephilia (Blanchard 1991) or transvestism. Anna-Marie suggests that a 'true transsexual' woman's authenticity is established by moving away from the idea that she wants sex change for 'sexual gratification' and closer to the idea that it is because of her wanting to *express* her gender identity.

A few participants suggested that the authentication process 'was just a matter of course' and that they were not concerned about telling the psychiatrist about specificities of their histories. The strategy, of these participants, for getting through the RLE and number of appointments needed to secure the 'diagnosis' and subsequent surgery, if this was sought, was guided by 'rehearsed narratives' (Chawla and Krauss 1994; Hines 2007). Thus, these patients offered stereotypical answers to questions that the psychiatrist asked.

Amongst the younger participants in this group, clinical authentication is seen as manipulable, but only to a certain extent. Oscar, a transman, suggests that his bodily requirements and queer political leanings, which opened up questions about the relationship between normative bodies and transgender and the notion that gender identity is fixed, led him to consider how his narrative could be tailored to NHS medical definitions, while retaining a certain amount of agency over his transition. Oscar at the time of the interview wanted to take hormones to become aesthetically less female or 'more physically trans.' He believed, however, that telling the clinician this would hinder, if not stop, his process of transitioning. Later in Oscar's interview he clarified why he wanted to initially look 'trans,' as opposed to masculine. It was because he was concerned about the effect transitioning would have on his relationship with his parents. Oscar suggested that he needed to transition slowly in order for his parents to get used to the physical changes.

> I do not want to take hormones in order to pass as male yet [. . .], but want the hormones to be more physically trans and less female. The struggle I am having with this is that I am aware of the affects that the hormones are going to have on other people.
>
> (Oscar, transman)

Benjamin however, understood that he must not disclose some of his feminine traits to the psychiatrist because he was concerned that it would be in breach of the clinical model's definition of what a 'true transsexual' (Benjamin 1966) is. He suggested:

> All men have a feminine side, but I did not dare show that to the psychiatrist.
>
> (Benjamin, transman)

Benjamin and Oscar's concerns centre the clinical model's construction of hegemonic masculinities (Connell 1995). For instance, Benjamin and Oscar believed that they needed to be careful not to disclose any form of femininity because they understood the psychiatrist had the power to halt the process of transition, despite them believing femininity was a part of their authentic self. Benjamin's concerns stemmed from being read as inauthentic by the psychiatrist and Oscar's came from fear of being drawn into a medical discourse that did not suit his plans.

Authenticity, then, is a precarious concept. Brian initially transitioned from male-to-female and had had sex reassignment surgery (SRS) in 2000. Brian had been living as Alison for a number of years, but during the times I interviewed Brian, he transitioned from appearing feminine to more masculine. Brian does not identify as male or female now and prefers to see hirself[3] as Cross-Gendered or Bi-Gendered. This case is similar to St. Jacques' (2007) 'Post-Transsexual' position, where the 'second' transition does not necessarily mean a reversion to an 'original' sex, but, as in Brian's case, it is a transition to an identity outside the medicolegal framework. Brian was authenticated as female by the first psychiatrist and unauthenticated as female by the second. While there was no pressure from the psychiatrist 'to go for reverse surgery,' Brian believed that the psychiatrist thought the only option was to have surgery that would try to rebuild a penis and allow him to live back 'fully' as male. This suggests that the psychiatrist assumed that the initial diagnosis was a mistake and that if Brian was not a transsexual woman then 'he' must have been a man all along. The 'mistake' was understood within a binary system of gender, as opposed to Brian's own identification of 'bi-gendered.' Brian did not believe the initial diagnosis to be a mistake and referred to hir situation as primarily a choice that became untenable whilst living as Alison.

The final set of authentication narratives, by some of the private patients, referred to the psychiatrist as simply rubber stamping their own decision to become transsexual, and providing the letter to authorise and enable technological and legal transition. Jess' narrative illustrated this:

> I phoned [the psychiatrist] to make an appointment and I have nothing but respect for [him] we had a long discussion and he said that I am 'definitely Gender Dysphoric,' which I knew, but it was nice for someone else to tell me that. He said as to whether you are a transsexual person or not it is up to you, you are going to have to work that out, it is your decision.
>
> (Jess, transwoman)

MONEY, TREATMENT AND AGENCY

In this research there was also a strong financial factor determining the kind of treatment some transsexual patients received. Quality of treatment in many cases was dependent upon whether the participant was a private or NHS patient. In most private practice cases, both the younger and older participants claimed they were lucky not to have to go through the process as a NHS patient. Patients who could afford to have private care found the process allowed them a certain amount of agency in relation to their treatment schedule, which was very important to them. For Penny, agency was being able to plan the transition in relation to her work commitments.

> I appreciated being allowed to go at my own pace and being given hormones diagnostically at the first visit. I did ask at that time if I could begin with hormone patches, rather than tablets, bearing in mind my age, forty-eight at that point. Given that it took a year and a half before I was able to change documents because of work and begin the RLT.[4]
>
> (Penny, transwoman)

For Jess, who transitioned in 2000, agency was about gaining respect from medical professionals. She stated:

> The positives were that they all respected my position and intelligence. Nobody treated me like a fool or as incompetent to understand the issues and consequences of transition and surgery. As a private patient, I was able [. . .] to set my own timescale and support team. [. . .] The biggest negative of course was the cost. Because I had no confidence in the NHS treatment of transsexual people at that time, I

believe it has since improved. And because the NHS was never going to fund what I considered necessary to a successful gender transition and for an acceptable post transition quality of life, I paid over £60,000 in transition and surgery costs. It was worth it but I do resent that after years of paying higher-rate tax and NI contributions [...] I could not get the treatment I felt I needed funded, at least in part by the NHS.

(Jess, transwoman)

Jess sees respect for her intelligence as an important element in the relationship between her and her private GIC, which made transitioning a mutually supportive arrangement. The arrangement seemed to give Jess agency, but this did come at significant financial cost.

There are more options to commencing transition outside the medical profession if one has the funds to buy body modification technology. Oscar suggests that there is a growth in Internet companies and illegal outlets selling hormones. Therefore, it seems there is less need for medical intervention in the early stages. This was the case for Oscar who was considering taking hormones unsupervised by a doctor or endocrinologist. He said:

The whole NHS route [...] I don't want to be part of that [...] The black market does seem quite appealing to me. What other options are available to me?

(Oscar, transman)

Oscar was the only participant in my study who suggested that he might initiate his body modification through non-medical sources. However, there is an obvious acknowledgement that transpeople are accessing hormones through other sources. Most of the literature surrounding this originates from the US, and focuses on how expensive treatment forces transgendered people to utilise black-market sources (Israel and Tarver 1997). Providing prescriptions to reduce the risks of black market hormone taking is also a recommendation in the *Standards of Care* (HBIGDA 2001). There were very few studies in the UK; however, one recent study by Vardi et al. follows the *Standards of Care* recommendation:

[i]n a harm reduction model (e.g., to prevent the use of black market hormones or decrease psychiatric consequences of denying the hormones), it can be appropriate to prescribe hormones with very minimal or no exam.

(Vardi et al. 2008)

Transpeople who take 'black market' hormones can be understood in a couple of ways. On one hand, it could be seen as transpeople agentically taking their health requirements in hand and reducing the intervention of an often difficult and demanding health system. On the other, it could be seen as a challenge to medical authority over the bodies of transpeople, which disallows many transpeople from actualising their body modification desires. What this section also illustrates is the influence of economic capital in relation to private health care access and the market in hormones. Transpeople's agency is also shaped through these access issues and through their (lack of) economic privilege.

CONSUMER RIGHTS AND NHS PROVISION: AUTHENTIC VS. COSMETIC

Most participants demanded medical services even though some were sceptical about the psychiatric process within the NHS. The processes involved in persuading their psychiatrist (gatekeeper) that they were legitimate candidates for hormonal and surgical intervention were viewed as ritualistic, lengthy and patronising. For example, Benjamin said:

> The positives are only that you get what you need from them. The negatives were lack of clinics so long travel involved, and very generalised and out of date questioning which resulted in standard answers.
>
> (Benjamin, transman)

Therefore, Benjamin provided a 'standard' narrative response, which is performed out of obligation rather than believed in wholeheartedly. Benjamin is both a passive recipient of clinical determinations, by responding to questions in such a way to secure his body modification, but simultaneously agentic in his securing of body modification by stage-managing the system in which he found himself. As with the majority of participants in this research, both Benjamin and Mariza understood that taxonomic legitimacy and a diagnosis are required to actualise transformation of their bodies.

Mariza rationalised her request for treatment as pragmatic, even a run of the mill solution. She thought surgical and hormonal intervention should be provided as in the context of other medical conditions:

> People with physical problems they do help, but the mental and any other problems are just as valid and are as much a contribution to the happiness of a person as getting rid of diphtheria or anything else. I remember the doctor telling me one time about hypochondria who really thinks they suffer with a disease, but I don't think I suffer from a disease I was just born with the wrong bits. These needed sorting out. However, a medical health service can't be called a medical health service unless there is a service and they sort them out. They cannot be selective about who does and who does not need services.
>
> (Mariza, transwoman)

According to Mariza, the NHS works hierarchically in relation to Gender Identity Disorder, which is deemed less significant than other conditions. This hierarchy affects the funding for therapy and surgery. In the mid 1990s, when participants such as Mariza were waiting for SRS, NHS budgets were being tightened and reformed with different accountability structures for health care provision, which was further constrained by 'clinical audit' mechanisms (Hughes Tuohy 1999). Health authorities radically changed the ways they purchased health care from providers (Hughes Tuohy 1999). Decisions to buy and then provide healthcare services to patients were made by managers. The provision of SRS and hormone therapy was reduced or cut by some health authorities. This is illustrated in a document that became known in the court case *Regina v. North West Lancashire Health Authority*, 21 December 1998. In 1995, this particular health authority introduced a policy entitled *Medical procedure of no beneficial health gain or proven benefit*, where it stated:

> [I]nterventions on the human body are not always related to ill-health but may be related to a desire to achieve an ideal body image or a bodily function that cannot currently be achieved. That is complicated by the fact that its supporters often describe the desire for intervention in medical terminology and indeed point out that the lack of complete well-being may itself be a health problem.
>
> (cited in Press for Change 1998)

This was followed by a section that specifically addressed transsexualism:

> Persons wishing to adopt the role of the opposite gender (male to female or female to male) have access to the general psychiatric or psychological services available within the contract portfolio. However no service will be commissioned extra contractually. The Heath Authority will not commission drug treatment or surgery that is intended to give patients the physical characteristics of the opposite gender.
>
> (cited in Press for Change 1998)

The plaintiffs' case was based on the argument that health authorities did not regard GID authentic and, therefore, de-prioritised treatment. The health officials had conflated a 'superficial' perception of transsexualism with other body image cases, such as breast augmentation or rhinoplasty, viewing all as cosmetic. According to the ruling, GID consists of a psychological dimension and a physical dimension, but the health service focused solely on the 'cosmetic' body image aspect downplaying Gender Dysphoria and rendering transsexualism imaginary and thus, 'inauthentic.'[5] This health authority's stance on transsexualism was ruled unlawful by Mr Justice Hidden (Press for Change 1998). The following quotation from Octavia provides a critique of depictions surrounding sex change surgery as cosmetic:

I don't think it is necessarily fair to spend public money on cosmetic surgeries; fair enough the sex change should be paid for by the public money because it saves a lot of money in the long run and stops a lot of suffering. If I can afford to pay for things myself I do not see why I should burden the tax payer [. . .] Well I know I can live with my nose if I have to, I don't have to have it chopped about and mashed up. I would like to but things I can live without I consider cosmetic but the actual change no. If I hadn't had that [sex change] done it would have finished me off.

(Octavia, transwoman)

Another interviewee, Jess, was not an NHS patient, but she had learned much through anecdotal evidence from other transpeople receiving NHS services and treatments. Jess claimed to have mentored quite a few transwomen through transition surgery in an attempt to turn this 'scary' and 'harrowing' process into something positive. Jess visited or phoned the transwomen she mentored daily for the first month and every week thereafter. In response to my questions about the psychiatrist and surgeons' attitudes in the clinical setting, Jess said:

The psychiatrists have focussed on justifying the controversial provision of expensive medical resources to PCTs [Primary Care Trust] by bringing about a resolution of a psychological 'disorder.' The surgeons don't really care beyond doing an acceptable job of genital reconstruction and both, understandably, wish to avoid post-treatment legal claims and keeping people off their backs.

(Jess, transwoman)

Jess sees the psychiatrists as 'justifying' surgical interventions in the treatment of Gender Identity Disorder to health authorities who must provide the funding. Jess suggests that there is pressure from health authorities to justify spending and curb any possible lawsuits for negligent treatment. Furthermore, she suggests that the treatment offered by the NHS is minimal and surgical intervention is not about alleviating Gender Identity Disorder through transformational bodily aesthetics per se, but doing just enough to keep both health authorities and patients 'off their backs.' This interpretation compliments the findings of West's research, which held that:

those who continued to [have the] operation with Charing Cross [gender identity clinic] report patronising attitudes, insensitivity and no sense of caring. The operative results, I have seen so far, are far inferior to those from other countries and invariably give problems post-op. Local psychiatrists can vary widely in their knowledge about GID and seem at times to be unsympathetic and unable to empathise.

(West 2004: 14)

Diane, who became extremely distraught during the interview, expressed dissatisfaction with her genital surgery and the subsequent response of the surgeon:

> it was ugly, it was not realistic at all, there was far too much tissue. I actually got really badly treated about it because I said, "look, this is not realistic, this is just a mess." The way I was treated was "well it looks alright to me, what else, do you want me to do?" He actually said at one point, "well I have cut off your penis, what else do you want me to do?"
>
> (Diane, transwoman)

Diane's rendition of the follow-up meeting between her and the surgeon, when the surgeon said "I have cut off your penis, what else, do you want me to do?" demonstrates a decisive insensitivity and uncaring attitude. Diane's comments here illustrate how this particular surgeon did not accommodate her in an ethical sense. There was a lack of an 'ethics of care,' proponents of which suggest good practice should allow a person to act authentically and with autonomy (Cardol et al. 2002). Questioning the surgeon's 'authority' was received negatively according to Diane. This 'questioning' attitude is further evidenced by psychiatrists in the medical literature who have characterised attitudes of transsexuals in the clinical setting as 'adversarial' (Newman 2000) or resentful toward the psychiatrist (Green, in Speer and Parsons 2006). What is seen as adversarial by psychiatrists, however, is simply read as assertive by transsexuals themselves. Kenneth said:

> Historically we have looked to the medical profession as gods. In fact, these people have strong opinion and do not treat people impartially. To do these professions you must have a very strong belief in yourself, and what you're doing and where you are going. When you get to that point where you are a leader in that profession, even though it is a microcosm of society, to change your opinion it takes a big man or big woman to do that. So as somebody who is trans it is down to me to have a responsibility in my own treatment [. . .] I think in doing that it is educating people. I think people should be allowed to have a dialogue with the medical profession, allow them to change their theories.
>
> (Kenneth, transman)

What Kenneth is attending to here is a hierarchal relationship between the psychiatrist and patient. Historically this meant absolute respect for the doctor and her/his 'wisdom.' Nevertheless, Kenneth's narrative spoke of the fallibility of doctors' theories, which made him question their judgments and be more proactive in researching his own treatment. These treatment dynamics were desired by a few participants in this research, which may account for the reports by psychiatrists of difficult encounters with transpeople (Newman 2000; Green, in Speer and Parsons 2006). Likewise, Karen challenged her psychiatrist when he used male pronouns with her:

> You are in a professional capacity where you give a service to people like me and you have just said something that is so unacceptable and so unprofessional. People could have gone out after that and done something to themselves, after that very simple statement. So I think it is a question of training and I see this across the system at every level. And we all know that psychiatrists are a bunch of dysfunctional people, they are more dysfunctional than we are.
>
> (Karen, transwoman)

Over the last few years, the UK government has worked with the Sexual Orientation and Gender Identity Advisory Group (SOGIAG). The SOCIAG is an umbrella group of stakeholder individuals and organisations, (such as Press for Change)[6] who assisted the Department of Health with the development and delivery of a social and health care programme to eliminate discrimination for Lesbian, Gay, Bisexual and Transgender people. This healthcare strategy covers both service users and employees. The group has four work streams: (1) Reducing Health Inequalities, (2) Better Employment, (3) Improving Services and (4) Transgender Health (Department of Health 2007). Participants in this research, when describing the changing climate in a user/provider context within healthcare, often used the discourse of 'health authorities should be providing a service.' Perhaps this enabled Karen to understand the power dynamics between 'client' and 'psychiatrist,' and feel able to demand more consumer rights in relation to her treatment. This may seem 'adversarial' or 'resentful' to the psychiatrists.[7] However, it could also be seen as the service users utilising the policy initiatives to their own advantage by demanding their rights as consumers of services within the NHS.

GENDER RECOGNITION AND THE 'MEDICOLEGAL ALLIANCE'

Prior to the Gender Recognition Act 2004 (GRA) (Office of Public Sector Information 2004) transpeople were able to change their names by deed poll; and have passports, driving licences and bank accounts in their new name and corresponding gender prior to any surgery or hormonal intervention. Sex/gender could not, however, be changed in relation to national insurance numbers and the birth certificate. When the GRA was passed in 2004 it was heralded as a huge advance for the rights of transpeople (Press for Change 2005), after more than thirty years of having only partial legal recognition (Sharpe 2007). However, amongst respondents in this research, the GRA provoked mixed reactions. Three significant themes emerged from the interviews, 'authentication,' 'agency' and 'ambivalence.'

Some interviewees viewed the GRA possibilities ambivalently in their current situation. Emily suggested:

> I haven't applied for the Gender Recognition Certificate, even though I could have. I will, but because I have been trans for so long, for about seven years, it doesn't seem particularly urgent and it doesn't actually affect my day-to-day life. I will get around to do it at some point especially when, although I am not satisfied with civil partnerships, I would like to marry a woman one day. I would like to be recognised as a woman when I do, do that.
>
> (Emily, transwoman)

At this point, to be recognised by law is of little consequence for Emily's identity as a transwoman. Emily's socio-legal discontinuity illustrates the complexity of her gender identity and sexuality, which form a composite identity with the potential for fluidity. Emily is aware that her legal status may change in the future; however, she is prepared to only use legal recognition if she needs to in a future contractual scenario, such as having a civil partnership. Similarly, Clifford said:

> I suppose at the moment getting a Gender Recognition Certificate is not really important to me so it has not influenced it [my life] that much. If the Act said that anybody who has not had treatments would not be considered then it might have had some influence in the long term.
>
> (Clifford, transman)

Clifford raises a number of issues about how trans bodies are (not) situated in law. The law, as it stands, allows Clifford the freedom to reflect on his body project without the mandates of law forcing surgical intervention on transpeople for legal recognition. Clifford continued:

> The Act is good for people who wish to be recognised as either male or female but in the long run I think I would rather see either three boxes or no boxes.
>
> (Clifford, transman)

In addition, Clifford highlights the growing 'transgender phenomenon' (Ekins and King 2006) in the UK and his ambivalence to the binary logic of the law. Clifford suggests that the GRA cannot accommodate those who do not identify with the male and female options and, in effect, misrecognises many transpeople. Similarly, Oscar recognises the positive aspects for those transpeople who want 'equal access' to citizenship rights in the binary system, but fears the underlying ideology upon which sexed identity is premised.

It is important for the recognition of trans identities and status in terms of transsexual peoples' financial privileges and in terms of citizenship and equal access, but I am sceptical about the basis of this and the reliance on certain medicalised narratives. The status of the transsexual and the hierarchy being created through that and reinforcing, the 'true' the 'real' and the 'authentic.' [At the point of saying true, real and authentic Oscar indicated that he wanted to use quotation marks around the words by gesturing with his fingers]. Also not recognising genderqueer and still only having two options to choose from. It is an important step but there is many flaws in it and should just be seen as the first step.

(Oscar, transman)

Interestingly, but not surprising, it was the younger transpeople, Oscar, Emily and Clifford, who belonged to queer activist organisations, who were ambivalent about institutional recognition. Oscar was grappling with different notions of authenticity within frameworks of socio-legal authenticity and personal authenticity. In Sartre's (1966) existentialist philosophical discourse around authenticity, he suggests people who have made their decisions based on pre-established codes of civil life—which is how the GRA is viewed—are inauthentic. The decisions are made in 'bad faith,' which is the primary obstacle to authenticity (Sartre 1966). In a Sartrean sense, the pre-established codes of male and female in the GRA foreclose the possibility of gender queerness and restrains freedom, the freedom Oscar is striving for. Clifford highlighted how 'bad faith' and inauthenticity may act empirically:

In terms of doctors and psychiatrists and having to prove and actually going out of their way to, in the case of transwomen who are overtly feminine beyond what she might feel comfortable with just to prove a point. So there are always transpeople going out of their way, beyond what they want, just to not leave doubt in people's minds. If you cannot show to prove it then you are going to have to do something to prove it.

(Clifford, transman)

Nonetheless, and somewhat paradoxically, transsexuals with non-normative bodies may also be seen to embody a symbolic critique of the binary sex/gender system, which contests the naturalness of sexed bodies. Transsexuals who actualise their desired bodies, or do not actualise normative bodies through surgery and hormones, undermine the once dogmatic sex/gender binary, which was based on corresponding bodily and gender presentation. Contestation of the symbolic understanding of 'natural' or normative bodies also undermines the notion that transpeople's so-called 'bad faith' in civil codes, such as the GRA, can never overcome and challenge the social conditions of its production. As Lois McNay (2000) contends, the possibilities and scope to re-enact in new social contexts is always evident because of individual subjectivity and agency.

The GRA provides new social contexts that allow agency in how far people may go to realising their (non-normative) gendered bodily aesthetic. Sartre's (1966) dichotomous assertion, that civil life suppresses authentic subjects and 'the desire to maintain distance from those structures, to call them into question and to change them' (Sartre cited in Zane Charme 1991: 253) is more authentic, and is witnessed in relation to trans embodiment. Transsexuals are re-writing the civil codes themselves, and thus, overcoming what it means to have normative bodies and normative civil lives, and they are staking claims about their own authenticity in diverse ways.

The medicolegal alliance in the UK has reduced, in many ways, the institutional constraints surrounding legal recognition of trans-sexed people in comparison to many other countries. The dependence of transsexuals' recognition by state institutions on the one hand has been a positive forward-looking regulative move. A new birth certificate, Gregory suggested, gave him both recognition and the feeling of authenticity:

> The first thing I thought, when the law was first passed, was at last I am a real person. I exist. When I got my birth certificate at the age of thirty-nine, I exist. Before, I felt like a part person in the eyes of the law but now I feel three-dimensional.
>
> (Gregory, transman)

Additionally, for Benjamin, Gender Recognition (GR) would allow him freedom to actualise dreams and plans that he had put off due to the sex stated on his original birth certificate:

> I am funny about sending my original birth certificate away and also when I am putting my previous name on forms as it is different identity. Just paperwork-wise, it's a completely different identity. So I think it [GR] will make me do things. I am going to learn to drive this year, but I might apply for that [GRC] first, because it will make me feel a bit better about sending my stuff off, that then will make quite a big difference.
>
> (Benjamin, transman)

The reification of transsexuality, through the regulatory practices of the Gender Recognition Act 2004, establishes authentic transsexuals according to Gregory and Benjamin. Thus, it seems that Gregory and Benjamin accept that their authenticity in part is awarded by the 'medicolegal alliance.' These participants celebrate their normativity and assimilation into a binary gender system. Hines argues:

> the GRA is unable to recognise the diversity of new (trans) masculinities and femininities as they are variously constructed and experienced.

Hence, rather than broadening the realm of citizenship in relation to gender diversity, the Act works to reinforce a normative gender model. (Hines 2007a: para 7.5).

Whilst this may be true on one level in relation to binary gender, Gregory illustrated that the GRA does in fact recognise 'new (trans) masculinities' within the law. Gregory was unable to have any body modification surgery due to physical impairments he sustained during childbirth. He was approved for surgery, but not operated on, giving him the required paperwork, which stated the planned surgery that is required by the Gender Recognition Panel (GRP) to approve his new birth certificate.

For the participants in this research, the discourse of authenticity was key to their social recognition, claims of embodiment and self-understanding within the structural parameters of medicolegal relations. Authenticity was qualified in various ways in relation to the medicolegal system. Rather than essentialising 'authenticity,' participants use it as an ontological category within lived relations, a concept to secure treatment and as a concept to open up the field of possibilities surrounding their embodiment choices.

CONCLUSION

The participants' narratives explored in this chapter suggest that experiences of accessing body modification technologies can be both positive and negative, experience of which is contingent on whether they were taken seriously or not by the GIC and GPs. Both quality and opportunity of treatment depended upon the 'luck of the draw' or a 'postcode lottery' for the participants in this research in relation to both GPs and psychiatrists. 'Luck' was often replaced with agency and respect if the participant was fortunate enough to have the capital to fund their body modifications privately, indicating that trans experiences are situated within a class system. Notions of agency and authenticity were complicated by intersubjective negotiations with those who act as gatekeepers to body modification technologies. According to some participants, there has been a shift in the provision of clinical treatments, which is marked by dynamic customer led negotiations, especially within the private healthcare sector. Nonetheless, new NHS healthcare policies gave some transpeople the confidence to challenge what they saw as unreasonable or unethical treatment. These experiences within the NHS or private practice all fed into complex embodiment stories of authenticity and agency. Agency was not seen in terms of voluntarism, where identity can be negotiated without constraints, but seen as meditative within more nuanced social relations. Therefore, the situation the participants found themselves in, generated reflexive agency in how best to secure body modification if so desired. This was also apparent in the legal domain.

The GRA has created novel parameters in which varied trans embodiments are recognised. The opening up of what is permitted in law in relation to body morphology creates socio-legal relations that allow participants to understand authenticity away from essentialised notions of bodily realness. Authenticity in law is an altogether different ontological claim and is seen as enabling autonomy and agency within lived relations and especially in relation to the medical establishment. Participants who embraced a more pluralistic outlook towards trans embodiment had some reservations about the underlying ideology of the GRA. Reservations ranged from reaffirming the medical autonomy over bodies and gender identity to the legal sanctioning of only two genders. However, these participants also empathised with those transpeople who identified as either male or female and who wished for citizenship rights awarded by the GRA. Most participants welcomed the GRA as a step in the right direction, by illustrating that the government recognised (some) transpeople as citizens.

These diverse views of participants in this chapter illustrate the phenomenological diversity within the trans population studied. Such an understanding is important because it shows that stereotypes often constructed within medical and academic literature are far from the norm in transpeople's lives. This will further generate understandings about the situational and agentic aspects of trans-sexing. Furthermore, the phenomenological, discursive and bodily diversity of transsexuals poses a critique of good/bad; natural/constructed, beautiful/ugly dichotomous theorising that often surrounds the transsexual subject in radical feminist texts (Raymond 1980; Jeffreys 2005) and in clinical depictions of the 'true transsexual' (Benjamin 1966; Green and Money 1969; Money and Ehrhardt 1972; Money 1996). I hope that this analysis will move the theoretical debate surrounding transsexuality toward a less deterministic understanding, which embraces more openly the agentic aspects of trans embodiment.

NOTES

1. The RLE is a process in which transsexuals live in their gender of preference for a length of time, in order to demonstrate to psychiatrists (and themselves) that they can function in the gender role.
2. The Harry Benjamin International Gender Dysphoria Association has been renamed the World Professional Association of Transgender Health (WPATH).
3. The gender-neutral pronouns hir and hirself are used here to indicate Brian's bi-gendered position.
4. RLT signifies the Real Life Test, which is often used in the trans community interchangeably with Real Life Experience (RLE).
5. Evidence of hierarchy in relation to doctors' perceptions of disease affects decision making within health services. As Album and Westin (2008: 188) suggest in their study in Norway 'medical activities are organized, [by] categorizing patients, planning and allocating work, setting priorities at all levels, pricing services, and teaching and developing medical knowledge. A

widespread, and at the same time tacit, prestige ordering of diseases may influence many understandings and decisions in the medical community.'
6. Press for Change is a longstanding political lobbying and educational organisation, which campaigns to achieve equal civil rights and liberties for all trans people in the UK.
7. A study in the US by Street Jr. et al. (2007: 594) suggests that physicians were more likely to be more "patient-centred" if they judged the patient to be 'more satisfied with care and more likely to adhere to treatment.'

REFERENCES

Album, D. and Westin, S. (2008) 'Do diseases have a prestige hierarchy? A survey among physicians and medical students', *Social Science & Medicine*, 66(1): 182–188.

American Psychiatric Association (1994) *Diagnostic and Statistical Manual of Mental Disorders: DSM-IV,* Washington, DC.: American Psychiatric Association.

Benjamin, H. (1966) *The Transsexual Phenomenon,* New York, Julian Press.

Blanchard, R. (1991) 'Clinical observations and systematic study of autogynephilia', *Journal of Sex and Marital Therapy* 17: 235–257.

Butler, J. (1993) *Bodies that Matter: On the Discursive Limits of 'Sex',* New York and London: Routledge.

Cardol, M. et al. (2002) 'On autonomy and participation in rehabilitation', *Disability and Rehabilitation,* 24(18): 970–974.

Chawla, P. and Krauss, R. M. (1994) 'Gesture and speech in spontaneous and rehearsed narratives', *Journal of Experimental Social Psychology,* 30: 580–601.

Connell, R. W. (1995) *Masculinities,* Berkeley: California University Press.

Department of Health (2007) 'An introduction to working with transgender people: information for health and social care staff'. http://www.dh.gov.uk/en/PublicationsandstatisticsPublications/PublicationsPolicyAndGuidance/DH_074257 (accessed 5 May 2007).

Ekins, R. and King, D. (2006) *The Transgender Phenomenon,* London: Sage.

Felski, R. (2006) '"Because it is beautiful": new feminist perspectives on beauty', *Feminist Theory,* 7(2): 273–282.

Green, R. and Money, J. (eds) (1969) *Transsexualism and Sex Reassignment,* Baltimore: The John Hopkins University Press.

HBIGDA (2001) 'The Harry Benjamin International Gender Dysphoria Association's standards of care for gender identity disorders, sixth version'. http://www.hbigda.org/socv6.cfm (accessed 1 August 2004).

Heinamaa, S. (1997) 'What is a woman? Butler and Beauvoir on the foundations of the sexual difference', *Hypatia: A Journal of Feminist Philosophy,* 12(1): 20–39.

Hines, S. (2007a) '(Trans)forming gender: social change and transgender citizenship', *Sociological Research Online,* 12(1). http://www.socresonline.org.uk/12/1/hines.html (accessed 3 January 2009).

———. (2007b) *TransForming Gender: Transgender Practices of Identity, Intimacy and Care,* Bristol: Policy Press.

Hughes Tuohy, C. (1999) 'Dynamics of a changing health sphere: the United States, Britain, and Canada'. http://www.cla.wayne.edu/polisci/parrish/US,%20UK&Canada.pdf. (accessed 3 January 2008).

Israel, G. E. and Tarver, D. E. (1997) *Transgender Care: Recommended Guidelines, Practical Information, and Personal Accounts,* Philadelphia: Temple University Press.

Jeffreys, S. (2005) *Beauty and Misogyny: Harmful Cultural Practices in the West*, London: Routledge.

Jeffreys, S. (2008) 'They know it when they see it: the UK Gender Recognition Act 2004', *British Journal of Politics and International Relations* 10(2): 328–345.

Kessler, S. J. and McKenna, W. (1978) *Gender: An Ethnomethodological Approach*, New York and Chichester: Wiley.

McNay, L. (2000) *Gender and Agency: Reconfiguring the Subject in Feminist and Social Theory*, Cambridge: Polity Press.

Millot, C. (1990) *Horsexe: Essay on Transsexuality*, New York: Autonomedia.

Money, J. (1996) 'Body-image disorder and gender identity', *Sexuality and Disability*, 14(2): 87–91.

Money, J. and Ehrhardt, A. (1972) *Man and Woman, Boy and Girl*, Baltimore: The John Hopkins University Press.

Newman, L. K. (2000) 'Transgender issues', in J. Ussher (ed.) *Women's Health: Contemporary International Perspectives*, Leicester: BPS Publishing.

Office of Public Sector Information. (2004) *Gender Recognition Act 2004*. http://www.opsi.gov.uk/acts/acts2004/ukpga_20040007_en_1. (accessed 3 January 2008).

Press for Change (1998) 'High Court: A, D and G v N-W Lancashire Health Authority: full text of the judgment of the High Court'. http://www.pfc.org.uk/node/317 (accessed 2 January 2008).

Press for Change (2005) 'Press for Change'. http://www.pfc.org. (accessed 20 December 2005).

Raymond, J. (1980) *The Transsexual Empire: The Making of the She Male*, London: Womens Press.

Rubin, H. (2003) *Self-Made Men: Identity and Embodiment among Transsexual Men*, Nashville: Vanderbilt University Press.

Sartre, J. P. (1966) *Being and Nothingness: An Essay on Phenomenological Ontology*, London: Methuen.

Sharpe, A. N. (2007) 'A critique of the Gender Recognition Act 2004', *Journal of Bioethical Inquiry*, 4(1): 33–42.

Speer, S. A. and Parsons, C. (2006) 'Gatekeeping gender: some features of the hypothetical questions in the psychiatric assessment of transsexual patients', *Discourse and Society*, 17(6): 785–812.

St. Jacques, J. (2007) 'Retrotranslations of post-transsexuality, notions of regret', *Journal of Visual Culture*, 6(1): 77–90.

Street Jr., R. L., Gordon, H. and Haidet, P. (2007) 'Physicians' communication and perceptions of patients: is it how they look, how they talk, or is it just the doctor?' *Social Science & Medicine*, 65(3): 586–598.

Vardi, Y., Wylie, K. R., Moser, C., Assalian, P., Dean, J., and Asscheman, H. (2008) 'Is physical examination required before prescribing hormones to patients with gender dysphoria?' *The Journal of Sexual Medicine*, 5(1): 21–26.

West, P. (2004) 'Report into the medical and related needs of transgender people in Brighton and Hove: the case for a local integrated service'. http://www.pfc.org.uk/files/medical/spectrum.pdf. (accessed 30 June 2005).

Zane Charme, S. (1991) 'Sartre's images of the other and the search for authenticity', *Human Studies*, 14(4): 251–264.

6 (In)Visibility in the Workplace
The Experiences of Trans-Employees in the UK

Em Rundall and Vincent Vecchietti

INTRODUCTION

This chapter explores trans-employees' self-reported experiences of inclusion, discrimination, and protection in UK workplaces, and how these are linked to their visibility or invisibility as trans or gender-diverse individuals. Primary data and existing literature are used in conjunction with our theoretical conceptualisations of (in)visibility, to set out and deconstruct various areas of difficulty faced by trans-employees in the work environment.

Since 1999 legislation designed to protect transsexual employees in the UK workplace has existed.[1] Despite this, trans-individuals are most likely to face significant and pervasive inequalities in the work environment (Whittle, Turner, Al-Alami 2007).[2] Employment is an area of key importance for trans-individuals because it enables financial access to healthcare and participation in family and social life (Whittle 2000). In many cases, gatekeepers of gender reassignment treat employment (or a place in education) as a prerequisite to medical and legal gender actualisation.[3] Additionally, the number of people seeking to actualise their gender-identity is steadily increasing (GIRES 2008a). Thus, a rising number of employees may face difficulties in the workplace.

Previous studies have assumed that individuals who appear visibly trans are more likely to experience prejudice and discrimination (Whittle et al. 2007: 8; Whittle 2006: xiv). This assumption has been upheld by recent research conducted in the UK, which found that moments of visibility or change, such as the point of transition, were trigger-points for discrimination in the workplace (Whittle et al. 2007). Discrimination based on visibility may continue after the initial point of transition, because not all trans-individuals will eventually completely pass in their preferred or legally acquired gender all or some of the time, for a variety of reasons.[4] Additionally, of the trans-employees who do 'pass' in their preferred or legally acquired gender, not all will choose to make their gender-diversity (including history) invisible all or some of the time, to all or some members of the workplace.

The individual's presentation of signifier-led gender-identity, in connection with the extent to which their gender-diversity, including history, is visible or invisible to the present or absent onlooker, is referred to in this chapter as (in)visibility.[5] Specific examples of trans-employees' self-reported experiences of inclusion, discrimination and protection are explored, and further explicated, through the notion of the bipartite agency of (in)visibility. Additionally, we consider context specific interactions within the workplace, which may shape the experiences of, subsequently navigate, and potentially police trans-employees.

The term 'transsexual' is problematic because it is rooted in a psychiatric definition of gender dysphoria, and is thus pathologised (GIRES 2008b). In view of this, we have exclusively chosen to use the term 'trans' in reference to 'transsexual' individuals, even though 'trans' more commonly signifies 'multiple terms that express transidentities' (Cromwell 1999: 26). This chapter focuses on the particular experiences of trans-individuals who identify within the socially sanctioned binary as the gender opposite to the one ascribed at birth. They are likely to seek to present their gender-identity within the socially accepted confines of gender binarism[6], and thus conform to the British medico-legal definition of 'transsexual.'[7] 'Transsexuals' are legally afforded protection from harassment and discrimination in the workplace, based on their prior, current or intended gender reassignment (The Sex Discrimination (Gender Reassignment) Regulations [SD(GR)R] 1999). This legal framework provides a context from which their experiences may be analysed.

This chapter contributes to empirical sociological research rooted in the experiences of trans-individuals in the UK (Monro 2000; Whittle 2006; Hines 2007; Sanger 2008). In the following subsection, the research methodology and the distribution of respondents are briefly outlined. Next, the multifaceted issue of (in)visibility in the workplace is theoretically conceptualised. We then focus in turn on the interaction between (in)visibility and participants' experiences of: inclusion; discrimination; and protection. Lastly, empirical and theoretical conclusions are drawn. Throughout this chapter, we argue that the experiences of trans-employees in UK workplaces will be shaped by their (in)visibility as gender-diverse individuals. Furthermore, the interlocution between the agency of the trans-individual and the present or absent onlooker will navigate and police one's expression of gender-identity. We also argue that stealth is not a secure position because (in)visibility is not a fixed state but constantly subject to the potential of reinterpretation.[8]

RESEARCH METHODOLOGY

The primary research was conducted as part of Rundall's (forthcoming) sociology PhD entitled 'Transsexual People in the UK Workplaces: An Analysis of Transmen's and Transwomen's Experiences.' The data was collected via a web-survey between April and July 2007 through closed and open-ended questions, and was anonymous. Snowball sampling via trans networks and organisations was used to contact prospective participants. The data was analysed with SPSS using frequencies and chi-square analysis, as well as thematic coding.

Participant Sample

A total of 106 trans-employees between 18–64 years old participated in this research project, representing the public, private, and voluntary sectors.[9] Table 6.1 presents participants' age distribution. Most (38.1 per cent) were between 40–49 years old, which is an older mode than those reported in other research projects on trans-people (Weitze and Osburg 1996; van Kesteren et al. 1996; Whittle et al. 2007). However, this mode is close to the average age of 39 years reported for the UK population in 2007 (ONS 2008). 75.1 per cent of respondents had already transitioned, 67.1 per cent of whom had transitioned during or after 2000. 17.1 per cent of participants were currently transitioning, and 4.8 per cent were about to transition. The distribution of respondents' gender-identities, shown in Table 6.2, is similar to recent distributions noted in research in the UK, Europe and North America (Whittle et al. 2007: 28). Table 6.3 shows participants' stage of transition. Most respondents had already transitioned and therefore may have experienced their workplaces at different stages of transition. This participant sample is not fully representative of the UK trans population, as there was an under representation of participants from ethnic minorities (2.7 per cent). This percentage is significantly less than the 7.9 per cent for the UK population (ONS 2004). Such underrepresentation has been reported in other studies conducted within the trans community (Whittle et al. 2007).

Table 6.1   Participants' Age Distribution

Participants' age	Percentage of participants
18–24 years	1.9%
25–29 years	7.6%
30–39 years	27.6%
40–49 years	38.1%
50–59 years	21.9%
60–64 years	2.9%
65+ years	0%

Table 6.2   Distribution of Respondents' Gender-Identities

Participants' gender identities	Percentage of participants
MTF individual/Woman with a trans-background	66%
FTM individual/Man with a trans-background	27%
Other gender-diverse person/preferred term	7%

Table 6.3   Distribution of Participants' Stage of Transition

Participants' stage of transitions	Percentage of participants
Already transitioned	75%
Begun transisitioning	17%
About to transition	6%
Do not intend to transition	2%

CONCEPTUALISING (IN)VISIBILITY IN THE WORKPLACE

We conceive of (in)visibility as the extent to which one's gender diversity, including history, is visible or invisible to the present or absent onlooker. In order that the trans-individual's preferred gender is visible, their bio-gender or gender-diversity must, to a certain extent, be invisible. Agency must be seen here in the context of the individual's extent of choice, and ability, to present as their preferred signifier-led gender. (In)visibility is not the same as stealth because it acknowledges that some trans-individuals may always appear gender-diverse, but the (in)visibility of all trans-individuals may be found in the signifiers they choose to use. Inter-dependent to the agency of the trans-individual, is the present or absent onlooker. It is they who, perhaps despite dissonant visual cues or existing knowledge, may potentially accept the (in)visibility of the trans-individual. The agency of the onlooker therefore completes the bipartite agency of (in)visibility, and forms the basis of acceptance or non-acceptance.

We find the terms 'sex' and 'gender' in mainstream sociology problematical when considering and recognising trans-individuals' identities. Some feminist and trans-focused academics argue that sex, like gender, is a social construction (Kessler and McKenna 1978; Hird 2000). Furthermore, that categorisation, particularly gender, need not be 'dual and oppositional' (Lorber 1994: 4; see also, Butler 1990). However, it is still frequently the case in sociology, and indeed in the wider social consciousness, that sex is considered to be an innate biological division, and a foundation of hierarchy and identity. Gender is considered to be a nuance of identity, which is at once born of sex, and also a creation and expression of socio-cultural influence. This is perpetuated by 'legal sex' as a classification framework. However, trans-individuals commonly report that they feel they were born with a gender-identity at odds with their biological sex. Therefore gender-identity cannot be born of socio-cultural influence. The following conceptualisation is from Vecchietti:

> In a heteronormative paradigm, one may conceive of 'sex' as the signified concept–thought: 'penis' or 'vagina.' One may conceive of 'gender' as the signifier: 'masculine' or 'feminine.' Therefore, the signifier 'masculine' refers to the concept-thought 'penis,' which results in the sign being 'read' as 'male.' The signifier 'feminine' refers to the concept-thought 'vagina,' and thus results in the sign being 'read' as 'female.' These two signs are iconic.
>
> (Vecchietti 2008: 5)

The 'meanings of these iconic signs are derived from the privileging of the signified (sex) over the signifier (gender)' (Vecchietti 2008: 5). However, 'the pre-GRS transman "has" the signifier "masculine" and the signified "vagina." The pre-GRS transwoman "has" the signifier "feminine" and the signified "penis"' (Vecchietti 2008: 5).

> Therefore, the privileging of the signifier 'gender' over the signified 'sex' is necessary in order to acknowledge the transsexual's signifier-led identity. This is made explicit with the introduction of the Gender Recognition Act 2004, in which the signifier (gender) is 'legally' privileged over the signified (sex).
>
> (Vecchietti 2008: 5)

Ekins and King also note that the Gender Recognition Act (GRA, 2004), in allowing people to legally change sex, 'not on the basis of genital reassignment (sex), but on the basis of role change (gender)' (2006: 230) marks an official separation of gender from sex in British law. Sanger (2008) makes a similar point. Although historically a person's gender has been assumed from their sex, this legal change indicates that a person's sex may now be assumed from their gender-identity. It is because of this privileging of the signifier 'gender' over the signified 'sex' that throughout this chapter we have chosen to use the term 'gender.' The use of 'gender' as an overarching term has been used before (Kessler and McKenna 1978, 2000), although the benefits and usefulness of this approach are disputed (Ekins and King 2006). We took this approach in recognition of the trans-individuals who may choose not to, or are unable to, undergo aspects of, or in some cases any, gender reassignment surgery, in addition to those who do, as this should in no way diminish their right to identify and be recognised as their preferred gender. Thus the physical body should not take precedence over a person's sense of identity. Additionally, this is particularly relevant to the work environment, where one does not usually see the genitals of one's colleagues; rather one interprets their gender, and thus assumed 'legal sex,' through external signifiers.

Discrimination based on gender, perceived gender difference, or gender non-conformity may be both overt and covert. Discriminatory practices may also become embedded behaviours (GIRES 2008b: 48). If one is perceived to disrupt socially sanctioned expressions and representations of gender, one is likely to face sanctions from other individuals in and around the workplace, which may navigate trans-employees in their approach towards (in)visibility in the workplace. The purpose of this policing may be considered to be threefold: to navigate the transgressor back towards the expected folds of gender-expression and representation; to make an example of the transgressor as a warning to other would-be transgressors; and to 'shore-up' the policing individual's position within the dominant 'correct' collective (Rundall 2005). An example of this can be seen in the experience of this MTF employee (age 50–59); when her employer moved to make her redundant, the message of reprisal served to police her erstwhile supporters:[10]

> Made redundant from senior position . . . still enjoyed mainstream support and respect from colleagues, peers and customers . . . except that they were hesitant to show support once it was known that I was being made redundant.

According to Whittle et al. (2007), the point of transition is a trigger-point at which trans-employees are likely to face inequality and discrimination. Rundall's data supports this, as 68.2 per cent of respondents felt they were treated differently by some or all members of the workplace after announcing their intention to, or commencement of, transition. An overwhelming number of these participants reported negative treatment. The following are participant's examples of this:

> Demoted through three levels of management.
>
> (MTF respondent, age 40–49)

> Made redundant.
>
> (FTM participant, age 30–39)

Treated as a joke, gossiped about.

> (Woman with a trans-background, age 40–49)

People were ok to my face but some were nasty behind my back.

> (Woman with a trans-background, age 30–39)

Additionally, many participants reported that colleagues ignored their right to privacy:

People felt they had a right to know every fact about me post-transition.

> (MTF professional, age 50–59)

However, by no means all experiences were negative. A number of participants experienced supportive and positive treatment:

Everyone made a real effort.

> (MTF employee, age 50–59)

People say they prefer the new me because I'm so much happier.

> (MTF respondent, age 40–49)

A highly significant (P=0.000) statistical interaction was found between passing and feeling accepted as one's preferred gender. This interaction could be seen to 'highlight the overt and covert navigation of ["trans"] towards the established folds of [visual] gender-binarism, essentially constructing [gender-variance] as sous rature (under erasure)' (Rundall 2005: 17, drawing on Derrida 1998).

Passing constitutes a facet of (in)visibility via its utilisation of signifiers. Analysis of the data indicated that passing is incremental: 'Neither my face nor voice are sufficiently feminine to enable me to pass without some explanation' (gender-queer female-identified participant, age 40–49); 'On looks I pass, but my voice lets me down' (FTM respondent, age 30–39).[11] An aspect of incremental passing is temporal: 'I cannot tell potential employers about past work without outing myself' (MTF respondent, age 25–29); 'I do pass but my background is well known in my current workplace' (MTF employee, age 30–39). We also found that passing may reach its limit in the present or absent onlooker's misuse of a pronoun, or divulgence of information: 'I pass okay, but my confidentiality was broken by my manager' (woman with a trans-background, age 40–49); 'Using the telephone sometimes raises questions in other people's minds about my gender' (MTF participant, age 50–59). Vecchielti (2008) conceives of passing as a structure of incremental signifiers, which exist in competition with opposing signifiers. Therefore, just as passing is incrementally assembled, it can also be incrementally disassembled. We take this approach in this chapter.

Whittle (2006; Whittle et al. 2007), amongst others, states that trans-women are more likely to experience discrimination or difficulty as they are less likely to pass than their transmale counterparts. The findings of this study highlight the differing extent to which (in)visibility may impact upon transmale and transfemale employees. The data showed that there is a difference in reported levels of passing between transmen and transwomen. These are compared in the following tables (Table 6.4 and Table 6.5).

Table 6.4   Comparison of Transmale and Transfemale Respondents' Self-Reported Passing Physically at Work

Pass Physically	FTM/Man with a trans-background	MTF/Woman with a trans-background
All of the time	76.9%	42.9%
Most of the time	11.5%	36.5%
Some of the time	7.7%	11.1%
Rarely	0%	1.6%
I do not think I pass at this time	3.8%	3.2%
I do not aim to pass at this time	0%	4.8%
Total	100%	100%

Table 6.5   Comparison of Transmale and Transfemale Respondents' Self-Reported Passing Vocally at Work

Pass Vocally	FTM/Man with a trans-background	MTF/Woman with a trans-background
All of the time	73.1%	23.8%
Most of the time	3.8%	38.1%
Some of the time	11.5%	19%
Rarely	3.8%	7.9%
I do not think I pass at this time	7.7%	7.9%
I do not aim to pass at this time	0%	3.2%
Total	100%	100%

The majority of participants (84.8 per cent) stated that where possible, they made use of socially recognised gendered signifiers to pass physically or express their gender-identity. For example, these participants commented:

> If I cut my hair and didn't wear makeup I might not pass as well.
> (MTF employee, age 30–39)

> I wear a shirt and tie at work. I keep my hair cropped very short and I'm trying to grow facial hair.
> (FTM professional, age 40–49)

The positive or negative responses of others may be seen to navigate and police trans-employees in their presentation:

> Avoiding ridicule and possible physical violence makes me consider using recognised gender signifiers just to have an easier life.
> (MTF respondent, age 40–49)

Several participants remarked that when visible, their gender-diversity had an unsettling effect on others.

> People feel more comfortable if they don't get mixed messages. I prefer to make others feel comfortable. When I first transitioned the message was obviously very mixed and it did cause difficulties for me.
> (MTF participant, age 60–64)

Like nontrans-employees, trans-employees express and present themselves through a societally defined pallet of cues. This research found that over half of the respondents initially utilise more determinate and iconic representations associated with their preferred gender, but gradually decrease emphasis on these, as they feel increasingly secure in their position as one of the many diverse individuals who make up their preferred gender cohort. Similarly, Hines (2007) found that during their Real Life Experience, transwomen feel bound by prescriptive gender ideals espoused by Gender Identity Clinics, but felt less need to adhere to these ideals post-transition.

> Initially I had very short hair to encourage people to see me as a man. Now I don't worry if my hair gets a bit long.
> (Man with a trans-background, age 50–59)

> I rely on [socially recognised gender stereotypes/signifiers] less, and bring my own personality out more. However, I feel this has to be within acceptable limits.
> (Transman, age 40–49)

Here, this transman acknowledges that despite a decrease in his reliance on more determinate representations of gender, he continues to feel navigated and policed in his use of signifiers by notions of 'limits' to acceptable gender representation.

INCLUSION AND (IN)VISIBILITY IN THE WORKPLACE

We have split the workplace into formal and informal situations for the purposes of analysing and deconstructing participants' self-reported experiences of inclusion and exclusion. The formal situation is taken to be the standard work environment. Informal situations include networks like the 'grapevine' or 'gossip-circles.' Inclusion or exclusion is dependent upon the present or absent onlooker's acceptance of the trans-individual's (in)visibility. The interaction between participants feeling their gender-identity is accepted by others, and participants, feeling included in the workplace, was found to be highly significant ($P=0.000$).

Formal Situations

Many participants' experiences in the formal work environment (including job interviews) showed that feelings of inclusion are frequently reliant upon the absent or present onlooker's interpretation of their identity. Here, intertextually, acknowledgement resituates this man with a trans-background (age 25–29) from a position of différance to identity:

> I was seen as weird and people were clearly uncomfortable when I looked androgynous at job interviews during my early stages of transition . . . Once I reached the point of passing consistently, people became more comfortable around me and much more accepting and friendly towards me as they saw me simply as an ordinary young man.

This is not to say that the visibility of an individual's gender-diversity is a precursor to exclusion. The following is an MTF professional's (age 40–49) positive experience of inclusion despite the visibility of her gender-diversity:

> I am 100 per cent accepted as a woman—the fact I was born with a penis is irrelevant to that. More, as people know about the changes I am going through they are very helpful in accommodating my wish to keep my workload below about 50 hours a week until after surgery, even though that means them taking up some of the burden themselves.

Despite possibly dissonant visual cues and knowledge of her gender-diversity, colleagues actively chose to acknowledge this trans-employee's gender, thus demonstrating the bipartite agency of (in)visibility. One could suggest that when others accept an individual's gender-identity, despite full knowledge of that person's gender-diversity, a greater feeling of inclusion is engendered. Previous empirical research suggests that individuals who succeed in getting support in the workplace whilst undergoing transition may find their employment life easier in the long run (Whittle 2002: 102). Despite this, many of the respondents who have a choice present as stealth. However, it is important to bear in mind that presenting as stealth at work is never a secure position because the (in)-visibility of one's gender-diversity is constantly subjected to the potential of re-interpretation:

> When I worked part-time at another school in the second year of my transition, initially no-one knew about my transition and so I was treated very warmly until an advisory teacher spilt the beans, and people suddenly went quiet when I entered the staff room.
>
> (Woman with a trans-background, age 40–49)

Thus from a place of identity, the interpretation of the present or absent onlooker can at once resituate the trans-individual to a place of différance. When faced with exposure of this kind, the data showed that many trans-employees feel that they have no option but to leave their job and seek employment elsewhere:

> If I get outed in any given work or social group, I have to move on.
>
> (MTF employee, age 40–49)

Informal Situations

As genderist (Hill and Willoughby 2005) and transphobic discrimination are prevalent in the UK workplace (Whittle et al. 2007), of those participants who are able, many present as stealth in the workplace. Here we see an MTF individual's (age 50–59) self-reported experience of this:

> An object of fascination and certainly of ridicule by most senior managers (all male). Everybody wanted to talk to me; I became their 'toy,' something that they could talk about to their friends. Reborn after redundancy, moving into work arenas where nobody knew of me and I passed muster. I was truly accepted, respected and have never looked back.

However, as we have already seen, (in)visibility is constantly subject to the potential of reinterpretation. In the following case, knowledge held by work colleagues was disclosed during informal situations exterior to the work environment:

Work colleagues in other departments have disclosed my trans-history to their friends if they meet me outside of work e.g.: pub/bar.

(MTF participant, age 50–59)

Many respondents elaborated that they felt included because they are treated as their preferred or legally acquired gender in informal situations, and that inclusion in informal interactions and situations cemented a feeling of acceptance at work. For example, many transwomen reported they felt accepted when included in conversations that they had been excluded from pre-transition:

The girls at work now accept me as one of them, and have no problem in discussing 'women's problems' with me.

(Woman with a trans-background, age 40–49)

In the following quotation, an MTF respondent (age 30–39) compares her experiences of inclusion in informal situations at her new job where she is stealth at work, with similar situations at her old job where she was visibly gender-diverse.

Women will discuss topics such as menstruation, sex, childbirth etc that they would not have done in the job I transitioned in. Similarly, men at my current school will be 'flirtatious' and 'chivalrous' in a way that men at my previous school didn't.

Our findings suggest that positive interactions may be seen to uphold and strengthen identity through 'conversation' between social agents, as Foucault theorised (Foucault, in Rabinow 1997). The following table (Table 6.6) compares transmen's and transwomen's levels of inclusion in informal situations.

Table 6.6 Comparison of Transmen's and Transwomens's Levels of Inclusion in Informal Situations

Levels of Inclusion/Exclusion	FTM/Man with a trans-background	MTF/Woman with a trans-background
Actively included	42.9%	49.1%
Mostly included	19%	25.5%
Mostly excluded	4.8%	10.9%
Actively excluded	9.5%	3.6%
We all continue as before	23.8%	10.9%
Total	100%	100%

When combining 'actively' and 'mostly' included, and 'mostly' and 'actively' excluded from Table 6.6, we find that 74 per cent of transwomen feel included in the workplace, whereas 61.9 per cent of transmen feel included. However when viewed in relation to passing, we see that 73.1 per cent of transmen pass physically all of the time, and 76.9 per cent pass vocally all the time.[12] However, 42.9 per cent of transwomen pass physically all the time, and 23.8 per cent pass vocally all the time. The interaction of this data strongly suggests that feelings of inclusion are not related to passing. Therefore we can intimate that although presentation as stealth in the workplace can lead to a greater feeling that one's gender-identity is accepted, it does not lead to feelings of inclusion; as illustrated in the following quotation:

> Whenever I have joined an existing team, or another person has joined my team, I have always told my team colleagues of my trans status. I have always had positive reactions in those circumstances, and, in a few cases, this has led to lasting friendships being formed.
>
> (MTF employee, age 50–59)

Despite perhaps dissonant cues or existing knowledge, these present or absent onlookers accepted this MTF employee (age 50–59). Furthermore, we suggest that in the wider context, it is not passing that leads to feelings of inclusion, but rather the present or absent onlooker's acceptance of the trans-individual, regardless of gender-diversity.

DISCRIMINATION AND (IN)VISIBILITY

Although the data shows that not all of the trans-employees with visible aspects of their gender-diversity faced discrimination at work, over half of respondents (57.8 per cent) reported negative experiences in the workplace, including harassment and, in several cases, abuse. The data highlighted the pervasive nature of trans-discrimination in the employment sphere, and we found that, as with inclusion, discrimination was contextually and situationally specific. In addition, our research found that on average 75.3 per cent of participants transitioned, began transitioning, or intend to transition, whilst at work. Concomitantly, 73.9 per cent of participants had changed their job, position, or sector of employment since starting to transition or transitioning. In many cases, experiences of discrimination navigated respondents to change or leave employment:

> Having been booted out of my job because I was transitioning, I realised that my only chance of survival was to be self-employed.
>
> (MTF respondent, age 40–49)

Discrimination is seen to have a policing and navigating affect on the trans-employee's colleagues and clients as well as on the trans-employee themselves, as seen earlier in this chapter. Furthermore, we suggest that the enactment of policing takes place on both conscious and unconscious levels. Indeed, the data shows that the perceived 'unsettling' of the gender binary in the workplace by the trans individual can create an anxiety that inculcates a 'violent' response from colleagues and employers. In an effort to restore 'normality' to the work environment, and to the perceived 'face' of their company to those external to it, they are motivated to discriminate. This MTF participant (age 50–59) reports that she was:

> Told not to allow other organisations or customers to see me. Made redundant.

In a separate, but not isolated, case, after an MTF employee (age 50–59) announced her intention to transition, management relentlessly harassed her in an attempt to force her from their employ (we discuss the significant and under-researched gulf between legislation and practice in the following text). Although she has won her case each time because the law is on her side, this kind of sustained harassment and discrimination is likely to take its toll:

> A petition was circulated . . . to ban my access to the Ladies changing rooms/toilet . . . Local management then tried to dismiss me for not declaring I was taking hormones on my medical application . . . Management tried this year to dismiss me on medical grounds [for a separate medical condition] . . . They've tried to start disciplinary action again . . . but backed off when I confronted them. I expect them to try again.

Furthermore, another MTF participant (age 50–59) reports that she was made redundant because management:

> . . . didn't want a transsexual to be the public face of the company.

Many trans-employees lost their jobs at the trigger-point of transition:

> I began transitioning . . . was forced out via redundancy.
> (FTM respondent, age 40–49)

> Public hate campaign forced out of work.
> (MTF individual, age 40–49)

In the following case, this FTM participant (age 30–39) was only able to regain employment once the 'unsettling' presence of his gender-diversity was no longer visible:

I was sacked and then stayed unemployed until I had transitioned enough to re-enter teaching.

In addition to those trans-employees whose employers moved to dismiss them as soon as they announced their intention to/began to transition, our data presented a number of instances where employers appeared to initially support the trans-employee. However, having been seen to be inclusive, after a period of between six and eighteen months, employers moved to either dismiss the trans-employee, force them to resign, or to accept redundancy. This woman with a trans-background's (age unspecified) experience is just one example of this:

> Senior management at my company started to bully and belittle me (over six months after my formal transition) . . . they were starting to make me ill, and I eventually resigned. My confidence and self-esteem were badly affected.

A statistically significant interaction was found between whether participants passed, and the types of negative experiences they reported due to their trans-identity or history (P=0.021). Table 6.7 presents the data from which the calculation was drawn. The result that passing impacted on the types of negative treatment experienced by trans-employees supports the notion that the policing of gender, and its expression, are both multifaceted, and contextually relative.

Fear of discrimination and negative reprisals were a major navigating and policing factor relating to whether participants felt able to express their gender-identity in the workplace, and whether they sought to hide their trans status and/or gender-diverse history, if that option was available to them. This MTF participant (age 40–49) says:

> Basically if I get outed in any given work or social group I have to move on. The level of transphobia in society is very high and it is more important that I earn a living than that I make a martyr of myself.

This woman with a trans-background (age 40–49) has mixed feelings about choosing to be stealth:

> Going through transition is a strange thing, because you don't 'come out,' you 'go in'—after transition your status has to be covered up, unlike GLB people who can be open about their history without creating problems. Trans-people still need to melt away into society, but changes like the GRA will only happen if some trans-people stand up, this is the dilemma. I'm afraid that personally I intend to try to melt away, even if I feel guilt about not supporting the trans community.

Table 6.7   Types of Discriminatory / Negative Workplace Experiences Reported by the Participant Cohort

Types of discrimi-natory/negative experiences reported	Percentage of participant cohort	Percentage of FTM/Man with a trans-background respondents	Percentage of MTF/Women with a trans-background respondents
Being ignored/given silent treatment	22.2%	28.6%	20.3%
Having work related requests constantly unfulfilled	16.7%	23.8%	14.1%
Being the focus of comments/gossip	41.1%	42.9%	40.6%
Bullying/harassment	20%	19%	21.9%
Work criticised unfairly/ unjustified complaints	25.6%	19%	28.1%
Verbal abuse	14.4%	9.5%	15.6%
Threatened with sexual abuse	0%	0%	0%
Sexual abuse	1.1%	0%	1.6%
Threatened with physical abuse	4.4%	0%	6.3%
Physical abuse	2.2%	0%	3.1%
Other	5.6%	4.8%	4.7

However, it is worth reiterating at this juncture, that passing is incremental, as explained previously, and is subject to physical, temporal, and situational factors, and therefore does not preclude discrimination. An individual's gender-diversity is constantly subject to the potential of reinterpretation, and therefore to the possibility of discrimination. Here, a man with a trans-background's (age 40–49) experience of being outed 20 years after transition highlights this:

> I had to have a CRB check done and the CRB told my personnel manager who told my boss. I was called a 'pervert' and made to feel uncomfortable in my job. The union rep was unsupportive and equally

verbally insulting. I felt that I had no option but to accept a package that was presented for me to leave with a payment of two months' salary and the promise of a good reference. I had not done anything wrong, except not tell my boss [about my transition] (after 20 years post-op).

In addition to those who lose their jobs, there are those who face more insidious levels of discrimination on a daily basis, as this woman with a trans-background (age 40–49) explains: 'I was initially ostracised. Over time, bullying and harassment became more subtle.' A transman (age 40–49) reports that he was: 'so severely bullied by staff that I was fired because of the amount of sick leave I was taking.' This FTM participant (age 30–39) simply says: 'not everyone has to go through all this crap and carve a career at the same time.' As deprivation through discrimination continues to effect trans-employees, protections are crucial, as detailed in the following subsection.

PROTECTION AND (IN)VISIBILITY

There have been several recent legislative changes to afford protection and recognition to those trans-individuals who conform to the medico-legal definition of 'transsexual,' both in the workplace and within their lives overall.[13] These include: The GRA 2004; The Employment Equality (Sex Discrimination) Regulations 2005; The Equality Act 2006; The Public Sector Gender Equality Duty 2006; The Sex Discrimination (Amendment of Legislation) Regulations 2008. All of these pieces of legislation are built on the bedrock of the groundbreaking ruling of the European Court of Justice in the case of *P v S and Cornwall County Council* (1996) which stated that it was illegal to discriminate against an employee because they 'intended to undergo, were undergoing, or had undergone, gender reassignment treatment.' The Gender Recognition Act 2004 has the most far-reaching implications of the aforementioned legislative changes, as it enables trans-individuals to be recognised as their preferred gender, and 'acquire' it, for all purposes under the law.[14] Once in receipt of a Gender Recognition Certificate (GRC), trans-individuals are granted a birth certificate in their new gender (Gender Recognition Panel 2008), and will no longer be 'outed' as a matter of course when required to present such documentation to their employer. Many of the respondents spoke positively about what the GRA means for them:

> Someone's right to employment and respect should not depend upon their ability to pass and that is why the legal protections offered by the GR Act are so important. Trans people have a lot to offer in the work place and a person's trans status should not be, and need not be, a barrier to them succeeding in the work place.
>
> (Woman with a trans-background, age 30–39)

Furthermore, this FTM's (age 30–39) response is representative of many responses:

> Great peace of mind, feeling safer in the workplace, knowing that I can apply for new jobs without having to reveal my trans status (which has nothing to do with the job at hand), unless I choose to reveal it, knowing that if I ever come up against a problem, I have some legal ground to fall back on, and most of all, having a proper birth certificate that I can provide when asked for.

However, whilst legislation gives discrimination a context from which trans-employees may seek recourse, it does not in itself prevent discrimination, as detailed previously. This has been recognised over the years by trans academics, activists, and organisations (Press for Change; Whittle 2002). Additionally, it is important to recognise that the aforementioned legal changes are largely due to the efforts of an increasingly visible and recognisable trans community within the UK. Indeed, without this increasing visibility, and without trans-individuals presenting a human face to gender-diversity, many of these changes could not have occurred. Table 6.8 shows that despite the many trans-individuals who choose, where the option is available to them, to present as stealth, many felt that a visible trans community was important.

Although many trans-employees themselves do not feel able to be visibly gender-diverse, several participants expressed inner conflict, as demonstrated by this MTF employee (age 40–49):

> I wish that I could do more for the trans community, but I have to constantly make choices between being honest about what I am and being able to earn a living. I have children to support . . . and they come first.

Table 6.8   Distribution of the Importance that Respondents' Placed on a Visible Trans Community

Importance of the Trans Community Being Visible in Society	Percentage of participants
Very important	39.8%
Somewhat important	31.2%
Don't mind	12.9%
Unimportant	7.5%
Would prefer the trans community to be invisible	8.6%

Overall, the data showed that the majority of participants feel it is important to have a collective 'face' to represent a visible 'trans community' and signify their presence within society.

A key aspect of (in)visibility is the interlocution between the agency of the trans-individual and the agency of the absent or present 'onlooker,' who chooses to use their agency to either accept or reject the trans-individual's signifier-led identity. However, fear that others will use their agency to discriminate and persecute, instead of to support and protect, prevents many of those trans-employees who have a choice, from being open about their trans status. An example of this is provided by this MTF participant (age 40–49) who is able to, and does, present as stealth. This is her experience pre-GRA:

> I did not declare my status unless I was required to produce my birth certificate. On occasions that I did, I did not get further than interviews for jobs.

Another respondent, a woman with a trans-background (age unspecified), reports her, by no means isolated, experience of transition at work:

> I was left to announce my transition to work colleagues, support staff, and outside agencies. The company took very few steps to make it easier for me. In hindsight they expected me to struggle and fail, and give up and resign. But I was successful and this forced their hand and they commenced tactics of bullying and intimidation so I would resign. After six months this is what I did.

Nevertheless, of those who have been open about their status, either through choice (or lack thereof), some have experienced a positive response, as is the case with this FTM employee (age 30–39):

> I have been quite involved with the trans community . . . Often we, as a community, do not offer others the chance to accept us as we hold fears—not without reason—of rejection and ostracisation. That balance of trust and fear has been interesting to work with and I have often been surprised how accepting others are.

The data found that participants' feelings of protection were significantly interlinked both with feeling supported, and feeling accepted as their preferred gender, in the workplace. Feelings of protection and support differed in relation to the different groups of people who impact upon trans-employees' work life, as demonstrated by Table 6.9. This table provides an indication that despite legislation, which in principle provides protection to trans-employees, many employees are in fact unsure of receiving these protections in the event of transphobic abuse from customers or clients. This is apposite because trans-employees may face significant discrimination from those outside the core team, as illustrated by the following example provided by a gender-queer, female-identified employee (age 40–49):

> The worst aspects are not colleagues but members of the public and subcontractors with whom I have to come into contact. The general public are generally rude, abusive, and unpleasant and make my job harder than it should be.

These results highlight the uncertain and potentially precarious situation trans-employees may feel themselves to be in if they experience transphobic discrimination from customers and clients. In addition, Rundall's (forthcoming) research found that 67.7 per cent of participants stated that their workplace had no policies or procedures in place to protect trans-employees. Research conducted by Whittle (2000; et al. 2007) highlights employers' continued slow response regarding necessary changes to policy and practice, despite legal obligations. Indeed, Rundall's research conducted with business Human Resources and Equality Officers, found that some employers are unclear about their obligations under new legislation regarding the protection of trans-employees. For example, several organisations stated that they require transitioning employees to be in receipt of a GRC in order to change their name and gender details at work. This is a gross misinterpretation of the GRA 2004. In erroneously denying employees the right to make these changes at work without a GRC, employers are essentially preventing employees from carrying out the necessary processes and changes that are an essential prerequisite of a GRC.[15] This supports difficulties raised by trans-people in Whittle et al. (2007: 41).

Although 'transsexual' employees are afforded legal protection in the employment sphere, less than half of the participant's employers included

Table 6.9 Percentages of Participants Who Felt Protected by their Employer from the Prejudice of Transphobia of: Colleagues, Employees, and Customers/Clients

	Percentages of participants who feel protected by their employer from the prejudice or transphobia of:		
	Colleagues	Employees (if participant is in supervisory position)	Customers/ clients
Yes	58.7%	60%	47.8%
Unsure	25.3%	25.71%	37.7%
No	16%	14.29%	14.5%

'gender-identity' in their Equal Opportunities and Diversity Statement. Indeed, even fewer implemented this protection through the use of diversity-training to make members of the workforce aware of issues faced by trans-employees. This lack on the part of employers constitutes a tacit consent to discriminatory behaviours. Targeted research is needed to investigate why, despite existing protections, many employers continue to fail to protect and support their gender-diverse employees. This research deficit has also been noted in other recent research (Whittle et al. 2007).

CONCLUSION

In writing this chapter we have addressed a recognised shortfall of empirical sociological research in the study of trans-employees in the UK. We have argued that the experiences of trans-employees in UK workplaces are shaped by their invisibility or visibility as gender-diverse individuals, and have identified the categories of inclusion, discrimination, and protection as the areas in which this is most explicitly illustrated. In conceptualising (in)visibility, we have explicated the bipartite agency of (in)visibility, incremental passing, and the mutable condition of (in)visibility relative to its constant subjection to the potential of reinterpretation, thus acknowledging that stealth is a situation of insecurity. Moreover, we have found that although presentation as stealth attempts to guard against discrimination, it does so at the risk of constant exposure, and at the expense of inclusion. Our analysis of the data found that despite greater risk of discrimination, those who do not pass experience a greater sense of inclusion.

Our findings are significant because they highlight restrictions to inclusion and protection faced by employees who may be set apart by: their history; perceptions of their gender; or their physical presentation. Such findings also have wider implications for inclusivity in the UK with regards to identity, intersectionality, agency, and debates surrounding gender expression as a whole. The egregious and pervasive nature of transphobic discrimination in the work place, despite legal protections, is deplorable. Further research is needed to discover why employers continue to fail trans-employees in this area. Rundall (forthcoming) examines the significant gulf between legislation and practice, via the responses of a limited number of business and trade-union equality and human resources managers. However, the topic warrants a much larger informant cohort, and this is something we seek to address in future research.

NOTES

1. The Sex Discrimination (Gender Reassignment) Regulations 1999.
2. Whittle et al. (2007) is the most up-to-date study of trans-individual's experiences in the UK with which to compare our findings.

3. Applicants must prove they have lived as their preferred gender for two years prior to applying for gender recognition (Gender Recognition Panel 2008), including at work. The 'Real Life Experience' (fully living in role) is a prerequisite of surgical treatments (GIRES 2008b: 11).
4. Once in receipt of a GRC, transsexual individuals 'can enjoy the rights and responsibilities appropriate to their acquired gender' (Gender Recognition Panel 2008).
5. After writing this chapter we found that the term '(in)visibility' has previously been used quite differently to our usage by Zitzelsberger (2005) to discuss embodiments of women with physical disabilities and differences.
6. As 'a [transsexual] person . . . feels a consistent and overwhelming desire to transition and fulfil their life as a member of the opposite gender' (Gender Trust 2008).
7. The diagnosis required by the GRP is 'a strong and persistent cross-gender identification' (Whittle et al. 2007).
8. Stealth: where a person lives as their preferred/acquired gender, and withholds their trans-status or history from others.
9. Although small in terms of the estimated trans-population of 21:100,000, i.e. 10,500 people (GIRES 2008a), the sample does provide an indication of trends in trans-employees' experience.
10. No names are used in this chapter due to anonymous participation.
11. The concept of incremental passing is drawn from Vecchielti 2008.
12. See Tables 6.4 and 6.5.
13. The diagnosis required by the GRP is 'a strong and persistent cross-gender identification' (Whittle et al. 2007).
14. Once in receipt of a GRC, transsexual individuals 'can enjoy the rights and responsibilities appropriate to their acquired gender' (Gender Recognition Panel 2008).
15. Applicants must prove they have lived as their preferred gender for two years prior to applying for gender recognition (Gender Rocognition Panel 2008), including at work. The 'Real Life Experience' (fully living in role) is a prerequisite of surgical treatments (GIRES 2008b: 11).

REFERENCES

Butler, J. (1990) *Gender Trouble: Feminism and the Subversion of Identity*, New York: Routledge.
Cromwell, J. (1999) *Transmen and FTMs: Identities, Bodies, Genders and Sexualities*, Chicago: University of Illinois Press.
Derrida, J. (1998 [1976]) *Of Grammatology*, trans. G. Spivak, Baltimore: The John Hopkins University Press.
Ekins, R. and King, D. (2006) *The Transgender Phenomenon*, London: Sage Publications Ltd.
The Employment Equality (Sex Discrimination) Regulations (2005). http://www.opsi.gov.uk/si/si2005/20052467.htm (accessed 12 August 2006).
The Equality Act (2006) http://www.opsi.gov.uk/acts/acts2006/pdf/ukpga_20060003_en.pdf (accessed 13 January 2007).
Foucault, M. (1997 [1984]) 'Sex, power and the politics of identity', in P. Rabinow (ed.) *Ethics: Subjectivity and Truth*, New York: New Press.
The Gender Recognition Act (GRA) (2004) http://www.opsi.gov.uk/acts/acts2004/ukpga_20040007_en_1 (accessed 5 July 2006).

The Gender Recognition Panel (GRP) (2008) http://www.grp.gov.uk/ (accessed 5 July 2006).

The Gender Trust (2008) http://www.gendertrust.org.uk (accessed 5 July 2006).

GIRES (2008a) *Gender Dysphoria, Transsexualism and Transgenderism: Incidence, Prevalence and Growth in the UK and the Implications for the Commissioners and Providers of Healthcare.* http://www.gires.org.uk/prevalence. php#LBGTSummit (accessed 12 November 2008).

———. (2008b) *Guidance for GPs, Other Clinicians and Health Professionals on the Care of Gender Variant People* Department of Health. http://www.dh.gov. uk/en/Publicationsandstatistics/Publications/PublicationsPolicyAndGuidance/ DH_084919 (accessed 2 October 2008).

Hill, D. and Willoughby, B. (2005) 'The development and validation of the genderism and transphobia scale', *Sex Roles*, 53: 531–544.

Hines, S. (2007) *TransForming Gender: Transgender Practices of Identity, Intimacy and Care*, Bristol: Policy Press.

Hird, M. J. (2000) 'Gender's nature: intersexuals, transsexuals and the "sex"/"gender" binary', *Feminist Theory*, 1(3): 347–364.

Kessler, S. and McKenna, W. (1978) *Gender: An Ethnomethodological Approach*, New York: John Wiley and Sons Ltd.

———. (2000) 'Who put the "trans" in transgender? Gender theory and everyday life', *International Journal of Transgenderism*, 4(3).http://www.symposion. com/ijt/gilbert/kessler.htm (accessed 2 October 2006).

Lorber, J. (1994) *Paradoxes of Gender*, New Haven: Yale University Press.

Monro, S. (2000) 'Theorizing transgender diversity: towards a social model of health', *Sexual and Relationship Therapy*, 15 (1): 33–45.

Office of National Statistics (ONS) (2004) *Population Size: Ethnicity and Identity.* http://www.statistics.gov.uk/cci/nugget.asp?id=455 (accessed 17 October 2008).

———. (2008) *Population Estimates.* http://www.statistics.gov.uk/CCI/nugget. asp?ID=6 (accessed 20 October 2008).

Press for Change. http://www.pfc.org.uk (accessed 20 June 2008).

The Public Sector Gender Equality Duty (2006) http://www.equalityhuman-rights.com/en/publicationsandresources/Pages/gedcopEnglandandWales.aspx (accessed 20 June 2008).

P v S and Cornwall County Council (1996) IRLR 347 ECJ http://www.pfc.org.uk/ node/362 (accessed 3 June 2006).

Rundall, E. (2005) 'What is a "Lesbian?" The deconstructive constructive of the category "lesbian" by the British "lesbian" community', unpublished MA thesis, Oxford Brookes University.

———. (forthcoming) 'Transsexual people in UK workplaces: an analysis of transmen's and transwomen's experiences', unpublished thesis, Oxford Brookes University.

Sanger, T. (2008) 'Trans governmentality: the production and regulation of gendered subjectivities', *Journal of Gender Studies*, 17(1): 41–53.

The Sex Discrimination (Gender Reassignment) Regulations (SD[GR]R) (1999). http://www.pfc.org.uk/node/295 (accessed 12 July 2006).

The Sex Discrimination (Amendment of Legislation) Regulations (2008) http:// www.opsi.gov.uk/si/si2008/uksi_20080963_en_1 (accessed 26 October 2008).

Van Kesteren, P. J., Gooren, L. J. and Megens, J. A. (1996) 'An epidemiological and demographic study of transsexuals in the Netherlands', *Archives of Sexual Behavior*, 25(6): 589–600.

Vecchietti, V. G. (2008) *Disrupted Sign*, unpublished paper.

Weitze, C. and Osburg, S. (1996) 'Transsexualism in Germany: empirical data on epidemiology and application of the German Transsexuals' Act during its first 10 years', *Archives of Sexual Behavior*, 25(4): 409–425.

Whittle, S. (2000) 'Employment discrimination and transsexual people', *The Gender Identity Research and Education Society*. http://www.pfc.org.uk/files/ Employment_Discrimination_and_Transsexual_People.pdf (accessed 23 June 2007).

——. (2002) *Respect and Equality: Transsexual and Transgender Rights*, London: Cavendish Publishing Limited.

——. (2006) 'Foreword', in S. Stryker and S. Whittle (eds) *The Transgender Studies Reader*, New York: Routledge.

Whittle, S., Turner, L. and Al-Alami, M. (2007) 'Engendered penalties: transgender and transsexual people's experiences of inequality and discrimination', *The Equalities Review*. http://www.pfc.org.uk/files/EngenderedPenalties.pdf (accessed 12 February 2009).

Zitzelsberger, H. (2005) '(In)visibility: accounts of embodiment of women with physical disabilities and differences', *Disability and Society*, 20(4): 389–403.

Part III

Transforming Identities

7 The Impact of Race on Gender Transformation in a Drag Troupe

Eve Shapiro

Imagine a drag show. A huge drag show. It's the Saturday night show at the fifth annual International Drag King Conference, and there are more than 1,000 people in the audience. The lights are down; the crowd quiets after cheering loudly for the previous number and a drag king in an Afro, 'pimp' duds, and big gold jewellery steps on stage. The crowd cheers and then, as flickers of recognition cross the faces of audience members, some of the cheers stop, abruptly. There is a ripple of whispers moving through the crowd. 'He's in blackface!,' 'It's true, he's White!' 'His name is Stephon.' I approached him earlier today and he told me that he "identified" with African Americans even though he was White,' 'No Way!' Your neighbour turns and says, 'Hey, I think people should get to perform whatever they want.' As the music comes up, many audience members cheer and begin dancing along to the rap song Stephon lip-syncs. Others turn their back on the stage, hoping to register their dissent visibly. The song ends, some people cheer, others stay facing the back of the room. The next act comes on, and the show continues. Time passes, and later in the show a large drag troupe takes the stage. The Disposable Boy Toys (DBT) are introduced, and they file on stage, dressed in circus costumes with glitter mustaches and sequined dresses.

The performers are dressed as boys and girls, fags, femmes, and butches. The music comes up and a refrain from the film musical Moulin Rouge begins to play. The performers begin to lip-sync and dance as if they had just stepped out of a Toulouse-Lautrec painting. Quickly, the performers gather in a half circle and the music changes. The song 'Woman Lose Weight' by Slick Rik and Morcheeba begins to play and a White performer from this group comes on stage wearing an Afro wig and performing all the stereotypical 'gangster' moves. Pantomiming the ridicule of a full-bodied woman, the performer sings the lyrics, 'Look, fat chicks, I don't mean to sound rude/I tell her nice hit the gym and don't eat so much food,' and then a few lines later, 'The only thing left for me to do/Is to kill her.' As this performance is enacted centre stage, other characters on stage pantomime being 'audience' members, whose thoughts are flashed on the screen behind them. One performer looks toward the crowd in a distressed manner while his question is flashed on the screen: 'Why do White kings always choose fucked up hip-hop numbers?' The crowd roars with applause. Another performer steps toward the vignette, and the screen changes to express her thought: 'I can't believe that White king is wearing an Afro.' Another, 'If she's fat what does that make me?' and on through the song. Without knowing about Stephon's number beforehand, the Disposable Boy Toys have brought to the International Drag King Conference a number that calls performances out for being racist, misogynist, and fat-phobic; numbers like Stephon's. The connection between DBT's number and Stephon's earlier performance is not lost on anyone.

Current debates within the drag king community about race and performance—played out in the drag numbers described previously—reveal deep divides and tensions. Discussions about race have become more prevalent at drag shows and conferences in the United States, and in public forums and listservs that are part of the drag king community. For example, at the 2006 International Drag King Conference, participants organised a race caucus. As one of the founders of the conference stated in a public post about the caucus she helped organise,

> I thought not that many folks care to talk about race, racism and how both intersect with [the International Drag King Conference]. I was wrong. We had probably between 75 and 100 people there, and lots of them were White folks (something I also didn't expect).[1]

Simultaneously, performers and audience members have begun to speak out about the ways that racist performance affects them. The virulent debates have centred, in part, on issues of cultural appropriation and race, and have devolved into mudslinging accusations of 'censorship' and 'racism'. And, all the while, some drag performers—both part of these discussions and in performance communities not-engaged with these debates—claim their performances devoid of social (or racial) meaning. Reflecting similar debates about racism within the larger North American LGBT community (Berube 2003; Ward 2008), drag performers and communities are strongly divided. Some performances—almost exclusively White—assert that drag is, and should be, 'just fun'. Others assert that drag is a meaningful cultural production that is always already engaged in a political and racial project and that to not acknowledge this is to perpetuate racism. A number of scholars and performers have examined the public debates about race and performance, and race and drag more specifically. What I examine in this chapter are the meanings and implications of race and racialised drag on individual performers themselves (in terms of their own identity interrogation). In my larger research project I found that drag troupes had the potential to, but did not necessarily, facilitate individual identity changes among participants. Examining the Disposable Boy Toys, I found that the group's collective processes, performance environment, beliefs, and collective identity cultivated a space that encouraged and enabled identity shifts. What I assert, here, is that identity interrogation and change within DBT was mediated by race.

What I found as I analysed data from four years of participant observation and ethnographic data collection was that despite often explicit intentions otherwise, the Disposable Boy Toys troupe was a racialised space (and sometimes a racist one) that better fostered identity exploration and support for White members than people of colour in the group. Informed by Anglo-centric body and behaviour norms that manifested in the music, venue, and topic choices made by performers, and shaped by the segregated LGBT community within which the group arose, DBT functioned as a safe space where White participants engaged in a variety of masculinities and femininities with which they could identity. Simultaneously, however, members of colour often felt marginalised within the group and caught between DBT and the local queer people of colour community. As a product of these dynamics and the associated inability (or unwillingness) of DBT to change, people of colour moved through the group much faster and found the group less personally transformative than White members.

MAKING SENSE OF GENDER, RACE, AND DRAG PERFORMANCE

There is a fair amount of research that has examined whether and how race mediates identity change (Streitmatter 1988; Grove 1991; Stanley 2004) and on the intersections of race, class, and gender (Connell 1995; Anderson and Hill Collins 2003). Little work, however, has focused on the relationship between race and (trans)gender identity (change) (Halberstam 1997; Namaste 2000; Koyama 2006; DeVries 2007). For example, social psychological and medical literatures on how individuals come to define themselves as transgender (Bockting and Coleman 1992) focus primarily on the internalisation of an incongruent gender identity in childhood but ignore differences across race. In addition, this research, as well as the broader literature on gender identity and transgender individuals has been silently but pervasively focused on White MTFs and more recently FTMs in the US (Halberstam 1998; Dozier 2005; Schrock, Reid, and Boyd 2005). When scholarship has interrogated race it has tended to do so within the context of non-western, non-White cultures (Herdt 1996; Kulik 1998).

Over the past 25 years drag performance in the United States has been used pervasively by sociologists and queer theorists as evidence for the constructed nature of gender (Tewksbury 1994; Schrock et al. 2005), as a means for theoretical elaboration, as a display of the artistic vibrancy of GLBT communities (Newton 1972; Schacht 1998; Piontek 2002), and more recently as a politically significant discursive and cultural protest (Halberstam 1998; Munoz 1999; Rupp and Taylor 2003). The meaning of these public performances has been debated throughout this literature arguing either that drag challenges (Butler 1990) or reinforces (Dolan 1985; Lorber 1999) hegemonic gender structures.

Like the limited scholarship of race and racism within LGBT culture and cultural production (Rodriguez 2002; Moore 2006; Ward 2008), there is limited scholarship on drag and race. While some theorising has been done about the performativity of race and ethnicity (Swarr 2004), conceptualised as 'colonial mimicry' (Bhabha 1994), 'mimetic identification' (Modleski 1997) and 'ethnic drag' (Sieg 2002), little of this work has explored the intersection of race and gender performance. Some scholars have made sense of 'crossethniking' (Munoz 1999) as akin to cross-gender performance and as potentially cathartic. For example, Rupp and Taylor argue that intentional 'crossethniking' was popular and politicised by drag queens at the 801 Cabaret in Key West, Florida (2003: 114). Similarly Katrin Sieg (2002) examines the history of cross-racial drag in Germany and argues that 'ethnic drag', like gender drag, has been deployed to both reinforce and challenge racism and racial hierarchy. Others have asserted that cross-racial drag performance is simply a new form of blackface, ripe with the same racist intentions (Jindal 2004). Richardson, writing about blackface 'without corking up' as well as the explicit blackface performed by Stephon (as described before), argues that, 'racial appropriation and impersonation [is] enacted through the use of Black musical styles and dance throughout the majority of drag king performances' (2006). What Richardson points to is how much of drag king performance relies on hip-hop music and dance, even as the performance scene remains predominantly White.

Research on Whiteness points to how hegemonic social, cultural, and body norms take Whiteness as the unmarked but ever present default. Despite the long history of Black male-impersonators,[2] a history that is significantly different from that of White impersonators, contemporary drag king performance remains deeply but silently raced. In 'Mackdaddy, superfly, rapper: gender, race, and masculinity in the drag king scene,' Judith Halberstam (1997) argues that hegemonic cultural norms make performing White masculinity—the hegemonic empty category—difficult. She argues, that 'masculinity within the drag king act is always inflected by race, class, and gender and by the histories of different lesbian communities and their different relationships over time to butch-femme styles and to female masculinity in general' (Halberstam 1997: 106). What Halberstam points to is how drag king performances are always informed by racialised histories and tied up with White privilege.

Although contemporary research suggests that race matters significantly in the life experiences of transgender individuals (Namaste 2000; Roen 2001) and research has connected drag to personal identity change (Shapiro 2007; Regales 2008), research has not examined whether or how race might mediate these identity shifts. Building upon the previously described research, and in line with Seig's (2002) findings that 'ethnic drag' both reifies and challenges racial inequality, I assert that drag king communities and performances both deconstruct and reinforce gender and racial hierarchies. Moreover, the meaning and import of these performances—for performer and audience—is racialised and gendered.

THE DISPOSABLE BOY TOYS

This chapter draws on data from a case study of the Santa Barbara, California drag troupe, the Disposable Boy Toys.[3] Founded early in the US drag-king renaissance of the 2000s, DBT was unique in its explicit feminist and political commitments.[4] Between its debut in May 2000 and its last performance in August 2004, DBT grew from a five-person drag king group to a self-titled 'political feminist collective.' During this time 31 individuals joined the group, recruited from both the local state university and surrounding community. Members were high-school students and professionals, lesbian, bisexual, and queer identified, seasoned performers and novices, activist and apolitical, young and middle-aged, raised poor, working-class, and upper middle-class. Members ranged in age from 17–36 and 23 of them were White, five were multiracial, one was Black, one was Asian/Pacific Islander, and one was Latina.

The troupe quickly moved from performances of masculinity by woman-identified performers, to performances of masculinity and femininity by woman and transgender-identified individuals. Participants described their performative characters as drag kings, transgender kings and queens, and bio-queens (women performing femininity).[5] Performances were primarily lip-synced and included dancing and acting in an effort to tell stories about a variety of social issues including racism, misogyny and sexism, body fascism, gender and sexual non-conformity, and local and national politics. Over four years the troupe performed more than 100 numbers in shows across the United States at political rallies, drag conferences, bar shows, and university events.

Members of the Disposable Boy Toys were all female-bodied at birth and raised as women. Participants did, however, hold a range of gender identities that changed throughout their tenure. No member, at joining, had taken medical steps to change their gender (through hormones or surgery), although a few did so after joining the group. Some members engaged in gender performances in line with their real-life identities (for example female women performing femininities), and others performed genders with which they did not identify (for example transgender men performing femininity). Members had varying definitions of transgenderism, and not all considered doing drag part of a transgender community or identity. I define transgenderism as the desire to change one's sex or gender after birth through social or biomedical means. I define drag as the intentional performance of gender for an audience (regardless of one's own gender status), and recognise that some activists and scholars situate drag performers within the transgender spectrum and some do not.

While DBT began as a close-knit friendship network from the local state university, it quickly expanded beyond a singular group of people. The troupe was a vibrant performance community for three years with a mostly-stable group of performers. One of the unique characteristics of DBT, and something that proved significant in my analysis of gender, sexual, and political identity change (Shapiro 2007), was the community-focused orientation of the group. In its maturation the Disposable Boy Toys intentionally cultivated a social movement collective identity through group rehearsals, peer mentoring, feminist-inspired consensus decision-making, shared earnings (including tips), and community-building events and retreats. In social movements scholarship the shared sense of 'we–ness' in a group is conceptualised as collective identity (Taylor and Whittier 1992). DBT's diverse group practices cultivated this collective identity by distinguishing group members from other performers, building a shared analysis of gender and drag, and orienting drag performance toward challenging gender norms and social inequalities. The result was a group that purposefully engaged in political and personal activism around gender, sexuality, and progressive politics.

In describing DBT members, most participants mentioned the lack of racial diversity within the group and offered up a variety of explanations including the constrained nature of friendship circles, musical and political choices made by DBT, and racial divisions in the queer community. This racial homogeneity and unintentional racialisation is not unique to DBT (Lewis 2004), and the group remained predominantly White across its history. In total only seven of 31 members identified as people of colour and/ or as multiracial.

Triggered by a significant shift in membership, DBT spent much of Fall 2003 focused on internal group dynamics. The troupe held several teach-ins and retreats to talk about leadership and collectivity, race and racism, the politics of performance, and the future of the group. By early 2004 participation in the troupe was waning and individuals simply stopped volunteering for shows. Without formally disbanding the group never performed together as DBT after August 2004, although a number of performers continued to do drag together in Santa Barbara as well as in other cities across the United States.

As part of its political maturation, DBT as a group came to understand performances across race as politically problematic. Academic members drew on feminist theorising such as standpoint epistemology (Haraway 1991) that critiqued speaking for social positions other than one's own to talk to other participants about the politics of drag. They argued that performances can engage in cultural appropriation and that gender, race, and class are always in interlocking relationships of subordination and domination (Andersen and Hill Collins 2003). From this the group drew a distinction between performing gender, and performing race. Many members (or at least the most vocal ones) saw performances of race as fundamentally different from cross-gender performances. DBT's official position was that histories of racism (e.g. blackface) meant that performances of non-White identities by White performers would always be imbued with racism. That is, they asserted that power matters—that being female-bodied and performing masculinity and femininity was dramatically different from being White and performing Blackness. Within this framework that placed power and social location in the centre, it meant something different to perform 'up' (women performing masculinity, for example) than it did to perform 'down' (White performers doing Blackness, for example). Because of differences in social power and histories of cultural appropriation one was seen as critique and the other as racist entitlement.[6] DBT's engagement with the political import of drag led to their critique of other drag performers (king and queen), and ultimately the creation of the medley described at the start of this chapter.

It is interesting, however, to note that while DBT was conscious of avoiding explicit racist portrayals, members did not talk about how performance expectations for people of colour in the troupe were also racialised; how they were asked to perform Whiteness as part of this 'compromise.' As such, discussions about race and drag were conceived of as about White performers and non-White performances. Similarly, because people of colour in DBT almost always performed masculinity, little conversation happened around non-White femininities.

RACIAL TENSION WITHIN DBT

Bill Dagger, who was the only Black member of DBT and the only non-passing person of colour during his participation, described feeling caught between DBT and people of colour in the community. He attributed his conflict to the fact that:

> DBT has a real tension with people of colour, queers of colour. They go to the extent of specifically boycotting the shows, will not attend if they know that DBT is going to be there. [They] have said that to me; 'I love you but I refuse to be there if DBT's performing.' So, I think that DBT has a particularly high tension with queer people of colour in this town that they don't know that they have.

Shocking, here, is the fact that many in DBT were oblivious to the fact that communities of colour in Santa Barbara explicitly boycotted their drag shows. How can we make sense of a performance group that thought of itself as anti-racist but was viewed by some as racist in its performances and politics? Part of how White privilege manifested in DBT was through participants' ability and willingness to ignore community tensions around race and dismiss critiques of its racial politics. Certainly not all White members were oblivious to these tensions, and several members who were engaged in anti-racist activism outside of the group tried to actively work against this. Regardless, DBT was never able to successfully repair its relationship with people of colour in the community, and perception of the group as racist by some never truly shifted.

These differences generated tension within DBT; there were many internal meetings held to address how to increase diversity in the troupe, network with people of colour organisations, confront individual racism, and adopt an anti-racist platform. Virginia Dentata, a White, femme-identified performer, related that 'the conversations about race made a big impact on me because people were in such different places about what it meant to be a White anti-racist, how people understood racism and whether they thought it existed in the group.' Virginia Dentata went on in her interview to suggest that the array of opinions about race was similar to what you would find among any group of White people, but that the group's internal dynamics inhibited any real change.

> By the end I think the people who identified as anti-racist in a political way felt alienated and angry and I think the people who felt like they were being accused of being racist felt alienated and angry and I think there were at least four people in the group (of eight or ten at the time) who felt like that whole thing was bullshit and are still really angry about it. So I don't think anything positive came out of those talks.

It is interesting to note that perception of DBT's success in addressing racism varied widely. For many members DBT did a lot of important education within the group around race; some members shared that DBT was the first place they ever talked about racism. For others, DBT was less racially progressive than the anti-racist groups they were involved in. It would also be misleading to suggest that White DBT members were always cognisant of racism in their performances, or that they cared. Some White participants thought DBT had gone too far in its attention to race. For example, toward the end of the group's tenure two long-time performers wanted to do a parody of BDSM master/slave dynamics to the Britney Spears song 'I'm a Slave for You.' When they began to rehearse the number several members raised questions about the racial politics of the song. Their critique was that the history of slavery in the US made the song racist and un-reclaimable, particularly when sung by a White pop star and performed by two White drag performers. Other members disagreed and argued that the popularity of the song, the master/slave archetype in BDSM communities, and the use of camp would be enough to counter the history of slavery evoked in the song. The debate between group members grew more and more heated during the rehearsal, and accusations of censorship and racism flew. Those in favour of the song felt that race was being treated as a special case, and those against argued that cries of censorship were being used to shut down a discussion about political responsibility. While a group vote ultimately kept the number from the stage, the decision was not at all unanimous and became an ongoing source of tension and frustration.

This disagreement, and the many other similar discussions, reveals varying levels of engagement with anti-racist ideology or activism. These ongoing and unresolved tensions were part of the group's inability to change its racial politics or demographics successfully. While the troupe was diverse in many other respects the oppositional consciousness that developed in DBT was racialised. This, along with its image as a 'White group', worked to perpetuate racial homogeneity throughout its tenure.

IMPACT OF RACE ON IDENTITY TRANSFORMATION WITHIN DBT

While the homogeneity within DBT, especially around Whiteness, and the shared social location and experience that went along with racial identity, helped White members build solidarity with each other, this sameness excluded others. Much of what kept participants engaged and open to personal identity transformation was the shared sense of family and community. DBT could not provide a representative community or inclusive space for participants of colour however. Moreover, how the group's collective identity was racialised was often invisible to White members.

These racialised experiences of community and solidarity, combined with an attendant lack of engagement suggest that the shared sense of community was critical for identity transformation. What I found was that DBT fostered personal identity changes by cultivating a variety of intra-group mechanisms. By creating an environment that helped members imagine gender differently, provided social and support resources, created opportunities to play with and enact new genders, and validated new and transformed gender identities, DBT encouraged members to redefine their own gender. These gender identity shifts happened both within and across gender categories and were pervasive. There were 26 of 31 members who described significant shifts in their gender identity during participation in the group. For example, nine members shifted from naming themselves as exclusively female to more complex identity formations. Instead of female women, members came to call themselves genderqueer, FTM (female-to-male), and transgender.[7] White DBT members, however, disproportionately experienced these identity shifts. The way in which race matters becomes clearer when we look at each mechanism for change individually.

Imaginative Possibility

DBT provided the *imaginative possibility* of alternatives to binary sex and gender categories within participants themselves. Like the Internet as a place where individuals can try on new self-conceptions before transferring these identities to 'real-life' (Turkle 1995), DBT provided members with new identity repertoires and scripts to draw on in the (re)construction of personal gender identities. While these imaginaries are still informed by social norms, my interview and observational data clearly demonstrates that DBT expanded the possible ways of being gendered that members could imagine for themselves and others.

The genders that were imagined, however, were raced White and this racialised imagining—a product of White privilege—was unintentional but very real in its consequences. Nate Prince, for example, felt that the manner in which he was supposed to do gender according to the group did not reflect his own Asian Pacific Islander-inflected gender norms. He commented that,

> When I first joined DBT I noticed that members of DBT didn't realise that the kind of masculinity they wanted to perform was a certain kind of masculinity, that it was racialised; it was a White, western masculinity. I remember being told my very first practice, don't move your hips so much. I grew up around men who always knew how to move their hips.

These expectations constrained the gendered imaginings of the group and as such reinscribed Whiteness as the unmarked but meaningful norm (Piontek 2002). Performances of femininities were also limited in these ways. And yet, the invisibility of Whiteness hid these negotiations, as most performers who performed femininities were White. When people-of-colour did create numbers around feminine characters, the numbers were rarely performed. Moreover, this limited repertoire of imaginative femininities shaped the larger culture of DBT and its shows. The outcome of these racialised imaginings of masculinities and femininities was that the group did not offer members of colour new ways to imagine racialised genders with which they could identify. This made DBT a very different kind of exploratory space for members of colour, which inhibited the imaginative possibility mechanism for personal identity change.

Resources

In addition to offering new ways to think about gender, the Disposable Boy Toys provided members a bridge to other gender organisations and support services. Conceptualised in social psychology in a variety of ways, including as toolkits (Swidler 1986), I refer to the tools and education that DBT provided to members as *resources*. DBT was a place to learn about transgender identity and community as well as to develop new paradigms for conceptualising gender identity. However, the resources provided, organisations networked with, and relationships held were racialised. While DBT did work with some groups and organisations focused on people of colour, by and large its engagements were about White transgender issues and not about race or the relationship between race and gender. For example, while DBT had strong connections to local and regional GLBT organisations, its ties to services and organisations directed specifically at queer people of colour were much more limited. The lack of an intersectional analysis reinforced the idea that DBT was engaged in education and activism around gender, and gender alone. In addition, by working primarily with transgender organisations that were implicitly White-focused (DeVries 2007), DBT did not help members of colour develop personal connections to queer or transgender organisations that might have represented and served their needs in a more holistic manner. This indirect, institutional racism is similar to how racial segregation is perpetuated in other GLBT organisations (Ward 2008).

Opportunities for Enactment

Alongside imaginative possibility and resources, DBT offered members a safe place to do gender in new and redefined ways. Drawing on the long history of dramaturgical analogies for identity negotiation (Goffman 1959) and postmodernist arguments that identity is constituted performatively (Butler 1990), I argue that the opportunity for enactment was a significant collective mechanism for gender identity shifts. Across the board DBT performers described how learning to do different genders was profoundly transformative. Both woman and man identified performers described taking on and adopting new masculinities and femininities in their performance and within their own sense of self. However, DBT's choice to avoid non-White, race-specific music and characters meant that the opportunities members had to perform new genders were almost completely restricted to White masculinities and femininities. While many White members saw what they were doing as anti-racist at best, and as neutral at worst, members of colour felt the impact of these choices. Nate Prince reflected that, 'DBT was made up of nonracist people who took to heart the idea that White people should not be performing hip-hop, and I understood. But at the same time it inhibited me in what I wanted to do and what I could do.' For performers of colour like Nate, DBT's racial homogeneity placed him in a double bind wherein he could participate in group numbers depicting White masculinities and femininities, or perform alone. Given that most DBT performances were group numbers, the impact of this is significant.

If drag in DBT was a place to practice masculinities and femininities one might inhabit, and this practice was critical for fostering individual identity shifts, the lack of performances of non-White gender effectively blocked this mechanism for members of colour. As Nate commented, he was unable to perform identities that reflected who he was or might be. Even more importantly, these dynamics were often invisible to most White

DBT members. While the group felt welcoming to most White members, for some people of colour in DBT the constant debate about race and simultaneous lack of opportunities to perform non-White genders made DBT a racist and unsafe space for self-exploration.

Role Support

Finally, in addition to helping members imagine and enact new genders, and connect to local and regional resources, DBT actively worked to validate and support participants' gender choices. This 'role support' (McCall and Simmons 1966), reflected back to performers their new and/or redefined personal identities and in the process helped to solidify these changes. DBT members took seriously the idea that they had to help each other find acceptance and support, on both a personal and community level, for whatever gender they came to identify with. However, like other mechanisms, role support was more real, more significant for White members. In fact, some members of colour did not find the Disposable Boy Toys group to be a safe space at all. Indeed, Bill Dagger, the only non-passing person of colour in the group while he was a member found DBT an explicitly unsafe environment for self-exploration. That is, while he recognised how DBT made the Santa Barbara community more trans-friendly, he was unable to use the space to interrogate his own gender:

> [DBT] seems to have been and continues to be a really powerful place for people to come out as trans . . . Unfortunately, it has maintained itself as very White even though people of colour have come in and out of the troupe. So, I'm not sure it's providing that kind of support for people of colour to do that transitioning . . . DBT was not the place that I felt safe enough to explore gender issues.

What Bill Dagger highlights is how these mechanisms for gender identity change functioned differently for people of colour. While DBT did offer support for identity choices, its racialised environment and White collective identity did not lead to identity work for people of colour in the way that it did for White members.

CONCLUSION

Given all of these contradictions within DBT, how can we make sense of the group's engagement with race and the implications of this for individual members? What does it mean that the same group that would put on the national drag stage an explicit critique of racial appropriation and racism in drag, simultaneously maintained a predominantly White troupe that some community members and even participants viewed as racist? Certainly it is more complicated than viewing Stephon's blackface performance as racist and the Disposable Boy Toys group as well meaning but stuck within hegemonic power relations. For sure some participants were critical of DBT's racial politics, but others were not. Further, even those that turned a critical lens on the group often fell short; efforts to recognise overt racism were much more successful than efforts to locate and address White privilege or racism in the group or performances of often unmarked, but always racialised genders. The group struggled to make room for non-White genders and performers, and all the while maintained a collective identity rooted in White norms and identities. And these contradictions manifested within the group as well. In rehearsals, meetings, and retreats DBT members often struggled to make sense of their own choices as (intentionally or not) imbued with White privilege and sometimes racism. Ultimately these tensions led to the downfall of the troupe.

The import of these struggles around race extended beyond the boundaries of collective identity, however; they also impacted the personal identity development of participants. Most members of the Disposable Boy Toys—23 of 28 members interviewed—identified participation in the troupe as *the* cause of significant personal gender identity change. Indeed members jokingly referred to the group as a 'gateway drug' for gender non-conformity. Participants moved from claiming mostly normative gender identities in line with their assigned sex-category, to naming themselves using a wide range of complex counter-hegemonic masculine and feminine gender identities. With one exception the members for whom this was not true were people of colour. These individuals either didn't need DBT to serve that function, or they didn't feel it was a place where they could do identity work.

The racial identities of DBT members, group choices around music and performance styles, and the existing racial demographics of Santa Barbara maintained DBT shows, rehearsals, and collective identities as racialised spaces. The unintended but very real consequences of these choices were a lack of resonance for queers of colour in the group. My data suggests that the outcome of racialised performances, a White collective identity, and the lack of racial diversity was that the mechanisms that fostered identity shifts were mediated by race.

The White identities performed by DBT did not resonate in the same way with members of colour. The collective mechanisms for gender identity shift that I documented are not inherent in drag, but rather a product of DBT's political commitments to collectivity, feminist politics, and progressive activism. The oppositional community of DBT was a critical venue for personal identity negotiation around gender for some members. I conclude, however, that the importance of these mechanisms was mediated by race; people of colour did not experience DBT as a space to do identity work in the same way as did White members. I assert, then, that gender identity development is affected by racial demographics in an oppositional community (Masquesmay 2003). Just as Halberstam (1997) argued that race mattered in both the production and meaning of drag king performances, this data suggests that race mediates the individual effects drag may have. More specifically, while DBT facilitated identity shifts for almost all White members of the troupe, members of colour neither experienced the same connection to the group, nor manifested similar gender identity changes. These findings warrant ongoing research into the ways that race matters within both gender identity formation and negotiation and within drag performances and communities.

NOTES

1. From the International Drag King Conference archives. http://idkearchives. blogspot.com/2006/10/djs-post-idke-8-friday-conference.html (accessed 22 December 2008).
2. For example Florence Hines, Storme Delarverié, and Gladys Bentley.
3. This study was undertaken between July 2002 and September 2004. In addition to four years of participant observation of group rehearsals, performances, and meetings, I conducted semi-structured interviews with 28 current and past members of the troupe, analysed more than 200 hours of video-recorded performance and workshop events, and examined archival materials from DBT and IDKE. Interviews ranged between 90 and 210 minutes and were recorded and transcribed. An endeavour in feminist participatory research (Wolf 1996), and cognisant of my status as both insider and outsider (Naples 2003), this project was rooted in a modified grounded theory approach.
4. The late 1990s and early 2000s were a time of rapid growth in the North American drag king community. The first International Drag King Conference was held in October 1999, and DBT was founded shortly after.
5. In this chapter I use the chosen drag names and gender pronouns of performers. These sometimes, but not always, correspond to the gender identities of performers outside of drag.
6. Interestingly, most participants made sense of drag queen performance with more nuance, recognising that drag queening could be (but certainly wasn't always) progressive and feminist.
7. Participants defined these different gender identities in a variety of ways. In line with larger GLBT community namings, genderqueer was an oppositional identity used to resist the male/female, masculine/feminine gender binaries. Some members who saw themselves as moving from a feminine to masculine gender identity or from a female to a male body used the term 'FTM' to describe their gender. Transgendered participants usually identified as masculine or male, but were not currently interested in taking medical steps to alter their bodies while transsexual members were hoping to alter their bodies to bring their sex-category in line with their gender identity. Most broadly, 'transgender' was used by a variety of participants to describe personal gender non-conformity. This often overlapped with genderqueer and FTM identities.

REFERENCES

Andersen, M. and Hill Collins, P. (eds) (2003) *Race, Class, and Gender: An Anthology*, Belmont, CA: Wadsworth.
Bhabha, H. (1994) *The Location of Culture*, London: Routledge.

Berube, A. (2003) 'How gay stays white and what kind of white it stays', in M. Kimmel and A. Ferber (eds) *Privilege: A Reader,* Boulder: Westview Press.

Bockting, W. and Coleman, E. (eds) (1992) *Gender Dysphoria: Interdisciplinary Approaches in Clinical Management,* New York: Haworth Press.

Butler, J. (1990) *Gender Trouble: Feminism and the Subversion of Identity,* New York: Routledge.

Connell, R. (1995) *Masculinities,* Berkeley: University of California Press.

DeVries, K. (2007) 'Exclusion/inclusion in developing collective identity: the experience of black transgenders in the southern U.S.', unpublished thesis, Southern Illinios University.

Dolan, J. (1985) 'Gender impersonation onstage: destroying or maintaining the mirror of gender roles?' *Women and Performance: A Journal of Feminist Theory,* 2: 5–11.

Dozier, R. (2005) 'Beards, breasts, and bodies: doing sex in a gendered world', *Gender & Society,* 19(3): 297–316.

Goffman, E. (1959) *The Presentation of Self in Everyday Life,* New York: Doubleday.

Grove, K. J. (1991) 'Identity development in interracial, Asian/White late adolescents: must it be so problematic?' *Journal of Youth and Adolescence,* 20(6): 617–628.

Halberstam, J. (1997) 'Mackdaddy, superfly, rapper: gender, race and masculinity in the drag king scene', *Social Text,* 52/53: 53–79.

Halberstam, J. (1998) *Female Masculinity,* Durham, NC: Duke University Press.

Haraway, D. J. (1991) *Simians, Cyborgs, and Women: The Reinvention of Nature,* Routledge: New York.

Herdt, G. (ed.) (1996) *Third Sex, Third Gender: Beyond Sexual Dimorphism in Culture and History,* New York: Zone Books.

Jindal, P. (2004) 'Sites of resistance or sites of racism?' in M. Bernstein Sycamore (ed.) *That's Revolting! Queer Strategies for Resisting Assimilation,* New York: Soft Skull Press.

Koyama, E. (2006) 'Whose feminism is it anyway? The unspoken racism of the trans inclusion debate', in S. Stryker and S. Whittle (eds) *The Transgender Studies Reader,* New York: Routledge.

Kulik, D. (1998) *Travesti: Sex, Gender, and Culture among Brazilian Transgendered Prostitutes,* Chicago: University of Chicago Press.

Lewis, A. E. (2004) '"What group?" Studying Whites and Whiteness in the era of "color-blindness"', *Sociological Theory,* 22(4): 623–646.

Lorber, J. (1999) 'Crossing borders and erasing boundaries: paradoxes of identity politics', *Sociological Focus,* 32: 355–370.

Masequesmay, G. (2003) 'Negotiating multiple identities in a queer Vietnamese support group', *Journal of Homosexuality,* 45(2/4): 193–215.

McCall, G. and Simmons, J. L. (1966) *Identities and Interactions,* New York: Free Press.

Modlewski, T. (1997) 'Doing justice to the subjects: mimetic art in a multicultural society: the work of Anna Deavere Smith', in E. Abel, B. Christian and H. Moglen (eds) *Female Subjects in Black and White,* Berkeley, CA: University of California Press.

Moore, M. (2006) 'Lipstick or Timberlands? Meanings of gender presentation in Black lesbian communities', *Signs,* 32(1): 113–129.

Muñoz, J. E. (1999) *Disidentifications: Queers of Color and the Performance of Politics,* Minneapolis: University of Minnesota Press.

Namaste, V. K. (2000) *Invisible Lives: The Erasure of Transsexual and Transgender People,* Chicago: University of Chicago Press.

Naples, N. (2003) *Feminism and Method: Ethnography, Discourse Analysis, and Activist Research*, New York: Routledge.

Newton, E. (1972) *Mother Camp: Female Impersonators in America*, Chicago: University of Chicago Press.

Piontek, T. (2002) 'Kinging in the heartland; or, the power of marginality', in D. Troka, K. LeBescoe and J. Noble (eds) *The Drag King Anthology*, New York: Harrington Park Press.

Regales, J. (2008) 'My identity is fluid as fuck: transgender zine writers constructing themselves', in S. Driver (ed.) *Queer Youth Cultures: Performative and Political Practices*, Albany: State University of New York Press.

Richardson, M. (2006) 'Going to make the man: queer gender performance and racial impersonation', paper presented at the annual meeting of the American Studies Association.

Rodríguez, J. M. (2002) *Queer Latinidad: Identity Practices, Discursive Spaces*, New York: New York University Press.

Roen, K. (2001) 'Transgender theory and embodiment: the risk of racial marginalisation', *Journal of Gender Studies*, 10(3): 253–263.

Rupp, L. J. and Taylor, V. (2003) *Drag Queens at the 801 Cabaret*, Chicago: Chicago University Press.

Schacht, S. P. (1998) 'The multiple genders of the court: issues of identity and performance in a drag setting', in S. P. Schacht and D. W. Ewing (eds) *Feminism and Men: Reconstructing Gender Relations*, New York: New York University Press.

Schrock, D., Reid, L. and Boyd, E. (2005) 'Transsexuals' embodiment of womanhood', *Gender & Society*, 19(3): 317–335.

Shapiro, E. (2007) 'Drag kinging and the transformation of gender identities', *Gender & Society*, 21(2): 250–71.

Sieg, K. (2002) *Ethnic Drag: Performing Race, Nation, Sexuality in West Germany*, Ann Arbor: University of Michigan Press.

Stanley, J. L. (2004) 'Biracial lesbian and bisexual women: understanding the unique aspects and interactional processes of multiple minority identities', *Women & Therapy*, 27(1/2): 159–171.

Streitmatter, J. L. (1988) 'Ethnicity as a mediating variable of early adolescent identity development', *Journal of Adolescence*, 11(4): 335–346.

Swarr, A. L. (2004) 'Moffies, artists, and queens: race and the production of South African gay male drag', *Journal of Homosexuality*, 46(3/4): 73–89.

Swidler, A. (1986) 'Culture in action: symbols and strategies', *American Sociological Review*, 51: 273–286.

Taylor, V. and Whittier, N. (1992) 'Collective identity in social movement communities: lesbian feminist mobilization', in A. Morris and C. Mueller (eds) *Frontiers in Social Movement Theory*, New Haven: Yale University Press.

Tewksbury, R. (1994) 'Gender construction and the female impersonator: the process of transforming "He" to "She"', *Deviant Behavior: An Interdisciplinary Journal*, 15: 27–43.

Turkle, S. (1995) *Life on the Screen: Identity in the Age of the Internet*, New York: Touchstone.

Ward, J. (2008) *Respectably Queer: Diversity Culture in LGBT Activist Organizations*, Nashville: Vanderbilt University Press.

Wolf, D. (1996) *Feminist Dilemmas in Fieldwork*, Boulder, Colorado: Westview Press.

8   Transgendering in an Urban Dutch Streetwalking Zone

Katherine Gregory[1]

'The State will not be my pimp, *the State will not be my pimp*,' Victoria stresses for a second time as she contemplates the benefits of not declaring income on her taxes when street working in a 'zone' designated for streetwalking. She pauses a moment to take a long drag on her cigarette, and without losing momentum exhales, 'I use my body to make this money, *they* will not have any of it.'

(Victoria van der Way in Gregory 2005)

Prostitution policy in the Netherlands is considered at the vanguard of legalised commercial sex. It has also proven to be innovative when addressing forms of sex work outside the realm of regulation. One type of commercial venue set up by city governments, are streetwalking areas, called *zones*. These sites are designated to accommodate drug-addicted female street-prostitutes as a method for removing them from red light districts where sex work is heavily regulated and frequented by tourists and clients alike. Over time, the zones have drawn other social groups such as transgendered and undocumented migrant sex workers, who are not drug-addicted but seek the site as an alternative to working in prostitution windows or private clubs. This study focuses on transgendered streetwalkers and explores how they make social meaning of their work, challenging the amount of symbolic capital assigned to this type of sex work, maintaining clientele relations, and performing transgendered identities. In particular, this chapter is a snapshot of a form of street prostitution that represents a crucial step in the social development of state-regulated prostitution in the Netherlands. It also suggests that many transgendered streetwalkers attach a positive value to their use of the site, countering what many window prostitutes, sex-worker advocates, and scholars (Dworkin 1987; MacKinnon 1991; Barry 1995) assign as a negative form of commercial sex (Gregory 2005).

Recognising how many transgendered streetwalkers frame their experiences counters the dominant negative association of many forms of commercial sex and exposes how these leading discourses impose sweeping interpretations on their narratives and perspectives. Instead of stitching together a universal interpretation of sex work, this chapter suggests that transgendered streetwalkers represent a complex cultural group of individuals with diverse professional and personal experiences. I would hope that this study is one of the first steps towards exposing how the dominant paradigms fail to address many of the needs and issues shaping the lives of streetwalkers.

Legalisation of sex work has made the Netherlands a desirable place for many 'Third World' and transgendered prostitutes to migrate to and survive in, however this system does not solve all issues related to prostitution. In the last 20 years, a massive influx of immigrants and undocumented migrants, many of whom are transgendered, has produced tensions within dominant society, and as a result, immigration policy reforms now threaten many migrants with deportation. This scenario produces a two-tiered system granting rights and benefits to some sex workers, while others, mostly migrants, face the same inequities produced in unregulated prostitution sites.

The Dutch 'rational' approach to prostitution offers a unique perspective on the lives of different types of sex workers and allows us to understand their quality of life based on the rights and privileges granted to them. Although the Netherlands is the location of many studies on sex work (Van Haastrecht et al. 1993; Altink 1995; Pheterson 1996; Chapkis 1997; Wijers and Lap-Chew 1997), the ongoing changes in the ethnic makeup and sexual identities of sex workers make it a challenging research setting. Dutch prostitution requires continuous reevaluation of social, economic, and spatial relations because diverse social factors such as a sex worker's citizenship; gender identity; language acquisition; erotic parameters, that is, what sexual services the sex worker is willing to perform or not perform; and ability to negotiate with clients when intersected with this context can dramatically affect conditions for prostitutes.

Feminist theorists (Dworkin 1987; MacKinnon 1991; Barry 1995) have organised around various polarising positions concerning prostitution. One of the dominant feminist projects interprets sex work as a form of gendered subjugation arising from male domination and patriarchy. In the writings of Andrea Dworkin, Catherine MacKinnon, and Kathleen Barry all forms of commercial heterosexual relations have been classified as male violence against women (Clough 1994; Chapkis 1997; O'Neill 2000). The basis of this interpretation further questions the effects decriminalisation might have on the working conditions of sex workers. In particular, the idea of 'legalised' conditions raises concerns that the institutionalisation of sex work will only become a normalised livelihood for women (Barry 1995). This stance fails to extend solidarity with the struggle of sex workers and pays little or no attention to different types of sex workers or the services they provide. Issues of transgendered sex workers, rarely, if at all, addressed in this discussion, are further pushed to the margins. For this reason, I present the view of transgendered sex workers as a primary filter to understand this topic.

TRANSGENDERED IDENTITIES

Queer theorists, activists, and transgenderists alike have contested Western notions of who or what counts as transgendered (Gamson 1995; Broad 2002). For some groups, the definition of 'transgendered' only includes 'those who change their gender but not their sex' (Broad 2002: 248). For others, it is a matter of 'not fitting' into a traditional idea of what is either masculine or feminine. Because of the broadness of this concept, the process of transgendered 'identity building strategies' might suggest that no universal identity claim applies to this group or that a transgendered performance functions more as an 'identity-blurring' tactic than the formation of a 'collective identity' (Gamson 1995: 590; Broad 2002: 244). The master category of gender is, therefore, challenged by transgendered identity politics taking on 'gay/lesbian ethnic identity' by using 'queer deconstructive politics' (Broad 2002: 243). Usually, the term 'transgendered' is used as an inclusive, umbrella term and identifies 'transsexual',[2] 'pre-operative transsexual', *'travesti'* and/or 'transvestite/cross-dresser'. For this chapter I have identified 'transsexuals' as a separate identity label from 'transgendered' persons because of the way transsexuals were segregated from the other transgendered people in the 'zone'.

'Travesti' is a common term used in Latin America (Kulíck 1998) and does not conform to standard northern Euro-American sexual typologies, as they consider themselves neither transsexuals nor transvestites (Kulíck 1998: 12). In addition to wearing female-coded clothing, *travestí*s have had some 'body modification' to enhance their feminine appearance. Many *travestí*s, particularly those from Latin America, ingest female hormones purchased in the underground economy, and have industrial silicone injected into their hips, buttocks, and possibly their breasts (Kulíck 1998). They do, however, retain their male genitalia and during sexual exchanges with clients sometimes perform with their penis depending upon the request of the client. During the course of my data collection, Dutch *'travestí*s' referred to themselves as 'transgendered'. As a result, I use the terms interchangeably when referring to them. Another group present on the street were transvestites and/or cross-dressers who dressed in women's clothing when streetwalking at night but 'lived' and identified themselves as men. Both *travestí*s and transvestites were spatially segregated from female and transsexual prostitutes but shared the 'transgendered' section of streetwalking areas (Gregory 2005).

Judith Butler's theory of 'denaturaliz[ation] of gender categories' and 'incoherent gender identities' (Bordo 1993: 289) asserts that even within an assigned transgendered space, daily enactments produce multiple categories of gender that operate as a disciplinary force and undermine the dominant sexual order. Here, 'performative theory' replaces notions of a 'core self' (Bordo 1993: 289). This rationalisation of transgendered performance inscribes a gendered coherency from those actors who occupy a central position within the transgendered space but also subordinates some members through enforced notions of transgenderism. Within such acts are moments that destabilise the dominant fictions of transgendering (a play on Butler's 'fictions of gender'), hence this spatial setting provides entry into how transgendered streetwalkers challenge social arrangements forced upon them in the zone.

In *Travesti: Sex, Gender and Culture among Brazilian Transgendered Prostitutes* (1998) Don Kulíck focuses on central elements in the construction of sexuality and gender of *travestí* sex workers, representing how Butler's gender theory applies to the practices of transgendered sex workers. In particular, his subjects reconfigure a gendered social order by resisting and negotiating their identities in and outside the *travesti* community. The study takes the position that 'transgenderism constitutes a privileged vantage point from which it is possible to oversee how sex and gender are conceived and enacted in everyday life' (Kulíck 1998: 10). Through such production, gender is exposed as a performance and debunked as an 'illusion that we are products of some natural process' (Kulíck quoting Shapiro 1998: 10).

Gender fluidity and 'shifting [gender] borders' in Brazilian culture are recognised in the writings of Mendès-Leite (1993) who refers to this phenomenon as 'ambigusexuality' because it stresses how gender roles are based on performative aspects of 'appearance' rather than sexual practices that remain 'ambiguous' (Nesvig 2001). Hence the gendered performance of the *travestí*, as a feminine identity, is affirmed by the presence of a hypermasculinised, 'heterosexual' male companion or client. However this public performance does not reflect what sexual roles each person is assigned in the sex act (Nesvig 2001). Sex roles are blurred or altogether changeable based on Mendès-Leite's account (Nesvig 2001). Whereas most streetwalkers whom I spoke to identified according to how they were physically situated in the organisation of the zone, this arrangement did not require that they conform their sexual services to any one set of practices.

METHODS

I began this study observing for hundreds of hours inside and outside windows in the red-light district of Amsterdam, and spent over 150 hours surveying, in the role of volunteer, at a health-care facility, called the Living Room, at the entrance of a streetwalking zone. During the course of a seven-month period spanning over two-and-a-half-years, between 1998 and 2000, I interviewed 22 sex workers, 17 of whom were 'transgendered' or transsexual and had worked sporadically on the streets. I conducted fieldwork at the zone during two separate periods, six months apart, interviewing 14 transgendered contacts there. Eleven informants held 'immigrant' or 'undocumented' status during the data gathering stage of my research.

Three transgendered informants, however, worked in the windows at the time of my study but had strong recollections of streetwalking.

To better understand how issues of sexual identity, migration, and erotic labour intersect and expose the material reality of sex workers, I conducted interviews with sex workers in their working environment and, when invited, in their homes. They shared their experiences with me through story telling, one-on-one interviews, and casual conversation, conveying the complexity of their social arrangements in their professional sphere and in their personal lives. Some interviews lasted hours at a time, while others were fragmented, often disrupted by the sex worker's need to return outdoors to work on the street. My shortest interviews were no less than 30 minutes each, but usually occurred more than once with the same informant. Overall, during a single shift at the Living Room,[3] I spent between eight and twelve hours during each observation and communicated with each informant up to six times during that same period.

Numerous ethical issues were addressed before I set out for my field setting. An Internal Review Board (IRB) at the university where I attended graduate school approved the protocol of this study under the condition that I did not use any electronic recording device because of the risk recordings might cause human subjects. Of course, this American-based IRB interpreted sex work through an American filter in which many forms of erotic labour are criminalised. They presumed my informants would face incarceration for their participation in the sex industry, which was not necessarily the case. The IRB was equally concerned for the well-being of migrants whom I interviewed under the condition of anonymity. Deportation was at the time and continues to be a driving concern for many undocumented migrants working in the underground commercial sex economy.

THE STREETWALKING ZONE

Municipalities across most major Dutch cities, including Den Apelhaven[4] where I gathered data (Gregory 2005), designated streetwalking zones in industrial areas that were commonly used for storing and transporting freights during the day. Street prostitution, organised seven days per week from 6pm to 6am, is intended to be confined to a cul-de-sac through which vehicles can drive. Working in the space requires streetwalkers to stand on a cramped sidewalk, waiting for clients to drive by, before negotiating services with the flick of a nod or a hand gesture and then entering their vehicles to exchange sexual services for money in the front seat of their car. A public health facility, called the 'Living Room', or *huiskamer* in Dutch, located at the entrance of the area provides health care and respite for streetwalkers. Staff members at the Living Room, along with local social workers, determine how social groups are segregated on the street, it is not decided by the sex workers themselves. Transsexuals and female-born streetwalkers are situated on a highly visible side of the street, while trans-gendered members are located in a smaller area near the exit. The demarca-tion of the street meant transsexual and female-born identities are blurred and *travestis* worked beside transvestites. Even though spatial segregation of the zone reinforces popular notions about sexual identities, the social actors in the space often destabilise those same binaries. Destabilisation often occurs when transgendered actors, particularly those who construct a hyper-feminine identity, do not conform to a culturally prescribed sexual role during the commercial exchange. No assumptions, therefore, could be made about what role the transgendered sex worker played during anal sex (as a bottom/insertee or a top/inserter).

SEX WORKERS' PREFERENCE OF PROSTITUTION SITES

Each prostitution site[5] has its benefits and drawbacks as a location for erotic labour. Window prostitution is often perceived as the choice location for legalised erotic labour. Some transgendered window prostitutes claimed the window sites provided added personal comfort and a degree of employ-ment stability. Having food and toiletries delivered to their window was an added advantage of working at this site. In contrast, working outdoors, exposed to the elements, with the vulnerability of entering an automobile, a procedure typical of streetwalking, seemed undesirable to them. This par-tiality illustrates only some of the elements that make a location preferable or undesirable.

Many transgendered streetwalkers, however, would strongly disagree with this construction of streetwalking or the benefits of working in the windows. Repeatedly, transgendered and female streetwalkers reported a preference for the zone because of the various ways the site represented commercial autonomy not found in windows or in the clubs. First, street-walkers paid no taxes on their income, unlike window prostitutes who must claim all earnings. Second, the windows constrained physical mobil-ity of the prostitute. Window prostitution limited access to clients, confin-ing sex workers to the parameters of a small (about 50 square feet) room rather than creating flexibility about where and when commercial sex could occur. Another criticism of window prostitution concerned a finan-cial commitment required for the duration of an eight-hour shift, five to seven days per week. Window prostitutes pay upwards of 100 Euros (150 to 200 guilders) per shift, averaging 600 Euros per week (1,200 guilders). Streetwalking zones provided a flexible work cycle. Should business slow down or other obligations require their attention, there would be no 'lost earnings' from rental overhead or negative recourse, because on the streets there is no landlord taking notice of their absence.

In the windows, a sex worker must have a worker's permit to rent a window. Standard practice in the windows requires some bodily display for all who work there. This requirement was framed as unacceptable for streetwalkers. Many streetwalkers expressed feelings of compromise when discussing bodily exhibition notably initiated in window prostitution and clubs. Contrastingly, as a standard practice on the street, streetwalkers stood and waited for cars to pass using minimal nonverbal communication with would-be clients. Streetwalkers were not expected to partially disrobe for 'inspection' or perform before would-be clients, as sometimes happens in the windows. This additional effort requires window prostitutes to attract attention to draw costumers into a negotiation but is unnecessary for streetwalkers. As a Dutch transsexual streetwalker, Victoria, explained, 'if a client [standing outside a window] wants me to turn around while I'm standing there, I'd tell him no way, I'm not a piece of flesh.' For this reason, the minimal amount of pandering to would-be clients appealed to many streetwalkers who sought the zone for work.

SYMBOLIC CAPITAL

Legalised prostitution is not without its points of tension. Questions such as whether a sex worker is voluntarily working in the industry or holding migrant status are a few of the ongoing issues facing prostitution policy in the Netherlands. Sometimes lost in these overarching concerns are the personal decisions sex providers must make regarding where to work. Often 'rationalising' justifications are asserted when choosing one commercial venue over another. As there are many different forms of commercial sex, each type of erotic labour holds a different set of meanings for anyone involved directly with prostitution. With the multiple prostitution communities in the Netherlands, sex workers (as well as advocates involved in prostitution issues) hold the belief that different types of prostitution sites confer varying degrees of symbolic capital to those who work there. Their reading of sexualised spaces enforces a hierarchy among prostitutes. Any number of physical and social conditions in the surrounding commercial venue could influence the amount of social capital assigned to the people who worked there. Luxury items found in a window interior, fluxes of human traffic, social exclusivity assigned to a site, degree of visibility of sex workers, whether solicitation occurred indoors or outdoors, or if an exchange transpired in an automobile, hotel, or window, all transferred some form of status.

Many sex workers and their advocates believed that the conditions found at streetwalking zones, in particular, held a lower social value when compared to other sexualised spaces. Many determinants affected the meaning attributed to the zone, including the presence of undocumented streetwalkers, drug addicted women, law enforcement, transgendered people, clients, and what agents utilise the area. Despite this reading of the space, the social meanings and arrangements assigned to the streetwalking zone were neither constant nor fixed for each agent situated there.

Unlike the regulation of windows where a prostitute generates a taxable income and pays a weekly rental fee, streetwalking zones remain a bastion of unregulated prostitution in the Netherlands. Often these sites carry a stigma stemming from the presence of drug-addicted prostitutes and their boyfriends and pimps selling and consuming hard drugs that negatively affect the symbolic value of the area. Because the layout of the site is a drive-through, most sexual exchanges occur in the front seat of the client's car rather than on a bed found in a window space. Furthermore, the presence of undocumented prostitutes from Latin America, Africa, and Eastern Europe is believed to lower standards and prices. The zone, therefore, becomes the only commercial place accessible for undocumented segments of the population, since window rentals require documentation of residency. The large community of transgendered prostitutes, who were both documented and 'undocumented,' were not drug-addicted and often described the work location as favourable.

Bourdieu's (1992, 1998; Bourdieu and Passeron 1990) definition of the 'field' suggests a way to frame the naturalisation of daily group relations among prostitutes. In this sense, all social action of members was the result of an internalisation of the habitus that reinforced group behaviour through shared rules, knowledge, and values (Margolis 1999). At the centre of this organisation were streetwalkers vying for different forms of capital.

The very notion of a 'hierarchy of sex workers' would serve to reinforce this field. A stratified group of transgendered prostitutes could explain the ways in which sex workers hold and vie for different social positions and amounts of symbolic capital. Whether their status was determined by factors such as whom a sex worker provides services to; the conditions under which the sex worker meets her client; how the commercial transaction takes place; how sex workers articulate their habitus through gestures, attire and movement; or their legal status, it all amounts to different forms of cultural and economic capital.

Any experienced streetwalker in the Netherlands would also know both the unspoken 'rules' of the street, and the ethics transgendered streetwalkers share with other sex workers to economically and socially survive on the street. This includes how she relates to regular customers, both hers and others', spatial parameters between sex workers, sites of operation, even attire that distinguishes one prostitute from the other. A breach of these rules occurred when a small group of young, well-dressed Eastern European prostitutes appeared for the first time in the zone. They were immediately bullied out of the space by the most senior member on the street, a Dutch transsexual. The police later told them to leave because a) they were undercutting their prices for services by not following the rules; and b) they were 'marked' differently in their attire, presenting themselves as 'other' than what was expected at that site.

CLIENTELE RELATIONS AND DESIRES

When sexual identities, practices, and meanings are framed as 'social products' from different cultural and historical perspectives rather than naturalised tendencies, the normalisation of multiple gender configurations begins to provide new dimensions to the politics of desire and the body. Research on Latin American sexual typologies supports this claim (Almaguer 1991; Mendès-Leite 1993; Carrier 1995; Balderston and Guy 1997; Kulick 1998; Prieur 1998; Nesvig 2001; Cantú 2002; Sigal 2002), suggesting that the Latin American social construction of 'homosexuality' is defined by the roles that each partner performs, unlike a Western definition where 'homosexuality' is based on the biological sex of the partners involved. Kulíck's research, in particular, contributes to how *travestís'* relations with their boyfriends challenge North American constructs around identity labels relegating certain sexual practices to the realm of 'homosexuality'. *Travestís* neither consider their male lovers 'gay' nor their relationships as 'homosexual;' instead gender and sex roles are interpreted through the filter of 'passive' and 'active' positions.[6] Distinctions found in the sexual typologies constructed across Latin American cultures differ widely from Western discourse on sexual identities and practices but are steadily influencing commercial sexual relations in the Netherlands. The large number of Latin American informants included in my sample described the impact Latin American *travestís* have had on client demands for their sexual services there (Gregory 2005). Clients in the zone, as it turned out, were inclined to 'cross the street,' seeking sexual services from different types of streetwalkers, further blurring sexual identities of actors in the zone and services provided by all sex workers. In this instance, self-described heterosexual clients would seek out the services of transvestites and *travestís.* However, the crossing of the street by clients also affected the work performance of biological women who felt a need to make anal sex available as part of the sexual services they performed.

Replication of this sexual typology was found in the gendered subgroups frequenting a Mexico City brothel identified in Prieur's (1998) ethnographic study. Labels identified in *Mema's House* both reinforce a heterosexual model on queer and transgendered relations and simultaneously expose marked distinctions in Latin American sexual identities. Each label reflects the multidimensional aspect of sexual practices and its impact on heterosexual status retention, masculinity, and *machismo.* Such social labels distinguish between *jotas* who are biologically born men but 'dress and act like women,' and *vestidas* who are defined as 'transsexuals and transvestites', but refute the label of 'homosexual' in Mexican culture. *Mayates*, meanwhile, are men who perform penetration in the dominant role, but are not socially defined as 'homosexuals' because of their 'active' position and the fact that many of them are 'socially heterosexual' and married to women, further paralleling the identity claims of many clients in the Dutch urban zone.

The data gathered for my study produced similar findings to Prieur and Kulíck. Gender blurring (Bornstein 1994; Calhoun Davis 2009) of sex providers in the zone was discouraged through the demarcation and enforcement of the street. An invisible partition distinguished the biology of one set of sex workers from the other, and ultimately the type of services they performed. Transgendered sex workers, however, reported that many of their clients were men who defined themselves as heterosexual but sought their sexual services. As a means of protecting their heterosexual status, many clients of transgendered sex workers attempted to conceal the pursuit of their desires in a number of ways. Often they drove their automobiles past female sex workers a few times before seeking services from a transgendered prostitute. They also engaged in their pursuit only after dark when 'crossing over' was less conspicuous. A client's 'crossing over' after nightfall also had a direct effect on transgendered streetwalkers' labour practices. This occurrence motivated streetwalkers to begin their daily operations long after dark, sometimes hours after the zone was opened. Research findings suggest that this tactic influenced their earnings and required an intensification of street working in the condensed time afforded them (Gregory 2005).

This type of transaction also revealed complex client relations, disqualifying a simplistic suggestion that it was a matter of client exploitation of subordinated sex workers. Contrary to popular belief, clients and transgendered sex providers held mutable social positions based on their individual interests and identity claims. This was particularly the case if the client needed to conceal his desires behind a 'heterosexual' identity. This kind of concealment could lead to more favourable social position from which the transgendered sex worker could negotiate in the commercial exchange. In order to assume any disruption of the social order of prostitution, relations on the part of transgendered sex workers, the influence of desire fulfilment, the social meaning attached to sexual practices by the participants, and any identity concealment on the part of 'heterosexual' clients, must be factored into the equation. Likewise, embedded in this scenario were other social determinants intersecting social relations between client and sex worker that were less favourable for migrants. For instance, if a sex worker held Dutch or EU citizenship, she was probably able to negotiate better in Dutch or English. A language barrier, however, for undocumented workers could dramatically influence their ability to negotiate. Not all clients were Dutch or Dutch speaking, and any indication of inexperience, or a lack of English language skills, could tilt the balance of power in the direction of the sex provider.

The streetwalker must take into account numerous bodily adjustments before entering the street or engaging in an exchange with a client. Unlike condoms that were distributed for free at the Living Room, transgendered streetwalkers were required to purchase lubricant and to apply it rectally before venturing out. The application of a lubricant gel signified a central part of a transgendered commercial sexual performance. For both sex worker and client, the condom, however, signaled the start of a sexual act

(Alexander 1994). Once the client negotiates with the streetwalker, the standard ten minute 'suck and fuck' is exchanged for 25 Euros, at which time the sex worker is expected to perform oral sex on the client, and then have anal sex until the client climaxes. What roles they play out depends on the client's needs and the transgendered sex worker's performative parameters.

Without the application of the lubricant, the physicality of the work would be too taxing, if not impossible, on their body. This intermediary facilitates genital penetration, and afforded the simulation of gendered arousal for transsexual streetwalkers. Some clients, they said, interpreted this effusion of fluid as a symbol of a reciprocal 'heterosexual' exchange; however, most transsexual sex workers would describe it as a means to producing a feminine performance comparable to that of female-born sex workers. Meanwhile, *travestís* and transvestites applied lubricant to facilitate an erotic exchange, making anal penetration possible. On occasion, a *travestí* sex worker reported how her clients could not distinguish them from female-born sex workers, and, assuming this to be true, the lubricant was a gendered prop. This 'misreading' of a *travestí* performance by a client was not the case for most *travestís*.

Relationships between many streetwalkers and their former clients occurred beyond the realm of the streetwalking zone, and sometimes proved fruitful for streetwalkers. In three separate cases, transsexual informants developed a solid clientele base but reported different outcomes when former clients became their long-term intimate companions. One Dutch transsexual described how she met her fiancé when he visited the streetwalking zone on a lark with his male relative. Another Dutch transsexual, who late in her career trained as a nurse but continues to work on the streets, named a list of former boyfriends whom she had first met as customers. Negotiating why she would continue working on the street proved challenging even when the new boyfriend had an aforementioned knowledge of her work and the relationship seemed stable. For undocumented transgendered streetwalkers, a monogamous relationship with an EU citizen could lead to permanent residency and access to social welfare services denied illegal residents if they were not able to register as domestic partners. This arrangement is possible because the Dutch government recognises 'same sex' monogamous relationships and affords them the same rights as heterosexual couples. However, if a relationship terminates, as was the case for an Ecuadorian transsexual who broke up with her boyfriend, chances of permanent residency are all but lost.

TO MIGRATE ACROSS THE STREET

Much has been written in an effort to deconstruct the naturalisation of sexual dualism in western society (Butler 1990; Lorber 1994; Sedgwick

1994; Namaste 2000; Calhoun Davis 2009). These works challenge reproductive heterosexuality and the 'hegemonic hold' it has on sexual identity. In an attempt to reconfigure popular concepts of gender, Butler calls for subversion, or 'gender trouble,' to expose how gender performances are enacted and notions of transgenderism understood in a singular way (Butler 1990: 24). Resistance takes many forms and is achieved through parody to destabilise notions of a 'naturalised' gendered self. On the street, subversion occurs explicitly through drag, linguistics, and an 'incoherent' gendered body. Performance theory applied to the multiple gender identities and sexual practices performed in streetwalking suggests a stabilising effect on the 'transgendered identity,' possibly signaling a 'normalisation' of a third gender or more genders (Bornstein 1994). 'Normalisation' of a third gender, however, does not make it any easier to classify practices that do not conform to a fixed meaning of what is 'transgendered'.

The bodily practices presented in Kulíck's (1998) data are of great value to the social reconstruction of gender inside and outside the *travestí* community. In particular, he contributes to a greater understanding of body modification and its links to an economy that has grown around injecting industrial silicone directly into the tissues of the body, hormone consumption, and hair extensions, resulting in the image of *travestí*s becoming a symbol of Brazilian femininity. Undocumented sex workers from Latin American, whom I interviewed, continued similar practices in the Netherlands where they use their earnings to buy hormones purchased in the underground economy and to ingest them without the supervision of a physician. Although Kulíck's informants were not considering a 'permanent' identity migration, many transgendered sex workers in my study contemplated this procedure but saw it as an enormous undertaking. Their understanding of transsexualism as a material and social reality in their professional lives implied direct economic consequences for them in terms of the commercial services they provided. Material factors that came into play when a transgendered sex worker considered sex reassignment surgery elicited tactics to ensure their economic and social survival on the streets and in the windows. Some transgendered prostitutes interviewed for this project were in the preoperative stages of a gender reassignment. How post-operative 'tools' meaning a surgically constructed vagina would impact on economic life for a trans-person depended upon the meaning she ascribed to a permanent gender migration. Nonetheless, each sex worker approached her identity claims and client relations differently regardless of what stage she was at in her gender migration.

Some streetwalkers in the Netherlands spoke of a transsexual migration as a fulfilling process; for others, the course was filled with emotional fear and economic uncertainty. The notion of a 'migration' as a physical act, for some sex workers, seemed an unnecessary process to achieve a gendered identity (Calhoun Davis 2009). But the process was also a privilege that was only afforded Dutch and EU streetwalkers who had state insurance coverage to pay for the cost of the procedure. Whether an informant was undocumented or a citizen of the Netherlands, the responses were highly subjective and depended on how a sex worker felt about her 'marketability' on the street and not just whether she had free access to a medical procedure. For one transgendered sex worker, a physical transformation held no significance to her material viability in prostitution. However, for others a sex reassignment meant their economic future looked less hopeful. In this case, the dominant emotion shared by numerous sex workers was that of fear when contemplating an invasive and total gender migration.

Three transsexual informants, interviewed for my study, expressed emotional satisfaction with their transsexual identities and reported positive client relations, working on the 'female side of the street'. Communicating their gender identity to clients, however, was a personal decision for many sex workers. One informant chose not to disclose her transsexual identity with customers; while the other two expressed a transparency around their recent transsexual identity when communicating with clients. Disclosing their sexual identity to clients, for the most part, did not, they said, result in any negative response and had no positive or negative impact on their economic viability on the streets.

Not all pre-operative transgendered people anticipated working in a favourable climate as post-operatives. In some cases, the commercial necessity for maintaining an 'intersexed' body guaranteed economic viability and the ability to continue providing niche sexual services to clients.[7] The penis, in this case, was an erotic tool, however, it held little erotic function or meaning in her personal life. The overriding perception was that a transsexual held second-class status when competing with female-born sex workers who were perceived as having a superior anatomy.

Some transgendered streetwalkers expressed fears around sex reassignment surgery/procedures. Even after having begun procedures to have her Adam's apple removed, one transgendered informant feared taking the final steps towards a post-operative life. Like many migrant transgendered sex workers who acquire female hormone medication from the underground economy because they don't have access to medical care, this informant ingested unmonitored female hormones for five years before seeking medical attention for regulating her hormone intake. The possibility of completing a sex reassignment and then working on the street as a transsexual felt uncertain for her. She assumed that following a sex-reassignment operation, she would not be able to maintain her clientele base.

Not everyone on the cusp of a sex reassignment anticipates such negative economic outcomes. A transgendered Ecuadorian faced other concerns about making a gender identity transition. She contemplated a vaginoplasty after having already delayed the procedure once before, when surgeons wanted to simultaneously augment her breasts. Despite medical recommendations to complete the sex reassignment in this way, she preferred having her breasts augmented first, and then once adjusted to the change, having her genitals reconstructed. Distress over the institutionalisation of the sex reassignment procedure meant she could not control the invasive process to which her body would be subjected. This situation occurs because in the Netherlands, a medical board determines who is an appropriate candidate and when they are 'ready.' Unlike many Latin American transgendered people who must pay for the procedure, Dutch transsexuals can have the procedure paid for by their insurance or the 'state'. Clearly, the benefit of being Dutch meant having a plethora of elective surgical options available to them.

Despite reservations over the sequence of the procedure, the informant expressed confidence that her clients would remain with her after the operation. When asked whether her clients sought her out for her penis or anal sex, (a practice customers might be less inclined to seek out from a female), she declared that all of her clients were just 'sexual' and 'don't care who they are with [because on] one day they go with a transgendered and the next to a woman. Mostly I suck. Sometimes they suck me. But usually they are surprised when they see my penis.' Hence the procedure was more for personal reasons than an economic one.

A few transgendered sex workers expressed the view that operative modification in the construction of a gender identity was irrelevant to how they viewed themselves or their material well-being. Two Romanian transgendered streetwalkers expressed how they could not find a justifiable reason for 'having to be a woman only [by] wearing a particular item or having the surgery'. While one of them appeared to have had breast augmentation and facial cosmetic surgery, the other admitted to having shaved her entire body to appear hairless. Both expressed 'that [body modification] won't make you happy, but it can be achieved by just accepting who you are in that moment.' Regardless of their opinion about sex reassignments, both informants sought some external modification to serve their transgendered and transvestite niche markets.

CONCLUSION

This chapter is a brief snapshot of some of the ways transgendered relations are shaped by a streetwalking zone and the social actors who occupy it. Popular assumption interprets transactional exchanges in the streetwalking zone as undesirable, assigning no symbolic capital to this type of sex work. While other activities take place in the space, such as drug sales and consumption, giving the appearance of an unregulated or 'disorderly' site, the main actors saw opportunities, and gave an alternate interpretation of its social meaning and value. The main advantage many transgendered streetwalkers considered was the sizable amount of autonomy they could assert and the untaxed income they could generate. Furthermore, unlike the clubs where sex workers may have little choice in who they must service and what sexual acts they must perform, the zone gave streetwalkers spatial options in which to better negotiate their services. The results contest popular notions of this type of commercial sex and identify how transgendered sex workers produce social hierarchies among themselves for the purpose of accumulating different forms of capital.

By focusing on the ways that spatial conditions favour the interests of transgendered streetwalkers, the function of this site may be perceived as a nexus for ongoing struggle and negotiation, rather than a blanketed negative form of sex work. Operating in a dynamic way as a field, with every agent strategising for economic and cultural capital, this depiction suggests that streetwalkers weigh the drawbacks to benefits when seeking a commercial space in which to work. With the zone now defunct in some areas of the Netherlands, social hierarchies among prostitutes still remain a fixture of Dutch prostitution, and are still largely dependent upon the commercial space and who occupies it. Many of the agents involved in prostitution: clients, boyfriends, junkies, the police, public health workers, or immigration police contribute to or hinder the daily struggle sex workers face when ensuring their safety, respect and economic livelihood. In the last 20 years, the issue of immigration has fostered more complexities to the commercial space. The complexities of sex work in the Netherlands have been compounded by a two-tiered system determining who has rights and who does not. All of these factors contributed to how transgendered sex workers operated within the site.

The rights of transgendered people in the Netherlands are considered to be at the forefront of progressive policy. Monogamous same sex couples have the same domestic rights as heterosexual couples. Pre-operative transgendered people who have Dutch residency or citizenship may apply to have a sex reassignment, and if approved, have the procedure covered by state insurance. By all accounts, many transgendered sex workers stated that their quality of life was measurably better in the Netherlands than in other countries where they had lived or worked. The one caveat, however, is that many transgendered sex workers whom I interviewed were also undocumented. In the months leading up to the closure of some streetwalking zones, greater measures of control were enforced by immigration police. Streetwalkers were forced to register and carry identity cards to enter the zone. Routine deportations took place, forcing the removal of many undocumented streetwalkers, including those who were transgendered. By giving a rare glimpse into the complex identities circulating around transgenderism, this chapter has touched upon the diversity of sex workers who are also transgendered, but suggests this diverse representation of sex workers makes it difficult to identify a unified narrative among them.

NOTES

1. I want to thank Angelo Cacciuto and Emily Wood for their feedback on this chapter.
2. This term refers only to 'post-operative' transsexuals.

3. The Living Room is a literal translation of *Huiskamer*, as the facility was called in Dutch. The site provided medical care, respite, food, condoms, and a space where drug users could inject heroin or smoke crack cocaine under the surveillance of public health workers.
4. The city where I conducted my streetwalking research had to be given an alias for the purpose of protecting my contacts.
5. This definition includes window prostitution, streetwalking zones, clubs, and escort services.
6. A sexual typology found throughout Latin America.
7. This means having male genitals and augmented breasts and hips. This also includes ingesting female hormones.

REFERENCES

Alexander, P. (1994) 'Sex workers fight against AIDS: an international perspective', in B. Schneider and N. E. Stoller (eds) *Women Resisting AIDS: Strategies of Empowerment*, Philadelphia: Temple University Press.

Almaguer, T. (1991) 'Chicano men: a cartography of homosexual identity and behavior', *Differences*, 3: 75–100.

Altink, S. (1995) *Stolen Lives: Trading Women into Sex and Slavery*, London: Scarlet Press.

Balderston, D. and Guy, D. J. (1997) *Sex and Sexuality in Latin America*, New York: New York University Press.

Barry, K. (1995) *The Prostitution of Sexuality*, New York: New York University Press.

Bordo, S. (1993) 'Feminism, Foucault and the politics of the body', in C. Ramazanoglu (ed.) *Up Against Foucault: Explorations of some tensions between Foucault and Feminism*, London: Routledge.

———. (1993) *Unbearable Weight: Feminism, Western Culture, and the Body*, Berkeley: University of California Press.

Bornstein, K. (1994) *Gender Outlaw: On Men, Women, and the Rest of Us*, New York: Routledge.

Bourdieu, P. and Passeron, J. (1990) *Reproduction in Education, Society and Culture*, London: Sage.

Bourdieu, P. (1992) 'In conversation: doxa and common life', *New Left Review*, 191: 115.

———. (1998) *Practical Reason: On the Theory of Action*, Stanford, CA: Stanford University Press.

Broad, K. L. (2002). 'GLB+T: gender/sexuality movements and transgender collective identity (de)constructions', *International Journal of Sexuality and Gender Studies*, 7(4): 241–264.

Butler, J. (1990) *Gender Trouble: Feminism and the Subversion of Identity*, New York: Routledge.

Calhoun Davis, E. (2009) 'Situating "fluidity": (trans)gender identity and the regulation of gender diversity', *GLQ: A Journal of Lesbian and Gay Studies*, 15(1): 97–130.

Cantu, L. (2002) 'De ambiente: queer tourism and the shifting boundaries of Mexican male sexualities' *GLQ: A Journal of Lesbian and Gay Studies*, 8(1/2): 139–166.

Carrier, J. (1995) *De Los Otros: Intimacy and Homosexuality among Mexican Men*, New York: Columbia University Press.

Chapkis, W. (1997) *Live Sex Acts: Women Performing Erotic Labor*, New York: Routledge.

Clough, P. T. (1994) *Feminist Thought: Desire, Power, and Academic Discourse*, Cambridge, MA: Blackwell.

Dworkin, A. (1987) *Intercourse*, London: Secker and Warburg.

Gamson, J. (1995) 'Must identity movements self-destruct? A queer dilemma', *Social Problems*, 42: 390–407.

Gregory, K. (2005) *The Everyday Lives of Sex Workers in the Netherlands*, New York: Routledge.

Kulíck, D. (1998) *Travesti: Sex, Gender and Culture among Brazilian Transgendered Prostitutes*, Chicago: University of Chicago Press.

Lorber, J. (1994) *Paradoxes of Gender*, New Haven: Yale University Press.

MacKinnon, C. (1991) *Feminism Unmodified: Discourse of Life and Law*, Cambridge: Harvard University Press.

Margolis, J. (1999) 'Pierre Bourdieu: habitus and the logic of practice', in R. Shusterman (ed.) *Bourdieu: A Critical Reader*, Oxford: Blackwell.

Mendès-Leite, R. (1993) 'The game of appearance: the "ambigusexuality" in Brazilian culture of sexuality', *Journal of Homosexuality* 25(3): 271–282.

Namaste, V. K. (2000) *Invisible Lives: The Erasure of Transsexual and Transgendered People*, Chicago: University of Chicago Press.

Nesvig, M. (2001) 'The complicated terrain of Latin American homosexuality', *Hispanic American Historical Review*, 81(3/4): 689–729.

O'Neill, M. (2000) *Prostitution and Feminism: Towards a Politics of Feeling*, Cambridge: Polity Press.

Pheterson, G. (1996) *The Prostitution Prism*, Amsterdam: Amsterdam University Press.

Prieur, A. (1998) *Mema's House: Mexico City on Transvestites, Queens, and Machos*, Chicago: University of Chicago Press.

Sedgwick, E. (1994) *Epistemology of the Closet*, Berkeley: University of California Press.

Sigal, P. (2002) 'Teaching radical history to cross the sexual borderlands: the history of sexuality in the Americas', *Radical History Review*, 82: 171–185.

Van Haastrecht, H. J., Fennema, J. S., Coutinho, R. A., van der Helm, T. C., Kint, J. A. and van den Hoek, J. A. (1993) 'HIV prevalence and risk behavior among prostitutes and clients in Amsterdam: migrants at increased risk for HIV infection', *Genitourin Med*: 251–256.

Wijers, M. and Lap-Chew, L. (1997) *Trafficking in Women Forced Labour and Slavery-like Practices in Marriage Domestic Labour and Prostitution*, Utrecht: STV.

9 Beyond Borders

Lived Experiences of Atypically Gendered Transsexual People

Sara Davidmann

ARE YOU A GUY OR A GIRL?

I've heard the question all my life. The answer is not so simple, since there are no pronouns in the English language as complex as I am, and I do not want to simplify myself in order to neatly fit one or the other . . . We have a history filled with militant hero/ines. Yet therein lies the rub! How can I tell you about their battles when the words woman and man, feminine and masculine, are almost the only words that exist in the English language to describe all the vicissitudes of bodies and styles of expression?

(Feinberg 1996: ix)

QUEERING THE TERRITORY

Building upon the work of Judith Butler (1990) and Michel Foucault (1984) and emerging in the early 1990s from the fields of lesbian, gay and feminist studies, queer theory constitutes a collection of foci on the relations between sex, gender and desire in relation to stereotypical heterosexual norms. Central to queer theory is a concern with the ways in which atypical configurations of gender, sex and desire challenge the concept of the 'natural' (Butler 1990, 1991, 1993; Spargo 1999; Sullivan 2003). Since queer theory's inception, the use of the term 'queer' has spread beyond academia into lesbian, gay and transgender communities where it is now commonly used as an umbrella term for sexual and gender identities beyond the norm (Jagose 1996; Wilchins 2004; Halberstam 2005).

Concurrently with the popularity of queer theory, the Western world has seen an increased social acceptance of lesbian and gay sexuality and a greater integration of openly lesbian and gay people into mainstream society as well as increased legal recognition. Following this, the mixing of gender characteristics that have long been a part of the experiences of some lesbian and gay people, for example, a woman displaying masculine characteristics, or a man appearing effeminate, would appear to have become more widely accepted in Western urban society (Shaw and Ardener 2005). In line with this, in the broad social sphere, the acknowledged gender boundaries appear to have expanded to accommodate a degree of female masculinity and male femininity. Judith Halberstam argues that it is because gender boundaries are flexible that this mixing of gender attributes can take place while maintaining the status quo of the binary sexes (1998: 20).

Further, gender is an interactive process (Garfinkel 1967; Kessler and McKenna 1978). While a person may identify beyond the categories of 'female' or 'male', and project this in the public domain, if the widely held belief in society is that there are only 'females' and 'males', and 'women' and 'men', then in practice an observer is likely to 'read' the person's gender as falling within one or other of the binary categories (Kessler and McKenna 2000).

Indeed, the assumption that there are two genders and that these are aligned with the polarities of biological sex is widely taken as a given in the Western world and believed to be a fact of life. Darwinian theories of evolution, and in particular, the concept that sexual behaviour serves reproduction, provide the foundation for the belief in the binary sex system (Herdt 1993: 24). This premise forms the basis for the 'natural attitude' towards gender (Garfinkel 1967). Building upon empirical research carried out in the 1970s, Suzanne Kessler and Wendy McKenna summarise the general perception of the 'natural attitude' as follows:

1. There are two and only two genders . . .
2. Gender exists as biological 'fact' independently of anyone's ideas about gender.
3. A person's gender never changes.
4. Genitals are the essential defining feature of gender.

(2000: n.p.)

In a more recent study, with material generated through questionnaires completed by 83 students in a human sexuality class, Kessler and McKenna argue that there is now a greater sense that gender is complex. However, they conclude:

Twenty-five years of our and others' theorizing about gender has in many ways unsettled the meaning of gender, but it has done no damage to the gender dichotomy . . . genitals are the essential defining feature of what it means to be a gender . . . just because more people acknowledge that gender features can be mixed together or that a person can move more easily between categories, this has not led to an expansion of or transcendence of the gender categories. There are still two and only two genders.

(2000: n.p.)

Thus, while in theory gender beyond the binaries may be recognised, nonetheless, in mainstream society, living openly beyond the two-sexes/two-genders systems would still not appear to constitute a socially viable option (Whittle 1996; Namaste 2000; Green 2004; Cromwell 2006). The experiences of transsexual people demonstrate this point. Of particular significance in this regard are the accounts of people who are unable to sufficiently resemble biological women or men and transsexual people who identify beyond the binary genders (Hill and Willoughby 2005; Davidmann 2007; Valentine 2007; Whittle et al. 2007).

In this chapter I shall discuss the experiences of two non-binary gendered transsexual people. Through their accounts, I shall explore the impact of everyday life on the transsexual person who openly transgresses the binary sex and gender borders. This chapter draws on photography and interview research carried out with 23 transsexual people over an eight-year period and specifically builds on the outcomes of a four-year doctoral photography and interview study carried out with eight transsexual people.[1]

'WRONG' BODIES OR 'RIGHT' BODIES

Underpinning the two-genders/two-sexes premise is the assumption that a person's sex and gender are not only aligned but also in accord with the genitals (Kessler and McKenna 2000). Following this formula, genital surgery is believed to be a necessary requirement, and is frequently perceived as the ultimate act for 'changing sex'. This idea can be traced back to the case of Christine Jorgensen, who underwent genital surgery in 1953 (Benjamin 1966; Stryker and Whittle 2006). Subsequent to the media attention surrounding the case, medical interest in transsexuality developed upon the principle that genital surgery is fundamental to transsexual identities.[2] Building upon the gender/sex/genitals/surgery equation a narrative has emerged in accounts of transsexuality that a transsexual person is born in the 'wrong body'.[3] Indeed, this notion has come to symbolise the transsexual condition.

The transsexual author Sandy Stone argues that: 'under the binary phallocentric founding myth by which Western bodies and subjects are authorized, only one body per gendered subject is "right". All other bodies are wrong' (1991: 297). Moreover, the FTM author Jason Cromwell asserts that the term 'wrong body' reflects the fact that transsexual discourses, arising from medical and psychological perspectives, are fundamentally moral discourses based on the assumption that 'trans behaviours of any kind are abnormal' (1999: 19).[4] Further, Cromwell suggests that it is through the 'wrong body' concept that: 'Biological determinists thus join transsexual discourses and medico-psychological practitioners in attempting to eradicate gender diversity.' (1999: 38)

While the medical and popular view is that the 'cure' for the transsexual condition is the 'exchange' of a male body for a female one, or vice versa, many transsexual people's accounts indicate that the ways in which they experience their bodies, and in particular the sexed/gendered parts of the body, are intrinsically more complex than the notion of 'right' or 'wrong' bodies would allow (Nataf 1996; Cromwell 1999; Hines 2007). My research suggests that specific combinations of female and male physical attributes may be significant in allowing for the corporeal manifestation of atypical transsexual genders. Thus for transsexual people who self-identify beyond the binary gender categories, the genitalia at birth can constitute an important part of their identity. In line with this, in the two brief case studies that follow, I aim to demonstrate that, contrary to the popular belief that a desire for genital surgery is an essential criteria of a transsexual identity, the focus of transsexual experiences does not always reside with the genitals. Consequently, some transsexual people do not wish to have the surgeries that have become widely known as 'sex change' operations. By offering a counter-narrative to the notion of 'being born in the wrong body', which configures around the genitalia as the signifier of female-ness or male-ness (Stone 1991: 297), the case study material will bring to the surface the concern that while some transsexual people are creating what could be construed as new configurations of sex and gender, the link between transsexual well-being and the broader social domain is more significant than is generally acknowledged. Further, despite the important social changes and shifts in theoretical perspectives that have taken place since the 1990s, everyday life for the transsexual person who openly transgresses the binary sex and gender borders remains highly problematic.

KITTY

Kitty was assigned 'male' at birth and raised as a boy. She now self-identifies as a 'she-male woman'. In other words, she sees herself as both a she-male and a woman. A she-male is a term used to describe someone born anatomically male, who undergoes physical changes in order to appear more female, usually taking female hormones and having breast augmentation, while retaining male genitalia. In talking about her gender identification Kitty claims:

> I know there are some natural born women who would say that I'm not the same as them. I say, well, I'm not the same as you . . . why can't there be two variations? . . . To me, at the end of the day, I guess I'm both. Ultimately I am a woman . . . you could also look on me as a she-male . . . She-male woman. One may seem on the surface to cancel out the other, but it makes sense to me.

The term 'she-male woman' is Kitty's own hybrid invention created in order to try to describe as closely as possible how she experiences her gender. Kitty continues to take female hormones, though she has had no surgery. Originally she had intended to have genital surgery but she decided against this. Kitty explains:

> My intention was to go for the full thing . . . I did want it but I guess I also felt that I needed it to be a full woman and I came to the conclusion I didn't need it—and I guess the interest in wanting it went away . . .

> I've decided now that I don't want the operation. If that changes later
> on in life then fair enough . . . but at the moment I'm happy enough.

Kitty's description articulates a potential fluidity of gender. She is comfortable with her body in its present form but she does not rule out the possibility of a future change. In discussing her male genitalia Kitty asserts: 'I don't particularly like them but I don't particularly dislike them either.' In terms of her sexuality, Kitty identifies as a lesbian and her male genitalia play a part in sexual relations. However, she asserts: 'I didn't really think it was supposed to be done.' Kitty sought guidance by contacting gender support organisations and she recalls that she was given pamphlets discussing, among other issues, sexual relationships. Nevertheless, they were written for people transitioning from one to the other of the binary sex/gender polarities. The advice was unhelpful to Kitty and she had to resolve on her own the concerns she had with regard to having sexual relations.

Kitty is now at ease with her body, both in physical relationships with others and as a reflection of her gender. Nonetheless, in the public domain she is unable to blend with expected gender appearances. Kitty has strong masculine features and she has not been able to afford the costly facial and cranial surgery or electrolysis to remove her facial hair that some trans women undergo in order to appear more stereotypically feminine. In the UK the National Health system covers the cost of genital surgeries, hormone treatment and chest surgery for people assigned female at birth. Other treatments are not available under the system. Thus the medicalisation of transsexuality emphasises the primacy of the sexed body over and above social integration. Additionally, because these aspects of trans embodiment are not state-funded, the person's financial status and social class are an issue.

Kitty has strong features that are generally associated with masculinity and in public spaces others frequently 'read' her as either a transvestite or a transsexual person. The reactions of others to Kitty's appearance make interacting in the public domain a continuous strain and cause her considerable emotional distress. She has been spat at on the street, shouted at, pointed at, accosted by drunks, and is frequently stared at. When I have been out with Kitty I have been aware of the measures she takes so as to go unnoticed by others. On the street she is highly sensitive to the positions of others' bodies in relation to her own and she will navigate her route when walking in an attempt to avoid face-to-face contact whenever possible. In cafés and bars she will sit opposite a wall so that her back faces outwards towards other people. I have been shocked by the reactions of others when Kitty has been unable to hide from view. One evening when we met for a drink in a crowded bar in London's Soho district I suggested that we finish our drinks outside, even though it was raining, because of the amount of unwelcome attention Kitty was receiving.[5] Another time, in a café near her home in Kilburn, London, we walked out because of the comments and jeers from three men at the table next to us. Unfortunately, Kitty is not alone in her experiences. Almost all the transsexual people who took part in my research have specifically highlighted incidents in public spaces that have been distressing because of how other people have reacted to them.[6]

The consistent abuse that Kitty receives in public spaces is because she is not able to 'pass' as a biological female. The term 'passing' is used to describe projecting and being accepted in a gender that is at odds with the person's assigned birth sex. For many transsexual people this involves using highly visualised, visualising and visible means in order to become 'invisible' in the social domain. The term 'passing' implies an act of secrecy and dishonesty, of playing a part that one has no right to play.

However, social interaction involves both a performance and a reading of the performance (Goffman 1959: 32). Judith Butler develops this theme with regard to gender and claims that the performance of gender de-stabilises the notion of a fixed gender identity (1990: 179). Building on Butler's hypothesis that gender expressions are not derived from an essential gender identity and Goffman's argument that social exchange involves the performance of the self, it follows that in everyday social interaction non-transgender people are also 'passing'. In other words, female and male gender presentations are not natural or neutral facts of life that emerge from an essentially gendered self. Individual presentations of the self are performative expressions that are developed in relation to culturally created and socially sustained models. In line with this, the trans writer and performer Kate Bornstein suggests: 'Everyone is passing; some have an easier job of it than others.' (1994: 127)

Further, Bornstein asserts that she first believed that the gender dichotomy was the only possibility. Consequently, she saw herself as: 'a mistake: something that needed to be fixed and then placed neatly into one of the categories.' (1994: 65) Bornstein claims that this is how most transsexual people feel (Ibid). The trans activist and legal expert Stephen Whittle expresses a rather different understanding of the relationship between transsexual people, the binary gender system, and the broad social domain. Building on the understanding of gender as: 'an idea, an invention, a means of oppression and a means of expression', Whittle argues: 'Many in the community would see themselves as existing outside of gender, of being oppressed by it but using its icons and signifiers to say who they are.' Further, Whittle suggests that many transsexual people decide not to declare their trans status because: 'they are seeking a form of sanctuary in the gender-roles they adopt' (1996: 212). Nonetheless, assuming a female or male gender, if one does not identify within either binary category exclusively, does not necessarily offer a satisfactory solution. In the semi-autobiographical novel *Stone Butch Blues* Leslie Feinberg characterises his experiences of 'passing'. Feinberg's main character Jess claims:

At first everything was fun. The world stopped feeling like a gauntlet I had to run through. But very quickly I discovered that passing didn't

just mean slipping below the surface, it meant being buried alive. I was
still me on the inside . . . But I was no longer me on the outside.

(1993: 173)

One can conjecture that, because of the continuous efforts that Kitty makes
to 'pass' and to become 'invisible' in the public domain, she may also feel
that she is being 'buried alive'. Further, this concern may shed light on why
Kitty contacted me in the hope that I might agree to work with her. Kitty
had seen a published photograph of mine, taken of Frances who identifies
as a 'pre-op transsexual'.[7]

The photograph, a naked full-frontal torso, clearly shows that Frances has
breasts and male genitalia. I later realised that the picture presents a body
image with which Kitty is able to identify. While images of she-males and pre-
operative transsexual people are accessible through the Internet and in some
pornographic publications, they are not generally available in the broad public
domain. Kitty has expressed feeling the need for validation and self-visibility.
On discussing the photograph in Figure 9.2 Kitty asserts:

As I understand it, the work we're doing . . . is very much a reflection
of me, which I've wanted for a long time. An opportunity for me to tell

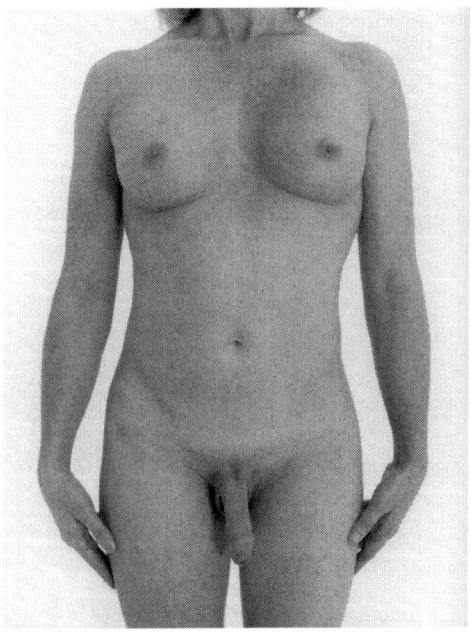

Figure 9.1 Frances, 2002. Photograph
by Sara Davidmann. C-type print, 60" x
40". Exhibited in *nu-gender*, APT gallery,
London, 2003.

myself as I am and show myself as I am . . . People basically see what they want to a lot of the time so I'm trying to leave something behind . . . that people can look at . . . and whether they believe it or not . . . I know that is Kitty up there.

Thus, while Kitty is unable to openly express her gender identity in mainstream social spaces, she suggests that photography may allow self-visibility without the danger inherent in being physically present. The significance of photographs in transsexual experiences has repeatedly come to the surface in my research. I would suggest that the reasons for this are three-fold.

First, the social expectation of photography is that it reproduces reality (Burgin 1982). Roland Barthes describes photographs as constituting 'a certificate of presence' (2000: 87). This, he argues, is because of the power of photographs to authenticate 'the existence of a certain being' (2000: 107). Hence, for people who have been unable to identify with their body and, as a consequence, have undergone extreme physical changes, the photograph provides a form of 'proof' of their new physical reality. Second, photographs constitute a form of evidence that the person 'is' who they believed themselves to be all along. This is because the photograph 'blocks memory, quickly becomes a counter-memory' (Barthes 2000: 91). Third, the indexical trace (the photograph can be understood as a trace that is left behind by the referent) additionally allows the subject to regard an image of themselves in their new form from an external position, which is aligned with that from which they view images of other people. Thus a photograph has the potential to contribute towards enabling the person to assume a new position in relation to other people through the act of inserting their own 'certified' image alongside representations of others.

Kitty asserts that she has wanted for a long time to: 'show myself as I am.' The widely held beliefs associated with photography allow Kitty to produce 'evidence', and thus to verify, that she is indeed as she sees herself in her mind. Further, seeing the photograph, the trace of the person that *was* there, that is in accord with the internal self-image, is an affirmative act. Thus, while in the public domain Kitty is the recipient of considerable verbal abuse because, as Kitty claims: 'People . . . see what they want to a lot of the time', photography allows for a different version of 'reality' that emerges from her self-perceptions.

Figure 9.2 is a photograph of Kitty taken in her flat during the course of our collaborative photographic work. Kitty was entirely responsible for constructing the image, creating an exotic background by arranging scarves and saris from her collection on the sofa. She specifically wanted to be photographed in her boots and feather boa and initiated the pose, making adjustments using a mirror until she was satisfied with her appearance.

A few weeks earlier, prior to our first meeting I had sent Kitty an email asking if she was able to name anyone with whom she identified. She promptly replied and included pictures of Mata Hari, Marilyn Monroe, Constance Bennett and Hedy Lamarr, all of whom are popular female film stars. In an accompanying text Kitty described characteristics of herself that she recognised in the images. Of the Mata Hari picture (Figure 9.3) Kitty wrote: 'This shot of Mata Hari for me represents so much.' In an interview she later explained: 'Mata Hari, to me, tends to sum up very much myself.'

When I took the photograph in Figure 9.2 I did not make a connection between the image that Kitty was creating and the Mata Hari picture. However, having studied the pictures at a later date I now believe that there is a resemblance between them. The similarity resides in the fact that both images depict generalised orientalist fantasies that are highly sexualised and consistent with the idea of the glamorous Orient. While Mata Hari is draped in lengths of fabrics, Kitty uses saris and scarves from her collection to create an exotic backdrop. Both Kitty and Mata Hari are transformed in these pictures into orientalised odalisques.[8] I would suggest that, for Kitty, the photograph in Figure 9.2 provides a record of the 'becoming' or 'being' that which she would like to be. When she saw the photograph for the first time she exclaimed: 'This is me . . . It's everything that I am.'

When I asked Kitty how she felt about her genitalia being visible in the photographs that we were taking she responded: 'it's part of me . . . I wish the emphasis was more on my face, or my breasts or something, but it's part of me . . . It's pictures of my body . . . and I'm proud of it.'

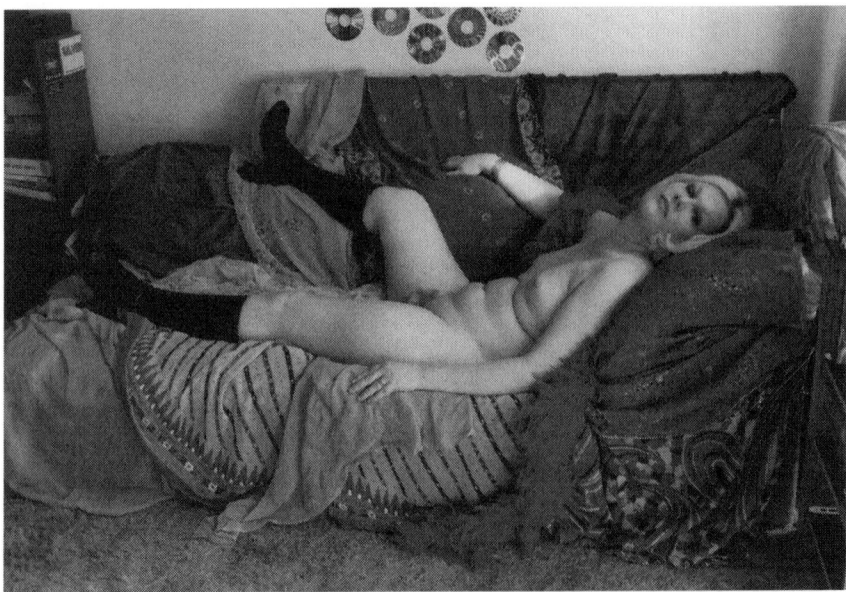

Figure 9.2   Kitty, 2003. Photograph by Sara Davidmann. C-type print, 30" x 40". Exhibited in *Somatechnics*, Macquarie University Gallery, Sydney, Australia, 2005.

Figure 9.3   Mata Hari, photograph c. 1910. Picture from Kitty's collection. Digital inkjet print, 10" x 8".

ROBERT

Kitty's assertion, that she is proud of her body, is echoed in the account given by another of the research participants, Robert. Robert also identifies beyond the gender dichotomy. Similar to Kitty, Robert has undergone some physical changes and also claims that he has no desire to alter his genitalia. While Kitty was assigned male at birth, Robert was assigned female.

Robert has had a bilateral mastectomy in order to remove his breasts and create a masculine chest, and he has testosterone injections every two weeks. The testosterone maintains the male aspects of Robert's appearance, such as facial and body hair, muscle strength and re-distribution of fat towards a more masculine body shape. Robert's physical appearance is now predominantly male. Nevertheless, in discussing his genitalia he claims: 'I don't ever see myself in my mind as having a penis and I never have done.' Robert has said that when he first came across the term 'transsexual' he knew that he 'fitted in there somewhere', while at the same time he thought that he was not transsexual because he did not want male genitalia. Robert identifies as gay and his genitalia play a part in sexual relationships.[9] Robert describes his body as it is now, with a masculine chest and female genitalia, as 'complete'. He argues:

> For some having a penis is a sign of completion, completeness with breasts and everything else, and for other people not having a penis and having a flat chest is absolutely fine. It's just where you put your boundaries, where you put your borders.

Robert's assertion here, that the placement of borders is significant in relation to atypically sexed embodiment, is reflected in the way in which he describes his gender. Robert claims:

> I'm not really a man, but I'm not a woman . . . I'm trans. So in some ways I'm not really transsexual either . . . I'm male, but I'm not a man. I'm neither a man nor a woman, but I'm male rather than female.

While 'trans' is widely used as an abbreviation for the term 'transgender', Robert's use of the term is rather different. For Robert, the term describes a position beyond the binary genders. Robert explains:

> There's a lovely saying that one door closes and another door opens but it's hell in the hallway . . . that's something I think a lot about. Being trans, you're in the hallway. A trans life is the one in the hallway . . . These doors open and shut but at the end of the day you can only open a door into the male world on one side and the female world on the other side and you have to join society on either side. But if you stay in the hallway, which I believe is much more freeing because you're not bound by either side, it's infinitely harder because you're not bound by either side but you're not belonging to either side. The hallway is a wonderful place. Hallways can have windows and they can have wonderful views.

Despite the perspective that Robert's trans status allows, he lives as a male in society. In his everyday life Robert is able to blend with expected gender appearances. In other words, he is 'seen' by others as male. How people are seen is fundamental to being able to function in society.[10] The FTM author Zachary Nataf asserts that: 'Very few people can cross-live, get employment successfully and be safe in the streets without hormones and some surgery.' (1996: 43) While the binary sexes and genders continue to be the only socially recognised positions, people who identify as trans but blend with female or male appearances will inevitably be perceived by others as belonging within the binary categories. Cromwell argues that in this context being seen as male does not constitute 'passing' as it is generally

Figure 9.4 Robert and the Mirror, 2003. Photograph by Sara Davidmann. C-type print, 30" x 40". Exhibited in *Somatechnics*, Macquarie University Gallery, Sydney, Australia, 2005.

understood. In other words, it is not an act of falsehood or of living a lie (1999: 39). Rather, what occurs here is the result of a process of negotiation between the individual's gender identity and the limitations of the socially sanctioned binary sexes and genders. Because Robert is perceived to be a biological male he is able to interact with ease with others in social spaces. However, whenever he feels it is necessary, for example on job applications, Robert has no hesitation in being open about his assigned birth sex and subsequent transition.

In contrast to the difficulties Kitty experiences in the public domain since taking oestrogen and living as a female, Robert encountered problems before undergoing any changes. In explaining people's reactions, Robert claims that before taking testosterone neither his appearance nor his body language conformed to stereotypically feminine principles. For example, on leaving school Robert was given a place at a prestigious music college and trained as a viola player. However, he was once fired from an orchestra and the reason he was given for this was that he looked: 'ridiculous in a skirt'. This issue, of the pre-transitional appearance being construed by others as

Figure 9.5   Robert in Dublin, 2006. Photograph
by Sara Davidmann. C-type print, 12" x 10".

androgynous and subsequently encountering difficulties in social interactions, was highlighted in the accounts of female-assigned participants.

Since taking testosterone and having chest surgery, Robert's life has changed dramatically for the better and he is now able to interact with confidence in public spaces.[11] However, in order to do so Robert has had to comply with expected appearances for males. Thus he has become 'invisible' as a trans person in the public domain. Stone argues that transsexual people are 'programmed to disappear', claiming: 'The highest purpose of the transsexual is to erase him/herself, to fade into the 'normal' population as soon as possible.' (1991: 295) In order to gain equality, transsexual people need to be visible in society. Yet, as I have demonstrated, when a person is recognisable as being transsexual—when they do not 'pass'—they run the risk of verbal or physical abuse in the public domain. The trans activist and author Jamison Green highlights the complexity of this issue when he asserts:

> Visibility remains a conflicted aspect of transsexual lives. How do we manage visibility? If we are visible then we risk being mistreated; if we

are invisible, no one will understand what our social or medical needs are. If we are visible, we risk being judged inferior or unreal, inauthentic; if we are invisible, we risk being discovered and cast out.

(2004: 180)

Stemming from his own experiences, which include being seen by others as being different, Robert was politically active for many years with the aim of bringing about positive changes for transgender people. For several years he was involved with Press for Change, an organisation that campaigns for equal rights for UK trans people, and for four years of that time he was a Vice President. He was on the Parliamentary Forum for Transsexuality, worked as a helpline volunteer for the FTM network and has been on the FTM London Committee. Robert also set up a London-based hospital visiting service in order to provide support for transsexual people having surgery.

Robert's political awareness underpinned his interest in taking part in my study. While Robert is able to interact with ease in mainstream society because he is seen as male, photography provides a way for him to be able to stand up and assert his trans identity. Kitty's need for validation and self-visibility surfaced strongly in her desire to work with me. For Robert, the photographs constitute both a personal affirmation and a political statement. Robert explains:

The only way you're going to know I'm trans is if I stand up and say so—and that's why I do it—because I can appear to blend in. If I don't stand up then what about those people who don't have the choice to blend. You're implying there's something wrong with being trans if you hide . . . I'm enjoying the opportunity to stand up and celebrate the body and celebrate the differences in the body . . . I'm trying to show an alternative way . . . I think the photos are very important.

Thus Robert suggests that photography may offer a way of enabling social visibility for non-binary identified transsexual people. Robert's argument builds on the trans photographer Loren Cameron's (1996) use of photography as a vehicle for FTM and self-visibility. Further, as previously discussed, photography has the potential to allow visibility without directly endangering the individual through their embodied presence. The accounts of Robert, Kitty, and the other participants who contributed to my research, demonstrate that this constitutes a crucial factor for people who do not appear, in the eyes of others, to belong within one or other of the polarised sex or gender categories.

CONCLUSION

In this chapter I have foregrounded the lived experiences of two self-identified non-binary transsexual people. Their accounts demonstrate that, contrary to the medical and popular view of transsexuality that construes a desire for genital surgery as an essential criterion of a transsexual identity, some transsexual people do not wish to have 'sex change' operations. Further, their experiences offer an alternative perspective to the medical and popular view that the 'cure' for transsexuality is the exchange of a male body for a female one, or vice versa. Through their accounts, I have aimed to present a counter-narrative to the notion of 'being born in the wrong body', which has come to symbolise the transsexual condition and configures around the genitalia as the signifier of female-ness or male-ness (Stone 1991: 297). The two case studies presented here reveal that the ways in which transsexual people experience their bodies, and in particular the sexed/gendered parts of the body, can be intrinsically more complex. Further, for transsexual people identifying beyond the binary gender categories, the genitalia at birth may constitute an important part of their gender identities.

Concerns of visibility and invisibility in the broad social domain, and the difference between private and public gender presentations, have formed an important part of this discussion. This is because these issues surfaced in the research as being highly significant in the lives of non-binary identified transsexual people. While some people do represent direct challenges to the sex and gender dichotomies, everyday life re-enforces the binary model. Thus few images explore beyond the polarised categories. Consequently the visual articulation of the categories defines and perpetuates the binary model, controlling and reproducing gender 'norms' to the exclusion of non-binary definitions. For many people who identify beyond the gender dichotomy this can result in a considerable difference between private and public gender presentations. In other words, the changes that are made to the body to bring it into alignment with the person's gender are at odds with the expected appearances of the two socially sanctioned sexes. Neverthe-less, in order to lead a satisfactory social existence, it is often still necessary to 'pass' as a biological female or male.

The policing of gender in mainstream public spaces, that repeatedly featured in the accounts of my research participants, not only contributes towards maintaining and reinforcing polarised gender presentations in every-day life, but also demonstrates that crossing the sex and gender borders con-stitutes a threat to some people. Everyday life for the transsexual person, and in particular the non-binary identified person, remains highly problematic.

Thus, despite the considerable theoretical advancements that have devel-oped in the past 20 years through queer theory and the popularisation of its concerns, with regard to the two-sexes/two-genders systems this appears to have had very little impact on mainstream society. Gender borders may have expanded to encompass a degree of 'mixing' of gender attributes, which results in female masculinity and male femininity becoming more prevalent in Western urban social spaces. Nevertheless, these factors do not appear to have succeeded in subverting the primacy of the binary categories of 'female' and 'male', 'woman' and 'man' in everyday life. Consequently, as the material presented here demonstrates, some transsexual people who identify beyond the sex and gender binaries may act strategically in order to function in society, nonetheless, ultimately they are left out 'in the hallway' between these positions. The hallway may have doors on either side through which a person might pass to enter the female or male worlds and thus join society. However, while these are the only doors, some people are unable to pass through either and are left with no other choice than to *live* in the hallway.

NOTES

1. See Davidmann (2006, 2007) for further details of the study.
2. There is evidence of 28 cases of transsexual operations prior to 1953 (King 1996: 85). Jorgensen was originally diagnosed as a homosexual man. Surgery and hormones were used to 'treat' Jorgensen's 'homosexuality'. After the incident had been reported in the press the medical team decreed the operation to be a 'sex-change' (King 1996: 92). The publicity surrounding Jorgensen's case enabled other transsexual people to come forward. In 1953 Jorgensen's psychiatrist, Dr Christian Hamburger, published a paper based on the letters of 465 men and women who wanted to 'change sex' (Hamburger 1953). This, in turn, led to an increase in the number of medical professionals interested in the field (Benjamin 1966: 148).
3. The use of the term 'the wrong body' has a history that extends beyond the recognition of transsexuality. In the late 1890s homosexuality was described as 'a feminine soul confined by a masculine body'. In other words homosexual people were considered to inhabit the wrong body (Ulrichs 1975 [1898], cited in Kennedy 1981: 106).
4. FTM is an abbreviation of 'female-to-male'. Both terms refer to transsexual people assigned female at birth. FTM is also used as an abbreviation for 'female-towards-male'. This acknowledges the person's history and socialisation as a female and recognises that the person is not the same as a biological male. Female-towards-male is also used when the person identifies as a 'female man'. In this case the person may or may not take testosterone or have surgery (Cromwell 1999: 28).
5. Soho is London's best known lesbian and gay area.
6. In a public talk in January of this year, hosted by the Wellcome Trust, Rikki Arundel, Director of *Gendershift*, suggested that somewhere in the region of 60 per cent of trans women and 50 per cent of trans men experience hate crime on the street.
7. *Time Out* London 8–15, 2003 listing for *nu-gender* exhibition, APT Gallery, London.
8. The photograph of Kitty is also highly reminiscent of another well-known odalisque, Édouard Manet's [1832–1883] painting 'Olympia'.
9. The fact that Kitty and Robert both identify as gay is a coincidence. Other non-binary identified transsexual people who have taken part in my research do not necessarily identify as gay.
10. This concern surfaced repeatedly in my research in different ways.
11. Robert's experiences in this regard are not uncommon among FTMs and trans men. The FTM research participants' accounts highlight that testosterone appears to readily override the effects of oestrogen on the body. Unfortunately, this process does not always work as effectively the other way around.

This is particularly evident in some cases where people transition later on in life when testosterone has had a long-term effect on the body.

REFERENCES

Barthes, R. (2000 [1980]) *Camera Lucida*, London: Vintage.
Benjamin, H. (1966) *The Transsexual Phenomenon*, New York: The Julian Press.
Bornstein, K. (1994) *Gender Outlaw: On Men, Women, and the Rest of Us*, New York: Routledge.
Burgin, V. (ed.) (1982) *Thinking Photography*, London: Macmillan.
Butler, J. (1990) *Gender Trouble: Feminism and the Subversion of Identity*, New York: Routledge.
———. (1991) 'Imitation and gender insubordination', in D. Fuss (ed.) *Inside/Out: Lesbian Theories, Gay Theories*, London: Routledge.
———. (1993) *Bodies that Matter: On the Discursive Limits of Sex*, London: Routledge.
Cameron, L. (1996) *Body Alchemy*, San Francisco: Cleiss Press Inc.
Cromwell, J. (1999) *Transmen and FTMs: Identities, Bodies, Genders and Sexualities*, Urbana and Chicago: University of Illinois Press.
Cromwell, J. (2006) 'Queering the binaries: transsituated identities, bodies and sexualities', in S. Stryker and S. Whittle (eds) *The Transgender Studies Reader*, New York: Routledge.
Davidmann, S. (2006) 'Border trouble: photography, strategies, and transsexual identities', *SCAN: Journal of Media, Arts, Culture*, 3(3). http://scan.net.au/scan/journal/display.php?journal_id=85 (accessed 12 July 2008).
———. (2007) 'Visualising the transsexual self: photography, strategies, and identities', unpublished thesis, University of the Arts London.
Feinberg, L. (1993) *Stone Butch Blues*, Ithaca, New York: Firebrand Books.
———. (1996) *Transgender Warriors: Making History from Joan of Arc to Dennis Rodman*, Boston: Beacon Press.
Foucault, M. (1984) *The History of Sexuality: An Introduction*, Harmondsworth: Penguin Books.
Garfinkel, H. (1967) *Studies in Ethnomethodology*, Englewood Cliffs, New Jersey: Prentice Hall.
Goffman, E. (1959) *The Presentation of Self in Everyday Life*, London: Penguin Books.
Green, J. (2004) *Becoming a Visible Man*, Nashville: Vanderbilt University Press.
Halberstam, J. (1998) *Female Masculinity*, Durham, NC: Duke University Press.
Halberstam, J. (2005) *In a Queer Time and Place: Transgender Bodies, Subcultural Lives*, New York: New York University Press.
Hamburger, C. (1953) 'The desire for change of sex as shown by personal letters from 465 men and women', *Acta Endocrinologica*, 14: 361–375.
Herdt, G. (1993) 'Introduction: third sexes and third genders', in G. Herdt (ed.) *Third Sex, Third Gender: Beyond Sexual Dimorphism in Culture and History*, New York: Zone Books.
Hill, D. and Willoughby, B. (2005) 'The development and validation of the genderism and transphobia scale', *Sex Roles*, 53(7/8): 531–544.
Hines, S. (2007) *Transforming Gender: Transgender Practices of Identity, Intimacy and Care*, Bristol: The Policy Press.
Jagose, A. (1996) 'Queer theory', *Australian Humanities Review*. http://www.australianhumanitiesreview.org/archive/Issue-Dec-1996/jagose.html (accessed 10 December 2008).

Kennedy, H. C. (1981) 'The third sex theory of Karl Henry Ulrichs', *Journal of Homosexuality*, 6(1/2): 103–111.

Kessler, S. J. and McKenna, W. (1978) *Gender: An Ethnomethodological Approach*, Chicago: University of Chicago Press.

———. (2000) 'Who put the "trans" in transgender? Gender theory and everyday life', *The International Journal of Transgenderism*, 4(3). http://www.symposion.com/ijt (accessed 10 February 2004).

King, D. (1996) 'Gender blending: medical perspectives and technology', in R. Ekins and D. King (eds) *Blending Genders: Social Aspects of Cross-Dressing and Sex-Changing*, London: Routledge.

Namaste, V. (2000) *Invisible Lives: The Erasure of Transsexual and Transgendered People*, The University of Chicago Press: Chicago.

Nataf, Z. (1996) *Lesbians Talk Transgender*, London: Scarlet Press.

Shaw, A. and Ardener, S. (eds) (2005) *Changing Sex and Bending Gender*, Oxford: Berghan Books.

Spargo, T. (1999) *Foucault and Queer Theory*, London: Icon Books.

Stone, S. (1991) 'The empire strikes back: a posttranssexual manifesto', in J. Epstein and K. Straub (eds) *Body Guards: The Cultural Politics of Gender Ambiguity*, New York: Routledge.

Stryker, S. and Whittle, S. (eds) (2006) *The Transgender Studies Reader*, New York: Routledge.

Sullivan, N. (2003) *Queer Theory: A Critical Introduction*, Edinburgh: Edinburgh University Press.

Valentine, D. (2007) *Imagining Transgender: An Ethnography of a Category*, Duham, NC and London: Duke University Press.

Whittle, S. (1996) 'Gender fucking or fucking gender? Current cultural contributions to theories of gender blending', in R. Ekins and D. King (eds) *Blending Genders: Social Aspects of Cross-Dressing and Sex-Changing*, London: Routledge.

Whittle, S., Turner, L. and Al-Alami, M. (2007) 'Engendered penalties: Transgender and transsexual people's experiences of inequality and discrimination', *Press for Change*. http://www.pfc.org.uk (accessed 15 January 2009).

Wilchins, R. (2004) *Queer Theory, Gender Theory: An Instant Primer*, New York: Alyson Books.

Part IV

Transforming Theory

10 Who Put the 'Hetero' in Sexuality?

Angie Fee

It is not so much that there have always been transgendered people; it is that there have always been cultures which imposed regimes of gender.

(Wilchins 1997: 67)

INTRODUCTION

This chapter is based on my Ph.D. research which explores how transgender identity is constructed and discursively produced in Western societies in the early twenty-first century; and also draws from my experiences in teaching Sexualities and Genders courses to postgraduate counselling and psychotherapy students. My teaching and research has led to my interest in examining the wider cultural conditions that shape and regulate our understandings of sex, gender and desire. In this chapter, I focus on one of these conditions; namely how heterosexuality has become an organising principle for understanding and experiencing sexual and gendered identities. By challenging the presumed naturalness of heterosexuality and the largely unquestioning acceptance of this category, I illustrate the limited conceptual space of heterosexual discourse that depends on binary sexed and gender categories for exploring and understanding erotic relationships.

In the last 50 years, feminist and gay theoretical scholarship has produced a substantial body of work concerning the categories of sex and gender. Debates have mainly taken place on the essentialist/constructionist continuum, which is best understood as connoting a space between fixed identities and fluid social processes. Theoretical scholarship has emerged from a diverse range of disciplines resulting in significant social and political shifts in the way that sexed and gendered identities were discursively produced; first, with sex seen as biological and natural, and gender as social and cultural; and more recently, with the idea of embodied gender and sex as the constructed category. Much has been written on what sex and gender are, and are not, and most of this work underplays the dominance of the heterosexual matrix—the conflation of sex-gender-desire which leads to the normalisation of heterosexuality—as the source of sex and gender categorisation.

This chapter moves beyond the essentialist/constructionist debates, to focus, instead, on a critique of the heterosexual matrix. My intentions are to question the predominant heterosexual discourse that is used to understand the concepts of sex and gender and to illustrate how discourse influences what is experienced and how experiences are described. It is with this in mind, that this chapter traces the development of the heterosexual matrix, mapping the rise of a hegemonic heteronormative regime which has become central to how people experience and understand their sexual and gender identities and to how we form erotic relationships. This chapter is divided into five sections. I begin by exploring Freud's development of the Oedipal complex and how it produces heterosexuality as a symbol of 'normal' and 'mature' adult sexual and gender identity. The second section reviews Foucault's (1984) argument that sexuality is not a natural fact of life but a constructed category of experience which has historical, social and cultural, rather than biological, origins. The third section introduces feminist theorists Butler (1990), Rich (1980), and Wittig (1998 [1992]) who continued to critique the unquestioned assumptions of heterosexuality and its capacity to shape identity and desire by creating a 'compulsory heterosexuality' (Rich 1980: 23). I then draw attention to the effects of heteronormativity; the term that is used to describe this social norm which has become naturalised. The fifth section explores the emergence of the non-normative gendered category of transgender and how it is contributing towards the interruption and subversion of the binary sex and gender categories created by the heterosexual matrix. Finally, I chart the development of theoretical scholarship that is challenging heterosexual ideology and which points to a reordering and reframing of the limited language available to describe transgendered people's identities, bodies and sexualities.

PSYCHOLOGICAL CONSTRUCTION OF HETEROSEXUALITY

The identity categories of sex, gender, and sexual orientation are central to people's descriptions of their identity. Sexologists (Hirschfield 1868–1935; Kraft-Ebbing 1840–1902) of the late nineteenth and early twentieth centuries, studied sexual and gendered diversity and this laid the groundwork in establishing normative opposing gender and sexed distinctions based on a dualistically opposed sex/gender system. These historical and cultural conditions had a profound and long lasting impact on the emergence of heterosexuality as a dominant discourse for how people organised their sexual and gendered identities.

Katz's (1995) exploration of the concept of heterosexuality as a twentieth-century creation explores how Freud's (1962 [1905]) theory of the Oedipal complex both relies on, and creates, the institution of heterosexuality. It is this particular matrix–with its arrangement of gender, sex and desire—that influences the way people experience and think about their sexual and gendered identities. The Oedipal complex resides in different-sex desire, subsequently leading to a heteronormative theory of dichotomous gender development, and it is a cornerstone of twentieth-century psychological theories. The Oedipal complex structures the direction of identification and desire, in that identification is what one would *like to be*, and desire is what one would *like to have* but one cannot identify and desire the same object. In this way, the concepts of identification and desire are gendered and heterosexualised. Homosexual desires are seen as heterosexual desires stemming from the wrong identifications. The Oedipus complex is the story that Freud creates about growing up and taming these initial multiple desires.

It is worth questioning whether Freud's 'normal' negotiation of the Oedipus complex is ever achieved. My own psychotherapeutic work with people is testimony to how fluid desire is and how it flows in many directions breaking up all kinds of imposed moral codes (Moon 2008; Sanger 2008). In Freudian terms, we can—at any point in life—still be at the mercy of the pre-Oedipal state of 'polymorphous perversities'—a time when neither we, nor the objects of our desire, were defined through sexual difference, a time before our gendered fate was sealed by strongly embedded cultural messages. If Freud's theory that all children are polymorphously perverse is to be believed, it is difficult to understand how these multitudinous, undifferentiated desires get so narrowly channelled into adult procreative heterosexuality. His theory of identity does not allow for diverse identifications and contradictions, and the free play of polymorphous perversities are constrained within the dominant cultural heterosexual matrix. The Oedipal system entrenches, and continues the reproduction of heterosexuality within the family, repressing anything that is different. In these ways, the Freudian view brought about increasingly rigid social classifications of drives, desires and sexual relationships.

The Oedipal trajectory manifests itself in the construction of dualistic and hierarchical gender categories whereby, traditionally, sexual orientation is dictated by gender identity. The Oedipus myth, by relying on a heterosexual psychic structure, accepts the social, political and religious forms of domination in modern Western society which effectively control and define desire. Western heterosexuality defines what is male and female, and gender is thus derived from it. This heterosexual matrix is unconsciously lived out to the extent that it is marked as natural and given (Warner 2002).

Katz (1995) describes Freud's theory of psychosexual development as an ethical journey, with the individual working through the various stages from immature to mature sexuality. Failure to achieve this progression results in the homosexual who is fixated at an early psychosexual stage; thus they are immature and polymorphously perverse—unsocialised and wild. Freud's linear psychosexual development implies that the ideal is an exclusive heterosexual who has learned to socially restrict his or her roving sexual instinct. This position is full of ethical meaning and, subversively, suggests that heterosexuals are made, not born (de Beauvoir 1987 [1949]).

As the preceding discussion has demonstrated, the Oedipal complex has been hugely influential in developing an associated heteronormative theory of sexed and gender development where difference or otherness is a condition of sexual desire. Richardson underlines how the privileging of heterosexual relations as the bedrock of social relations has reinforced the idea that 'heterosexuality is the original blueprint for interpersonal relations' (1996: 3). As such, heterosexual identities remain unremarkable, escaping critical scrutiny (Yep 2003: 29). Society uncritically incorporates and maintains 'heterosexuality' as an unchanging, unquestioned, ahistorical idea, instead of seeing it as it actually is: one particular arrangement of the sexes and their pleasure. The next section examines how this alternative view was advanced by Foucault (1978), who challenged the heteronormative underpinnings of the institutions of western society.

HISTORICAL CONSTRUCTION OF HETEROSEXUALITY

Foucault (1978) emphasises sexuality as having complex roots in western culture and history. The first volume of his *History of Sexuality* is a powerful account of different views of sex and sexuality across various cultures and periods of time. His 'archaeology of sex' illustrates how our sexual beliefs and values are influenced by the social institutions and discourses of the time in which we live. He challenges the idea that sexuality is a natural 'truth', arguing that it is a constructed category of experience which has historical and cultural origins. Foucault (1985) examines discourses from the ancient Greeks to the Enlightenment with a view to examining how discourses on sex and sexuality produce categories of sexual practices and sexual identities which marked people out as particular types. For instance, the Greeks did not have the same social organisation of sexed difference and eroticism as that which prevails in contemporary Western society, and they did not have a heterosexual/homosexual dualism. Foucault (1978) notes how the Greeks saw sex as one of many social activities compared to the dominant attitude in the Enlightenment where sexual activity reflected our 'true' identity. Individuals, and not just their acts, were labelled as normal and abnormal. This continues in modern discourses where there is a desire to classify and categorise particular sexualities and new ways of viewing people are produced. A key point in the history of sexuality occurred when people's sexuality was no longer used simply to classify them, but also to ascribe values and rights/privileges to these categories. This interest in sex in western societies is an example of what Foucault (1984) calls 'power-knowledge' which limits the possibilities of subjectivity—both of who we can be and the kinds of relationships that are possible. Thus we can begin to understand why he views sex and sexuality as phenomena that have much to do with social discourse and laws, and less to do with bodies and desires.

Foucault (1984) describes the defining event of the eighteenth century as the heterosexualisation of modern society where forms of knowledge established norms that were linked to the social order of the time. Garlick's (2003) paper, *What is a Man?*, explores Tim Hitchcock's (1996) account of heterosexualisation at work in eighteenth-century England, which involved a redefinition of what constituted 'sexual intercourse'. At the beginning of the century it was characterised by kissing, caressing, touching, and masturbation (what we now call foreplay by heterosexual definition). This changed at the end of century when it became more phallocentric; thus sexual intercourse referred explicitly to putting a penis in a vagina. Certainly, reproductive activity increased in the eighteenth century and Garlick (2003) cites Abelove's (1992) suggestion that this may be linked to the emphasis on production in the Industrial Revolution where the focus was on sex for reproduction rather than for pleasure. In this way, heterosexuality emphasises reproduction as an acceptable normative practice, but again this was responding to a broader need in society. It is within this context that homosexuals came to be seen as a 'species', one that did not fit with the nineteenth-century medical science framework.

Foucault (1978) highlights the regulating of sexuality, asserting that the category of modern homosexuality grew out of a specific historical context. At this point, the binary opposition between homosexuality and heterosexuality began to be formulated. Foucault (1978) argues that the normalisation of these ideas came about by repeating cultural practices and techniques, which continue to infiltrate minds and bodies and which, in turn, cultivate beliefs and behaviours as seemingly natural qualities embedded in the individual psyche. Foucault's (1984) answer to this tendency is to demand an analysis of the historical, cultural and social politics of the time. He is less concerned with the essence of sexuality than with how it functions as a structure of power in society. Foucault's ideas paved the way for feminist theorists Butler (1990), Rich (1980), and Wittig (1992) who continued to critique the unquestioned assumptions of heterosexuality and its capacity to shape identity and desire by creating a 'compulsory heterosexuality' (Rich 1980: 23).

COMPULSORY HETEROSEXUALITY

> Heterosexuality offers normative sexual positions that are intrinsically impossible to embody, and the persistent failure to identify fully and without coherence with these positions reveals heterosexuality itself not only as a compulsory law, but as an inevitable intrinsic comedy . . . a constant parody of itself.
>
> (Butler 1990: 122)

Much feminist writing has sought to argue that gender roles are not bio-logically given and natural, but socially and culturally constructed (Rich 1980; Butler 1990; Wittig 1992). In a highly influential book, Rich (1980) questions the assumption that women are naturally heterosexual and explores the links between heterosexuality and procreational economics. Rich's (1980) essay on compulsory heterosexuality was pioneering in her depiction of heterosexuality as yet another socially produced fiction that constructed and maintained a binary heterosexual order on which the foundation of gender was built. She emphasises how heterosexuality, as an institution, maintains the oppression of women. French feminist theorist Wittig (1992) continues this debate, arguing that the categories of men and women, indeed all sexual categories, are the products of a gender hierarchy which is institutionalised as heterosexuality. Rich (1980) and Wittig (1992) challenge the idea of heterosexuality as 'natural', and view it as a social construct. Whether sexuality is seen as a something that is psychologically achieved or socially constructed, Freud, albeit perhaps unwittingly, and the feminist theorists, draw attention to the notion that heterosexuality is not a 'natural' state.

Wittig (1992) and Rich (1980) paved the way for Butler's (1990) post-modern critique of heterosexuality as an unexamined discourse. Butler's (1990: 151) translation of the unrelenting tyranny of heterosexuality is described as the 'heterosexual matrix', which designates that grid of cul-tural intelligibility through which bodies, genders and desires are natura-lised. Butler (1990: 15) argues that this results in the heterosexualisation of desire which requires and institutes the production of discrete and asym-metrical oppositions between feminine and masculine. The normalisation of heterosexuality is a social phenomenon and promotes a sexuality that is based on the principle that opposites attract which, in turn, perpetuates the reproduction of a binary gender system. In this way, heterosexual iden-tity is affirmed and stabilised through sexual and gendered categories that become norms. Butler (1990) argues that this exclusive binary framework of sexual duality has key consequences in how desire is constructed and in how homosexuality is interpreted as a failed development. Sex, gender, and sexuality are thought of as distinct variables described as having binary characteristics: bodies are either female or male; gender presentation, behavioural dispositions, and social roles are either masculine or feminine; and sexuality is either heterosexual or homosexual (Lorber 2000: 144). The gendered idea of biological sex produces the binary notion of 'opposite sexes' that maintain the workings of the heterosexual matrix. These then become the basis of social identities that often remain unquestioned.

Butler's (1990) critique of the heterosexual matrix exposes the unques-tioned intelligibility of individuals who conform and define within a binary oppositional relation. The heterosexual matrix describes the boundaries of expression and social acceptance by defining what is natural and unnatural within the governing law, and this matrix is reinforced by those that fall outside it. Butler (Butler, Osborne and Segal 1994: 4) is alert to the possible reification of the heterosexual matrix, as explored in *Gender Trouble* (1990), whereby it becomes a 'kind of totalizing symbolic'. Butler (1993) uses the term 'heterosexual hegemony' in her subsequent publication *Bodies that Matter* as a way of suggesting that this matrix is open for rearticulation. In this way, Butler draws attention to how any discourse can become hegemonic and produce identities that then become normative by repeating and producing specific modes of expression and behaviour. From this point, the following section examines the ways that heterosexuality has become hegemonically embedded as a deep social norm and considers how it influences the ways in which people identify their sexual and gendered identities, and impacts upon the kind of relationships they have.

Heterosexuality is not simply a form of sexual expression or practice; it is institutionalised through the law and the state and is embedded in social interaction and practice. Normative heterosexuality describes a particular traditional gender arrangement and is based on the western sex/gender model—one based on difference, particularly the physical difference between sexes; and then gender is mapped onto this. In the 1990s, the theoretical concept of heteronormativity became established in gender/feminist/queer studies (Rosenberg 2008), and was used to describe the social norm of heterosexuality which has become embodied and is lived without question.

One of the most common heteronormative assumptions is that woman and men are 'made for each other', with vaginal penetration by a penis seen as '*the* sex act' (Hitchcock 1996: 79). This assumption remains entrenched, along with the belief that male and female sexuality are naturally different. These assumptions are continually produced and reproduced in social practice. One example of how this happens comes from Celia Kitzinger's (2005) work on displays of heterosexual identity through talk. She found that many people have a normative understanding of families as related by law and blood. Studying everyday social interactions make visible the mundane ways in which people, not on purpose, reproduce a world that marginalises non-heterosexuals. She illustrates how the role of biological parents in families is prioritised over non-biological parents. An example of this is the mother of a lesbian whose partner gave birth to a daughter. When this mother was asked to treat the child as her 'granddaughter' she could not do so and called her 'my daughter's friend's daughter' instead (Epstein 1994: 83). The heterosexual family produces familial terminology that takes for granted non-recognitional person references such as wife, husband, and son—membership categories that do not require you to use the person's name. There is no name for an intimate caring social unit that does not rely on a normative understanding of family as something which comprises of one father and one mother.

Heterosexuality is a particular historical arrangement of human relationships, of the sexes, their pleasures and desires, and it can limit our vision of any other sexed community. Dominant western heteronormative discourse dictates how the categories of sex, gender, and sexuality should interact with each other and this has had significant limitations for the development of categories outwith a binary system. Can we create a space outside the assumptions of heterosexuality? Would this change the way we understand ourselves, and open new possibilities for sexual expression, awareness and acceptance? There is an important developing body of work that poses challenges to the heterosexualisation of identities and desires (Califia 1997; Hines 2007; Monro 2007; Moon 2008; Sanger 2008). My own research and psychotherapeutic work makes it clear that there are multiple ways of being identified, embodied and having sexual relationships, and yet, the dominance of the hegemonic heterosexual discourse is still evident as a constraint on self- identification. In order to begin to imagine a space without sexed and gendered binary identities we need to become more aware of how they are woven into everyday social life and practices that take for granted such presumptions. These include the idea that there are only two sexes; that it is natural for people of opposite sexes to be attracted to each other; that these attractions may be publicly displayed and celebrated; and that the social institution of marriage and the notion of family are all organised around opposite sex coupling. Thus 'same sex' couples are, if not 'deviant', at least seen as 'alternative'. In these ways, heterosexuality is continually reproduced as natural and unproblematic, and in consequence, anything else is seen as unnatural, problematic and less valuable.

So far, this chapter has illustrated the significance and influence of cultural and collective processes on how people understand and experience sexed and gendered identities, and how heterosexuality has become a naturalised status. I will now turn to an examination of the emergence of transgender as a category within the dominant culture of heterosexuality.

EMERGENCE OF TRANSGENDER

According to Fuss (1989: 109), the greatest contribution that social constructionists have made to the theory of homosexuality is their collective subversion of the traditional, legal, and sociological approaches to gay identities, which usually begin with the question, 'is homosexuality innate or acquired?' Redirection away from this question has enabled sexuality and gender studies to move out from the realm of ontology and into the realm of discursive formations; asking new questions, such as, how are identities produced? Awareness of the social construction of identity categories such as sex, gender and sexuality offers a rich insight into how modern Western sexed and gender identities are read within the 'heterosexual matrix of meanings' (Jackson 1999: 172). The destabilisation of sexual and gender identities brought about by these shifts in theorising, opened up new ways of thinking about identities and practises outwith binary sex and gender ideology. Some people challenged gender diversity as pathology, and created the conditions for the emergence of the identity category of 'transgender' in the late twentieth century. This new category opened up a middle ground, previously inaccessible within the medically-based transsexual model, which made available a range of transgender 'identities'.

Transgender is a concept that emerged in the 1990s and is an inclusive term for people who have broken away from society's expectation that sex and gender are essential, binary categories. Transgenderists do not necessarily see themselves as transsexuals or transvestites, or, indeed, claim any clear cut identities. The category of transgender is itself multiple and contested and incorporates a principle of diversity rather than uniformity, moving from dichotomy to continuity where it is not so easy to categorise people into male-female dualities. The term transgender moves away from a physically-based definition (sex of the body) and encompasses a social definition whereby a transgendered identification may refer to people who live as *social* men or *social* women who may, or may not, seek sex reassignment surgery (Cromwell 1999). They live their lives in a gender that opposes -according to dominant discourse- their biological sex.

Claiming a right to speak for themselves is a key development in recent transgender writing and politics and has provided an increasing focus of study for Western trans and intersex activists (Devor 1989; Stone 1991; Feinberg 1993, 1996; Bornstein 1994, 1998; Stryker 1994, 2006; Prosser 1995, 1998; Whittle 1996a, 1996b, 1999, 2006a, 2007; Wilchins 1997; Halberstam 1998, 2005; Namaste 2000, 2005; Kuhling and Kinsman 2002-3; Devor and Matte 2004). As the transgender political and social activist movement has developed, the diversity and variance of gender identities has become more visible. The category of transgender is expanding to include a wider variety of behaviour that can be grouped together and, in the process, it undermines the established notion of fixed and binary gender categories.

It is worth noting however, that using the category of transgender as an umbrella for a variety of identities is problematic and its many meanings currently remain in dispute. I intentionally use a simple definition from Gilbert, as it refers to a mind/body dissonance of some kind without being specific. According to Gilbert (2000: 2), 'when applied to an individual, "transgendered" signifies some degree of discomfort, all or some of the time with one's birth-assigned gender designation.' This is not so much an externally assigned category as it is a self-defined one that moves away from medical definitions and describes a range of deviations from gender norms. This situation means that there is a need to develop language and terminology that describes new self-definitions in ways that do not rely on existing binary categories.

These shifts in thinking have demanded continuous discussion and debate within the transgender community and a need to constantly revise the language and discourse available for trans people. Current transgender literature and research are challenging the medical definition of trans-sexuality, with trans identity emerging as a new category that has possibilities that go beyond the binary structure of sex and gender. Emerging self-definitions such as transman, transwoman and genderqueer, pave the way for transgender people to be more visible and to take charge of building their own trans theory, instead of relying on the medical model of mental illness. Even here though, the power of heteronormativity is apparent in the continued use of the terms trans-man and trans-woman.

Stryker (2006) describes transgender studies, with its focus on questions of embodiment and positionality, as emerging at the intersection of feminist and queer studies. Transgender studies broadly describe anything that disrupts, denaturalises and rearticulates the normative linkages between sex, gender and sexuality (Stryker 2006). It is worth clarifying that the term 'transgender' can be used as a generic term to denote the whole field of gender identity transgressions known as 'trans theorising', and that it can also be associated specifically with a postmodern queer position that is opposed to stable identities (Beasley 2005). Stryker (2006) points out how the emergence of transgender studies parallels the rise of queer studies and despite similarities, their relationship with each other is often problematic and contested. However, it is worth noting that queer scholars have used the transgender phenomenon to open up new ways of thinking about identities and practices outwith the heterosexual discourse of 'oppositional' categories such as man and woman. This represents a move away from the essentialist/constructionist debate, and focuses on *how* people's bodies extend into available spaces and form sexed and gendered identities.

While transgender studies strongly invest in the 'transgressive' potential of transsexualism, this investment is by no means agreed upon by the transgender community. Hird's (2002: 577) exploration of the development of theories on transsexualism exposes a shift from the transsexual as 'authentic' (a 'real' man/woman) to issues of 'performativity' (the transsexual as hyperbolic enactment of gender), to the notion of 'transgressive' that can potentially collapse the sex/gender binary. Yet as Hird (2002) points out, the notion of transgression is a complex one as not all transsexuals want to be seen as subversive or queer.

DECONSTRUCTING HETEROSEXUAL IDEOLOGY

In the last 30 years, gender and cultural studies, feminist theory and queer theory have all made significant contributions to the destabilisation and demystification of heteronormative ideology. One of the first feminist critiques of the social structuring of heterosexuality emerged from the development of sexual politics with the feminist movement linking 'the sexual' with power and politics. Feminist theory (Crawford 1993; Jackson 1995, 1996, 1999, 2006; Richardson 1996) examines how 'normative' heterosexuality affects the lives of heterosexuals. Jackson is keen to remind us of a neglected legacy that 'institutionalised, normative heterosexuality regulates those kept *within* its boundaries as well as marginalising and sanctioning those *outside* them' (2006: 105). This illustrates a key point; that heteronormativity is concerned with not only normative sexuality but also with normative ways of life.

The processes of normalisation that sustain the current heteronormative paradigm have been taken up by queer theorists such as Butler (1990, 1993, 1997a, 1997b, 1999, 2004), Stone (1991), Sedgwick (1985, 1990), Warner (1993, 1999), Halperin (1990, 1995), Seidman (1996), Halberstam (1998, 2005), and Garber (1992). They all significantly build on Foucault's (1978) argument that sexuality is discursively produced, and extend it to include gender. Queer theorists argue that it is possible to have a society that is not organised by a heterosexual norm and that sexuality and gender need not be reducible to each other. In other words 'queer' is concerned with challenging basic hegemonic assumptions about the social and political world by subverting the normative rules of the heterosexual matrix and opening up spaces between the sexual and gender binaries. As Warner (1993) emphasises, 'queer' does not define itself against the heterosexual but against the very notion of the normal.

Feminist psychoanalysts (Benjamin 1988, 1996, 1998; Dimen 2002, 2003; Goldner 2002) are contesting the normalising knowledge of heterosexuality. Benjamin (1998) and Dimen (2002) have been questioning whether a single unified gender identity is necessary to be considered healthy. Maybe, they suggest, it is actually the attempt to create a single gender identity which creates pathology (Goldner 2002), These analysts have begun to question the taken for granted assumptions of everyday thinking on gender, advocating new ways of bringing this thinking into the consulting room. This means being able to stay with multiple meanings, shifting identifications, as well as bearing contradictions and ambiguities that cannot be understood within the gendered, binary language of psychotherapy. At the same time, it is necessary to resist the temptation of assuming a gender free space, a liberal post-modern stance of flexibility and ambiguity, which denies the inevitable gender ideology that society has internalised. Even though I advocate challenging the gender binary, the reality that gender is a central organising principle cannot be ignored. The thought of not having a stable gender identity is a frightening one for many—what would our point of reference be if we were not categorised as a man or a woman?

Being part of an established and recognised group in society is an important aspect of developing self-esteem and an identity. The formation of an individual's identity requires recognition that the individual exists, and in this way, people are dependent on what is outside of them to reflect back a sense of being. In my work as a psychotherapist and trainer, I am witness to how it is a struggle for many people to become an intelligible and recognisable human within the current theoretical and political discourse of heteronormativity and the laws of desire that operate within this. Heterosexuality is a potent sign and it influences how we live our lives, how we learn and how we see desire and this is why it is so difficult to destabilise. We rarely study the norm or social process of normalisation—it is easier to probe and study the abnormal and the deviant, hence the many studies and research projects on transvestites, transsexuals, gays and lesbians. Although society has become more affirming of diversity and difference, heterosexuality is still treated as a monolithic and unitary concept (Crawford 1993; Eliason 1995; Jackson 1996, 1999; Smart, 1996; Yep 2003)

CONCLUSION

One of the questions that began to emerge in the course of my work on trans identities and experiences was one posited by Butler when she cited the laws of intelligibility by which a human being emerges; 'Who can I become in such a world where the meanings and the limits of the subject are set out in advance for me?' (2004: 184) Butler (2004) raises important questions about who counts as a person, and what the conditions and norms are that enable someone to qualify as a coherent and real citizen. My work as a psychotherapist and trainer make it clear that transgendered people struggle to become intelligible and recognisable humans within the current theoretical and political discourse of heteronormativity, and within the laws of desire that operate within this discourse. People need to be able to put their existence into words and this is difficult in a world that already has the groundwork of heteronormativity well constructed, meaning that possible categories are already constituted—the social organisation of bodies into two 'sexes' is seen as two inflexible categories of man and woman.

As I have shown, this division is grounded in the naturalised belief that women are anatomically female and men are anatomically male. These meanings are deeply entrenched in everyday thinking and talking. Current hegemonic conceptions state that if one is to exist at all, one must be a man or a woman. It could be argued that in trying to align their bodies to their internal identities, transgendered people are buying into this hegemonic link between bodies and gender. At the same time, it can be argued that in order to achieve intersubjective recognition, it is necessary to be seen as belonging to the only viable categories of the time—man or woman. The development of possible new sexed and gendered identities has been limited by the historical, social, and political parameters of heteronormativity. The right to claim membership in socially recognised sex, gender and sexual orientation groups is particularly essential for transgendered people in order to construct sustainable ways of living.

My own research suggests that it was the desires of transgendered people that forced them to move beyond categorised notions of being; to move forward into alternative ways of being and belonging. Their long-ing bypassed the constriction of individualised identities while still relying on the only discourse they knew—the hegemonic discourse of the hetero-sexual matrix. Their experiences illustrate how sex, gender and desire are grounded and organised within the heterosexual matrix, and how this influences both their sexed and gender identities and how they lead their erotic lives. Not surprisingly, this discourse then informs the telling of the transgender narratives as they attempt to make sense of their developing identities. Sadly, my own work suggests that currently there is little room for thinking about gender and sexuality outwith the heteronormative para-digm. Transgendered people identify themselves in ways that are conflated with the discourse and language that is available at any given time; influ-encing both how they experience themselves and how they describe their experiences. In other words, discourse and language operate to consolidate and maintain the heterosexual matrix as the main mechanism for describ-ing their experiences. As Wittgenstein (1922) cited in Lazenby (2007: 46) notes, 'the limits of my language mean the limits of my world.' Butler (1990) emphasises the role of language in reproducing the heterosexual matrix whereby individuals cannot identify themselves outside of this language, or indeed any language. Language has become impoverished in terms of what is available for thinking about sex, gender and desire and this affects how people can put their existence into words. Butler (1990) reminds us of how dependent our existence is on a language that people never made, but which leads to decisions being made about people's lives.

Society puts limits on the ways that an individual can make sense of his or her life and, as I have shown, part of this process is the creation of hege-monic binary categories of identity like heterosexual/homosexual, man/woman. We cannot understand our lives without the constraints of the heterosexual matrix because our identities have been and continue to be constructed and constricted by the dominant heteronormative discourse. We tend to collude in reproducing this matrix by still using it as a major lens through which we think about people. Engaging with alternative ways of thinking about desire means questioning the predominant heterosexual discourse, and relies on examining the language that we employ to under-stand the concepts of sex, gender, and sexuality.

Transgender identities illustrate the need for a language that repre-sents the diverse plural identities that are subsumed under the category of transgender. To generalise the term transgender would to be to miss out on the opportunity it provides to examine how the institution of hetero-sexuality shapes our thinking about the erotic and polices the boundar-ies of desire. The category of transgender has the potential to question what is possible in the arena of sex, gender, and sexuality, particularly when the body is not seen as natural or fixed. Importantly, this revelatory and liberating capacity of transgender research should not be confused with setting up transgendered people as objects of fascination. Instead, their experiences simply make it easier to think about the limitations of heterosexual ideology, and to expose the contradictions and subversions that most human beings experience. Heterosexuality needs to be deconstructed and the discourse reformulated, if the lived experiences and aspirations of most people, not only transgendered people, are to be heard and accommodated.

REFERENCES

Abelove, H. (1992) 'Some speculations on the history of "sexual intercourse" during the "long eighteenth-century" in England', in A. Parker, M. Russo and P. Yaeger (eds) *Nationalisms & Sexualities*, New York: Routledge.

Beasley, C. (2005) *Gender and Sexuality: Critical Theories, Critical Thinkers*, London: Sage.

Benjamin, J. (1988) *The Bonds of Love: Psychoanalysis, Feminism, and the Problems of Domination*, New York: Pantheon Books Inc.

——. (1996) *Like Subjects, Love Objects: Essays on Recognition, Identification, and Difference*, New Haven: Yale University Press.

——. (1998) *Shadow of the Other: Intersubjectivity and Gender in Psychoanalysis*, London: Routledge.

Bornstein, K. (1994) *Gender Outlaw: On Men, Women, and the Rest of Us*, New York: Routledge.

——. (1998) *My Gender Workbook: How to Become the Kind of Man or Women You Always Thought You Could Be . . . or Something Else Entirely*, New York: Routledge.

Butler, J. (1990) *Gender Trouble: Feminism and the Subversion of Identity*, New York: Routledge.

——. (1993) *Bodies That Matter: On the Discursive Limits of 'Sex'*, New York: Routledge.

——. (1997a) *The Psychic Life of Power: Theories in Subjection*, Stanford, California: Stanford University Press.

——. (1997b) 'Performative acts and gender constitutions: an essay in phenomenology and feminist theory', in K. Conboy, N. Medina and S. Stanbury (eds) *Writing on the Body: Female Embodiment and Feminist Theory*, New York: Columbia University Press.

——. (2004) *Undoing Gender*, New York: Routledge.

Butler, J., Osborne, P. and Segal, L. (1994) 'Gender as performance: an interview with Judith Butler', *Radical Philosophy*, 67: 32–39.

Califia, P. (1997) *Sex Changes: The Politics of Transgenderism*, San Francisco: Cleis Press.

Crawford, M. (1993) 'Identity, "passing" and subversion', in S. Wilkinson and C. Kitzinger (eds) *A Feminism and Psychology Reader*, London: Sage.

Cromwell, J. (1999) *Transmen and FTMs: Identities, Bodies, Genders and Sexualities*, San Fransisco: Cleiss Press.

De Beauvoir, S. (1987 [1949]) *The Second Sex*, trans. H. M. Parsley, London: Penguin Books.

Devor, H. (1989) *Gender Blending: Confronting the Limits of Duality*, Bloomington: Indiana University Press.

Devor, A H. and Matte, N. (2004) 'ONE Inc. and Reed Erickson: the uneasy collaboration of gay and trans activism, 1964–2003', *GLQ: A Journal of Lesbian and Gay Studies*, 10(4): 179–209.

Dimen, M. (2002) 'Deconstructing difference: gender, splitting, and transitional space', in M. Dimen and V. Goldner (eds) *Gender in Psychoanalytic Space*, New York: Other Press LLC.

———. (2003) *Sexuality, Intimacy, Power (Relational Perspectives Book Series)*, New York: Routledge.

Eliason, M. J. (1995) 'Accounts of identity formation in heterosexual students', *Sex Role*, 32: 821–834.

Epstein, R. (1994) 'Lesbian parenting: cracking the shell of the nuclear family', in M. Oikawa, D. Falconer, and A. Decter (eds) *Resist: Essays Against a Homophobic Culture*, Toronto: Women's Press.

Feinberg, L. (1993) *Stone Butch Blues: A Novel*, New York: World View.

———. (1996) *Transgender Warriors: Making History from Joan of Arc to Rupaul*, Boston: Beacon Press.

Foucault, M. (1978) *The History of Sexuality: An Introduction (Vol. 1)*, New York: Pantheon Books.

———. (1984) 'Nietzsche, genealogy, history', in P. Rainbow (ed.) *The Foucault Reader*, New York: Pantheon Books.

———. (1985) *The History of Sexuality: The Use of Pleasure (Vol. 2)*, New York: Vintage Books.

Freud, S. (1962 [1905]) *Three Essays on the Theory of Sexuality*, trans. and ed. J. Strachey, New York: Basic Books.

Fuss, D. (1989) *Essentially Speaking: Feminism, Nature and Difference*, Routledge: London.

Garber, M. (1992) *Vested Interests: Cross Dressing and Cultural Anxiety*, New York: Routledge.

Garlick, S. (2003) 'What is a man? Heterosexuality and the technology of masculinity', *Men and Masculinities*, 6(2): 156–172.

Gilbert, M. A. (2000) 'The transgendered philosopher', *International Journal of Transgenderism*, 14(3). http://www.haworthpress.com/store/product. asp?sku=J485 (accessed 12 May 2009).

Goldner, V. (2002) 'Toward a critical relational theory of gender', in M. Dimen and V. Goldner (eds) *Gender in Psychoanalytic Space*, New York: Other Press.

Halberstam, J. (1998) *Female Masculinity*, Durham, NC: Duke University Press

———. (2005) *In a Queer Time and Place: Transgender Bodies, Subcultural Lives*, New York: New York University Press.

Halperin, D. (1990) *One Hundred Years of Homosexuality and Other Essays on Greek Love*, New York: Routledge.

———. (1995) *Saint Foucault: Towards a Gay Hagiography*, New York: Oxford University Press.

Hines, S. (2007) '(Trans)forming gender: social change and transgender citizenship', *Sociological Research Online*, 12(1). http://www.socresonline.org. uk/12/1/hines.html (accessed 26 May 2009).

Hird, M. J. (2002) 'For a sociology of transsexualism', *Feminist Theory*, 36(3): 577–95.

Hitchcock, T. (1996) 'Redefining sex in eighteenth-century England', *History Workshop Journal*, 41: 73–90.

Jackson, S. (1995) 'Heterosexuality, power and pleasure', *Feminism and Psychology*, 5(1): 131–135.

———. (1996) 'Heterosexuality as a problem for feminist theory', in L. Adkins and V. Merchant (eds) *Sexualising the Social: Power and the Organisation of Sexuality*, New York: St Martin's Press.

———. (1999) *Heterosexuality in Question*, London: Sage.

———. (2006) 'Gender, sexuality and heterosexuality', *Feminist Theory*, 7(1): 105–121.

Katz, J. (1995) *The Invention of Heterosexuality*, London: Penguin Books.

Kitzinger, C. (2005) 'Heteronormativity in action: reproducing the heterosexual nuclear family in after-hours medical calls', *Social Problems*, 52(4): 477–498.

Kuhling, C. and Kinsman, G. (2002-3) 'Addressing the politics of social erasure: making transsexual lives visible—an interview with Vivian K. Namaste', *New Socialist Magazine*, 39: http://www.newsocilaist.org/magazine/39/article04. html (accessed 12 April 2009).

Lazenby, J. M. (2007) *The Early Wittgenstein on Religion (Continuum Studies in British Philosophy)*, London: Continuum International Publishing Group.

Lorber, J. (2000) 'Using gender to undo gender: a feminist degendering movement', *Feminist Theory*, 1(1): 79–95.

Monro, S. (2007) 'Transmuting gender binaries', *Sociological Research Online*, 12(1). http://www.socresonline.org.uk/12/1/hines.html (accessed 16 March 2009).

Moon, L. (2008) 'Queer(y)ing the heterosexualisation of emotion', in L. Moon (ed.) *Feeling Queer or Queer Feelings? Radical Approaches to Counselling Sex, Sexualities and Genders*, East Sussex: Routledge.

Namaste, V. K. (2000) *Invisible Lives: The Erasure of Transsexual and Transgendered People*, Chicago: University of Chicago Press.

———. (2005) *Sex Change, Social Change: Reflections on Identity, Institutions, and Imperialism*, Toronto: Women's Press.

Prosser, J. (1995) 'No place like home: the transgendered narrative of Leslie Feinberg's *Stone Butch Blues*', *Modern Fiction Studies*, 41(3/4): 483–514.

———. (1998) *Second Skins: The Body Narratives of Transsexuality*, New York: Columbia University Press.

Rich, A. (1980) *Compulsory Heterosexuality and Lesbian Existence*, London: Onlywomen Ltd. Press.

Richardson, D. (1996) 'Heterosexuality and social theory', in D. Richardson (ed.) *Theorising Heterosexuality: Telling it Straight*, Buckingham: Open University Press.

Rosenberg, T. (2008) 'Locally queer: a note on the feminist genealogy of queer theory', *Graduate Journal of Social Science*, 5(2). http:// www.gjss.org (accessed 3 May 2009).

Sanger, T. (2008) 'Queer(y)ing gender and sexuality: transpeople's lived experiences and intimate relationships', in L. Moon (ed.) *Feeling Queer or Queer Feelings? Radical Approaches to Counselling Sex, Sexualities and Genders*, East Sussex: Routledge.

Sedgwick, E. (1985) *Between Men: English Literature and Male Homosexual Desire*, Columbia: Columbia University Press.

———. (1990) *Epistemology of the Closet*, Berkeley: University of California Press.

Seidman, S. (1996) 'Introduction', in S.Seidman (ed.) *Queer Theory/ Sociology*, Cambridge, MA: Blackwell.

Smart, C. (1996) 'Collusion, collaboration and confession: on moving beyond the heterosexuality debate', in D. Richardson (ed.) *Theorising Heterosexuality: Telling it Straight*, Buckingham: Open University Press.

Stone, S. (1991) 'The empire strikes back: A post-transsexual manifesto', in: D. Epstein and K. Straub (eds) *Body Guards: The Cultural Politics of Gender and Ambiguity'*, London: Routledge Publications.

Stryker, S. (1994) 'My words to Victor Frankenstein above the village of Chamounix: performing transgender rage', *GLQ: A Journal of Lesbian and Gay Studies*, 13: 237–254.

Stryker, S. (2006) '(De)subjugated knowledges: an introduction to transgender studies', in S. Stryker and S. Whittle (eds) *The Transgender Studies Reader*, New York: Routledge.

Warner, M. (1993) 'Introduction', in M. Warner (ed.) *Fear of a Queer Planet: Queer Politics and Social Theory*, Minneapolis: University of Minnesota Press.

———. (1999) *The Trouble with Normal: Sex, Politics, and the Ethics of Queer Life*, New York: The Free Press.

———. (2002) *Publics and Counterpublics*, New York: Zone Books.

Whittle, S. (1996a) *The Transvestite, the Transsexual and the Law*, 3rd Edition, London: Beaumont Trust.

———. (1996b) 'Gender fucking or fucking gender?' in R. Ekins and D. King (eds) *Blending Genders: Social Aspects of Cross-Dressing and Sex Changing*, London: Routledge.

———. (1999) 'Transgender rights: the European Court of Human Rights and new identity politics for the new age', in A. Hegarty and S. Leonard (eds) *Human Rights: An Agenda for the 21st Century*, London: Cavendish Publishing.

———. (2006a) 'Foreword', in S. Whittle and S. Stryker (eds) *The Transgender Studies Reader*, New York: Routledge.

———. (2006b) 'Where did we go wrong? Feminism and trans theory- two teams on the same side?' in S. Stryker and S. Whittle (eds) *The Transgender Studies Reader*, New York: Routledge.

Whittle, S. and Turner, L. (2007) '"Sex changes"? Paradigm shifts in "sex and gender" following the Gender Recognition Act', *Sociological Research Online*, 12(1). http://www.socresonline.org.uk/12/1/whittle.html (accessed 12 February 2009).

Wilchins, R. A. (1997) *Read My Lips: Sexual Subversion and the End of Gender*, Ithica: Firebrand.

Wittig, M. (1998 [1992]) 'The straight mind', in S. Jackson and S. Scott (eds) *Feminism and Sexuality*, New York: Harvester Wheatsheaf.

Yep, G. (2003) 'The violence of heteronormativity in communication studies: notes on injury, healing, and queer world-making', in G. A. Yep, K. Lovaas and J. P. Elia (eds) *Queer Theory and Communication: From Disciplining Queers to Queering the Discipline(s)*, New York: Harrington Park Press.

11 Corporeal Silences and Bodies that Speak

The Promises and Limitations of Queer in Lesbian/Queer Sexual Spaces

Corie J. Hammers

INTRODUCTION

'Queer' has multiple meanings and functions. The word 'queer', once derogatory, is now a site of empowerment, and denotes a wide assemblage of abject identities and non-normative practices (e.g., bisexuality, transgender, polyamory). Additionally, queer is both a theoretical and political project. Queer political activism is a reaction to the assimilationist agenda of the gay rights movement, and is embodied in such organisations as ACT UP and Queer Nation, where confrontational tactics were deployed to challenge heterosexual privilege and the supposed etiological foundations of (pathological) sexuality. This admixture of theory and practice/activism sets queer apart in terms of its philosophical and social pursuits.

Queer emerged from the rubble of the gay liberationist agenda of the 1970s and 1980s. Gay liberationism, which was akin to an ethnic identity model (Seidman 1994), espoused and embraced 'gay' and 'lesbian' as core sites for mobilisation and used a 'politics of normalization' (Meeks 2001) for assimilation purposes (although lesbian feminists were carving out their own separatist politics and community). Yet, it soon became clear that the mobilising force of 'gay' and 'lesbian' and the notion of a unitary gay identity could only be sustained via the refutation of difference. For instance, sex rebels and lesbians and gay men of colour challenged queer solidarity by showing that this 'liberation' was in fact based on a white (male) middle class subject (Hemphill 1991) who was, relatively speaking, sexually 'normal'. As a result, this 'gay subject' could no longer hold as the anchor for the gay and lesbian movement.

What was needed, according to poststructuralists and queer theorists, was an anti-essentialist politics that would decenter the heterosexual regime and contest the central underlying problem—the homo/hetero binary itself (Butler 1990). According to Sedgwick (1990), the whole of Western culture is predicated upon the heterosexual/homosexual sexual code (Seidman 1994). Furthermore, poststructuralism is highly distrustful of identities, since to evoke any one identity operates to exclude and conceal other identities/differences. Rather, queer must be able to validate and affirm multiple differences simultaneously, while refusing any one particular identity/difference to symbolise the epistemic authority of 'queer'. Taken together, the central tenets of queer theory, rooted as it is in poststructuralism and antifoundationalism, include: the denaturalisation of binaries and categorical thought, including most notably, sexual identities and the hetero/homo divide; the critique of the stable and univocal subject; a sex-radical/sex-positive ethos; the critique of heteronormativity; celebration of difference; and a confrontational attitude with visible and vocal displays of queerness, since it 'pivots on transgression or permanent rebellion' (Seidman 1994: 173). As will be shown, these queer principles inform and infuse the lesbian/queer sexual venues examined here.

There has been increased mobilisation among some lesbian/queer sex-positive communities to create an embryonic sexual entertainment infrastructure—that is, to appropriate public space for sexual pleasure and sexual entertainment purposes. The two Canadian lesbian/queer bathhouses (located in different cities at undisclosed locations) examined here regularly, although episodically, take over gay male bathhouses every few months. Although few and far between, one organiser (the bathhouses have their own organising committee) commented that 'they expect these [events] now. If we didn't have one, people would be really upset.' Obviously, lesbian/queer-only play and sex parties did not begin with the arrival of said events. They have their own, albeit undocumented, history. There is some evidence (see Leap 1999) to suggest that in the early nineties lesbian/queer sex 'nights' were being organised at various lesbian bars in New York City and San Francisco. With the emergence of the lesbian bar scene in the mid to late twentieth century (Kennedy and Davis 1994), there arose a more public and visible lesbian culture. One outcome emanating from this burgeoning entertainment infrastructure was broadening of sexual possibility, and new sexual codes (such as butch/femme) within the lesbian community. Yet, to reiterate, empirical investigations dealing explicitly with lesbian/queer sex and desire are few and far between.

What sets these bathhouse events apart are their *public* and accessible nature, and visibility. That is, sex events for lesbian/queer communities are almost always private, invite-only and underground. Thus, only a select cadre attends. Furthermore, while male bathhouses demand anonymity and invisibility, these lesbian/queer events defy 'normal' bathhouse conditions with their extensive public advertising (in mainstream and queer media outlets) and long queues, which often extended several blocks—only to conclude at some of the busiest intersections in town.

Employing qualitative techniques—interviews (face-to-face and phone interviews) and participant observation—I examine two Canadian lesbian/queer bathhouses. Fieldwork and interviews for this ongoing project began in Fall, 2004 as part of my Ph.D. dissertation research. As was illuminated in interviews with bathhouse organisers, 'queer' figured as central to the organisers' larger goal: creating an inclusive event, one wherein transmen, transwomen and transgendered individuals attended. Advertisements and flyers stressed that all were welcome except bio-males. Exactly who was allowed in was kept, according to organisers, 'intentionally loosely defined'. As one organiser noted, 'it is about celebrating our diversity. This is for all of those who at some point were, have been, are going to be, or consider themselves now to be female bodied.' Thus, queer was strategically deployed to cater and attract a broad(er) coalition of subjects, identities and sex/gender configurations. Moreover, it was understood that the event's very 'success' hinged on being as inclusive and open as possible.

Queer sex and queer sexual subcultures signify non-normative sexual economies, a resistance to heterosexual hegemony, and the celebration of diversity. Thus, many believe queer to be *the* exemplar of radical behaviour and subversion, but showing how queer might operate on the ground to create such conditions continues to be permanently deferred. Although I outline ways in which these bathhouses foster agentic conditions, I question what a queer logic can actually 'do' whenever real corporeal bodies are at stake. More specifically, how do trans-bodies and non-trans privilege figure in queer sexual spaces? Elsewhere I discuss the extensive white privilege that permeates these spaces (Hammers and Sheff). With this research I offer a glimpse—albeit a contextually bounded one—into the workings of queer within and through these sexual spaces. In short, I explore how these spaces deploy 'queer' in the name of inclusivity and sex radicalism, only to reproduce various privileges, while concealing their own normalising mechanisms.

Before discussing my findings, I review some of the literature that discusses the sexuality-space nexus and the linkages between queer theory and sociology. Next, I offer a brief overview of the methods used to conduct this research. I conclude that although these spaces enable an embodied desire and spatial praxis which undermines hegemonic notions as it relates to 'female sexuality' and sexual abjecthood, these spaces also contain their own marginalising and regulatory mechanisms such that only those with the right 'bodily capital'—non-trans and white subjects—emerge as full participants.

SEXUALITY AND SPACE

Over the past several decades, social scientists have taken a keen interest in the relationship between space and practice (Knopp 1992; Valentine 1995). Sociologists have contributed substantially to this area, with empirical analyses addressing the linkages among space, identities, practices and subjectivities. Scholars note that spaces have their own codes of conduct, which provide the 'road map' for certain behaviours and interactional styles. For instance, Weinberg and Williams (1975) describe how bathhouses contain both explicit and tacit codes of conduct. These rules, coupled with spatial arrangements (dim lighting, loud music) that inhibit visibility and verbal communication, create an anonymous environment which works to facilitate sexual interaction.

That corporeal dimensions and subjectivities are contingent upon, and shift with space, supports queer contentions. More specifically, these studies elucidate the indeterminancy and fluidity of subjects. Sociology has increasingly begun incorporating the insights of queer theory into its own research endeavours and epistemological framework (Namaste 1994). While some (see Green 2007) see queer theory and sociology as fundamentally 'in tension', since queer is concerned with radical deconstruction and thus, permanent indeterminancy, others see sociology and queer theory as being able to mutually inform one another. For instance, Stein and Plummer state that while sociology can give to queer theory 'a more grounded, more accessible approach' (1994: 185), sociology should heed the insights of queer theory—in particular, the problematisation and deconstruction of identities, and its interrogation of the centre as opposed to simply the margins (as sociology has historically done). Some sociologists, particularly those working in the area of sexuality studies, are attempting to 'queer sociology' (Seidman 1997; Hines 2007). To queer sociology is to question and critique the sociological canon itself (e.g., its role in maintaining heteronormativity), while developing a more careful and nuanced approach to identity formations and subjectivities—their history, contingency, fluidity, and instability—and their intersections with 'other markers of social difference and systems of oppression' (Seidman 1997: 95).

Feminists have long acknowledged the lack of public space for women in general, and lesbians/queers in particular (Segal 1994). The sexual entertainment infrastructure exemplifies the degree to which public space is male space. Men of all sexual persuasions have a variety of venues to choose from: cabarets, strip clubs, 'family friendly' restaurants (with scantily clad women servers), and bathhouses. Women and lesbian/queer individuals have not had such choices. For one, lesbian/queer communities have to contend with both homophobic and patriarchal oppression (Valentine 1995). Additionally, the lack of economic resources, familial obligations and fear of male violence undermine the creation of lesbian/queer public sexual venues. Instead, what is available is often a peripatetic, episodic event wherein gay male venues agree to hold lesbian/queer events (Valentine 1995)—the pattern found here. Lesbian spaces—in particular, lesbian bars—were (and still are) some of the only places where lesbians and sexual deviants could go to find acceptance, sexual partners, and a sense of belonging (Kennedy and Davis 1993; Wolfe 1997).

Until fairly recently, the study of sexuality was a marginalised area of sociological interest, since sex and desire were seen as 'natural', biological categories. Sociologists (and other social scientists) studying sexuality have undermined this notion, showing instead the socio-cultural, historical and contextually bounded linkages to sexuality. Additionally, feminist scholars have thrown heterosexuality into the limelight, exposing its institutional and ideological apparatus, and the disciplining and regulatory effects of normative and compulsory heterosexuality (Jackson 2006; Wiegman 2006). Moreover, there is today a sizeable and growing body of scholarship examining gay male sexualities and gay male sexual subcultures (Humphreys 1975; Leap 1999). Although there are some notable exceptions (see Valentine 1995; Cooper 2007), overall, lesbian/queer sexual subcultures have simply not been interrogated to the same degree.

BACKGROUND AND SETTING

This project includes approximately 35 hours of participant observation at five bathhouse events, and 33 semi-structured interviews with bathhouse patrons. Most interviews were face-to-face and conducted on site (at the bathhouse) or at a neutral location in the area. Phone interviews were conducted when time did not permit face-to-face interviews. When not conducting interviews, I took mental notes of the scene, paying particular attention to patron interactions and demographics of the population. These bathhouses vary greatly in terms of locale and size. One bathhouse is located in one of Canada's largest cities, a city known for its progressive politics and visible queer communities. This bathhouse, referred to as bathhouse A, is also quite large, containing four floors and an outdoor swimming area. The other bathhouse, bathhouse B, is located in one of the least populous of Canada's provinces, in a city of slightly more than 300,000 inhabitants. This bathhouse was small, with one floor and no outdoor area.

Very few trans-identified individuals were present at any given event I attended. This held even when attendance levels reached upwards of 300 people at bathhouse A. Simply relying on visual cues is obviously inadequate, but because bio-males were not allowed entry, it was fairly easy to discern the transmen in the crowd—at least those transmen who were transitioning or had gone through sex transition. Additionally, I always asked the transmen and transwomen I interviewed to provide figures as to how many trans-identified individuals they believed came to these bathhouse events. Of the 33 bathhouse interviewees (interviewed at five separate bathhouse events), five individuals were trans-identified (two transmen, one transwoman, and one person was transgendered). Of my entire sample, less than one-third identified as lesbian, with the majority identifying as queer or bisexual. In some respects, it was quite a diverse scene. Straight, bisexual, queer, and transfolk were all inhabiting one space—and an explicitly sexual one to boot. A variety of body sizes, ages (there were people in their sixties), body styles, dress, and a range of butch-femme configurations were present. Certainly, unconventional displays of gender and sexuality were part and parcel of the bathhouse scene.

I embodied the role of 'disengaged participant', in that my activities were limited to interviewing and observation as opposed to directly engaging in sexual activities. Although I did participate in the voyeuristic sense (which no doubt carries its own ethical dilemmas), to have been an 'engaged participant'—in this case, have sex—would violate the basic principles of feminist research (Acker, Barry and Esseveld 1983). Questions and observations revolved around such things as embodiment issues, the impact of the space on sexuality, desire and notions of self, patrons' feelings/emotions while at the event, participants' expectations, and activities that patrons had engaged in or anticipated engaging in. It is argued that space-making, a space-making informed by queer, can redirect and recreate the borders in an attempt to rid spaces of privilege—privilege which is, in theory, anathema to a queer logic. The spaces interrogated here function as case studies to address this assertion. Before doing so, some background information regarding these sexual spaces is in order.

SPATIAL ARRANGEMENTS AND PHILOSOPHY

Bathhouses serve important functions for the gay male community in myriad ways. Bathhouses enable men to act out desires and engage in sex (Bérubé 1996), are key sites for queer community activism (Kinsman 1996), and have been conduits in the fight against the spread of HIV/AIDS—being some of the only places to provide accurate information on safer sex techniques. However, the harsh aesthetic standards and racism that often permeate the bathhouse scene have also been pointed out (Bersani 1987).

The lesbian/queer bathhouses challenge this masculine environment and philosophy by being a space exclusively for lesbian/queer and trans-identified individuals. These spaces defy a number of other hegemonic ideologies: patriarchal attitudes and the denigration of women's bodies and sexualities; the lesbian feminist sexual 'prescriptivism' (Echols 1984) of the past, which set strict standards on what was considered 'good, feminist sex' (e.g., monogamy, non-penetrative sex); and the heteronormative sex/gender regime—at these events queer sexualities and bodies are validated. Ultimately, according to organisers, the objective is creating an avowedly feminist, queer and sex-positive space that is safe, where individuals can explore their sexuality, and according to one longtime organiser, 'discover their desire on their own terms.'

Organisers intentionally modify the space in the attempt to create just such a milieu. For instance, there are 'get-to-know-you' games to provide a sense of comfort and familiarity, and both bathhouse A and B have 'themed rooms', some examples of which include: a g-spot room, SM room, lap-dance room, and Temple Priestess room—wherein the 'Priestess' fulfills patron requests. The rooms were staffed by volunteers, who are there specifically to service patron requests. According to the organisers, the themed rooms not only provide a safe outlet for sexual satiation, but facilitate sexual interaction, and create an environment wherein patrons can be sexual without having to seek out sex and thus, risk rejection.

SEXUAL ARTICULATION AND AGENCY: QUEER MOBILITY

Informed by observations and interview data, I argue that in many ways these spaces function as counterpublic spheres (Fraser 1992), in that 'members of subordinated social groups invent and circulate counterdiscourses to formulate oppositional interpretations of their identities, interests and needs' (1992: 123). What were these emergent forms of resistance and re-interpretations of self? Without fail, when I asked interviewees what they enjoyed most about these spaces and why they believed them to be significant, it was not sex per se, but the 'watching of others' that seemed to hold particular resonance. This is not to deny that some individuals came to these events specifically for sexual satiation or to expand their sexual horizons. Rather, this voyeurism seemed to have salutary and ramifying effects that went beyond mere titillation.

When individuals were probed to discuss this 'watching of others' in greater detail, interviewees discussed how the mere sight of nude, queer and non-normative bodies 'getting off', as one participant put it, was, in and of itself, empowering. It was this ability to see 'real bodies, not plastic ones'—seeing images of themselves in others—that validated their own bodies and desire. The pleasure in seeing queer bodies is a response to the hegemonic phallocentric, heteronormative and standardised representations of both heterosexual and queer women's bodies and desire (Gelder and Brandt 1997). It is in these subaltern spaces where alternative configurations become thinkable and possible. For instance, Taylor, a 'butch-dyke-boi', stated that he believed people came to the event to 'see if they are normal.' Taylor states:

> they are seeing all sorts of gender freaks doing stuff they are interested in doing . . . They see themselves in some of these folks and it just makes people feel okay about themselves.

In addition to being a place of queer affirmation, interviewees expressed feeling secure in their bodies, in part because many of those bodies that were nude and exposed were far removed from conventional standards of beauty. Participants often used 'fat-positive' to describe these milieux.

Conversely, many discussed the power that came from being on the receiving end of someone else's gaze. Shannon, a lesbian and regular bathhouse attendee, connected her bathhouse participation to her increasing self-confidence. Shannon had always felt 'invisible', attributing this to her weight and butch appearance, but at the bathhouse people look at her and affirm 'who she is'. She describes a lifetime pattern of sexual passivity and suppressed desire that shifted with these bathhouse experiences. The appreciative expression Shannon experienced from other patrons enabled her to 'feel sexy and alive' for 'the first time' (she was in her late twenties). While invisibility 'brings about a negative emotional reaction—social shame [and] humiliation' (Westhaver 2006: 634), Shannon's visibility and recognition *as a sexual subject* transformed her corporeal demeanour and notions of self.

Additionally, according to organisers, a significant aspect of the themed rooms is that they foster verbal communication—patrons must communicate in clear terms with the volunteer exactly what it is they want to do. Giving voice to desire and the concomitant bodily praxis that follows—that is, having an embodied sexuality—is a resistance to the 'inhibited intentionality' (Young 1990) or docile bodies that society expects of women (and those socialised as women). The body as generative in meaning-making, such as through the carnal dimensions of subjectivity (McNay 1999) where bodily power is keenly felt, suggests that bodily and sexual agency are key sites of mobilisation. Michelle, a bisexual and regular attendee, attributes her own communicative skills and bodily awareness to the bathhouse. Michelle eloquently describes her own embodied desire:

> You have to practice communicating, that is central to this place [the bathhouse]. It is about also being emotionally aware . . . In exploring my body here, rather than just going through the movements, my brain is more connected to how my body moves, what my body needs, what it likes, dislikes . . .

Within these spaces heterodox behaviours and practices (public sex, non-monogamy) and unconventional bodies converge and are to be celebrated. This validation, coupled with the sexual services and opportunities available, were the necessary ingredients that, according to many interviewees, allowed for enlarged spatial boundaries and alternative sexual scripts. Many saw their own 'sexual evolution' as being directly tied to their bathhouse experiences, with 'empowerment' and 'confident' used to describe this process. Finally, this claiming of one's body and 'finding one's sexuality' was expressed by several individuals who were survivors of sexual abuse. For instance, one survivor asserted that the bathhouse had gotten her 'reacquainted with her body', having felt 'frozen [sexually] for all of these years.'

Thus, in some ways, these bathhouses work to counter heteropatriarchy, where research continues to show that women have difficulty articulating and satiating their *own* desires (Tolman 2005). This disembodied desire results in women's 'estrangement from her bodily being' (Bordo, 1990: 40)—those 'docile bodies' (Foucault 1978) far removed from bodily awareness and agency. On the other hand, an embodied desire incorporates feeling, thinking and bodily awareness—an awareness that many of my subjects displayed. Obviously, not all those who are/were socialised as women succumb to patriarchal messages, with lesbians and queers in many ways better able to overcome the phallocentric pressures of femininity.

As my data suggests, many individuals took advantage of the sexual opportunities that were available. Those who did often, in quite passionate terms, connected these bathhouse experiences to enlarged and empowered sexual subjectivities and notions of self. These individuals were the paradigmatic cases, those who seemed to 'showcase' the empowering appeal and resistive potential that inhered within the bathhouses.

CORPOREAL SILENCES

As previously stated, 'queer' functions as an umbrella term for a wide range of non-normative subjects and sex/gender practices—in short, those subjects which do not conform to the heteronormative sex/gender regime. Thus, an incredibly diverse population is consolidated under one word—queer. Obviously, this can create its own set of problems. That is, this queer heterogeneity might (unwittingly) install homogeneity, since significant differences amongst queers are erased under the aegis of 'queer'. In this attempt to be 'multicultural, multigendered, [and] multisexual' (Gamson 1995: 396), queer ends up:

> denying differences either by submerging them in an undifferentiated oppositional mass or by blocking the development of individual and social differences.
>
> (Seidman 1993: 133)

An illustrative example is the use of queer to represent or include those who identify as transgendered or transsexual (or somewhere in between). Many trans-identified individuals strongly oppose the term queer when it is used to represent them. For one, queer elides trans-experience and subjectivity. Obviously, transmen and transwomen, *because* of their trans status, have their own unique experiences, struggles and traumas that most 'queers' will never experience. Trans subjects' struggle for gender determination, recognition, and basic rights is not the *same* struggle that gays and lesbians endure (see Namaste 2000). Furthermore, queer's exaltation of indeterminancy belies and dismisses the desire some trans people have in (re)claiming a non-transitive state of permanency and stability (Hale 1998).

QUEER IM/MOBILITY

Two expressions of queer mobility at the bathhouses are highlighted: sexual exploration and thus, spatial and corporeal mobilisation; and the non-determinacy of bodies in terms of gender variance and sexual fluidity. Additionally and relatedly, queer provides recognition to the culturally unintelligible—those non-normative bodies and sexualities that heteropatriarchy invisibilises and ignores. The feminist and queer frameworks that undergird the bathhouses intend to do just that—provide recognition to abject subjects. Under such 'ideal' conditions differences are affirmed and celebrated. Herein lies the problem. As already mentioned, these sexual spaces are overwhelmingly non-trans and white. This lack of diversity was curious, but particularly so at bathhouse A, located in a city known for its active trans and queer of colour communities. Bathhouse A also put on 'Women of Color and Trans-only Events', which, while laudable, signals the very strong possibility that queers of colour and/or trans folk do not feel comfortable at 'regular' bathhouse events.

My data suggests—at least at the sites I examined—that non-trans status and whiteness mark sexual subversion and 'public sex.' In other words, it is the transparent white and non-trans subject that *does* public sex and traverses these particular spaces with ease. Ahmed's insights regarding the phenomenology of whiteness could also be applied to trans-status and non-normative corporeal formations. Ahmed, in describing how space-building is yoked to unmarked whiteness, states:

> Spaces acquire the 'skin' of the bodies that inhabit them . . . Spaces also take shape by being orientated around some bodies, more than others . . . When we describe institutions as 'being' white, we are pointing to how institutional spaces are shaped by the proximity of some bodies and not others: white bodies gather, and cohere to form the edges of such spaces.
>
> (Ahmed 2007: 157)

As a result, 'non-white [and non-trans] bodies feel uncomfortable, exposed, visible, different, when they take up this space' (Ahmed 2007: 157).

Within sexual spaces, bodies are hyper-salient, visible and vulnerable. Of the transmen and transwomen I interviewed and observed, although some were at times partially unclothed (e.g., topless or wearing a swimming suit for instance), never did I observe a scantily clad or completely nude trans-individual. Additionally, throughout the duration of those five events I attended, I never did see transmen/women directly participating—that is, having sex or utilising the themed rooms. Trans-subjects were literally, that is physically, on the margins of these spaces—inhabiting less space and removed from the sexual centre, often confined to one area of the venue. If nudity is encouraged and one sign of 'liberation'—which it was—and voyeuristic pleasure in 'watching others' who are *actively* participating sexually is cited as one of the main reasons people come to these events, then one must question who it is they are watching (and admiring). This spatial marginalisation and bodily immobilisation supports Ahmed's

(2007) insights regarding the connective tissue between the phenomenology of difference and space—that is, at the bathhouse spatial arrangements tend toward and cohere around normative (less queer) bodies.

Although I never did 'see' a trans-phobic or racist incident, interviewee data clearly indicate that phobic attitudes were present. Many trans and non-trans subjects alike noted that many trans-people they knew do not come because they understand it to be an event that is not for them (and of course, many transmen/women simply do not want to attend). The majority of trans-individuals I interviewed expressed reservations and insecurities when it came to their own participation, commenting, for instance, that they 'understood' how people probably felt about them. One fully transitioned 43-year-old transman, Eric, a participant at bathhouse A, mentioned that he 'needed to be careful' so as 'not to offend anyone'. Eric wanted me to understand from the outset his desire not to ruffle any feathers. Alluding to his masculine body and physical appearance as problematic, Eric chose 'not to participate'—meaning directly, either in organised activities or play sessions. When asked why he had come to this event (a question I asked all interviewees), Eric mentioned that prior to his transitioning he identified as a dyke and had belonged to the lesbian/dyke community for decades. Despite his transition, he still 'supports this community', even though things have changed. Unfortunately, as is shown in the following section, interviewee comments affirm Eric's concerns regarding his participation as a transman.

CORPOREAL EXCESS AND THE POLITICS OF NON/BELONGING

Instability arises from the disjuncture and refusal of one-on-one correspondence between the signifier and signified. Butler comes to apply these deconstructionist principles to the material body, since 'language and materiality are fully embedded in one another' (Butler 1993: 69). Under a queer theory project the body takes on new or alternative meanings—this is the process known as resignification—and the body itself comes to be *the* site of radical subversion (Butler 1993). Butler's notion of performativity is emblematic of this resignification process. While 'real bodies'—those that align with heteropatriarchal standards—are given recognition, queer embodiments problematise the naturalisation of the hegemonic sex/gender regime. Butler attempts to highlight gender's 'realness', as well as its flexibility and fabrication, which queer illuminates with its emphasis on non-normativity, fluidity and disjuncture. That is, gender is neither wholly determining nor voluntarist, but contingent and shifting. Moreover, as Butler argues, subjects always fail in the process of attempting to live up to any gender/sexual ideal—including heterosexuality (Butler 1993).

Although Butler's notion of performativity is not to be literalised (Jagose 1997), and Butler herself argues strongly against an interpretation of her work that suggests a voluntarist, willy-nilly concept of gender, queer theorists have done little in the way of explicating the logistics. That is, how exactly is a radical de/re/constructionist project to emerge? At the bathhouse, individuals are encouraged to utilise the space in non-conforming and queer ways, to change their scripts, to morph—at least for that time. Yet, my fieldwork suggests that non-normative bodies, even within non-normative settings, get mired, measured and reduced by way of heteronormative constructs. In other words, in these sexual zones of excess and non-determinancy, a one-on-one correspondence between gender identity and body morphology gets (re)inscribed and enforced, while subjectivities—that interiority which cannot be 'read' off the surface—are evacuated.

When it comes to perceptions and reactions vis-à-vis the transsexual body, context is paramount. What were participants' responses within these purportedly queer *and* sexual spaces? One of them was a preoccupation with masculinity and 'maleness' which emerged within participant subjectivities. Interestingly, it was maleness as opposed to femaleness or femininity that marked one's (non)belonging. Interviewee data suggest that some participants carried excess levels of masculinity that seemed to transgress the threshold of acceptability, determinations of which relied on visual cues of the physical body. Meanings generated from these visual cues operated alongside, not a queer frame, but a normative masculinity-femininity continuum, thus placing bodies into fixed gendered and sexed categories—manifestations of which are discussed in the following paragraphs. Although several interviewees indicated a strong discomfort with both transmen and transwomen, it was the transman that seemed to cause the most trouble. Remarks about the presence and inclusion of transmen included such statements as 'men don't belong here', 'these are men, not women', 'this is a women's-only space', to one participant's visibly frustrated assertion that 'why do men insist on coming to events where they don't belong?'

Jake, a 24-year-old transman, despite his discomfort, regularly attended bathhouse A events. He knew many of the organisers and had, previous to his transition, identified as a lesbian. When asked why he felt uncomfortable at the bathhouse, Jake felt as though he 'stuck out' and knew that people 'stared at [him], wondering if he was really a man or not'. Accordingly, Jake 'knew that some people didn't want [him] there'. Like Eric, Jake took part in the event, but never directly and never sexually. One of his main activities consisted of continuously traversing the space, a tactic undertaken to look busy and preoccupied. Eric, who, as previously mentioned, had identified as a dyke before transitioning, was highly aware of his surroundings and people's perceptions of him. That is, he just assumed—rightly or wrongly— that he made people uncomfortable. Although he had not experienced any discrimination (although I spoke with him at the very beginning of the event), Eric carefully monitored his behaviour, and stuck to observing as opposed to participating. During the event, Eric lounged outside in the swimming pool area.

To reiterate, these events were explicitly trans-inclusive. Yet, among the interviewees, it was a main organiser of bathhouse A, Valerie, who, when probed to discuss the details of their bathhouse policy, began exhibiting strong discomfort and outright transphobia (despite being a policy that she helped to craft). During the interview Valerie begins demarcating between trans-folk who are 'men' and those who 'fit in', asserting that those who are 'men' do not belong. I quote Valerie at length:

> In my opinion if you identify as a man, you don't belong. There are some trans folk who blend in fine . . . I would rather not have men there even if they used to be women. Again, if someone is trans and they fit in, they are queer identified and they fit in, and it is hard, I don't want to be the one to define it, because there are some who fit in, but once they are men then they don't. I think they need to be respectful of women's space, especially when they used to be women.

When asked to describe what made some*body* transgress—crossing that line of acceptability, Valerie's demarcation hinged on physicality, noting for instance that one particular individual (referring to Eric) 'had balls', and moreover, stated how some transmen 'who were allowed in' were simply 'hairy guys' who 'had no business being here'. At one point Eric had decided to swim with his swimming trunks on, thus outlining a bulge—a transitioned FTM body—that Valerie deemed highly offensive. As for the 'hairy guys', although Valerie had 'total respect for them' because they had started the dyke leather community, 'they were men immersed in maleness', and 'clearly did not belong'. Valerie's ultimate criterion hinges on those who 'fit in'—a nebulous, ineffable term—that is fortified by Valerie's claim that people *know* whether or not they belong. Although Valerie states that 'some trans do fit', it is the fully transitioned subjects or those who take hormones (thus, looking indistinguishable from 'real men'), whose 'male energy' permeates (read: taints) the space, that do not belong.

Valerie's criteria of who 'fits in' accomplishes two things: it evacuates interiorities, and, at least tacitly, mimics lesbian fears and exclusions of the past, wherein butches (and now transmen) were considered 'intruders' of women's space and predatory individuals. But, what separates butch masculinities from transsexual masculinities, and what is it about these masculinities that makes them inherently pernicious when it comes to these events? Again, this is not to deny that significant differences exist between those who transition and female-born butches. But such differences are in many ways not so clear-cut (see Halberstam 2003). I dwell on this precisely because it is this amorphous construct—masculinity—that seems to function as *the* marker, that delineation, that presages who belongs. Regarding the erasure of subjectivities, we continue to believe that surfaces, corporeal cues, tell all. Thus, trans-phobia within these sexual spaces is, in part and to reiterate, about 'excessive' masculinity, an excess that evokes concerns over safety and objectionable behaviours. But what about butches (or femmes) who are 'more masculine' than transmen? For instance, at one point I observed a butch, as a 'top' participant in an SM scene, slap, without solicitation, a passer-by's buttock, wherein the butch proceeded to beat her chest—a sign of conquest if ever there was one. A quick rebuke from the woman followed. In these sexual spaces, the butch is still read as 'female'—masculinity tacked onto a female body—thus, evading censor and self-monitoring.

In other spaces/contexts, the butch is rooted, while it is the transperson who exemplifies fluidity, mobility, and transgression (Halberstam 2003). A reverse pattern seemed to operate at these sites. That is, in sexual spaces such as the bathhouse, where desire and exposure converge, it is the butch body that is perceived as mobile—thus, queer—while the transmale body—masculinity yoked to a male body—is rooted, anchored, and univocal. In short, unlike the butch body, with the transmale body the visible disjuncture disappears, rendering him, not transgressive, but rather, frighteningly still and grounded. His seeming coherence and unambiguous display of masculinity suggests a masculine desire, a desire that has and can explore, a masculine privilege that assumes an entitlement to desire and sex. In short, he displays (whether real or perceived) the very signs of an agentic masculine body (entitlement, invulnerability), while simultaneously assumed (wrongly) to be a phallocratic agent. This essentialised and totalising portrayal of the transmale subject is fundamentally at odds with queer.

If contesting and rupturing normative constructions of gendered/sexed bodies is a queer objective, then under this logic, trans-bodies should be *the* sign of gender queerness. At the very least, this body, like all bodies, should be unexceptional, a body that blends in to the spatial cacophony, belongs, fits. Obviously, transsexualism, along with any other non-normative gender configuration, is not inherently radical (or queer). But Valerie's assumptions simply (re)calibrate bodies according to the normative sex/gender regime, thus, turning a heterogeneous field of non-normative bodies into a monochromatic landscape. According to Valerie, Eric, being physically male, thus masculine, possesses a 'male masculinity', which exceeds, and is thus qualitatively different from, other forms of masculinity that *are* acceptable—such as that which emanates from butch and femme bodies.

Lastly, in thinking about the bathhouse scene, it is important to reiterate that the staff, organisers, security personnel and volunteers (such as those in the themed rooms) were non-trans and overwhelmingly white. Juxtaposing this scene with organisers' stated goals—sexual exploration and the taking up of space—and being mindful of the fact that the themed rooms were considered to be crucial vector points for sexual facilitation and exploration, it will be much less likely that those of colour and/or trans-identified will see these venues as inviting spaces. One woman of colour stated that 'you don't see yourself in the person at the door, in the people posted at security, in the people doing the lap dances and the other activities . . . ' (Garro 2006). Not recognising yourself in others, coupled with feeling (doubly) marked, creates an acuity of self and body that is inhibitive, rather than liberatory or agentic. In short, these queer, sex-radical spaces have parameters—a register that governs what is and is not acceptable. These corporeal limits in turn determine the spatial politics of (non)belonging.

CONCLUSION

In this chapter I have attempted to illuminate the ways in which non-trans privilege operates in sexualised spaces—in this case, two Canadian lesbian/ queer bathhouses. Queer is employed in these spaces to signify a sex-positive/ sex radical philosophy, celebration of difference and non-normative gender/ sex configurations, and a resistance to heteropatriarchal forces that belittle and degrade women's and queers' sexualities and desire. The objectives are twofold: to explore and resuscitate those libidinal and bodily desires that are suppressed or stigmatised in society—thus, facilitating bodily empowerment and recognition; and inclusivity, where neither overt nor tacit exclusions operate. This latter objective—inclusivity—is a necessary and critical precondition for the former. In other words, these public and sexual events, unlike gay male sexual zones, would simply not work without this inclusion (queer) criterion—an understanding not lost on the organisers.

Lesbian/queer spaces have their own logic that emerges out of a social structure that is homophobic, misogynist, and patriarchal. Moreover, because there are so few lesbian/queer *public* sexual spaces, such spaces cater and attract a broad array of sexualities and sexual interests—as opposed to particular sexual niches (e.g., SM/leather). This dearth of public space, coupled with the sexual politics that such spaces engender, translates into events that, unlike most gay male sexual zones, contain low levels of both vertical differentiation as it relates to 'tiers of desirability' and horizontal differentiation as it relates to social/sexual types and one's 'erotic capital' (Green 2008). In other words, within this one available space multiple fields of sexual interest and desire converge, such that no one prevailing aesthetic standard of desirability exists. While such a plurality induces a democratising field of relations, it does not eradicate privilege.

Bodies circulate in these spaces with different degrees of bodily capital. By 'bodily capital' I refer not to aesthetic standards of attraction and eroticism per se (although this has linkages to my larger meaning), so much as a particular corporeality that exposes the fears of the sexual centre and the operative exclusionary mechanisms that prevail. For one, queers of colour and trans-folk are underrepresented in such spaces, both in terms of sheer participation, their inclusion on the organising committee, and as staff and volunteers. Other mechanisms curtail bodily and sexual expression such as (actual or perceived) discrimination, in the form of trans/racial eroticisation and transphobia.

Although some bodies actively take advantage of these sexual opportunities, it is the 'least queer' among them. Those too queer—and queer here means too physically outside normative sexed/gendered bodies—are outcastes even in spaces where queer is deployed to celebrate such configurations. Fieldwork revealed a current of transphobia at these venues. The transmen and transwomen were, like queers of colour, literally on the margins. Trans individuals were confined to smaller, outer areas of the venue, and rarely intermingled with the scene. Eric, a transman, came to the event knowing he might feel uncomfortable, but wanted to 'show his support'. Interviewee comments suggested that unambiguous trans-bodies—those with secondary sex characteristics and/or transitioned/ing bodies—'did not belong', since they were 'men with male energy'. Under this logic, subjects pass ('fit in') when *lacking* external cues of ('real') masculinity (a phallus or a hirsute body), while maintaining a body-sex-gender disjuncture.

Given the bathhouses' philosophy, this heteronormative and reductive assortment of bodies—the very 'thing' it is purportedly contesting—is ironic to say the least. Trans-masculinities violate 'women's' space, while 'other' masculinities—those *not* yoked to 'male' bodies—are accepted and even encouraged, even if the subjectivities/behaviours attached to these non-trans bodies are objectionable and misogynist. Conversely, transmen's subjectivities—even those closely tied to and affiliated with feminist, queer and lesbian communities—are evacuated when automatically flagged as contaminating. The politics of belonging debate has had a long and checkered past within the lesbian-feminist community (the Michigan Womyn's Music Festival's 'womyn-born-womyn' policy is a case in point). Yet, some quarters of the lesbian/feminist/queer pro-sex communities have attempted to overcome these border wars, seeing queer and its philosophy as an effective strategy to extricate women's space from political immobilisation, by refashioning, expanding and de-centring 'women's space' to forge coalitional alliances. Although 'queer' seemed to wield much promise, as the bathhouses illuminate, queer is a limited, if not ineffectual, strategy for such change. The salience of some bodies over others suggests that 'other' bodies will continue to be 'marked', even in purportedly democratic and queer spaces. In spaces that are sexually charged, this visibility becomes ever more intensified. Despite a celebration of difference and non-normativity, 'Other' bodies do not possess the bodily capital necessary to fully access the sexual opportunities that are available. As I have tried to show, these sexual spaces reproduce and replicate certain privileges—in this case, non-trans privilege—thus, revealing their own normative and disciplining processes.

REFERENCES

Acker, J., Barry, K. and Esseveld, J. (1983) 'Objectivity and truth: problems in doing feminist research', *Women"s Studies International Forum*, 6(4): 423–435.
Ahmed, S. (2007) 'A phenomenology of whiteness', *Feminist Theory*, 8(2): 149–168.

Bérubé, A. (1996) 'The history of gay bathhouses', in Dangerous Bedfellows (eds) *Policing Public Sex*, Boston: South End.

Bersani, L. (1987) 'Is the rectum a grave?' *Cultural Analysis/Cultural Activism*, 43: 197–222.

Bordo, S. (1989) 'The body and the reproduction of femininity', in A. Jaggar and S. Bordo (eds) *Gender, Body and Knowledge*, New Brunswick, NJ: Rutgers University Press.

Butler, J. (1990) *Gender Trouble: Feminism and the Subversion of Identity*, New York and London: Routledge.

———. (1993) *Bodies that Matter*, New York: Routledge.

Cooper, D. (2007) '"Well, you go there to get off": visiting feminist care ethics through a women's bathhouse', *Feminist Theory*, 8(3): 243–262.

Echols, A. (1984) 'The taming of the id', in C. Vance (ed.) *Pleasure and Danger*, Boston: Routledge.

Foucault, M. (1978) *The History of Sexuality*, New York: Random House.

Fraser, N. (1992) 'Rethinking the public sphere: a contribution to the critique of actually existing democracy', in C. Calhoun (ed.) *Habermas and the Public Sphere*, Cambridge: MIT.

Gamson, J. (1995) 'Must identity movements self-destruct? A queer dilemma', *Social Problems*, 42(3): 390–406.

Garro, J. (2006) 'Sugar shack shakes it up', *Xtra*, February 16. http://www.xtraca. com (accessed 10 February 2008).

Gelder, L. and Brandt, P. (1997) *The Girls Next Door*, New York: Simon and Schuster.

Green, A. (2008) 'The social organization of desire: the sexual fields approach', *Sociological Theory*, 26(1): 25–50.

———. (2007) 'Queer theory and sociology: locating the subject and the self in sexuality studies', *Sociological Theory*, 25(1): 27–45.

Halberstam, J. (2003) 'Transgender butch: butch/FTM border wars and the masculine continuum', in W. Kolmar and F. Bartkowski (eds) *Feminist Theory: A Reader*, Boston: McGraw-Hill.

Hale, C. (1998) 'Consuming the living, dis(re)membering the dead in the butch/FTM borderlands', *GLQ*, 4(2): 311–348.

Hammers, C. and Sheff, E. 'The transparent white subject and the racial (re)production of sexed spaces', manuscript under review.

Hemphill, E. (1991) *Brother to Brother*, Boston: Alyson.

Hines, S. (2007) *TransForming Gender: Transgender Practices of Identity, Intimacy and Care*, Bristol: Policy Press.

Humphreys, L. (1975) *Tearoom Trade: Impersonal Sex in Public Places*, Chicago: Aldine.

Jackson, S. (2006) 'Gender, sexuality and heterosexuality', *Feminist Theory*, 7(1): 105–121.

Jagose, A. (1997) *Queer Theory: An Introduction*, New York: New York University Press.

Kennedy, E. L. and Davis, M. D. (1993) *Boots of Leather, Slippers of Gold: The History of a Lesbian Community*, New York: Penguin Books.

Kinsman, G. (1996) *The Regulation of Desire*, New York: Black Rose Books.

Knopp, L. (1992) 'Sexuality and the spatial dynamics of capitalism', *Environment and Planning D: Society and Space*, 10(6): 651–669.

Leap, W. L. (1999) *Public Sex/Gay Space*, New York: Columbia University Press.

McNay, L. (1999) 'Gender, habitus and the field', *Theory, Culture and Society*, 16(1): 95–117.

Meeks, C. (2001) 'Civil society and the sexual politics of difference', *Sociological Theory*, 19(3): 325–343.

Namaste, K. (1994) 'The politics of inside/out: queer theory, poststructuralism, and a sociological approach to sexuality', *Sociological Theory*, 12(2): 220–231.

Namaste, V. (2000) *Invisible Lives*, Chicago: University of Chicago Press.

Segal, L. (1994) *Straight Sex: The Erasure of Transsexual and Transgendered People*, London: Virago.

Sedgwick, E. K. (1990) *Epistemology of the Closet*, Berkeley: University of California Press.

Seidman, S. (1993) 'Identity politics in a 'postmodern' gay culture: some historical and conceptual notes,' in M. Warner (ed.) *Fear of a Queer Planet*, Minneapolis: University of Minnesota Press.

——. (1994) 'Symposium—queer theory sociology: a dialogue', *Sociological Theory*, 12(2): 166–177.

——. (1997) *Difference Troubles*, Cambridge: Cambridge University Press.

Stein, A. and Plummer, K. (1994) '"I can't even think straight": "queer" theory and the missing sexual revolution in sociology', *Sociological Theory*, 12(2): 178–188.

Tolman, D. (2005) *Dilemmas of Desire*, Cambridge: Harvard University Press.

Valentine, G. (1995) 'Out and about: geographies of lesbian landscapes', *International Journal of Urban and Regional Research*, 19: 96–112.

Weinberg, M. S. and Williams, C. (1975) 'Gay baths and the social organization of impersonal sex', *Social Problems*, 23(2): 124–136.

Westhaver, R. (2006) 'Flaunting and empowerment: thinking about circuit parties, the body and power', *Journal of Contemporary Ethnography*, 35(6): 611–644.

Wiegman, R. (2006) 'Heteronormativity and the desire for gender', *Feminist Theory*, 7(1): 89–103.

Wolfe, M. (1997) 'Invisible women in invisible places: the production of social space in lesbian bars', in G. Ingram, A. Bouthillette and Y. Retter (eds) *Queers in Space: Communities/Public Places/Sites of Resistance*, Seattle: Bay Press.

Young, I. (1990) *Throwing Like a Girl and Other Essays in Feminist Philosophy and Social Theory*, Bloomington: Indiana University.

12 Towards a Sociology of Gender Diversity
The Indian and UK Cases

Surya Monro

Western transgender (trans) and intersex scholarly engagement with post-structuralism has mushroomed in recent years, including accounts by Feinberg (1996, 1998), Bornstein (1994, 1998), Whittle (2002) and Stryker and Whittle (2006). More recently, Western feminists and sociologists who draw on poststructuralism, such as Monro (2000, 2005, 2007a, 2007b), Hird (2000, 2002, 2006), Hines (2006, 2007), and Sanger (2008) have begun to explore the implications of affirmative trans and intersex identities for gender theory. There is recognition amongst these authors that poststructuralist accounts, whilst crucial to theorising gender diversity, require framing in such a way as to be mindful of the social, material, and corporeal formation of gendered experiences. These approaches are arguably sociological in that they address the structuring of human experience within both public and private realms, as opposed to, for instance, the focus on the discursive construction of social life favoured by cultural studies. Structural approaches fit well with broader developments within the field of gender and women's studies, in particular those associated with intersectionality, in which the mutually constitutive nature of social characteristics is interrogated. Recent trends within the field of intersectionality point to a need for attention to structural inequalities and power relations (Grabham et al. 2009).

This chapter aims to provide a snapshot of developments leading up to the formation of a sociology of trans and intersex, to provide an empirically-driven overview of one approach to the sociological theorisation of gender diversity, and to indicate future directions for the development of the field. The chapter draws on intersectionality theory to a degree, but space precludes a full exploration. To some extent it also speaks to Roen's (2001) important critique of the ethnocentrism of much trans theorising. The chapter is set within the context of the considerable body of cross-cultural work concerning gender diversity, including that of Herdt (1994), Masequesmay (2003), Boellstorff (2004), Blackburn (2005), and Peletz, (2006). By taking two localities as comparative sites, and ensuring that complexity in both sites is made evident, the author hopes to avoid 'idealising' a non-Western 'primordial location' where gender diversity flourished before the 'Fall into Western Modernity' (Towle and Morgan 2006: 666).

The chapter begins by providing an outline of developments of relevance to the sociology of transgender, in rough chronological order, and the three ways of conceptualising gender diversity that emerged from my empirical work. I conclude with a discussion of possible future directions for the sociology of gender diversity. Whilst I focus on trans and intersex subjects, following McCall's (2005) intracategorical intersectionality approach (in which a marginalised social group is taken as a point of departure for the development of analysis) I recognise that a fuller sociological account would require a broader problematisation of the gender binary system and related homosexual/heterosexual divide and interrogation of the raced, classed, aged, and able-bodied nature of this. Definitions and a description of the methodology are described elsewhere (Monro 2007a); space limitations prevent inclusion.[1] However, diversity is of importance across the trans and intersex communities, and it is important to point out that many trans and intersex people identify as male or female and would not necessarily relate to the theories of gender diversity that I outline in the following section.

THE SOCIOLOGY OF TRANSGENDER: SETTING THE SCENE

Western sociological and poststructuralist thought regarding gender variance has been preceded by developments in Indian scholarship, which I shall outline briefly before discussing Western approaches. Vanita and Kidwai (2000) describe the long tradition of Indian philosophical enquiry into gender diversity. Sex and gender are questioned in Buddhist, Hindu and Jain traditions, and:

> The philosophical basis of this questioning closely resembles the deconstruction of gender in our own times by such thinkers as Monique Wittig and Judith Butler. What these thinkers would call the social construction of gender that only appears to be 'natural', ancient Indian philosophers would call 'illusion' that only appears to be 'real'.
>
> (Vanita and Kidwai 2000: 23)

Vanita and Kidwai also argue that

> There is a direct connection between the nonreality of gender and the nonabsoluteness of heterosexuality. If the two categories, "man" and "woman" are not ultimate categories but are merely created by society to foster certain social roles and uphold institutions such as marriage, parenthood and patrilineal inheritance, then the heterosexual relation ceases to be the most important one.
>
> (2000: 23)

Importantly, they note that the notion of reincarnation renders categorisation, including sex/gender[2] and species categorisation, fluid and mutable. For Vanita and Kidwai, then, sex, gender, and sexual orientation categories are constructed; as with Western social constructionist approaches, this does not necessarily mean that sex/gender and sexuality categories are easily malleable, or that corporeality and social structuring factors are unimportant.

Western sociological theories of gender diversity draw on the interactionist accounts of early sociologists such as Garfinkel (1967) and Kessler and McKenna (1978), the scholarship of trans and intersex theorists, and the new wave of feminist sociologists engaging with the field. Ekins and King (2006) discuss the way in which pioneering books by transgender theorists such as Feinberg (1996, 1998), Bornstein (1994, 1998) and Wilchins (1997) 'established what was effectively a new paradigm for the conceptualisation and study of transgender phenomenon' (2006: 21). These books, and the work of other transgender and intersex authors such as Stone (1991), Prosser (1998), Chase (1998) and Halberstam (2002), engaged with, and informed, poststructuralist theory. Poststructuralist and interactionist accounts of trans and intersex share an ontological foundation in which both sex and gender have socially constructed components.

Another development in the field of trans studies has been the recent emergence of UK feminist and sociological accounts of trans and intersex that are grounded in research with trans and intersex people. These authors include Hird (2000, 2002, 2006), Monro (2000, 2005, 2007a, 2007b), Roen (2001, 2002), Tauchert (2002), Hines (2005, 2006, 2007) and Sanger (2008). The work of these authors stands in contrast to that of most of the earlier feminist work on trans, which stigmatises trans people and demonstrates an inability to deal with people who move beyond or between sex/gender and sexual orientation binaries (see for instance Raymond 1994). This new wave of writing shows greater acknowledgement of the differences within the trans and intersex populations. It complements other literature on trans, including the work of Namaste (2000), Dreger (2000) and Ekins and King (2006).

Overall, it can be argued that poststructuralism, and Indian philosophies that share common ground with poststructuralist thinking, provide important tools for understanding sex/gender diversity (Monro 2001, 2005). Notions such as sex/gender as being illusory, and understandings of the discursive construction of sexed/gendered subjectivity, are important for unpicking how people are normatively conditioned into binaried sexual and gender identities. The conceptual disassociation of sex/gender identities (and for some Indian theorists, core identities) and bodies also allows theorisation of more complex forms of gender. However, a number of problems with poststructuralist approaches have also been raised, pointing to the need for a more sociological position, which accounts for corporeal, material, and social structures. Difficulties with poststructuralism have included a tendency to overlook the importance of the body (Hird

2000; Monro 2000, 2005), a focus on performativity and transgression as opposed to the lived experiences of many trans people (Hines 2006), and the deconstruction of sex/gender categories as a basis of political organisation (Wilchins 1997). Another issue is that some transgender and other people experience themselves as having an essential self, or gender identity, that is 'other' than their body or social conditioning (Monro 2007b), although this issue could be dealt with using Vanita and Kidwai's (2000) approach, which models subjects as having a core self or 'soul' that does not have to be embodied to exist. It is important to point out that notions of the body and social structures as illusionary can be interpreted in different ways; Govender (2007) describes the way in which some Hindus see the doctrine of reincarnation as legitimising complacency or fatalistic attitudes towards social structures, whereas others actively work to address social and material inequalities. It is therefore possible to argue that understandings of sex/gender as illusory need to be informed by attention to the structuring of embodied experience.

To summarise, a sociological approach to sex/gender diversity acknowledges corporeality, and material and social structuring forces, whilst moving beyond unproblematised notions of sex/gender binaries. This chapter now presents three approaches to theorising sex/gender diversity. The approaches presented in the following section form ideal types and they may in practice overlap, or be used strategically by individuals in different ways at different times.

THEORISING SEX/GENDER DIVERSITY

The first ideal type, *'expanding sex/gender binaries'*, involves theorising femininities and masculinities as diverse, including people who have bodies or social roles that are different to those traditionally associated with women and men, for example, intersex people living as male or female (see Dreger 2000). As Halberstam (2002) suggests, the elasticity of sex/gender binary categories allows sex/gender diversity to be subsumed into 'male' and 'female'—at least to an extent. The expansion of binary categories is conceptually related to notions drawn from masculinity studies. The notion of masculinities as plural involves moving away from an understanding of masculinity as white, middle class, heterosexual and able-bodied, towards thinking about masculinities as multiple, and some masculinities as hegemonic (see Hearn and Morgan 1990). The understanding of femininities and masculinities as plural is helpful in theorising sex/gender and sexual diversity, because it is a pragmatic strategy for the majority of the population, enabling many people with diverse sexualities and sexes/genders to gain social rights and acceptance.

The 'expanded sex/gender binaries' model is, arguably, an adaptive mechanism, allowing management of the social structures which entrench gender binaries for most, but not all, people. Third sex/gender Hijra people have been documented in India for over 4,000 years (PUCL-K 2003), and these individuals are not accountable for within the 'expanded male/female categories' model. Some Kothis may also fit poorly into such a model. The model further fails to include those Western subjects who identify as other than female or male.

The second approach, *'moving beyond gender'*, follows the work of Lorber (1994), who argues for moving towards a non-gendered social order, based on equality, without gender categorisation. Her notion of degendering can be conceptually linked with the notion of gender liminality and also of the gender transcendence discussed by Ekins and King (2006). Such an approach is evidenced in some of the trans scholarship, for example Stone (1991) and Bornstein (1994) describe transsexuality as a place outside of duality.

Notions of moving beyond gender, and gender liminality, are useful for conceptualising gender diversity. With regard to Indian notions of sex/gender, the concept of a soul that has successive incarnations, perhaps in bodies with different sexes, implies liminality at the times when the soul is without a sexed body. There are also elements of degendering in some Hijra discourses, where Hijras are seen as occupying a particular place in Indian society because they are outside of male or female categorisation systems. Discourses concerning degendering have become apparent to a degree in the UK. A number of contributors to my 1996–1998 research in the UK (see Monro 2005, 2007a) discussed the need for a less heavily gendered society—for example, the use of 'male' and 'female' on forms when sex/gender is irrelevant to the matter at hand. In a society where there is less concern with gender, androgynous and gender ambiguous people would face less barriers to social inclusion, and gender norms overall would be less heavily enforced.

There are, however, some difficulties with 'degendering' approaches, which relate primarily to issues of corporeality, materiality and social structure. Some corporeal characteristics (such as childbearing and parturition) are, with the exception of a few trans men who have given birth, experienced only by female bodied people; these have significant social and material implications. Social structural issues are also apparent in the recurrent discourse concerning the necessity of categories as a basis for cultural and political organisation (see for example Wilchins 1997). If strategies focused on erasing gender are pursued, the minority gender groups, such as Hijras, Kothis, intersex people and androgynes are likely to be disadvantaged because the default dominance of men and non transgender people will remain unchallenged. In addition, degendering, if pursued in a prescriptive manner, would deny people the choice to identify in a sexed and gendered way.

A third strategy to theorising sex/gender diversity concerns conceptualising sex/gender as plural, and as a spectrum, a field, or intersecting spectra or continua. Sex and gender are seen as being more finely grained than is the case with the binary system, and as being formed via the interplay of different characteristics associated with sex/gender and sexuality, and other structuring factors such as ethnicity, class, and nationality. Sex/gender pluralism involves 'calls for new and self-conscious affirmations of different gender taxonomies' (Halberstam 2002: 360). It involves conceptualising gender as 'fields' or 'groupings' of—in some cases overlapping—masculinities, femininities, and gender diverse identities; and sex as a continuum. The existence of non male/female sex/gender possibilities also entails the acknowledgement that the categories of 'lesbian', 'gay', 'bisexual' and 'heterosexual' cannot encompass all sexual orientation options (see also for example Hines 2007, Sanger 2008).

The development/recognition of identities that are intersex, androgynous, third and other sex, or gender diverse in other ways, moves beyond the poststructuralist deconstruction of gender and sexuality binaries towards reconstruction—potentially towards a more diverse and tolerant society. Theoretically, gender pluralism draws on both poststructuralist and corporeally-grounded approaches. It is similar to the work of Hird (2006), who discusses the 'new materialism', outlining the biological differences amongst non-human species. Continuing to argue against biological determinism, she convincingly suggests that binaried models of sex and gender are limited, given the plethora of other alternatives. Gender pluralism is quite clearly the most relevant conceptual approach for cultures which already have third or other sexes and genders, such as those found in India. Kothi and Hijra identities fit easily within the sex/gender pluralist model, and the concept of reincarnation is extremely compatible with notions of sex/gender pluralism—it includes those who incarnate in a variety of sexes/genders at different times. Some of the Western literature also supports the spectrum model of sex and gender, for example Rothblatt (1995) discusses what she terms 'gender continuum theory', a shift away from bipolar sex/gender categories towards a multiplicity of genders. There was support for sex/gender pluralism amongst some of the UK research contributors, who discussed the way that they would prefer to identify as something other than female or male if this was socially possible. However, debates about the viability and advisability of a plural gender system will continue; key concerns are with the possible development of a third/multiple sex 'ghetto' (see for example Towle and Morgan 2006). Such debates demonstrate the key importance of social structuring factors to gender politics.

To summarise, the conceptual framework that is emerging draws on the work of, in particular, Vanita and Kidwai (2000), Hird (2000, 2002, 2006) and Ekins and King (2006), as well as Monro (2000, 2005), and is as follows: Sex, gender, and sexual orientation are all constructed and mutable (via agency or otherwise) to a degree, and they are interrelated in complex and dynamic ways. People may experience characteristics such as sex and gender as fixed, although ultimately they are mutable (even if only through processes of aging, death, and reincarnation if the latter is seen as valid). Different sexed and gendered levels form spectra which combine and interact in ways that are unique to each individual. These spectra are present on different levels: genetic, endocrinological, gonadal, secondary sexual characteristics, core identity/identities (which can include spiritual identity/identities and political beliefs), social identity/identities, and sexual identity or identities.[2] The spectra are structured by physiological, psychological, social, cultural, and other factors (including economic) in a variety of ways. The spectra are cross-cut and shaped by a range of other social structuring factors centred on ethnicity, nationality, geographical location, socio-economic class, ability, familial structure, political and/or faith factors, and other physical and cultural factors.

SEX AND GENDER DIVERSITY IN INDIA AND THE UK

Arguably, it is important to ground conceptual debates in contextualised lived experience. This section aims to do this by discussing the situations regarding gender diversity in, firstly, India, and then in the UK.

An empirical account of Indian gender diversity cannot be presented without contextualising it historically. 'The Hijra communities in India have a recorded history of more than 4,000 years' (PUCL-K 2003: 17). These people, who are born as intersex or as male (some undergo castration), currently form a third sex/gender community in India, tracing their origins to the myths in the ancient Hindu scriptures of the Ramayana and Mahabarata. Historically, Hijras belonged to the 'Eunuch' culture that was common across the Middle East and India, where Eunuchs worked as guards, advisors, and entertainers (PUCL-K 2003). Other forms of sex/gender diversity were also socially accepted in ancient India. Historically, sex/gender variant women took roles as mercenaries, advisors, and religious people, and same sex sexual expression is also documented, often taking place alongside opposite sex relationships (see Penrose 2001); 'traditionally, sexuality has always been more fluid, less rigidly categorised [than in the West]. For many Indians Western naming does not correspond to the amorphous nature of sexual experience' (Seabrook 1997).

The data gathered in New Delhi in 2003 indicated that there are different systems of gender and sexuality classification operating simultaneously, set against the backdrop of ancient systems of sex/gender variance, dominant patriarchal norms, and post colonialism. These systems are being integrated to some extent by the growing LGBT communities, which bridge indigenous and western systems of categorisation, and are reportedly inclusive of Hijras and Kothis. The empirical material indicated that there seems to be some overlap and conflation of the categories that are assumed in the West, for instance:

Hijras are akwas (not castrated) and nirvana (castrated)—some Hijras are akwas, so biologically they are men—they are mostly homosexual though they may be married with kids, but this is due to convenience, they are not bisexual. These are the Kothis, who cross over into the Hijra communities. Less than 1% are intersex and 5% have been castrated . . . they would not speak about this to most people because it is not in their interest.

(Sexual Health Organisation worker).

Kothis belong to a community of gays—I define 'gay' as being a woman in a man's body. I want to have sex with a man as if I was a woman. I want a vagina in my body, instead of having a penis. How can I satisfy myself? Kothis want to look like girls, like Hijras do, but Kothis are those who have a penis—Hijras don't have a penis.

(Kothi contributor)

In some cases, therefore, Indian sexualities and genders are related in ways that are different to the Western relationship between male/female binaries and heterosexual/lesbian/gay/bisexual identification. In other words, sexual orientation is not necessarily based on the gender binary system; genders may instead be based to an extent on sexual experience or identity (this is the case in a number of other non-Western locations, see for instance Pantaziz and Bonthuy's (2007) South African account). The relationships between different sex/gender/sexuality systems are complex. For example I asked the Kothi contributors whether Kothis are different from transsexuals. One Kothi reported that they are different because 'a Kothi is a man who has a woman's heart, who thinks like a female.' However, another said that

> my feeling is that transsexuals and Kothis feel the same, but, the transsexual is castrated and the Kothi is not. Kothis have a difference of sex organs—I have a penis but I can satisfy another heterosexual man— but he can't satisfy me because I don't have a natural sex organ.

A further Kothi contributor said that 'transsexuals are those who have made a change in their sexuality by surgery—an artificial vagina'. Contributors varied concerning their use of the term transgender. Some did not relate to or use the term but others said, for instance, that 'transgender is a term without social stigma. That is why I use it,' and 'transgender and Kothi are the same'. There was not much discussion concerning intersex, but a larger sample could provide more material on this.

Material, corporeal and social factors are central to shaping Indian gender diversities. With the advent of British colonialism, the established social position of sex/gender variant people was systematically undermined, for example the British removed the land rights of the Hijra communities

(Seabrook 1997). The relatively strong social positions which at least some Hijra people occupied disappeared. Current literature indicates that most Hijras belong to the poorer castes and classes, and economic marginalisation structures their experiences very heavily. As Gupta says, 'Hijras might have an accepted place in Indian society, but it is a place pretty much at the bottom of the heap—making them not only a sexual but also a highly deprived social minority' (2002: 21). The research contributors discussed the difficulties that Kothis and Hijras face, including having to remain closeted within families due to heavy levels of stigmatisation, abuse, and economic marginalisation. For instance one person said that:

> It is very difficult for Kothis to find other work [than begging and sex work] because they don't want to be exposed. They are forced to go to the police station and because they don't want to be exposed Kothis give the police money. Also the police make money from the Kothis by taking bribes but they are not satisfied by this and they also want to have sex with the Kothis. They force it. Kothis say that every policeman is a bisexual. This situation is common, especially for sex workers—it is an everyday problem. Hijras get less trouble from the police.

Contributors discussed the factors affecting choices concerning surgery. For example, one person said that 'Hijras earn a lot of money doing marriages. Sometimes I think that if I change sex I'll look like a girl and the bloke I like will want me'. Another pointed out that getting a sex change in India is very risky, due to medical difficulties and cost.

Gendered social structures are an important factor in shaping people's identities and experiences in a society where 'No one seriously disagrees with the fact that women lead difficult lives, they suffer gross discrimination and injustice' (Geetha 2002: xiii). According to the research contributors, gender or sexually variant Indians who are born female have fewer options than those born as male. They can identify as lesbian or transsexual, but these possibilities are often only available to the middle and upper classes. In theory, people born as male, on the other hand, can identify as gay, transgender, cross dresser, Kothi or Hijra. Intersex people are likely to become Hijras, either through choice, or because of rejection by their families.

In addition, identity choices in India are heavily structured by caste/class and location. Seabrook (1997) discusses the way in which most of the men who call themselves gay in India are middle class, privileged, and English speaking. According to Seabrook (1997), the undefined same sex expression that was present prior to British rule still takes place to an extent in the slums and villages, whilst amongst the less affluent urban dwellers a 'gendered' system of male classification has emerged. Men who have sex with men are divided into two categories—the 'karte hain' (those who do) and the 'karvate hain' (those who are done to).

Findings also indicated that structuring factors such as faith and tradition benefit certain Indian sex/gender variant people. One contributor pointed out that Hijras occupy a position in society that is simultaneously revered and stigmatised, and that they cultivate the mystique associated with this. They are seen as having the power to curse or bless people, due to their spiritual heritage, and they are also seen as having a huge potential for embarrassment because they threaten to expose themselves physically if they are not paid for attending events such as weddings. The Hijras utilise these sources of power, retaining a somewhat secure position in society. This means that they can beg, and are less harassed by the police than other sex/gender and sexual minorities. A review of the journalistic coverage of gender diversity also showed that there are some designated political seats for Hijras. Hijra involvement in party politics is well documented in the newspapers, and Hijras are using their third sex status to their advantage, marketing themselves as 'incorruptible Eunuchs' (Chakraborty 2002) . As one contributor said, 'they are seen as not being part of the mainstream, which then allows them to have a place in the mainstream'.

To summarise, it appeared that three main types of gender and sexual classification are current in India—unclassified sexual activity, the Hijra and Kothi systems (where what would in the West be termed transgender and same sex expression are merged, and are structured by the sex/gender binary system), and Western systems. These three forms of categorisation illustrate intersectionality because their operation is a product of caste, class, and colonialism related inequalities, as well as the gender and sexuality inequalities that permeate Indian society. The Hijras, by occupying a social position in opposition to the binary system, have carved out a social space in which mainstream norms are rejected or revised, perhaps challenging, but not escaping, other structuring factors.

Documented sex/gender diversity in the UK is a much more recent phenomenon than that in India, although, as described previously, the field has blossomed in recent years. As in India, gender diverse people in the UK can be seen to disrupt sex/gender binaries, but gender diversity is structured rather differently. Indian people born as female who identify as gender diverse appear at least as socially excluded as UK trans men. However, whilst the Hijra and Kothi subject positions in India are confined to a large degree within certain denigrated social positions, they exist in a more socially recognised way than do trans and intersex people in the UK, at least until recent UK advances in some areas of transgender equality (Whittle 2002; Whittle et al. 2007).

The empirical data included in this section aims to demonstrate the ways in which trans and intersex disrupt sex/gender and sexuality binaries, lending support to the gender pluralist and other models outlined previously. This material is included with awareness that the sample was not fully representative and that many trans and intersex people wish to assimilate into mainstream society as men and women (see Monro 2005). However, this is not the case for all gender-diverse people, and therefore there is a need for theories to be overhauled in order that they become more inclusive. UK gender diversity is, like Indian gender diversity, subject to a high degree of structuring by social, material and corporeal forces.

Findings from the 1996–1998 and 2003 research projects demonstrate a variety of ways in which UK sex/gender and sexual orientation binaries can be disrupted by people with trans and intersex identities. Some of the research contributors identified as other than male or female. For example, Simon Dessloch, a FTM trans person, said that he felt himself to be in-between, or neither, or both, or third sex. Similarly, Christie Elan Cane, who started life as female, said in 1998:

> I don't feel male or female, and I say that I'm basically third gender because I can't identify as male or female . . . I mean I'm still trying to unravel how I wanted to be, I wondered whether maybe I could be part of both, which is not how I feel any longer but I sort of went through several stages along, trying to express and figure out how I felt, but now I feel I'm neither. I can't relate to male and female.

Sex/gender binaries are sometimes destabilised by sex/gender fluidity. For example, contributor Zach Nataf described how, during the early stages of his transition from female to male, he felt more like a man on some days and more transgendered on others, and that this depended to an extent on who he was with (see also Bornstein 1994). 'Gender fuck' also disrupts gender binaries. 'Gender fuck' refers to conflicting sex/gender signals—in some cases these are consciously taken on as part of identity (see Halberstam 2002). Kate N' Ha Ysabet explained that:

> . . . if I have a penis and big tits that's gender fuck, if I wore makeup and butch clothing that's gender fuck. And what's quite interesting is that androgyny is acceptable because there's a reason for that, but gender fuck isn't, because people go 'oh, OK' but with gender fuck its this thing of 'shit, I'm getting two sets of signals' and it feels like you're having a drum and bass mix on one side and classical music on the other and you're going 'Oh my God which am I going to listen to?'

Non-gendered, 'third space' (see Nataf 1996), multiply gendered (sometimes called 'gender pluralist'), androgynous or multi-gendered people may desta-bilise the discrete gender binaried system. Intersex provokes a questioning of the sex/gender binary system on two levels—physical, as the various conditions subsumed under the umbrella term of intersex involve physiological characteristics (for example chromosomal, hormonal and gonadal) which are other than (or a mixture of) those conventionally associated with males and females; and identity, as research contributions showed that in some cases intersex people wish to have an identity that is other, or in addition to, male or female. Intersex is perhaps the most profoundly disruptive identity (Monro 2000, 2005). As intersex person Michael Noble posts on the UK Intersex support website:

> ... rather than accepting the fact that sex, gender and identity exists within a spectrum of unlimited potentials, science and medicine have sought to 'modify' people in order to fit them into what is considered to be the 'norm' ... Intersex is not an identity nor a gender, but rather it's the biological variation which exists between the polar binaries of the male and female sex. Gender and sexuality classifications have little meaning, or relevance for the Intersexed because they are terms derived from the concept of the binary opposites—while the Intersexed themselves exist beyond the binaries ... '
>
> (Noble 2008)

The Western system of sexual orientation categorisation is also problematised by UK sex/gender diversity (see Rothblatt 1995), physically, in terms of sexual expression, and socially, in terms of identity. Whilst the majority of people can relate to notions of same sex or opposite sex attraction, the categories of lesbian, gay, bisexual, and heterosexual are insufficient in describing, for example, attraction between an androgyne and someone who identifies as gender transient. Sexual orientation categories based on the sex/gender binary system are disrupted by physical sex diversity. The genitals of some sex/gender diverse people are physiologically 'other' than those usually associated with women and men (although, of course, they may identify as male or female). For example at the 1998 Transgender Film Festival, Del LaGrace Volcano (an initially female-bodied person who took testosterone) displayed photographs of his and other people's phalloclits, which resemble small penises enwreathed in labial lips. Sex between people with non-standard genitals is unlikely to fit heterosexual, gay, or lesbian sexual norms.

Non-binary forms of sexual orientation identification (such as omnisexual) are not current in the UK, although anecdotal evidence suggests that unnamed/uncategorised sexual activity is not uncommon. When trans and intersex people's sexuality supersedes the binary system, individuals and groups continue to an extent to use existing definitions, even when they do not fit very well. One example of this would be Annie Cox, a trans person who defined herself as a 'woman who loved women' although she has a penis. Overlap of LGBT and heterosexual categories can occur when people move through a number of different spaces or identities, problematising assumptions underpinning mainstream forms of sexual orientation category, where a single sexual identity that is taken over a period of years is assumed.

The UK situation for gender-diverse people is structured along a number of corporeal, social, and material axes. Whittle (2002) addresses the legislative underpinnings of trans inequality, and documents the high levels of employment discrimination and institutionalised transphobia facing trans people in the UK. Monro (2005) outlines the ways in which linguistic forms and the bureaucratic division of people into 'male' and 'female' categories serve to render people who do not identify as female or male culturally unintelligible. I also documented the economic, spatial (given the incidence of violence and harassment of trans and intersex people), legislative, medical, educational, and relationship exclusion that trans and intersex people faced at that time, and the ways in which these structures are underpinned by discursive formations which are homophobic, ethnocentric, and patriarchal. The corporeal element of structuring is discussed to a degree, both in terms of the limitations and difficulties associated with surgery and hormone treatment, and in the social privileging of certain bodies over others.

Whittle et al. (2007) provide a very comprehensive account of trans experiences of inequality post-Gender Recognition Act (2004), based on a qualitative review of 86,000 emails, 16,000 online postings and a survey with 872 responses. They demonstrated that despite the advances in legal recognition that the Act provides for many UK trans people, they still experience high levels of inequality, primarily in employment, access to healthcare, leisure, education and social relations (the family and friends). For example, 73 percent had experienced harassment in public places, and 64 percent of young trans men and 44 percent of young trans women had been bullied or harassed at school, by pupils and in some cases teachers. They note for instance that '42% of people not living permanently in their preferred gender role were prevented from doing so because they feared it might threaten their employment status' (Whittle et al. 2007: 15). Unfortunately similar studies are not available concerning the UK situation for intersex and androgynous people.

ANALYSIS AND CONCLUSION

The sociology of gender diversity, including trans and intersex, has moved forward from its interactionist roots into engagement with poststructuralism. Poststructuralist theory has been used to disaggregate gender, sex and sexuality, to inform understandings of the discursive production of subjectivity, and to facilitate the conceptualisation of sex/gender as complex, multiple and fluid. However, there is a need for a 'materialist turn' in thought concerning gender diversity, grounding poststructuralist gender analysis in the 'realities' of social structures, material forces, and embodied subjectivities; this chapter aims to contribute to such a turn. Without attention to the social and material, as well as corporeal, structuring factors that shape gendered subjects' lived experience, gender theory can become dehumanising, politically retrogressive, or appropriative of trans and intersex people's experiences. Attention to cross-cultural diversity concerning sex/gender, if combined with analysis of the ways in which sex/gender is materially and socially structured in different contexts, moves the sociology of sex/gender diversity away from an ethnocentric focus.

In this section I would like to comment on the three approaches to conceptualising gender diversity outlined in the preceding section, before indicating some of the directions in which the sociology of trans and intersex may be usefully progressed. The three models of sex/gender outlined before are all currently in evidence both in India and the UK. However, certain subject positions are erased by the different types. The 'expanding genders' model erases some physiologically intersex people, and people who do not identify as male or female. The 'degendering' model erases people who identify strongly with—or are forced to identify strongly with—a particular gender, and 'sex/gender pluralism' erases those people who do not identify with gender at all (although arguably degendering could also form a category amongst gender pluralists). Broadly speaking, in India the use of Kothi and Hijra positions as a basis for rights claims (something that can be aligned with the gender pluralist approach) has purchase, whilst in the UK, the 'expanding genders' model is more generally utilised. In India, three different forms of conceptualising the relationship between sex/gender and sexuality are at play, and these are heavily structured by location, caste, gender and class. In the UK, only one model prevails, that of a gender binaried system with lesbian, gay, bisexual and heterosexual sexualities predicated upon it. It is possible to argue that individuals as well as social groupings will use these different approaches in varied ways at different times, depending on the ways in which they interface with corporeal, social, and material structures. As Roen (2002) says, movement between subject positions can be frequent and strategic, as people respond to conflicting discourses by positioning themselves in varied ways. Overall, the fictious nature of systems of categorisation is apparent, but that does not mean that categorisation is invalid, providing as it does a basis for social organisation.

The sociology of gender diversity, including trans and intersex, can be further developed along a number of lines. In the UK, considerable work has been carried out in relation to the structural constraints affecting trans people (for example Whittle et al. 2007), but there is a gap concerning the structural constraints affecting intersex, androgynous, non-gendered/ multiply-gendered and other-gendered people. More research about the social, material and corporeal structures impacting on Indian gender-diverse people is also needed, especially hidden populations (such as gender-diverse people who were born as female). In addition to work concerning social structure, there is scope for an extension of the sociology of transgender via serious engagement with intersectionality theory. This would build on the work of authors such as Juang (2006), in dealing with the racialised nature of gender diversity, and the classed nature of trans and intersex identities (for example vis a vis access to surgery). A related direction for research concerns an extension of cross-cul-tural comparisons, including post-colonial analysis as a means of interrogat-ing the ways in which Western notions of gender and sexuality are exported to, and remodelled by, Southern actors. A further avenue for enquiry concerns the ways in which sexed/gendered identities are strategically utilised, by indi-viduals and by activist groups, to further equality (or at least to survive), and the intersectional and cross-cultural patterning of these.

NOTES

1. The author would like to acknowledge and thank the ESRC, who funded the original research, and the research contributors.
2. The term 'sex/gender' is used here to emphasise the interrelated nature of these social characteristics as well as their mutability.

REFERENCES

Blackburn, M. V. (2005) 'Agency in borderland discourses: examining language use in a community centre with Black queer youth', *Teacher's College Record*, 107(1): 89–113.

Boellstorff, T. (2004) 'Playing back the nation: Indonesian transvestites', *Cultural Anthropology*, 19: 159–195.

Bornstein, K. (1994) *Gender Outlaw: On Men, Women and the Rest of Us*, New York: Routledge.

———. (1998) *My Gender Workbook*, New York: Routledge.

Chakraborty, T. (2002) 'Patna eunuchs in power play', *Telegraph*, 6 March 2002.

Chase, C. (1998) 'Affronting reason', in D. Atkins (ed) *Looking Queer: Body Image and Identity in Lesbian, Bisexual, Gay and Transgender Communities*, New York: Harrington Park Press.

Dreger, A. D. (ed.) (2000) *Intersex in the Age of Ethics*, Hagerstown, Maryland: University Publishing Group.

Ekins, R. and King, D. (2006) *The Transgender Phenomenon*, London, Thousand Oaks and New Delhi: Sage Publications.

Feinberg, L. (1996) *Transgender Warriors: Making History from Joan of Arc to Dennis Rodman*, Boston: Beacon Press.

———. (1998) *Transliberation: Beyond Pink or Blue*, Boston: Beacon Press.

Garfinkel, H. (1967) *Studies in Ethnomethodology*, Englewood Cliffs, NJ: Pren-tice Hall.

Geetha, V. (2002) *Gender*, Calcutta: STREE.

Govender, P. (2007) *Love and Courage: A Story of Insubordination*, Auckland Park, South Africa: Jacana.

Grabham, E., Herman, D., Cooper, D., and Krisnadas, J. (eds) (2009) *Intersection-ality and Beyond: Law, Power, and the Politics of Location*, London: Rout-ledge/Cavendish Publishers.

Gupta, A. (2002) 'Transgender law and civil rights', *From the Lawyers Collective.* http://www.lawyerscollective.org/hiv-aids/publications/articles?page=1 (accessed 8 October, 2009).

Halberstam, J. (2002) 'An introduction to female masculinity: masculinity with-out men', in R. Adams and D. Savran (eds) *The Masculinity Studies Reader*, Malden, Massachusetts and Oxford: Blackwell Publishers.

Hearn, J, and Morgan, D. (1990) *Men, Masculinities and Social Theory,* London: Unwin Hyman.

Herdt, G. (ed.) (1994) *Third Sex Third Gender: Beyond Sexual Dimorphism in Culture and History,* New York: Zone Books.

Hines, S. (2005) '"I am a Feminist but . . . ": transgender men, women and feminism', in J. Reger (ed.) *Different Wavelengths: Studies of the Contemporary Women's Movement,* London/New York: Routledge.

———. (2006) 'What's the difference? Bringing particularity to queer studies of transgender', *Journal of Gender Studies,* 15(1): 49–66.

———. (2007) *TransForming Gender: Transgender Practices of Identity, Intimacy and Care,* Bristol: The Policy Press.

Hird, M. J. (2000) 'Gender's nature: intersexuals, transsexuals and the "sex"/"gender" binary', *Feminist Theory,* 1(3): 347–364.

———. (2002) 'For a sociology of transsexualism', *Sociology,* 36(3): 577–595.

———. (2006) 'Animal trans', *Australian Feminist Studies,* 21(49): 35–48.

Juang, R. M. (2006) 'Transgendering the politics of recognition', in S. Stryker and S. Whittle (eds) *The Transgender Studies Reader,* London and New York: Routledge.

Kessler, S. and McKenna, W. (1978) *Gender: An Ethnomethodological Approach,* Chicago: University of Chicago Press.

Lorber, J. (1994) *Paradoxes of Gender,* New Haven: Yale University Press.

Masequesmay, G. (2003) 'Negotiating multiple identities in a Vietnamese support group', *Journal of Homosexuality,* 45(2/4): 193–215.

McCall, L. (2005) 'The complexity of intersectionality', *Signs,* 30(3): 1771–1800.

Monro, S. (2000) 'Theorizing transgender diversity: towards a social model of health', *Sexual and Relationship Therapy,* 15(1): 33–45.

———. (2001) 'Gender love and gender freedom' in: E. McWilliams (ed) *Unseen Genders: Beyond Binaries,* New York: Peter Lang.

———. (2005) *Gender Politics: Activism, Citizenship and Sexual Diversity,* London: Pluto Press.

———. (2007a) 'Transmuting gender binaries: the theoretical challenge', *Sociological Research Online* 12(1). http://www.socresonline.org.uk/12/1/monro.html (accessed 10 December 2007).

———. (2007b) 'Transgender: destabilising feminisms?' in V. Munro and C. Stychin (eds) *Sexuality and the Law: Feminist Engagements,* London: Glasshouse Press.

Namaste (2000) *Invisible Lives: The Erasure of Transsexual and Transgendered People,* Chicago: University of Chicago Press.

Nataf, Z. (1996) *Lesbians Talk Transgender,* London: Scarlett Press.

Noble, M. (2008) 'I am me and I am OK'. http://www.ukia.co.uk/voices/mnoble.htm (accessed 29 December 2008).

Pantaziz, A. and Bonthuys, E. (2007) 'Gender and sexual orientation', in E. Bonthuys and C. Albertyn (eds) *Gender, Law and Justice,* Cape Town: Juta.

Peletz, M. G. (2006) 'Transgenderism and gender pluralism in Southeast Asia since early modern times', *Current Anthropology,* 47(2): 309–40.

Penrose, W. (2001) 'Hidden in history: female homoeroticism and women of a "third nature" in the South Asian past', *Journal of the History of Sexuality,* 10(1): 3–39.

Prosser, J. (1998) *Second Skins: The Body Narratives of Transsexuality,* New York: Columbia University Press.

PUCL-K (2003) *Human rights violations against the transgender community: a study of Kothi and Hijra sex workers in Bangalore, India.* Bangalore: People's Union for Civil Liberties, Karnataka.

Raymond, J. (1994) 'The politics of transgender', *Feminism and Psychology,* 4(4): 628–633.

Roen, K. (2001) 'Transgender theory and embodiment: the risk of racial marginalisation', *Journal of Gender Studies,* 10(3): 253–263.

———. (2002) '"Either/or" and "both/neither": discursive tensions in transgender politics', *Signs,* 27(2): 501–522.

Rothblatt, M. (1995) *The Apartheid of Sex: A Manifesto for the Freedom of Gender,* New York: Crown Publishers.

Sanger, T. (2008) 'Trans governmentality: the production and regulation of gendered sexualities', *Journal of Gender Studies,* 17(1): 41–53.

Seabrook, J. (1997) 'Not "straight", not gay', *The Pioneer,* 30 September 1997.

Stone, S. (1991) 'The empire strikes back: a post-transsexual manifesto', in D. Epstein and K. Straub (eds) *Body Guards: The Cultural Politics of Gender Ambiguity,* London: Routledge.

Stryker, S. and Whittle, S. (2006) (eds) *The Transgender Studies Reader,* New York: Routledge.

Tauchert, A. (2002) 'Fuzzy gender: inbetween male and female embodiment and intersex', *Journal of Gender Studies,* 11(1): 29–38.

Towle, E. B. and Morgan, M. (2006) 'Romancing the transgender native: rethinking the use of the "third gender" concept', in S. Stryker and S. Whittle (eds) *The Transgender Studies Reader,* London and New York: Routledge.

Vanita, R and Kidwai, S (2000) 'Introduction' in R. Vanita and S. Kidwai *Same-Sex Love in India: Readings from Literature and History,* Houndmills, Basingstoke: Palgrave Macmillan.

Whittle, S. (2002) *Respect and Equality: Transsexual and Transgender Rights,* London: Cavendish Publishing Limited.

Whittle, S., Turner, L., and Al-Alami, M. (2007) *Engendered Penalties: Transgender and Transsexual People's Experiences of Inequality and Discrimination,* Manchester: Press for Change/Manchester Metropolitan University.

Wilchins, R. A. (1997) *Read My Lips: Sexual Subversion and the End of Gender,* Ithaca, New York: Firebrand Books.

13 Beyond Gender and Sexuality Binaries in Sociological Theory
The Case for Transgender Inclusion

Tam Sanger[1]

INTRODUCTION

Despite escalating academic interest in transgender identification, especially within the humanities but also increasingly within the social sciences, most sociologists have not taken on board the radical potential of trans identities for challenging the taken-for-granted gender and sexuality binaries which underpin sociological theory (Hines 2007a; Monro 2007).[2] I argue in this chapter that consideration of those who do not straightforwardly identify within the gender binary of male/female or the sexuality binary of heterosexual/homosexual, offer new directions for sociology in their repudiation of such binary positionings. These theoretical directions may take the form of, for example, a queer sociology (Seidman 1996; Hines 2006), gender pluralism (Halberstam 2002; Monro 2007, Chapter 12, this volume) or degendering (Firestone 1971; Lorber 1994, 2000; Hawkesworth 1997).[3]

In order to contextualise my assertion that theorisation of identity should not be limited to binary possibilities, I draw upon recent interview data focusing on the experiences of trans people and their partners in the UK and Ireland (Sanger 2007a). This data, in line with that collected by scholars such as Gagné and Tewksbury (1998), Namaste (2000), Hines (2007b) and Monro (2007), indicates a growing diversity and fluidity of gendered and sexual identities in contemporary society. This diversity has so far not been captured within mainstream sociological analyses, but could offer a means of furthering theorisation of gender and sexuality, as well as including a broader spectrum of individuals more generally. Further, as trans identities are becoming more visible in society, there is a need for sociology to engage with trans narratives. This would involve recognition of the ways in which trans people both engage with, and disengage from, social structures and discursive frameworks.

TRADITIONAL SOCIOLOGY AND BINARY THINKING

Traditionally, as in other academic disciplines, sociological reflections have been predicated upon binary conceptualisations. As Patricia Hill Collins states:

> Grounded in binaries such as White/Black, man/woman, reason/emotion, heterosexual/homosexual, Eurocentric/Afrocentric, and self/other, science manufactured views of a world compartmentalized into either/or oppositional categories. Defining one side of the binary by the absence of qualities characteristic of the other side afforded one side normality and relegated the other to a deviant, oppositional Other.
>
> (1998: 145–146)

Gender has been theorised in terms of maleness and femaleness, with sexuality tending to be considered within a heteronormative framework (Seidman 1997; Fee Chapter 10, this volume). Relatively recently, the construction of gender and sexuality, and the related study of embodiment and intimacy, have become more significant within sociological theory. Yet there remains a great deal of work to be done in uncovering the contingency of these aspects of the self on hegemonic discourse and on relations with others. Work on transgender subjectivities offers one avenue through which to explore these aspects of self and society.

Critical sociologists have been working towards expanding our frames of reference in relation to multiple identity markers, such as 'race' and ethnicity, class, age, and (dis)ability, whilst also, more recently, working towards a more intersectional approach to identity (see, for example, Delgado and Stefancic 1997; Riddell and Watson 2004; Yosso 2006; Taylor, Hines and Casey forthcoming). Limitations of early sociological approaches in relation to the gender binary, many of which persist to this day, include the taking for granted of gender norms, and the social construction of gender only being explored at a very basic level.[4] Early exceptions to this framework were advanced in the work of sociologists such as Garfinkel (1967) and Kessler and McKenna (1978), who advocated the use of an ethnomethodological approach to study transgender identity practices, thereby furthering understanding of the social construction of gendered subjectivities. Ekins and King (1996) added to this exploration throughout the 1990s, mapping a diversity of trans identities and thus moving away from the homogenous understanding of trans previously employed within both psychology and sociology (see, for example, Money and Ehrhardt 1972; Money and Tucker 1976; Green 1992; Hausman 1995; Mason-Schrock 1996; Lewins 2002). However, as Hines states, for a contemporary understanding: 'ethnomethodological studies of transgender problematically assume a heteronormative analysis, which collapses the categories of gender and sexuality and is unable to account for the contemporary diversity of transgender identity positions' (2007b: 32–33). This shortcoming indicates the importance of studying gender and sexuality in tandem. The collection *Queer Theory/Sociology* (Seidman 1996) is particularly pertinent in relation to how sociology could engage with sexuality studies beyond binary configurations. Specifically, in bringing a queer perspective to sociological studies of sexuality, the heterosexual/homosexual dichotomy is problematised, and exploration of identities such as bisexuality emerges. As I have detailed elsewhere disruption of gender norms often also leads to the rethinking of sexuality (Sanger 2007b).

More recently there has been increasing interest in those who identify as trans in the media, as well as trans people agitating for equal rights and recognition in the law, and thereby raising the profile of trans issues and the problems of marginalisation and exclusion many trans people face in their everyday lives (Hines 2007a). Additionally, the question of what consideration of trans people's experiences can bring to sociology as a discipline has been raised (Roen 2001; Hird 2002; Hines 2007a, 2007b; Monro 2007). I argue that this interest is, however, still relegated to the margins of sociological theorising, despite the potential for sociological inquiry envisaged by Hird in 2002:

> Transsexualism is a complex social phenomenon, and involves many issues, not least of which are the contradictions and divisions within transsexual narratives. Further sociological analysis might fruitfully be applied to analysing these contradictions and divisions in terms of their transgressive potential. Indeed, it is the possibility of transcending sex and gender altogether that offers, from a sociological perspective, the most interesting possibilities.
>
> (p. 591)

It is at this juncture that I wish to set out the usefulness of transgender studies to sociology and vice-versa, further illustrating these through consideration of my own empirical work with trans people and their intimate partners. In discussing the importance of bringing together sociology and transgender theory I am not only claiming that consideration of transgender identities could add greater depth to sociological theory, but also that studies of transgender would be enriched through employing a sociological lens.

TRANSGENDER STUDIES

Transgender studies emerged in the late 1990s as a loosely defined academic field of study, arising from the desire of academics studying transgenderism to be heard, as well as to engage with the diverse voices of trans people in a critique of social norms relating to gender and sexuality. Many of those scholars who work in transgender studies identify as trans themselves and have been motivated to challenge societal (mis)understandings of trans, due to the injustices trans individuals face throughout the world (Califia 1997; Prosser 1998; Stryker 1998; Namaste 2000; Whittle 2002; Rubin 2003). Stryker defines transgender studies as follows:

Most broadly conceived, the field of transgender studies is concerned with anything that disrupts, denaturalizes, rearticulates, and makes visible the normative linkages we generally assume to exist between the biological specificity of the sexually differentiated human body, the social roles and statuses that a particular form of body is expected to occupy, the subjectively experienced relationship between a gendered sense of self and social expectations of gender-role performance, and the cultural mechanisms that work to sustain or thwart specific configurations of gendered personhood.

(2006: 3)

Thus, transgender studies is a critical approach, which problematises the assumption that sex is a rigid marker of identity through exploration of instances where this assumption is challenged. Whilst focused upon trans people's experiences, transgender studies works to make visible those norms that are taken for granted and tend not to be brought into question, but which impact on how individuals are subjectified in society. As such, it has resonance for every individual, and not just those who identify as trans (Hird 2002; Sanger 2008a). Some of the cultural mechanisms that determine how gendered personhood will be evaluated are legislation, discrimination, social expectations, medical possibilities, and recognition from others. These are some of the areas currently being studied in relation to trans from a sociological point of view (see, for example, Stryker and Whittle 2006; Hines 2007b; Monro 2007). Trans people are, more than ever before, organising collectively and gaining a voice, or indeed, a plethora of voices, in challenging their exclusion from society, with transgender studies offering an academic platform for this activist counter-discourse.

Stryker argues that 'transgender studies is following its own trajectory and has the potential to address emerging problems in the critical study of gender and sexuality, identity, embodiment, and desire in ways that gay, lesbian, and queer studies have not always successfully managed' (2004: 214). As such, transgender studies could be labelled post-disciplinary and is thus well placed to draw from the strengths of various disciplines, including sociology, as well as moving in new directions and addressing previously ignored subject groups.

Transgender studies shares many of its ideologies with queer sociology, where 'new sociological queer perspectives emphasize the unstable, multiple character of identities, the performative aspects of identity, and identity as a mode of social control' (Seidman 1996: 19). The notion of a queer sociology arose through dissatisfaction with the overly textual and abstract nature of queer theory. Within queer theory there exists 'a strong commitment to creating/maintaining a theoretical space for polyphonic and diverse discourses that challenge heteronormativity' (Goldman 1996: 170), which involves challenging the primacy of heterosexuality and introducing new ways of defining sexuality and other identities that challenge the boundaries of societal norms. However, this challenge has tended to remain at the level of theory, without discussing lived experiences. Hines has proposed 'that queer sociology may release "transgender" from the trap of homogeneity by addressing the material and embodied contours of transgender lives' (2006: 64). It is this call to a more materially informed and less homogenised sociological account of trans with which I engage through consideration of my own empirical research later in this chapter.

The growing awareness of trans people's experiences both socially and legally indicates that this is a topic which should be taken seriously by sociologists (Hines 2007a). Increasing interest in, and community organising in relation to, marginalised populations often precipitates theoretical change within the social sciences. For example, according to Seidman, '[s]ociology's silence on "sexuality" was broken as the volume level of public sexual conflicts was turned up so high that even sociologists' trained incapacity to hear such sounds was pierced' (1996: 4). With trans community voices becoming more apparent and transgender studies continuing to expand and call to attention the importance of recognising the gender diverse, I argue that it is time for sociologists to recognise the significance of cultural shifts in understandings of gender and sexuality, and to incorporate this recognition into explorations of the social.

SOCIOLOGY AND TRANSGENDER

As mentioned in the previous section, sociology as a discipline has been slow to recognise the significance of transgender studies, lives and identities. Gender and trans theorists within the arts and humanities have been much more influential and have contributed a great deal to the expansion of thinking and theorising about gender and sexuality (for example, Butler 1999[1990], 2004; Halberstam 1998, 2005). Indeed, it is difficult to discuss gender and sexuality without reference to transgender studies in the current climate, and sociologists could gain a great deal from engaging with transgender debates, as well as vice-versa.

As Plummer and Stein have argued, '[t]he process of paradigm shifting entails two dimensions: (1) the transformation of existing conceptual frameworks and (2) the acceptance of those transformations by others in the fields' (1996: 140). Currently, transgender studies carried out within the rubric of sociology are offering new insights into theories of gender and sexuality. However, sociological surveys still contain questions asking for a box to be ticked indicating maleness or femaleness (Williams 2006; Browne 2008) and sociological theory is, in general, still predicated upon the supposition that gender identification adheres to one side or the other of the normalised gender binary formulation (Hines 2007b; Monro 2007).

We are, in addition, limited by language. Most languages just do not have words to encompass a wide diversity of identity markers. This is why

trans people and trans theorists are coining new terms, such as cisgendered, genderqueer and bi-gendered.[5] Queer collectives and queer theorists have done the same, reclaiming the term 'queer' and inventing terms
such as pansexual and omnisexual.[6] In this way, those who are excluded
from mainstream academic theory, who are rendered mentally ill, who are
often denied full citizenship, and who are figured as objects of ridicule,
may assert their own language through which to resist societal norms and
the harm they cause to those who do not fit. Recognition of such terms by
social theorists may work to aid inclusion of those on the margins.

Sociologists have moved from the generalised usage of male pronouns
to utilising both male and female. A question which I believe is worthy of
consideration is whether we can move to the use of non-gendered pronouns
in order to include everyone. This could occur in the form of using 'they'
instead of 'he/she' or another non-gendered pronoun form such as 'ze'
(Foertsch and Gernsbacher 1997). For many this will seem unnecessary,
but this is a change which would not disenfranchise anyone and would aid
inclusion of those who currently feel excluded by gender binary adherence
in theory. This type of alteration would not mean a movement beyond gender categorisation entirely, as the male and female categories could still be
employed in more specific circumstances, but additional possibilities would
be given theoretical space to develop.

Whilst consideration of those who do not conform to binary norms may
be seen as a minority issue and therefore not important enough to transform or expand how we theorise society, I shall move on to elucidate how
the study of trans could in fact add a great deal to a number of areas of
sociological inquiry. In addition, the level of misrecognition and violence
against trans people in society, and particularly those who do not conform
to gender norms, means that excluding these individuals can have serious
consequences (see Namaste 2000). As Butler has argued, '[o]n the level
of discourse, certain lives are not considered lives at all, they cannot be
humanized, they fit no dominant frame for the human, and their dehuman-
ization occurs first, at this level' (2004: 25). Thus, discursive frameworks,
including that of sociological theory, impact on the material lives of individuals and groups. If certain people are not recognised as holding valid
identities they may be written out of society altogether.

NEGOTIATING NORMATIVITIES: BINARIES AND LIVED EXPERIENCE

I shall now consider my own research in which I explored the experiences
of trans people and their partners in the UK and Ireland. For the purpose of
this chapter I will focus in particular on the ways in which a number of those
I interviewed visualised binary thinking as exclusionary and outdated. This
consideration builds upon my previous work exploring the limitations of living and theorising within a binary gender framework (Sanger 2008a).

The project involved interviews with trans people and their partners, with questions relating to issues such as the law, medicine, intimacy, gender, sexuality, and embodiment (Sanger 2007a).[7] Whilst some individuals were happy to remain within binary gender and sexuality norms, others were consciously working to challenge these, through negotiation within their intimate partnerships, and through their dealings with medicine, the law and social others. In contradistinction to Gagné and Tewksbury's (1998) findings, over half of those I interviewed discussed the limits of gender and/or sexuality binaries in some manner, perhaps indicating that resistance to binary norms is increasing over time.[8] Quotations from interviews with participants who identified outside of the female/male and/or homosexual/heterosexual binaries will be used here to illustrate how lived experiences and understandings of identificatory possibilities are currently being shaped and reimagined in relation to gender and sexuality.

The theoretical framework guiding the research incorporated Foucault's notion of governmentality, as well as theories of relationality, whilst engaging with a queer theoretical perspective. Foucault's removal, expressed through his exposition of governmentality theory, of the 'taken-for-granted' character of how things are done, resonates with my problematisation of the 'taken-for-granted' norms of gender and sexuality (see Dean 1999: 38). The importance of considering relationality lies in the difficulties trans people encounter in gaining recognition through their relationships with both other individuals and groups, and with social institutions, such as the law and medicine. The sociological approach of symbolic interactionism similarly offers a means of foregrounding the centrality of such relationships (Mead 1934). My theoretical approach also draws upon queer theory and the work of Judith Butler (1999 [1990], 2004), in critically examining the interrelations between identity and social norms, particularly with respect to discourses surrounding gender and sexuality.

When questioned about both gender and sexuality, a number of research participants produced complex narratives of change over time and flexibility, dependent upon the situations or partnerships they found themselves in (see also Dozier 2005: 314; Hines 2007). Sam understood the gender binary as limiting and incapable of encapsulating all possible individual experiences:

> I'd really like everyone to just be able to, if someone doesn't feel male, female, feels both, feels something else, it would be nice if there was some representation of that. Or alternatively there was no representation of gender and everyone was just a person. That would be nice.
>
> (Sam, genderqueer, age 24)

Sam's problems with gender arise because of the societal acceptance of only maleness and femaleness, and the imposition of these categories on every individual. There is very limited cultural awareness of anything 'beyond' binary gender, despite a more homogenous notion of transsexual identities gaining greater acknowledgement, so that Sam, who identifies as genderqueer, faces a lack of understanding and recognition within society at large. Sam's position indicates the need for a greater openness to gender diversity, which, in terms of sociological theory, could be enacted through employing an approach to gender (and sexuality) that allows for variation in individual experiences of gender. Lorber's notion of 'degendering' speaks to Sam's call for there to be 'no representation of gender' According to Lorber, rejecting binary gender categories, at least in societies where a high level of gender equality allows for this, could decrease gender inequalities and work to alter social structures (1994, 2000). Lorber asserts that 'as pervasive as gender is, because it is constructed and maintained through daily interaction, it can be resisted and reshaped by gender trouble-makers' (2000: 83). Sam, and others who took part in this research, act out such 'trouble-making', thereby setting up the possibility of undermining people's perceptions of gender, as well as those social institutions that undergird hegemonic gender norms.

Of those who did not adhere to binary norms in relation to gender and/or sexuality, a number argued that the reification of binary understandings of identity within society was stifling and did not allow for them to freely articulate their sense of self due to the risk of misunderstanding from others. For example, Lee articulated the struggle involved in labelling sexuality in a way that would be understood by others:

> I'm not keen on the binary gender thing so saying I'm bisexual is ah, (pause) it's not accurate, but given that people have enough problems getting their head round the concept of someone who is attracted to both genders I can't be bothered to explain pansexual, especially since that implies [. . .] everything.
>
> (Lee, trans man, age 25)

Lee had to resort to the use of a category that relied upon the gender binary, as he perceived this to be the limit of others' understanding. The interconnections between binary gender and binary sexuality are clearly significant for Lee, as his belief that gender goes beyond male and female cannot be encompassed within society, and concomitantly any understanding of sexuality which does not rely upon this binary is also held to be unfeasible. A queer sociological approach would make room for Lee's challenging of both gender and sexuality, and allow exploration of the contingency of these aspects of subjectivity on one another, as well as uncovering the ways in which the identity articulations of Lee and others like him are limited through social control.

Partners of trans people often spoke of how their views of gender and sexuality were shaken by their relationships. It was through their growing awareness of the possibilities of change and the limits of binaries that they reconsidered their own identities and prejudices in relation to the world around them. Susan stated,

> meeting Tim kind of opened up ideas around [...] what gender was all about and what sexuality was all about and [...] what people did with their gender and how it was a bit more fluid, so I guess from that it made me question whether bisexuality actually covered what I was doing with my life and [...] the kind of things I was directed to [...] so that probably opened up my mind more to kind of ideas around pansexuality or omnisexuality, as the new term for being attracted to people regardless of their gender.
>
> (Susan, non-trans woman, age 27)

Some partners of trans women also came to recognise their own internalised homophobia, which had heretofore limited them to heterosexuality. Helen discussed her realisation of her bisexuality: 'when I started realising that the thought of her with a female body was attractive, [...] it sort of makes you realise feelings and thoughts that have been suppressed' (non-trans woman, age 56) with Myfanwy positing that 'nobody models anything else [other than heterosexuality] for you' (non-trans woman, age 51). Thus neither Helen nor Myfanwy became aware of possibilities beyond heterosexuality until their partners told them they were trans and they found that they felt able to remain within their relationships.

Marina found that her articulation of a questioning position with respect to gender, and her identification as neither male nor female, opened up the possibility of such reconsiderations to others:

> I've run into lesbian friends [...] who, the more I came out as trans or as questioning gender the more they felt comfortable asking me [...] what was going on for me and how did I think about certain things, and they went ahead and tried a few things, at least in terms of exploring about themselves. And I've had a few friends who've come out as trannies because of me (both laugh), or at least they'd explored the in between space as well [...] so it was really nice cos it was like I was able to pass on some of [...] my things that I [...] had a hard struggle with, and once I was able to digest better then it was easier for them to.
>
> (Marina, genderqueer, age 35)

This passing on of discursive possibilities, particularly in relation to those identities rarely societally acknowledged, broadens gender possibilities and destabilises assumptions of male and female as the sole valid gender identities, at least for some. Marina's narrative of resistance showed others that they are, as Foucault argued, freer than they might think, and therefore able to resist dominant knowledge forms (Foucault, 1988 [1982]: 10). Inclusion of non-binary identity possibilities in social theory would similarly broaden the range of self-conceptualisations available to individuals, as explored through gender pluralist theorisations (Monro 2007).

A further arena in which those who do not identify as male or female are disenfranchised is through legal recognition, as this recognition, where available, is offered within a binary framework, where an individual who is assigned the male gender at birth has the opportunity to alter the gender recorded on their birth certificate to female and vice versa, but those who wish to have no gender attributed to them are forced to remain within binary possibilities (Hines 2007a, 2007b, 2009, Chapter 4 this volume; Sanger 2008b). Such limitations indicate the ways in which 'private troubles' link to 'public issues', and thus the usefulness of employing a sociological framework (Mills 1959).

Examination of hegemonic discursive frameworks leads to the question: 'Would a "self" without sexuality [...] be understood as a self at all?' (Fraser 1996: 254) This is particularly pertinent when considering those who do not define their sexuality within accepted categories. These individuals' identities cannot be articulated within hegemonic frames of reference and are therefore denied public recognition, thus invoking a lack of 'self,' where selves are perceived to be inherent and stable entities. This is also the case for those who do not identify as male or female, and are similarly denied a recognised sense of self. As '[b]eing fully human (in Western culture) entails being recognized *as a subject* by another human subject' (Mitchell 2000: 64, emphasis in original), recognition from the other is in fact crucial to each subject, and must be available in order for individual subjectivities to be livable (also see Butler 2004). Thus I argue that expanding mainstream sociological theory to encompass the possibility of genders and sexualities outside of the hegemonic binary framework would increase inclusion, as well as open up a wider range of possibilities for individuals more broadly.

Binary thinking and theorising have serious political, social and personal consequences, as they lead to a lack of recognition of anyone who does not adhere to accepted binary norms, as evidenced in the examples discussed previously. Exploration of the identities and relational lives of trans people sheds a great deal of light upon the norms by which societies are governed. This is the case for those who adhere to gender and sexuality norms as well as those who reject them, as Hird explains: 'Intersexuals and transsexuals who attempt to "fit" into a sexually divided world reveal the regulatory mechanisms through which sexual difference is enforced; whereas intersexuals and transsexuals who refuse an either/or "sexed" identity disturb the infallibility of the binary' (2000: 359). Lorber has also argued for the expansion of sociological thinking, stating: 'Data that undermine the supposed natural dichotomies on which the social orders of most modern societies are still based could radically alter political discourses that valorize biological causes, essential heterosexuality, and traditional gender roles in families and workplaces' (1996: 155). If we limit our studies to only those who live within the norms of society, or remove studies of 'others' to the margins of sociology, we reinforce societal norms and do not open up space for either recognition and acceptance, or for change.

THE VALUE OF A SOCIOLOGICAL APPROACH

Whilst there are currently major impasses with respect to mainstream sociology recognising transgender identities and non-binary categorisations, there are a number of ways in which the sociological study of trans could add to existing knowledge bases, and it is these to which I now turn.

Sociology's focus on social interaction has the potential to alter societal conceptualisations of trans through a movement away from the dominant discourses of medicine and psychology, which assume the naturalness of the sexed body and thereby work to homogenise and pathologise trans people (Money and Ehrhardt 1972; Money and Tucker 1976; Green 1992). Sociological approaches offer the possibility of engaging with the lived experiences of trans people and bringing these experiences to bear on social theory, rather than working from an existing template of scientific norms. As discussed by those who call for a queering of sociology (Seidman 1996; Hines 2006; 2007a), this is a particular strength of sociological research in the study of marginalised groups and offers the potential for challenging dominant discourse in relation to, for example, gender and sexuality.

The examination of trans subjectivities engages with key contemporary issues in sociology, which I will now briefly examine in order to locate transgender studies within a sociological framework, and to indicate the relevance of studies of trans identity to sociology as a discipline.

Firstly, of significance to both sociologists and transgender theorists, is the impact of bio-technologies on social identities (Doyle and Roen 2008). Feminist and Foucauldian scholars have been particularly critical of the role of bio-technology in the control of populations and the reinforcement of societal norms, as in Foucault's notion of 'bio-power', or the governance of bodies (Foucault, 1991[1977]). The societal risks and benefits of bio-technologies are of great significance to sociology in a world which is relying increasingly on bio-technological innovations. For some, bio-technologies are seen to inform and transform identity (Kleinman 1991; Shiva and Moser 1995; Hird 2004). It has been argued variously that the technology of genital reassignment surgery produced trans subjectivity (for example, Hausman 1995), and, conversely, that trans people have exercised agency in demanding necessary surgical alterations (Meyerowitz 2002). However, surgical alterations and medical interventions are not central to all trans people's experiences of their identities, and as such the debate around trans and bio-technology can be seen to have moved beyond the previous framing around genital reassignment surgeries (Califia 1997; Denny 2004;

Hines 2007b; Sanger 2007b). The diversity of experiences of trans people with respect to bio-technologies cuts to the heart of what it is to be a subject in contemporary Western society, as well as highlighting the necessity of exploring embodiment as concretely experienced in relation to social life and institutions, rather than purely as an abstract concept (Davis 1997).

Trans identities also speak to the significance of the nature/culture dichotomy, as their consideration problematises the relationship between sex (nature) and gender (culture). There is a further challenge to 'the natural' and its relationship to culture which has arisen through the study of transgender identities, via a movement away from the 'born in the wrong body', medicalised paradigm to a more complex positioning which is difficult to place on one side or the other of this dichotomous imaginary (Denny 2004). Trans people variously identify as having been born in the wrong body, embrace their socially unacceptable body in relation to their gender identification, and also inhabit many positions in between, as has been shown in recent empirically-based sociological studies of trans such as Hines' (2007b), Monro's (2007) and Sanger's (2007a). The narratives of trans people who both embrace and challenge gender norms indicate the fragility of rigid dichotomous thinking with respect to 'nature' and 'culture', sex and gender.

The governance of individuals and groups through medicine and the law, which is crucial to the (re)formation of identities of those who are categorised (by themselves and/or others) as trans, flags up important sociological issues, relating to the structure/agency debate and possibilities of resistance to social norms (Sanger 2008a). Sociology offers a means of studying this socially and culturally mediated identity formation (Hines 2007a, Chapter 4, this volume; Sanger 2007b, 2008b; Davy Chapter 5, this volume).

Discrimination and marginalisation are also central concerns, as trans identities continue to be limited through social expectations (Gagné and Tewksbury 1998; Hird 2002) and concomitant fears of harassment and violence (Namaste 2000). Despite recent legal changes, trans people continue to be discriminated against in relation to, for example, employment (Whittle et al. 2007; Rundall and Vecchietti Chaper 6, this volume), health care (Burns 2006; Davy Chapter 5, this volume), and education (Rooke Chapter3, this volume). For those who do not identify as either male or female, or wish to remain married as well as changing the gender recorded on their birth certificate, the legal system also remains a site of marginalisation (Sanger 2008b; Hines Chapter 4, this volume).

Early sociological studies such as Becker's (1963) on deviance and Goffman's (1968) on social stigma continue to offer useful explorations of why some identities come to be stigmatised and marginalised. Investigation of trans marginalisation may be enriched through incorporation of existing sociological insights into how individuals and groups relate to one another, reasons for stigmatisation, and ways of moving beyond generalised assumptions about groups on the borders, as these are all extremely relevant to trans people's lived experiences. Homogenous understandings of trans are often employed within academia as well as societally, and even within marginalised groups there are hierarchies and disagreements as to how best to end discrimination. I argue that sociological approaches offer useful tools in studying such issues. Sociology particularly offers the possibility of those on the receiving end of such exclusion becoming involved in evaluating and contemplating their enforced (or sometimes welcomed) deviant status.

Consideration of these sociological issues could work to expand understandings of the position of trans people in society. This more socially-engaged approach resonates with Seidman's (1997) call for a move from 'sociological theory' to 'social theory.' He argues that sociological theories have become too focused on uncovering a generalisable formula for society, whereas '[s]ocial theories are typically closely connected to contemporary social conflicts and public debates' (Seidman 1997: 44). Such engagement with the particularities of what is happening 'on the ground', I would argue, makes for a more constructive, 'public sociology', with the capacity to co-construct knowledge with individuals in ways which may elicit social change (see Burawoy 2007). This type of sociological knowledge construction fits in well with the aforementioned aims and objectives of transgender theorising.

CONCLUSION

The ways in which trans people may adhere to or resist hegemonic norms shed light on the possibilities for moving beyond normative understandings of both gender and sexuality, as well as highlighting the more general regulation of individual and group identities through societal regimes of truth (Sanger 2007a, 2008a). Unstable and fluid understandings of identity are largely absent from mainstream sociological theory, with the result that gender and sexuality become channelled into narrow and limiting options. Thus theory remains both limited and limiting. New sociological approaches may be uncovered through exploration of previously unexplored or underexplored identity categories. I argue that examination of trans identities offers such possibilities.

As I have detailed throughout this chapter, lives are currently being lived which challenge binary understandings of gender and sexuality. Sociological examination of such lives offers the possibility of recognising and exploring this diversity of gender and sexuality, and thereby challenging the marginalisation of those who do not fit within normative ideals. In addition, investigation of trans identificatory strategies works to make more visible some of the processes and intricacies of identification which exist with respect to *every* individual, and as such, this area of research is extremely relevant and informative for sociology as a discipline (Lorber 2000; Hird 2002; Sanger 2008a).

Approaches such as a 'queer sociology' (Seidman 1996; Hines 2006), 'degendering' (Lorber 1994, 2000) or 'gender pluralism' (Monro 2007) offer space for studies of identity to move beyond limiting conceptual frameworks and to challenge existing norms relating to gender and sexuality. Frameworks such as these allow for the experiences of those who do not adhere to binary configurations of identity and who tend to be erased from social research and society as a whole, such as Sam, Lee, Marina and Susan, and many others who identify with trans in differing ways. Those studying trans from a sociological perspective have, I argue, already begun the process of bringing together transgender studies and sociology in a fruitful way, and I argue that this endeavour has a great deal of potential for expanding 'public sociology' and social theory, and as such building a platform from which to critique hegemonic gender norms, and the impact of these on both trans individuals and broader populations.

NOTES

1. I would like to thank Sally Hines and Lisa Smyth for their very useful comments on earlier versions of this chapter.
2. I use the term 'trans' to refer to any individual who identifies with a gender other than that assigned at birth. This may mean someone assigned the male gender at birth identifying as female or vice-versa, or identifying with neither or both of the commonly accepted binary gender categories.
3. It is because of these complex intersections that I am considering theorisation of both gender and sexuality within this chapter. The living of gender outwith binary possibilities leads to a movement of sexuality beyond hetero- and homosexuality due to sexuality being based on gender relationality.
4. Particularly in undergraduate textbooks, which have a large readership, the social construction of gender tends to be considered in relation to girls being dressed in pink and boys in blue, and each being given different toys to play with and being expected to fulfil different roles in society. As Marx Ferree, Lorber and Hess argue, 'most introductory sociology textbooks still treat gender as an individual attribute and gender inequality as an outcome of childhood socialization' (1998: xv). Such explanations stop short of analysing the full extent of the damage these norms can do, or considering the possibility of gender norms being deconstructed.
5. Cisgendered refers to non-trans people, genderqueer indicates a positioning as neither male nor female, and bi-gendered individuals identify as both male and female.
6. Pansexuality and omnisexuality indicate sexual attraction independent of the gender of the object(s) of attraction.
7. This research was carried out between 2002 and 2006, with interviews taking place, mainly in participants' homes, during the period of November 2003 to June 2004. The majority of interviews were carried out in England, with a small number taking place in Ireland.
8. Hines (2007b) also indicates that her research sample included a higher number of individuals who did not unproblematically adhere to binary gender norms, as compared to Gagné and Tewksbury's (1998) findings. Gagné

and Tewksbury said of their sample that '[a]mong non-political transgendered respondents [60 out of 65 interviewees] . . . the overwhelming majority adhered to the belief that males should be masculine, females should be feminine, and that identity as a gay male should be avoided' (1998: 84).

REFERENCES

Becker, H. S. (1963) *Outsiders*, New York: The Free Press.
Browne, K. (2008) 'Selling my queer soul or queerying quantitative research?' *Sociological Research Online*, 13(1). http://www.socresonline.org.uk/13/1/11.html (accessed 11 June 2009).
Burawoy, M. (2007) 'Private troubles and public issues', in A. L. Barlow (ed.) *Collaborations for Social Justice: Professionals, Publics, and Policy Change*, Lanham, MD: Rowman and Littlefield Publishers, Inc.
Burns, C. (2006) 'Collected essays in trans healthcare politics: documenting the scandal of how medicine lost the trust of trans people'. http://ai.eecs.umich.edu/people/conway/TS/Health/Essays_In_Trans_Healthcare.pdf#search=%22collected%20essays%20in%20trans%20healthcare%20politics%22 (accessed 13 May 2009).
Butler, J. (1999 [1990]) *Gender Trouble: Feminism and the Subversion of Identity*, New York and London: Routledge.
———. (2004) *Undoing Gender*, New York and London: Routledge.
Califia, P. (1997) *Sex Changes: The Politics of Transgenderism*, San Francisco: Cleis Press.
Davis, K. (1997) *Embodied Practices: Feminist Perspectives on the Body*, London: Sage.
Dean, M. (1999) *Governmentality: Power and Rule in Modern Society*, London, Thousand Oaks and New Delhi: Sage Publications.
Delgado, R. and Stefancic, J. (1997) *Critical White Studies: Looking Behind the Mirror*, Philadelphia: Temple University Press.
Denny, D. (2004) 'Changing models of transsexualism', *Journal of Gay and Lesbian Psychotherapy*, 8(1–2): 25–40.
Doyle, J. and Roen, K. (2008) 'Surgery and embodiment: carving out subjects', *Body and Society*, 14(1): 1–7.
Dozier, R. (2005) 'Beards, breasts, and bodies: doing sex in a gendered world', *Gender & Society*, 19(3): 297–316.
Ekins, R. and King, D. (eds) (1996) *Blending Genders: Social Aspects of Cross-dressing and Sex-changing*, London: Routledge.
Firestone, S. (1971) *The Dialectic of Sex: The Case for Feminist Revolution*, New York: Bantam.
Foertsch, J. and Gernsbacher, M. A. (1997) 'In search of gender neutrality: is singular *they* a cognitively efficient substitute for generic *he*?' *Psychological Science*, 8(2): 106–111.
Foucault, M. (1988 [1982]) 'Truth, power, self: an interview with Michel Foucault', in L. Martin, H. Gutman and P. Hutton (eds) *Technologies of the Self: A Seminar with Michel Foucault*, Amherst: University of Massachusetts Press.
———. (1991 [1977]) *Discipline and Punish: The Birth of the Prison* (trans. A. Sheridan), London: Penguin Books.
Fraser, M. (1996) 'Framing contention: bisexuality displaced', in D. E. Hall and M. Pramaggiore (eds) *RePresenting Bisexualities: Subjects and Cultues of Fluid Desire*, New York: New York University Press.
Gagné, P. and Tewksbury, R. (1998) 'Conformity pressures and gender resistance among transgendered individuals', *Social Problems*, 45(1): 81–101.

Garfinkel, H. (1967) *Studies in Ethnomethodology*, Englewood Cliffs, NJ: Prentice Hall.

Goffman, I. (1968) *Stigma: Notes on the Management of Spoiled Identity*, New York: Touchstone.

Goldman, R. (1996) ' Who is that queer queer? Exploring norms around sexuality, race, and class in queer theory', in B. Beemyn and M. Eliason (eds) *Queer Studies: A Lesbian, Gay, Bisexual and Transgender Anthology*, New York: New York University Press.

Green, R. (1992) *Sexual Science and the Law*, Cambridge and London: Harvard University Press.

Halberstam, J. (1998) *Female Masculinity*, Durham, NC and London: Duke University Press.

——. (2002) 'An introduction to female masculinity: masculinity without men', in R. Adams and D. Savran (eds) *The Masculinity Studies Reader*, Malden, MA and Oxford: Blackwell.

——. (2005) *In a Queer Time and Place: Transgender Bodies, Subcultural Lives*, New York: New York University Press.

Hausman, B. (1995) *Changing Sex: Transsexualism, Technology and the Idea of Gender*, Durham, NC: Duke University Press.

Hawkesworth, M. (1997) 'Confounding gender', *Signs*, 22(3): 649–685.

Hill Collins, P. (1998) *Fighting Words: Black Women and the Search for Justice*, Minneapolis: University of Minnesota Press.

Hines, S. (2006) 'What's the difference? Bringing particularity to queer studies of transgender', *Journal of Gender Studies*, 15(1): 49–66.

——. (2007a) '(Trans)forming gender: social change and transgender citizenship', *Sociological Research Online* 12(1). http://www.socresonline.org.uk/12/1/hines. html. (accessed 10 October 2009)

——. (2007b) *TransForming Gender: Transgender Practices of Identity, Intimacy and Care*, London: Policy Press.

Hird, M. J. (2000) 'Gender's nature: intersexuals, transsexuals and the "sex"/"gender" binary', *Feminist Theory*, 1(3): 347–364.

——. (2002) 'For a sociology of transsexualism', *Sociology*, 36(3): 577–596.

——. (2004) *Sex, Gender and Science*, Basingstoke: Palgrave MacMillan.

Kessler, S. J. and McKenna, W. (1978) *Gender: An Ethnomethodological Approach*, Chicago and London: The University of Chicago Press.

Kleinman, D. L. (1991) *Science and Technology in Society: From Biotechnology to the Internet*, Malden, MA, Oxford and Victoria: Wiley-Blackwell.

Lewins, F. (2002) 'Explaining stable partnerships among FTMs and MTFs: a significant difference?' *Journal of Sociology*, 38(1): 76–88.

Lorber, J. (1994) *Paradoxes of Gender*, Newhaven, London: Yale University Press.

——. (1996) 'Beyond the binaries: depolarizing the categories of sex, sexuality, and gender', *Sociological Inquiry*, 66(2): 143–159.

——. (2000) 'Using gender to undo gender: a feminist degendering movement', *Feminist Theory*, 1(1): 79–95.

Marx Ferree, M., Lorber, J. and Hess, B. B. (1998) *Revisioning Gender*, London and Thousand Oaks, CA: Sage.

Mason-Schrock, D. (1996) 'Transsexuals' narrative construction of the "true self"', *Social Psychology Quarterly*, 59(3): 176–192.

Mead, G. H. (1934) *Mind, Self and Society*, Chicago: University of Chicago Press.

Meyerowitz, J. (2002) *How Sex Changed: A History of Transsexuality in the United States*, Cambridge, MA and London: Harvard University Press.

Mills, C. W. (1959) *The Sociological Imagination*, New York: Oxford University Press.

Mitchell, S. A. (2000) *Relationality: From Attachment to Intersubjectivity*, London: The Analytic Press.

Money, J. and Ehrhardt, A. (1972) *Man and Woman/Boy and Girl*, Baltimore: Johns Hopkins University Press.

Money, J. and Tucker, P. (1976) *Sexual Signatures: On Being a Man or a Woman*, London: Harrap.

Monro, S. (2007) 'Transmuting gender binaries: the theoretical challenge', *Sociological Research Online* 12(1). http://www.socresonline.org.uk/12/1/monro.html. (accessed 10 October 2009)

Namaste, V. (2000) *Invisible Lives: The Erasure of Transsexual and Transgendered People*, Chicago: The University of Chicago Press.

Plummer, K. and Stein, A. (1996) '"I can't even think straight": "queer" theory and the missing sexual revolution in sociology', in S. Seidman (ed.) *Queer Theory/Sociology*, Malden, MA and Oxford: Blackwell Publishers Ltd.

Prosser, J. (1998) *Second Skins: The Body Narratives of Transsexuality*, New York: Columbia University Press.

Riddell, S. and Watson, N. (eds) (2004) *Disability, Culture and Identity*, Harlow: Prentice Hall.

Roen, K. (2001) 'Transgender theory and embodiment: the risk of racial marginalisation', *Journal of Gender Studies*, 10(3): 253–263.

Rubin, H. (2003) *Self-made Men: Identity and Embodiment among Transsexual Men*, Nashville: Vanderbilt University Press.

Sanger, T. (2007a) 'Desiring difference? Transpeople's intimate partnerships and the cultural construction of gender and sexuality', unpublished thesis, The Queen's University of Belfast.

——. (2007b) 'Queer(y)ing gender and sexuality: transpeople's lived experiences and intimate partnerships', in L. Moon (ed.) *Feeling Queer or Queer Feelings? Radical Approaches to Counselling Sex, Sexualities and Genders*, New York: Routledge.

——. (2008a) 'Trans governmentality: the production and regulation of gendered subjectivities', *Journal of Gender Studies*, 17(1): 41–53.

——. (2008b) 'Transpeople's intimate partnerships and the limits of identity politics', in Z. Davy, J. Downes, L. Eckert, N. Gerodetti, D. Llinares and A. C. Santos (eds) *Bound and Unbound: Interdisciplinary Approaches to Genders and Sexualities*, Cambridge: Cambridge Scholars Publishing.

Seidman, S. (1996) 'Introduction', in S. Seidman (ed.) *Queer Theory/Sociology*, Oxford: Blackwell Publishers Ltd.

——. (1997) *Difference Troubles: Queering Social Theory and Sexual Politics*, Cambridge: Cambridge University Press.

Shiva, V. and Moser, I. (1995) *Biopolitics: A Feminist and Ecological Reader on Biotechnology*, Basingstoke: Palgrave MacMillan.

Stryker, S. (1998) 'The transgender issue: an introduction', *GLQ*, 4(2): 145–158.

——. (2004) 'Transgender studies: queer theory's evil twin', *GLQ: A Journal of Lesbian and Gay Studies*, 10(2): 212–215.

——. (2006) '(De)subjucated knowldege: an introduction to transgender studies', in S. Stryker, and S. Whittle (eds) *The Transgender Studies Reader*, New York and Abingdon: Routledge.

Stryker, S. and Whittle, S. (2006) *The Transgender Studies Reader*, New York and Abingdon: Routledge.

Taylor, Y., Hines, S. and Casey, M. (eds) (forthcoming) *Theorizing Intersectionality and Sexuality: Sexual Advances*, Basingstoke: Palgrave Macmillan.

Whittle, S. (2002) *Respect and Equality: Transsexual and Transgender Rights*, London: Cavendish Publishing Limited.

Whittle, S., Turner, L. and Al-Alami, M. (2007) 'Engendered penalties: trans-gender and transsexual people's experiences of inequality and discrimination', *The Equalities Review.* http://www.pfc.org.uk/files/EngenderedPenalties.pdf (accessed 13 May 2009).

Williams, C. (2006) 'Still missing? Comments on the twentieth anniversary of "The missing feminist revolution in sociology"', *Social Problems,* 53(4): 454–458.

Yosso, T. (2006) *Critical Race Counterstories along the Chicana/o Educational Pipeline,* New York and London: Routledge.

Contributors

Sara Davidmann is a photographer and Research Fellow at London College of Communication, University of the Arts London. Her research interests are in gender, sexuality, embodiment, visibility and photography. In particular, her work is concerned with the use of photography as a medium for allowing agency with regard to transgender representation, developing new collaborative methods for documenting transgender lives and photography's potential to reveal unique insights into lived experiences. She is the author of *Crossing the Line*, Dewi Lewis, 2003; *trans agenda: transsexual portraits* Source, 2004; and *Border Trouble: Photography, Strategies, and Transsexual Identities* SCAN: Journal of Media, Arts, Culture, 2006. Her photography has been exhibited internationally in Europe and America. Exhibitions include: Paris Photo, Basel Art Fair, *Somatechnics*, Sydney, *Transfabulous*, London, MOMA Oxford. She is the award holder of an Arts and Humanities Research (AHRC) Fellowship in the Creative and Performing Arts. Previous awards include a Fulbright Hays scholarship, an Association of Commonwealth Universities Fellowship, two AHRC awards and a Promising Researcher Fellowship.

Zowie Davy is an ESRC research assistant at the University of Leeds. She completed her Ph.D. in September 2008 and her work focused on transgender embodiment and the medicolegal system in the UK. Zowie's research interests are in transgender studies, sociology and on the medicalisation of 'deviant' genders, sexuality and citizenship, queer, feminist and phenomenological methods. She has contributed to and is co-editor of *Bound and Unbound: Interdisciplinary Approaches to Genders and Sexualities* (2008): Cambridge Scholars Press, and contributor to *The Greenwood Encyclopedia of LGBT Issues Worldwide* (2009).

Richard Ekins is a jazz record producer and Professor of Sociology and Cultural Studies in the School of Media, Film and Journalism at the University of Ulster at Coleraine, UK, where he has directed the Transgender Archive since 1986. He is a member of the International Academy for Sex Research and the British Psycho-Analytical Society, and is an editor of the *International Journal of Transgenderism*. He is particularly interested in a grounded theory approach to the sociology of intimate detail. His authored and edited books include *Blending Genders: Social Aspects of Cross-Dressing and Sex-Changing* (with Dave King), Routledge, 1996; *Male Femaling: A Grounded Theory Approach to Cross-Dressing and Sex-Changing*, Routledge, 1997; *Virginia Prince: Pioneer of Transgendering* (with Dave King), Haworth, 2005; and *The Transgender Phenomenon* (with Dave King), Sage, 2006.

Angie Fee works in private practice as a psychotherapist, supervisor and trainer. She is a trainer in Sexualities and Genders and teaches this topic on post graduate counselling and psychotherapy programmes in London, Sweden and Amsterdam. She is completing her Ph.D. thesis 'Transgender identities: within and beyond the constraints of heteronormativity' at Edinburgh University. Her clinical and research work explores the gender experiences of people who define themselves as transgender. The longer term purpose of her research seeks to contribute to the development of a new, non-binary or 'trans', form of gender-inclusiveness.

Katherine Gregory is a research scientist for a governmental agency addressing public health issues in New York City. She is an interdisciplinary scholar and media producer who has taught in the University of Wisconsin System and other educational institutions in the United States. Routledge Press published her doctoral dissertation titled The Everyday Lives of Sex Workers in the Netherlands (2005). This two and half year study explores the coping strategies and working practices of transgendered and migrant sex workers in the Netherlands. She has contributed to numerous anthologies and continues her research on social media communities and sexual identity.

Corie J. Hammers is currently an Assistant Professor in the Women's, Gender and Sexuality Studies Department at Macalester College. She teaches courses on gender, sexuality, feminist/queer theories and methodologies, and GLBT issues. She continues to research women's sexual spaces, and is particularly interested in the relationships between queer theory and feminism, and the intersections between queer theory, sexuality and race. She has published in a variety of journals including *Sexualities, Journal of Contemporary Ethnography*, and *Journal of Gender Studies*. She is currently at work on a book which brings together her research on lesbian/queer sexual spaces (bathhouses and BDSM/kink sites), the politics of identity within these venues/sex-positive communities, and the agentic and disciplining aspects of these spaces. Her latest project involves examining the (in)visibility of lesbianism—particularly lesbian coaches—within collegiate sports.

Sally Hines is a lecturer in Sociology and Gender Studies at the University of Leeds, UK. Her research interests fall within the areas of identity, gender, sexuality, and the body. Her work is particularly concerned with transformations in gendered, sexual and embodied identities. She is currently award holder of an ESRC research grant, which is exploring the impact of the UK Gender Recognition Act on individual and collective transgender identities and intimate practices. She has published widely in international refereed journals including The *Journal of Gender Studies, Sociology, Critical Social Policy* and *Sociological Research Online,* and has authored numerous book chapters. Her recent sole-authored book, 'TransForming Gender: Transgender Practices of Identity, Intimacy and Care', is published by Policy Press (2007). She is co-editor (with Yvette Taylor and Mark Casey) of *Theorizing Intersectionality and Sexuality* (Palgrave Macmillan, 2010).

Dave King is a Senior Lecturer in Sociology at the University of Liverpool. His research interests span the broad areas of gender, sexuality and deviance/control. He is particularly interested in gender deviance and medical forms of social control and has carried out research into the social aspects of transgenderism for a number of years. He is an editor of the *International Journal of Transgenderism.* His recent publications include; 'Telling Body Transgendering Stories', with Richard Ekins in K. Backett-Milburn and L McKie (eds), in *Constructing Gendered Bodies,* (Palgrave, 2001), and 'Gender Migration: A Sociological Analysis (or the Leaving of Liverpool)', (*Sexualities.* 6:2 2003). His latest book with Richard Ekins is called *The Transgender Phenomenon,* published by Sage in 2006. He has also co-authored a book with Karen Evans called *Studying Society* (Routledge, 2006)

Surya Monro is one of the key contemporary feminist sociologists working in the field of transgender. She contributes to three areas of scholarship: [i] An exploration of the implications of transgender for gender theory, feminisms, and citizenship; [ii] Local government and initiatives concerning lesbian, gay, bisexual and transgender equality; [iii] Sociological and anthropological analysis of gendered processes and parliament. She is currently a co-applicant (with Professor Diane Richardson at the University of Newcastle) on a large ESRC funded project concerning sexualities and transgender initiatives in local government, a Visiting Research Fellow at the University of Newcastle. She also works as a Research Fellow at Huddersfield University with specific interest in LGBT Equalities and governance. She has published substantially in international refereed journals in the areas of sex/gender diversity and has presented papers at a range of national and international conferences. Her book *Gender Politics: Citizenship, Activism and Sexual Diversity,* came out in 2005 (Pluto Press). She has also written and taught courses on gender, sexuality and Women's Studies at the Universities of Sheffield, Keele and Brighton.

Alison Rooke is a lecturer in the Department of Sociology, Goldsmiths, University of London. Alison has written on issues relating to cosmopolitanism, visibility, embodiment and belonging in classed and queer cultures. Alison's work focuses on gendered and sexual subjectivities, grounding queer theorising in everyday lived complexity. Her Ph.D. research, 'Lesbian landscapes and portraits: the sexual geographies of everyday life', was a visual ethnography exploring the interconnections of spatiality and subjectivity for working class lesbian and bisexual women. As well as teaching visual sociology, her work is concerned with participative and collaborative arts and the social, economic and cultural impact of creativity.

Em Rundall is a Ph.D. Student in the Department of International Relations, Politics and Sociology at Oxford Brookes University. Her Ph.D. focuses on Trans-employees' experiences in UK workplaces. She is an associate member of FTM London, and contributed to the literature review on trans employment issues in the 2007 research paper by Whittle, S., Turner, L., and Al-Alami, M., entitled 'Engendered Penalties: Transgender and Transsexual People's Experiences of Inequality and Discrimination' which was commissioned by the Equalities Review. Her interests include gender expression, identity construction, sociological theory and issues surrounding employment equality.

Tam Sanger is currently writing her first book, to be published by Palgrave Macmillan (forthcoming). She has authored a chapter in *Feeling Queer or Queer Feelings? Radical Approaches to Counselling Sex, Sexualities and Genders* (Moon 2007) focusing on counselling trans people and their partners, as well as an article in *The Journal of Gender Studies* (2008) which is a discussion of the ways in which gender is lived and regulated. A second book chapter has focused on the implications of the Gender Recognition Act for trans recognition and identity politics, and was published in Z. Davy et al. (eds) *Bound and Unbound: Interdisciplinary Approaches to Genders and Sexualities* (2008). Tam is a teaching fellow in gender and sociology at The Queen's University of Belfast and is interested in studying asexuality and polyamory, as well as continuing to investigate trans identification and the societal regulation of gender and sexuality.

Eve Shapiro is an Assistant Professor of Sociology at Westfield State College. Eve received her Ph.D. in Sociology from the University of California, Santa Barbara and has received a number of awards for her scholarship, including two University of California Graduate Division dissertation awards, the American Sociological Association sexualities section Graduate Paper Award, and an honourable mention for the 2004 Martin Levine Dissertation Fellowship. Her current research elaborates whether and how both cisgender and transgender individuals narrate gender throughout their lives, making sense of it in conversation with identity, community, and nation. This project is guided by a theoretical and empirical interest in how individuals and communities imagine and create social change at individual, collective, and societal levels. Her forthcoming book *Gender Circuits: Bodies and Identities in a Technological Age* examines whether and how new information and biomedical technologies are changing the gendered lives of all individuals.

Vincent G. Vecchietti is an independent academic who read English at Oxford, and has a particular interest in theory, with an emphasis on signification, identity, and power. In addition, he is a playwright and photographer. He is also a member of FTM London.

Laurel Westbrook is an Assistant Professor of Sociology at Grand Valley State University. She recently completed her Ph.D. in Sociology at the University of California, Berkeley, where her dissertation investigated the ideas about gender, sexuality, and violence that have been produced, circulated, and reinforced in 'non-fiction' narratives told about the murders of transgendered people in the United States. Her recent publications include 'Doing gender, doing heteronormativity: "gender normals," transgender people, and the social maintenance of heterosexuality,' co-authored with Kristen Schilt, in *Gender & Society* (23:4. 2009), 'Vulnerable subjecthood: the risks and benefits of the struggle for hate crime legislation,' in the *Berkeley Journal of Sociology* (52 2008), 'Where the women aren't: gender differences in the use of LGBT resources on two college campuses,' forthcoming in *The Journal of LGBT Youth* (6:4. 2009), and 'On writing public sociology: accountability through accessibility, dialogue, and relevance,' co-authored with Damon Mayrl in *The Handbook of Public Sociology* (Routledge, 2009).

Index

Printed in Great Britain
by Amazon